New Zealand Adopts Proportional Representation
Accident? Design? Evolution?

KEITH JACKSON
ALAN McROBIE

Ashgate
Aldershot • Brookfield USA • Singapore • Sydney

Ashgate Publishing Limited
Gower House
Croft Road
Aldershot
Hants GU11 3HR
England

Ashgate Publishing Company
Old Post Road
Brookfield
Vermont 05036
USA

Published in New Zealand by
Hazard Press Limited, 62 Gloucester Street, Christchurch

British Library Cataloguing in Publication Data
Jackson, Keith
  New Zealand adopts proportional representation : accident?
  design? evolution?
  1.Proportional representation - New Zealand 2.New Zealand -
  Politics and government - 1972-
  I.Title II.McRobie, Alan
  328.9'3'07347

Library of Congress Cataloging-in-Publication Data
Jackson, William Keith, 1928-
    New Zealand adopts proportional representation accident? design?
  evolution? / Keith Jackson, Alan McRobie.
      p. cm.
    Includes bibliographical references and index.
    ISBN 1-84014-472-6 (hardcover)
    1.Proportional representation--New Zealand. I. McRobie, Alan,
  II. Title.
  JF1075.N45J33 1998
  328.3'347'0993--dc21
                                                              98-24974
                                                              CIP

ISBN 1 84014 472 6

Printed and bound by Athenaeum Press, Ltd.,
Gateshead, Tyne & Wear.

Contents

List of Figures

List of Tables

Preface

Widely regarded as a fairly quiet, largely conservative society, New Zealand seems to break out every now and again, even to the extent of surprising itself. The Liberal government's reforms of the 1890s, or the contrasting reforms of the Labour governments of the 1930s and 1980s — both of which attracted world-wide interest at the time — are cases in point. The decision to adopt a system of proportional representation, taken by a series of referendums in the early 1990s, is another such example.

Depending upon your point of view, New Zealand was an extreme, or almost perfect example of the simple plurality or First-past-the-post majoritarian electoral system. For most New Zealanders the change to proportional representation represented a radical step — virtually into the unknown. It was also a step strongly opposed by the majority of politicians. Throughout our research for this book we were constantly reminded of Sir Humphrey Appleby's observation (when discussing 'Power to the People' with Bernard Woolley) that, "Oppositions always want to change the system that is keeping them out of office. But once they are in office they want to keep it. For instance, no one *in office* has ever wanted to change our electoral system to proportional **representation**".[1]

This study is an examination of why, how, and with what effect, such a radical change was undertaken in a political environment which, while lively, was far from the catharsis of revolution. Tracking down the various aspects of what, initially, appeared to be a simple undertaking has proved to be a fascinating task. During our research we received invaluable help from politicians, officials, academics, and others too numerous to list in detail. Indeed, some might not wish to see their names associated with the final result! We must, however, acknowledge our deep appreciation to the Electoral Commission, without whose financial assistance this book would probably not have eventuated, and to its Chief Executive, Dr Paul Harris, who originally suggested that we examine how and why New Zealand adopted the MMP form of proportional representation and who, throughout, has proved to be an excellent and discerning critic; to all members of the 1985–86 Royal Commission on the Electoral System, in particular its chairman, Sir John Wallace, Sir Kenneth Keith, Professor Richard Mulgan, and Mrs Whetumarama

---

1   Jonathan Lynn and Antony Jay, *The Complete 'Yes Prime **Minister'***, London, BBC Books, 1989, p. 396.

Wereta, all of whom unstintingly gave of their time in answering the many questions asked by two sceptical political scientists who were only too ready, it must have seemed to them, to put the worst interpretations on their actions! Others who have helped by talking with us, and reading and/or commenting on early drafts of particular chapters — and to whom we owe a considerable debt — are Peter Andrew, Hon Michael Bassett, Hon Max Bradford, Lawrence Bryant, Hon David Caygill, Colin Clark, Rt Hon Helen Clark, Hon Michael Cullen, Rod Donald, MP, Hon Peter Dunne, Wayne Eagleson, David Flux, Hugh Garland, Professor Colin Hughes, Rt Hon Jonathan Hunt, Owen Jennings, MP, Neil Kirton, MP, Dr Ngatata Love, Hon Murray McCully, David McGee, Malcolm Mackerras, Lowell Manning, Bill Moore, Brian Nicolle, Richard Northey, Rt Hon Sir Geoffrey Palmer, Hon Ruth Richardson, Sir John Robertson, Phil Saxby, Peter Shirtcliffe, Verna Smith, Priscilla Tate, John Terris, Hon Simon Upton and Phil Whelan. Thanks are also due to Seishi Gomibuchi for permission to use his most helpful thesis dealing with Sir Geoffrey Palmer's contribution to electoral reform policy, and to Stephen Church for his excellent research assistance.

Last, but certainly not least, how, these days, do you thank the most valuable contributors of all without sounding patronising? Their contributions may have been more indirect, but without the 'book-writing tolerance' of our long-suffering — but no less feisty — wives, Jenny and June, it would have been for nought. Having said that, neither they, the Electoral Commission, nor any other of our 'intellectual creditors' are responsible for the final product — that rests with us alone.

Keith Jackson and Alan McRobie
Christchurch
New Zealand

x

List of Abbreviations

AJHR	*Appendices to the Journals of the House of Representatives*
CA	Court of Appeal
CAB	Cabinet papers
CFPP	Campaign for First-past-the-post
CIR	Citizens' Initiated Referendum
CPR	Campaign for Proportional Representation
CRC	Canadian Royal Commission on Electoral Reform and Party Financing
DNZB	Dictionary of New Zealand Biography
Dom.	*The Dominion* (Wellington)
DST	*Dominion Sunday Times* (Wellington)
EC	Electoral Commission
ELSC	Electoral Law Select Committee
EP	*Evening Post* (Wellington)
ERP	Electoral Referendum Panel
FPP	First-past-the-post electoral system
HC	High Court
IDEA	International Institute for Democracy and Electoral Assistance
Ind.	*The Independent* (Auckland)
LC	Legislative Council
Listener	*New Zealand Listener* (Auckland)
MHR	Member of the House of Representatives
MLC	Member of the Legislative Council
MMP	Mixed Member Proportional electoral system
MP	Member of Parliament
NA	National Archives
NBR	*National Business Review* (Auckland)
NZG	New Zealand Government Gazette
NZH	*New Zealand Herald* (Auckland)
NZLP	New Zealand Labour Party
NZLR	New Zealand Law Review
NZNP	New Zealand National Party
NZPD	New Zealand Parliamentary Debates
ODT	*Otago Daily Times* (Dunedin)
PR	Proportional representation

Press	*The Press* (Christchurch)
PV	Preferential Voting system
RC	Representation Commission
RCES	Royal Commission on the Electoral System
SM	Supplementary Member electoral system
SNTV	Single Non-transferable Vote electoral system
SS	*Sunday Star* (Auckland)
SST	*Sunday Star-Times* (Auckland)
ST	*Southland Times* (Invercargill)
STV	Single Transferable Vote electoral system
TDN	*Taranaki Daily News* (New Plymouth)
TH	*Timaru Herald* (Timaru)
TPK	Te Puni Kokiri (Ministry of Maori Development)
WT	Waitangi Tribunal

Glossary of Maori Words
used in text

haka	ritual chant of defiance accompanied by stylised dance
hui	assembly; meeting; gathering (political and social purposes)
iwi	tribe; people
iwi-runanga	assembly; tribal council
kanohi-ki-te-kanohi	face-to-face
kawanatanga	government; governance
kereru	native wood pigeon (a protected species)
kingitanga	kingship
kohanga reo	language nest (for immersion learning of Maori language)
marae	place of assembly; spiritual and symbolic centre of tribal affairs
pakeha	person of non-Maori descent (usually European)
tangata whenua	original inhabitants ('people of the land')
Te Puni Kokiri	Ministry of Maori Development
te tino rangitiratanga	the unqualified exercise of chieftainship (self determination)
tikanga Maori	Maori custom
whare wananga	educational institutions (house of instruction)

1 The Setting: Constitutional Evolution

Times change, and we change with them.
— William Harrison, *Description of Britain*, 1577.

As German political scientist, Dieter Nohlen, has pointed out:

> Fundamental changes in [electoral systems] are rare and arise only in extra-ordinary historical situations... Those discussions which span the possible range for reform from the majority/plurality system to PR, suggest a freedom of choice that obviously does not exist. (Nohlen, 1984:218.)

Thus, countries rarely change their electoral systems unless in times of severe political, economic or social upheaval such as war, revolution, economic depression, or the collapse of empire. True, there are exceptions such as France and Greece. In France, majoritarian systems using single-member con-stituencies have been replaced by proportional representation (PR) on four separate occasions, and subsequently restored. On the last occasion that PR was resorted to, in 1985, President Mitterrand's unpopular Socialist government used it in order to minimise losses in the 1986 general election. Subsequently, fear of the rise of right-wing extremists led by Le Pen caused a reversion to the more traditional absolute majority system.

Greece, in common with other countries, has also used changes of electoral systems for political purposes. Following the 1950 general election under PR, which produced a hung parliament, for example, the Greeks reverted to First-past-the-post (FPP) when the United States ambassador announced that further economic aid was contingent upon Greece adopting that system (Harrop & Miller, 1987:61).

In Britain, the traditional system, known varyingly as simple plurality, relative majority, or, more commonly, as First-past-the-post (FPP) has almost been abolished on at least two occasions, in 1918 and 1930. The form of proportional representation most generally favoured in English-speaking countries in the past, the Single Transferable Vote system (STV) was used to replace FPP for Northern Ireland elections in 1973. Meanwhile, Eire's parliament, the Dail, twice voted to abolish STV, which had originally been established in 1920, only to have its decisions overturned in referendums held in 1959 and 1968, albeit by narrow margins (Lijphart & Grofman, 1984:11).

In more recent times a spate of changes has taken place in Eastern Europe following the collapse of the Soviet Empire, while elsewhere countries as far apart as Italy and Japan have also changed their systems for a variety of reasons such as corruption or disruptive factionalism.

In general, changes in electoral systems in the twentieth century have trended from majoritarian to proportional. Recently, however, there has been some movement in the opposite direction. For example, Italy has moved from proportional to semi-proportional, while Japan has moved from a Single Non-Transferable Vote system (SNTV) — which, in a strict sense, was not proportional — to a semi-proportional system. The most favoured system in recent times appears to have been a form of 'Additional Member' system. For our purposes this can take one of two main forms. Both are two-level systems combining single-member constituencies elected by simple plurality with a larger constituency or constituencies elected by PR. The first, a system known in New Zealand as 'Supplementary Member' (SM), is semi-proportional, for proportionality applies *only* to the allocation of list seats to parties and not to the single-member constituencies. The second form, the German-type 'Additional Member System' (AMS), which has been labelled Mixed Member Proportional (MMP) in New Zealand, is fully proportional because the party vote determines the *overall* total of seats — both constituency and list — each party receives. Thus SM is *semi-proportional* while MMP is a *fully proportional* system.

The former communist world apart, by moving against this ebbing tide of proportionality New Zealand appears to be something of a rarity. Moreover, it has done this in a unique manner, using two popular referendums to achieve the change. As a stable, respectable, Westminster-style democracy it changed its system at a time of some political dislocation, but this was in no way comparable to the governmental instability and corruption that characterised much of post-war Italy, the one party dominance and party factions that characterised Japanese politics, or the deliberate electoral manipulation seen in Greece and France.

Indeed, many New Zealanders looking back on the decision to change the electoral system have tended to attribute it to an uncharacteristic collective rush of public blood to the head. Even members of the same political party have differed fundamentally on the causes of change. M.K. (Mike) Moore, third ranked minister in the Palmer Labour Government (1989–90) and successor to Palmer as party leader, stated unequivocally that, "[t]he letters I receive about proportional representation are not about the strength of proportional representation; they represent the contempt the people have for politicians — not the system" (*NZPD*, 1990:1619).

Yet the principal architect of change, Geoffrey Palmer, had no doubt that:

> Criticisms of a government's activity at this time are not the primary arguments in favour of that reform. The arguments in favour of reform are very clear. Most democracies recognise that there are serious undemocratic elements in the First-past-the-post system. They recognise that many electors have wasted votes, and that in a sensitive, modern democratic system it is important to have all colours of opinion represented in the democratic Chamber of Parliament. In other words, the democracy needs to be more sensitive and more representative. (*NZPD*, 1990:1879.)

Clearly, there were a number of contributory factors, political, social and constitutional which, given a longer view, may be seen to have played a part in a complex background to what appeared on the surface to be a fairly straightforward decision.

Without question, those who see the adoption of the Mixed Member Proportional (MMP) system of representation as merely the consequence of a sharp public reaction against the perceived inadequacies of the two-party system with its political broken promises are in the majority. But this easy assumption begs a number of questions. Amongst others: how was it that the question of a change of electoral system was on the political agenda at all? Why was it finally brought about by a government which regarded itself as moderate-conservative and contrary to the wishes of the leaderships of *both* major parties in a classical two party system? How is it that the favoured alternative electoral system came to be the (then) West German type, a form remote from the political consciousness of New Zealanders? How was it that the decision to change the system came to be vested in the shape of a popular referendum, and then, not one, but two referendums? How much were people aware of what they were voting *for*, as distinct from what they were voting *against*? Was it, indeed, the sudden rush of blood to the collective voter's cranium, or could, and should, the change be viewed in a longer term context?

There is a need for such questions to be set against the profound changes that the country had already experienced as a result of fundamental economic and social changes which had been taking place from the 1960s onward. It is arguable that these changes had served to steadily expose the inadequacies of the old two-party system which, in turn, became more and more inadequate in meeting the demands of an increasingly complex bi- (even multi-) cultural society. In this sense, and without drawing too long a bow, it is possible to view the adoption of MMP as one of the delayed consequences of what might be termed a 'decolonisation process' which characterised the 1960s and 1970s. But change is seldom attributable to a single cause. Thus, it has been suggested that there are six important factors which help to shape and determine the initial evaluation of institutional or constitutional change proposals. These are cited as events, individuals, organisations, the media, issues, and perceptions of self-interest (Longley, 1989:3). All play a role to a greater or less degree in the adoption of MMP in New Zealand and will be found interwoven throughout the chapters which follow.

First, however, it is necessary to place the adoption of MMP in context. The past two decades of the twentieth century have been noteworthy for their rate of economic and social change compared with what had gone before. Given the generally conservative nature of New Zealanders, particularly as expressed in the outcome of previous referendums, it is difficult to believe that a change as potentially momentous as the adoption of a new and radically different electoral system could have taken place at an earlier time. Why then were the 1990s so different from what had gone before?

To place the changes of these two decades in historical perspective it is useful to bear in mind the social and political development of New Zealand from colony to independent state. This may be characterised as taking place in three main stages.[1] First, the 67 years between 1840 and 1907 (Treaty of Waitangi to Dominion status) saw the *transformation* of New Zealand from a group of Maori tribal societies with a handful of settlers to a centralised, social welfare oriented, predominantly egalitarian, *European* society.

The institutions adopted were close imitations of the Westminster model: a monarchy, two chamber parliament and the FPP electoral system based originally upon a five year term. Special provision for Maori representation was introduced in 1867; manhood franchise followed in 1879, when the term of parliament was also reduced from five to three years, and female franchise was granted in 1893. Already, the British model had acquired distinctly New Zealand characteristics, but the structural shape remained firmly British.

Second, the 65 years, from 1907 until 1972 (Dominion status to the election of the third Labour Government), witnessed continued development and change, social, political and economic (e.g., the First Labour Government was elected in 1935) but, above all, they represented the *consolidation* stage of what continued to be an essentially European society with recognisably British institutions. Despite the acquisition of autonomous Dominion status, New Zealand remained tied to Britain and, for practical purposes, was an economic *colony* exporting raw materials, predominantly to the one market from which it imported its manufactured goods. Compared to the other Dominions this period of dependence, although mutually beneficial for both countries economically, was unnaturally prolonged, with important social and political, as well as economic consequences for New Zealand.

The status of this British-type society began to change with what amounted to economic decolonisation from the 1960s onwards. The diversification of trade after 1961 (when Britain first attempted to enter the European Community), for example, resulted in New Zealand's exports to the United Kingdom declining from 53 per cent in 1960 to 6.2 per cent by 1996. Politically, and constitutionally, changes began to take place. In 1950 New Zealand had adopted the unusual course for an old established Westminster-type system of abolishing its upper house of parliament (which had existed for nearly a century) and becoming a unicameral state. In 1962 it became the first of the Westminster system countries to adopt the Ombudsman system, both signs of the decreasing significance of the British example.

It is the period since 1972, however, which has witnessed the rapidly growing pace of change that has marked the third, or *adaptation* stage. During this period major changes have taken place in New Zealand in the structure of the public service, bi-cultural relations, industrial relations, the fundamental structure of the welfare state and foreign policy. Reforms have included, *inter alia*, radical reform of the public service, local government reform, freedom of information legislation, human rights legislation, a new Constitution Act (albeit hardly a formal constitution in the accepted sense), a Bill of Rights Act, provision for citizens' initiated referendums (CIR) and the referendums on the question of a change of electoral system.

Similar problems and solutions, along with the need for parliament to become both more efficient and effective in its performance, have long been the subject of debate in other Westminster systems including Britain. The difference is that in New Zealand the far-reaching economic reforms of the 1980s and 1990s were more draconian and compacted than elsewhere, and the public reaction stimulated growing interest in achieving more effective forms of political pluralism. This, in turn, has been paralleled by a steadily increasing emphasis upon bi- and multi-culturalism during the 1970s and 1980s. In particular, there has been increasing emphasis upon the accommodation of the needs of the Maori population and culture more adequately than in the past, and this has paralleled the *pakeha* (persons of non-Maori descent — usually European) reaction to the unsatisfactory features of majoritarianism (in effect, the obverse side of an unfocused inclination towards greater political pluralism).

Although the emphasis is still largely upon the pakeha majority rectifying past injustices, the pressure is for a more balanced relationship between the two races based less on numbers and more upon the original principles of partnership contained in the Treaty of Waitangi. Such pressures conflict head-on with the principles of simple majoritarianism. Hence, the contemporary continuing pressure for change in New Zealand with a growing acceptance of the country as an independent, basically bi-cultural nation has, in turn, had important implications for the long established principle of majoritarianism.

If the majoritarian system never explicitly excluded Maori, little intentional permanent provision was made for the effective expression of the viewpoint of what rapidly became a racial minority (the four Maori seats came to acquire a permanent 'temporary' status). Miscegenation was proceeding rapidly and it was confidently expected that, ultimately, Maori would integrate with Europeans. Despite extensive intermarriage, however, a sense of *tangata whenua*, or distinct identity as 'people of the land', persisted and, after languishing in pakeha consciousness, has enjoyed a substantive revival in the second half of the twentieth century.

In particular, many specific Maori grievances have persisted for well over a hundred years. Thus the growth of international concern about race matters since the mid-twentieth century, coupled with better education, served to encourage a greater sense of Maori self-identity just at a time when New Zealand was becoming more conscious of itself as an independent South Pacific nation.

This revival of Maori aspirations, therefore, has to be seen in relation to what amounted to the 'decolonisation' of New Zealand in the 1960s. Britain's decision to seek membership of the European Economic Community had a major impact on the New Zealand economy particularly in matters of trade. In addition, virtually free traffic in people between Britain and New Zealand began to be restricted as immigration restrictions and work permits were required by Britain. The close identification with that country which had permeated New Zealanders' thought came under growing pressure as Britain turned more to Europe. For a variety of reasons it became clear that the previously close relationship between Britain and New Zealand was no longer on the British political agenda. This, in turn, helped foster a growing sense of separateness and independence in New Zealand. New Zealand was a country which was pushed reluctantly into independence.

This lessening of ties with Britain, coupled with the world-wide growth of race issues, led to Maori reassessing their own position and reviewing the circumstances under which they had originally lost control of their native land. They began to see themselves no longer as a minority group in a British Dominion, which in turn was part of a greater whole, the Commonwealth. Rather, as New Zealand was forced to turn in on itself, their position became much clearer as the aggrieved partners in what had once been their land.

It is in this adaptation stage, therefore, that the limitations of the majoritarian system are most tellingly revealed. It is arguable that the existing system was well-attuned to a simple, pioneering, dependent, essentially mono-cultural state with a small population, such as New Zealand was until the mid-twentieth century.

Although conscious of themselves as an autonomous unit within the British Empire and, later, the Commonwealth, pakeha New Zealanders until mid-century had regarded Britain as 'home' and had not been accustomed to think in terms of dependence or independence. With Britain's declared intention of entering the European Community, that option was no longer available and so it was that, belatedly, the stirrings of feelings of true independence began to make themselves felt.

With the steady decline in trade and emotional ties, the extent of the previous reliance upon British models of institutions and behaviour also began to decline. If, in the 1950s and 1960s, New Zealand had led the way in adopting the 'foreign' concepts of unicameralism and of the Ombudsman, by the 1970s a groping towards independence was to turn into an era of assertive New Zealand nationalism, contrasting sharply with the faithful ally and supporter role which the country had almost invariably played in the past.

With a greater consciousness of themselves as a distinct South Pacific nation on the part of pakeha New Zealanders went a growing consciousness that Maoridom too had come to mean something more than the notable achievements of the Maori Battalion in World War II or token *haka* (ritual chant). In particular, it rapidly became clear that New Zealand, far from achieving the 'race miracle', was not exempt from race issues, a developing world-wide phenomenon at the time.

And so the deficiencies of the two-party majoritarian system were further highlighted. Whereas federal systems with highly developed, devolved, regional government centres, or separate executives frequently succeeded in providing a wide range of input agencies for democratic participation, this is less likely to be the case in strictly majoritarian systems. Basic societal assumptions were changing in New Zealand but the constitutional and political arrangements failed to reflect this adequately.

In the 1980s, in what Colin James (1986) has dubbed 'the quiet revolution', fundamental economic and social upheavals added to the accelerating rate of change which had come to characterise the country as it shed much of its welfare state chrysalis and emerged into world markets as a lean, hungry, capitalist economy. There was, therefore, a sense of inevitability that political change, and constitutional change, would have to follow far-reaching economic and social changes, but it was by no means obvious that this would involve such a dramatic shift to what had hitherto been regarded as an alien form of electoral system and a new interest in the workings of continental European legislatures rather than the traditional British model.

The Constitutional Perspective

Viewed from a constitutional perspective, it is possible to argue that the adoption of some form of proportional electoral system appears to be a logical consequence of what had gone before. Logically, New Zealand might have been expected to adopt proportional representation in 1950 when it abolished the old second chamber of parliament. Such a development would have had the effect of widening the representative nature of the lower house in order to compensate for the removal of the Legislative Council. The fact that this was not even seriously considered is an indication of the stranglehold that British tradition and thought continued to hold at that time.

New Zealand's constitutional development has been a largely incremental process, designed by and for settlers, and following an unbroken course from colony through Dominion status to independence. In 1852 a colonial constitution was devised by Britain but, initially at least, this provided only for representative, not responsible, government. Replete with provisions for Superintendents and Provincial Councils, development could well have taken a federal rather than a unitary direction, as occurred in Canada and later Australia. This would have served to limit the degree of unalloyed majoritarianism that was to emerge subsequently in New Zealand. The principal potential safeguard against that was an appointed second chamber. This was partly intended in the mid-nineteenth century as an informal bar on republicanism.

Once the original institutions were established institutional choice was determined by political culture and expediency. Legitimacy was fostered by the mid-nineteenth century parliaments frequently referring back to Westminster for guidance and consciously seeking to mould themselves on the British parliament. Yet this was also a culture impatient of any impediments to the will of the elected majority. In this sense the New Zealand version of the Westminster model was soon to run ahead of its mentor.

The provinces were abolished in 1876; the powers of the Governor were limited in 1892 when he was required to follow the advice of his local ministers; the Legislative Council, the upper house of parliament, was tamed by reducing life tenure to seven year terms, also in 1892, and it was finally abolished in 1950. Meanwhile, legal independence was achieved with the *Statute of Westminster Adoption Act 1947*.

By 1950, of the 82 sections of *The New Zealand Constitution Act 1852* originally passed by the Westminster parliament, no fewer than 70 had been repealed and 11 amended. Only two clauses, albeit amended, could be said to be of substantive effect. New Zealand had reached what Geoffrey Palmer has characterised as "a stripped version of the Westminster model; some might call it the racing model" (Palmer, 1992:184).

Lacking a formal written constitution or an upper house, developed regional or local government, without proportional representation and with two highly cohesive political parties, New Zealand was more lacking in constitutional safeguards than any comparable western democracy. It had become the most highly majoritarian democratic nation in the world.

There is evidence to suggest, however, that the abolition of the Legislative Council was the 'final straw' and pressure began to build for new safeguards to be established. Thus, if the period between 1852 and 1950 had seen the dismantling of much of the original structure, since 1950 a process of constitutional rebuilding has been under way, beginning with the important *Electoral Act 1956* which, with its reserved (entrenched) sections, represented something approaching a quasi-constitution in function. In particular, some of the Acts of a quasi-constitutional nature passed from 1950 on (sometimes in response to obligations adopted under United Nations' auspices) seem to indicate a desire to limit the otherwise overweening powers of majority single party governments.

The *Electoral Act 1956*, complete with its entrenched clauses, represented a part step in the direction of formal limitations upon government (albeit morally rather than legally binding). In addition to the establishment of the Ombudsman in 1962, the *Electoral Act* was followed by: a Race Relations Conciliator (1971), the Waitangi Tribunal (1975); the Privacy Commissioner (1976); the Human Rights Commissioner and the Equal Rights Tribunal (1977); the *Official Information Act 1982*; *Constitution Act 1986*; the *New Zealand Bill of Rights Act 1990* together with the *Citizens Initiated Referenda Act 1993* and a new *Electoral Act 1993*.

The impact of these measures varies considerably. The 1986 *Constitution Act*, for example, does not fulfil the usual purposes of a written constitution. It is not entrenched, except for the term of parliament (which was transferred from the 1956 *Electoral Act*). As Palmer has commented:

> It is the closest New Zealand has yet got to a written constitution; yet it is rather fragmentary. Much of the detail which matters is to be found elsewhere... There is much important constitutional material not contained in it. (Palmer, 1992:47.)

On the other hand, the *Official Information Act*, the *Bill of Rights Act*, the *Public Finance Act, Reserve Bank Act, Fiscal Responsibility Act* and, potentially, the *Citizens Initiated Referenda Act* and new *Electoral Act* represent important additions to the political and constitutional framework. Despite the fact that nearly all these measures are unentrenched, they represent further moves in the direction of seeking to place limits upon governments, whether formal or informal.

Coupled with the increased use of referendums, even before the *Citizens' Initiated Referenda Act 1993* (see Simpson, 1992), and the increasing role of the courts in interpreting legislation (particularly in relation to the Treaty of Waitangi), there were increasingly discernible moves away from the unalloyed majoritarianism of the Westminster model as described by Lijphart (1984: 1–21), even before the implementation of MMP.

Quite apart from the adoption of MMP, many of these preceding measures suggest growing dissatisfaction with the 'stripped' version of the Westminster model. Far from appearing 'out of the blue' therefore, the introduction of MMP follows a long series of less dramatic constitutional changes and the decision to displace the majoritarian model cannot be viewed in isolation.

Most of the constitutional changes which preceded the adoption of MMP were largely premised upon the long-held assumption that New Zealand is basically a homogeneous society (or that if it is not, it ought to be). Today, that assumption can no longer be taken for granted. The adequacy of single-party majorities to meet contemporary needs in circumstances of parliamentary sovereignty and an unwritten constitution have come into question, thus opening the way for the adoption of proportional representation as a device for removing the undesirable features of majoritarianism. It is notable too that, unlike all earlier constitutional changes, this one was finally decided by the people at a referendum in the face of opposition from the political elite.

Another factor helping to make change possible was the decline of the two major political parties (Fig. 1.1). From 1935 until 1994 New Zealand represented the classic two-party system. One of the two major parties had always won and maintained a clear majority of seats. Certainly, since 1954,

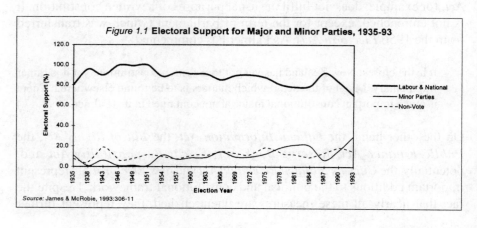

Figure 1.1 **Electoral Support for Major and Minor Parties, 1935-93**

Source: James & McRobie, 1993:306-11

when the Social Credit Political League entered the race, there was always third party intervention in elections but no third party ever won more than two parliamentary seats at one election. Even during World War II there was a separate War Cabinet but no coalition government. It was not until 1994 that a sitting government became a minority as a result of defections.

Nevertheless, the two-party hegemony began to be seriously upset in the 1970s. Following a twelve year period of National Party dominance, Labour was elected in 1972 only to be resoundingly defeated a mere three years later. A revivified National Party, in turn, suffered a strong electoral rebuff at the 1978 general election and by 1981, with Social Credit polling over 20 per cent of the vote, it was clear that public confidence in both major political parties was in decline. Lifetime habits of voting were breaking down in what was to become a process of dealignment.

In effect, New Zealand was suffering the effects of a combination of economic factors. The oil crises of the 1970s, coupled with Britain's entry into the European Community, had dealt a body blow to the New Zealand economy. Despite some heroic efforts at trade diversification, the economy had become inflexible, curbed by bureaucratic regulations as well as trade union and employer rigidity. Yet, with a declining economy, both major political parties continued to electioneer in the only way they knew how, by offering the voters benefits in one form or another. New Zealand elections were largely auctions with the two major parties competing with each other to offer the best 'deals'. When the need was to distribute 'scarcities' rather than 'benefits' both major parties continued to offer 'benefits' which both knew the country could no longer afford. When finally forced to 'bite the bullet' in government, both major parties successively did succeed in adopting courageous policies, but only at the cost of discrediting themselves because of the stark contrast between promises and performance.

The extent of the breakdown in support for the two major political parties at this time may be gauged by the degree of electoral volatility. The average volatility rate for elections between 1954 and 1969 (defined as 'fluctuations in voting results between elections'), was 6.6 per cent; between 1972 and 1990 the rate doubled to 13.3 per cent, with the elections of 1984, 1987 and 1990 generating the highest volatility scores of all, averaging 17.3 per cent. In 1990 it reached a new peak of nearly 20 per cent. So, if in 1963, 89 per cent of voters voted for the same party that they had supported in 1960, a comparable figure for 1987 and 1990 would be 64 per cent (Aimer and Vowles, 1993:14).

The dealignment which this represents is also reflected in a marked decline in the membership of the major political parties. In the 1960s and 1970s both major parties used to claim 200,000 members each in election years, dropping to approximately 100,000 at other times. By the 1990s, the National Party was widely considered to have fewer than 50,000 ordinary members even in an election year, with the Labour Party less than that. Both, however, carefully maintained the confidentiality of any specific figures. Electoral Commission research conducted in 1994 asking whether respondents had *ever* been a member of a political party, elicited a 19.2 per cent 'yes'. Asked if the respondent was *currently* member of a political party, only 6.5 per cent answered 'yes' (Harris, 1997b:16).

If the immediate cause of the problems preceding the adoption of MMP was, in this sense, the political parties and their policies, rather than the electoral system, it is clear that the nature of that system was an important factor in this competitive situation where voters took a stand mainly for, or against, a particular government. At the same time, the electoral victories of a National Party government in 1978 and 1981 on a minority of the total vote (although extremely rare occurrences) served to undermine public confidence in the electoral system. This was then reinforced in 1984 when a new party, the New Zealand Party, attracted a great deal of media attention and succeeded in winning more than 12 per cent of the vote but no seats.

If it is a rare occurrence for a nation to change its electoral system, it is even rarer for that choice to be left to the voting public. That reform was on the formal political agenda at all was the result of an unusual admixture of principle, miscalculation and political opportunism. Originally motivated by idealism as much as anything, the establishment of a Royal Commission seemed a harmless enough proposal. Deeply influenced by the need to cater for a bi-cultural society, the Commission itself formulated the type of change it deemed desirable; the public, disenchanted with politicians and politics for other reasons, was looking for some alternative, any alternative, to the political status quo. The political leaders, trapped in their two-party games, were unable to resist the temptation to try to outbid their rivals and then proved to be absurdly overconfident that, fundamentally, the public would continue to share their own belief in the status quo. The proclamation of that belief, perceived by the public as vested interest, merely served to further disillusionment.

Viewed in terms of a specific policy choice therefore, the choice faced by the intelligent voter in the November 1993 referendum was not just a simple question of a straight choice between a majoritarian or a proportional type system. The choice involved an individual's views on executive dominance, largely subsumed in views of broken party promises and a decade of far-reaching economic and social change. It may also have involved attitudes towards New Zealand as a homogeneous or bi-cultural society. But for many, it was a question of whether feelings of general dissatisfaction with the working of the existing system were outweighed, or not, by the fears and apprehensions attending the unknown consequences of the introduction of an alternative electoral system. To some extent the weight of these unknown consequences was alleviated by the commitment that the electoral system would be reviewed again by the House of Representatives after a sufficient trial of the MMP system. But above all, there was the danger that a failure to vote for MMP was likely to be taken by the politicians as a signal that major reforms to the system were not required, merely further tinkering.

The Conceptual Perspective

In his book *Democracies* published in 1984, Lijphart described the New Zealand system as:

> a virtually perfect example of the Westminster model of democracy ... In nearly all respects, [he wrote] democracy in New Zealand is more clearly majoritarian, and hence a better example of the Westminster model, than **British democracy**. (1984:16, **19**.)

He also quoted Rose to the effect that New Zealand is "the only example of the true British system left" (**ibid., 19**). For Lijphart the Westminster model was characterised by:

- Concentration of executive power with one-party and bare majority cabinets;
- Fusion of power and cabinet dominance;
- Unicameralism;
- A two-party system;
- A one-dimensional party system;
- A plurality system of elections;
- Unitary and centralised government;
- An unwritten constitution;
- Parliamentary sovereignty and a representative democracy.

Yet, within ten years of the publication of Lijphart's book, a number of changes suggested a substantial move away from some of the majoritarian principles which had served the country since responsible government was established in 1856.

There is a view that, too often, the simple majoritarian system fails to convey adequate signals; is prone to promote rather than to resolve differences; fails to represent minority interests adequately and thus fails to meet sufficiently the criteria for either representative or participatory democracy. In a highly cohesive two-party system, adversary politics can be seen as both promoting and exacerbating conflict (Johnson, 1975:76) and, because of its essential artificiality, ultimately calling the credibility of both political parties and parliament into question.

Thus no less than four of Lijphart's criteria came under questioning or attack: the concentration of executive power; the two party system; the simple plurality system of elections and even unicameralism. In particular, the decision to change to a Mixed Member Proportional electoral system represented a fundamental move away from the traditional majoritarian system. But to what? For Lijphart the alternative to majoritarianism is consensus, but the introduction of MMP does not, of itself, introduce a consensual model. The eight majority-restraining elements making up his consensus model are:

- Executive power-sharing — as distinct from the concentration of executive power;
- Separation of powers, formal or informal, i.e. a more balanced relationship between executive and legislature;
- Balanced bicameralism and minority representation;
- Multi-party system;
- Multi-dimensional party system, i.e. representation of the various lines of cleavage in a plural society;
- Proportional Representation;
- Territorial and non-territorial federalism and decentralisation, i.e. providing autonomy for groups within society (e.g. cultural councils);
- Written constitution and minority veto.

These eight elements aim at *restraining* majority rule by requiring or encouraging the sharing of power among executive and legislature; sharing power among parties; the delegation of power where practicable (territorially or non-territorially) together with formal limits on power (e.g. formal constitution, minority veto).

Of these eight characteristics the advent of MMP was likely to introduce *three*. Obviously proportional representation was one of these while executive power-sharing and a multi-party system were probable consequential outcomes. Beyond that, there were a number of other possible outcomes which could result.

First, as the Royal Commission anticipated, representation of Maori has improved as has representation of women, Pacific Islanders and Asian New Zealanders (McRobie, 1997:330-335). An improvement would have been expected anyway with the increase in the size of the House to 120 members. It still remains to be seen, however, whether Maori will succumb to the siren song of a separate Maori party, a possibility offered by the adoption of MMP.

The likelihood of a multi-dimensional party system is not high, however, for apart from differences of race and gender, there are relatively few cleavages that require additional representation in New Zealand society. Further constitutional change, such as federalism seems inappropriate for a small population, although this need not necessarily preclude greater devolution, particularly where Maori interests are concerned. On the other hand, a formal written constitution, normally an important feature of states where different races live together, could come to be seen as a desirable outcome of the changed system.

Hence, if the constitutional changes made before the 1993 referendum are best viewed as the beginnings of a trend away from the majoritarian Westminster system (in particular, the *Citizens Initiated Referenda Act* and the type of changes made to parliament's Standing Orders), we need to accept that the fundamental policy change to MMP, far from being an end in itself, is likely to be the harbinger of a further series of consequential changes.

Consequential Changes

It will be seen that the specific move away from the traditional majoritarian system took place for a number of different reasons. A crucial consideration was the widespread perception that the two party system was no longer working as well as it once did; that it was no longer so responsive as in earlier times. This perception was closely linked to the problem of executive dominance which was possible because of the high degree of party cohesion which had been developed by the two principal political parties.

To this was added a developing concern at the disproportional effects of the simple plurality electoral system. Majorities of votes could be grossly distorted as majorities of seats and minorities of the total vote could even be expressed as a majority of seats. It also discriminated heavily against third party representation, a factor which became increasingly important as the process of voting dealignment became more pronounced in the 1970s and 1980s. For the last two decades of FPP some 17.7 per cent of the voting population preferred parties other than the two major political parties at general elections and was denied effective representation. For third party supporters and Maori, in particular, the two-party system proved unsatisfactory and it is arguable that others might have defected from the major parties but for the constraints imposed by the two-party system. This problem of providing more adequately for ethnic representation is a matter which was clearly of major concern to the Royal Commission on the Electoral System (RCES, 1986a:81).

In terms of goals, therefore, negatives prevailed. The causes of the reaction against the status quo were much clearer than the potential benefits or disadvantages of change. As Mulgan put it before the 1993 electoral referendum, "political support for electoral reform ... is more conservative than radical in its inspiration" (Hawke, 1993:54).

This might be seen as reflecting the fact that for much of the twentieth century the two-party system appeared to work satisfactorily and was the cause of few major complaints. The failure to produce acceptable results in the last two decades of the twentieth century followed the protest movements associated with the Vietnam war and coincided with the severe economic downturn associated with the increased oil prices of the 1970s, adverse terms of trade, and the entry of the United Kingdom into the European Community.

Conclusion

There are a variety of approaches possible to explaining New Zealand's adoption of MMP. The simplest is the knee-jerk reaction of profound disillusionment with the performance of successive governments. That, however, raises the question of just how and why the means of *expressing* and *formulating* that knee-jerk reaction happened to be in place at the right time to allow for its focused expression.

Alternatively, we may substitute a pro-active approach. It might still be argued, for example, that what happened in 1992 and 1993 was merely a continuation of the 'quiet revolution' of which James (1986) had written in the 1980s. Undoubtedly, in New Zealand today, the reality of independence has outrun the symbols and old ties. In one important sense the referendum decision could be viewed as an important indicator of the country's growing self-confidence, representing a readiness to adopt yet another change to add to a long line of upheavals in the past three decades. These changes have ranged from the introduction of decimal currency to the *Employment Contracts Act* and substantial re-structuring of a hitherto sacrosanct welfare state.

In another sense MMP could be viewed as the coping stone completing the adaptation stage of constitutional development which arguably should have taken place at the time that the upper house, the Legislative Council, was abolished in 1950. Other changes taking place more or less concurrently such as the *Bill of Rights Act*, the increased size of the House of Representatives or the *Citizens Initiated Referenda Act*, might also be seen as fitting into that mould.

For some time the New Zealand Westminster model has been emancipated from slavish imitation of the specific practices of Westminster. Now the adoption of a new electoral system opens up a new era of change. To continue change of this order is to add further upheavals to the long line which many have faced in their lifetimes. To put a stop to change is hardly a valid option. The question uppermost to-day is not *whether* to change or not, but what rate of change to adopt, whether to continue radical change at a fast rate, whether to revert to incrementalism, or to continue at perhaps some intermediate rate. The adoption of MMP may well prove to have been a decisive step in reaching that decision.

So while MMP may be the coping stone completing the adaptation stage of constitutional development and moderating future change, like the dialectic it is also likely to constitute the beginning of a new transformation stage. In this stage a relatively newly independent multicultural state will have to struggle to implement a balanced pluralist regime while at the same time meeting a new order of problems likely to be associated with the twenty-first century. It seems likely that a phase of experimenting with different forms, techniques and processes, is just beginning, perhaps not unlike the turn of last century, except that the scale of the problems confronted is likely to be greater and the pace of change is likely to be more continuous and faster.

Note

1   These development categories are adapted from those used by Samuel P. Huntington in Huntington & Moore, eds. (1970:24).

2   Early Electoral Experiments

A variety of circumstances exist in New Zealand which do not exist in Great Britain and which make it desirable that any system of government adopted here should rest upon well-understood law, and be adapted to the peculiar circumstances and requirements of the colony.
— Report of the Constitutional Reform Committee, 1891.
AJHR, 1891 (Session II), I.10, p 1.

As we have already noted, New Zealand has been described as "a virtually perfect example of the Westminster model of democracy", one where power is concentrated in the hands of the leaders of the political party winning a clear majority of the seats in the legislature at the most recent general election. Given this scenario, elections are essentially contests between two overwhelmingly dominant political parties, with the party which wins a majority of the single-member electorates (decided by simple plurality) forming a single-party government. Executive dominance is maintained by the application of rigid party discipline and, in New Zealand's case, is further strengthened by the absence (since the beginning of 1951) of the constraining influence of a second chamber. Once in power the cabinet dominates both the executive and legislative functions of government. This is parliamentary democracy at its most streamlined. A more recent view is that the ideal Westminster model — one which promotes consensual and effective government, and shackles power with accountability (Norris, 1997:228) — does not adequately describe New Zealand's political system as it operated in the First-past-the-post (FPP) electoral environment.

Yet, despite appearances, New Zealand's electoral system has never been frozen in time. New Zealand's politicians have frequently revisited the country's electoral laws, not only to amend them to keep pace with the rapidly changing political, economic and social conditions but also to propose alternatives which, in the eyes of some Members of the House of Representatives (MHR)[1] at least, would more fairly reflect the principles on which they believed the country's electoral law should be based. Several reasons can be advanced to explain this seemingly greater willingness to experiment. New Zealand was settled during the 'Chartist decade' (1838–48) and many of its leading settlers were strongly influenced by Chartist ideals, including triennial parliaments, household suffrage, the abolition of the property qualification and the secret ballot. The nature of New Zealand's early settlements and the character of the settlers provided conditions favourable to the dissemination of radical Chartist

18

and liberal ideas of representation. During the late 1840s and early 1850s settlers, particularly those in the Cook Strait settlements, waged an intensive and largely successful campaign to secure political rights to which they believed they were entitled. Their demands reflected the liberal objective of popular participation in politics by 'active' citizens, but Chartism's influence resulted in their demands being far more radical than the political rights then accepted as proper in Great Britain (Wood, 1969:140; Herron, 1960:28–44).

If there is a single theme underpinning the development of New Zealand's electoral system it is one of adoption and adaptation. The basic constitutional and electoral framework was bequeathed by the *New Zealand Constitution Act 1852* (McLintock, 1958: 417–33), and Governor Sir George Grey's 1853 electoral proclamation (*NZG*, I:3:14 May 1853) which breathed life into a bare-bones framework. From the time that the New Zealand parliament assumed control of the electoral system in 1858, it has been modified frequently to meet the needs and demands of the local community. Sometimes New Zealand looked to Great Britain for inspiration; on other occasions the parliament looked across the Tasman to the Australian colonies (for example, the adoption of the secret ballot[2]); while others (for example, separate representation for the country's indigenous peoples and the development of provisions for regular reapportionments carried out by an independent commission) were unique to nineteenth century New Zealand. Some developments, such as the qualifications required to be registered as an elector, were settled relatively easily while others, such as the goal of one person-one vote-one value, were achieved only after lengthy and acrimonious debate.

From the outset New Zealand's legislators were not averse to proposing changes to many aspects of the electoral law as they strove to develop a framework that reflected representational principles and values they deemed to be important. Among these were questions about who or what was to be represented, how representation was to be achieved, and how the electoral system might be structured to ensure fairness to all. As a consequence, a number of core values — individual (as opposed to community) representation, equality of all votes, and the neutral, impartial administration of the electoral law — are, today, central features of New Zealand's electoral system.

This is not to say that all proposals for change were greeted with unbridled enthusiasm. The parliamentary records are littered with rejected and lapsed bills proposing changes — different voting systems, state initiated and citizens' initiated referendums, proposals to choose the country's Governor by popular election, and for MHRs to elect the Executive — which were promoted with considerable alacrity and persistence. Only the second ballot mechanism — used in the 1908 and 1911 elections — was approved and put into practice, albeit fleetingly. The other proposals indicate clearly, however, that the concept and process of representation was a live issue during the period when individual representation was giving way to government by party.

Most of the proposals for radical reform were concentrated in the four decades between 1890 and 1930. This period falls neatly into two halves: between 1890 and c.1912 the main advocates of reform were government supporters. After the Reform Party won office following the 1911 election, however, the main advocates for electoral reform were to be found amongst Labour party politicians intent upon implementing their party's policy of proportional representation, referendums, the initiative, and recall (Harris & Levine, 1994:138). The franchise had been steadily broadened throughout the second half of the nineteenth century and by the mid-1890s the goal of universal adult suffrage had been reached. Once this had been achieved, efforts were concentrated on making the electoral system more democratic, even more representative, and more fair. That most of these endeavours failed can be attributed to the development of party politics and the accompanying desire to control the legislature. Politicians of all hues increasingly evaluated proposals for changes to the electoral system in terms of party political advantage or disadvantage. Inevitably, this made it more difficult for MHRs to assess proposals on their intrinsic merits and most, therefore, were rejected. By the mid-1930s, when the two-party system became firmly established, the zeal for electoral reform had waned perceptibly as both Labour and National recognised the benefits to themselves of the FPP electoral system. Thereafter, until the late 1970s, most debate on matters electoral focused on ensuring that the 'other side' did not legislate any undue advantage for itself when in power. Only when people began questioning whether the long-held values of fairness and equality were still being met, was the debate broadened to include the electorate at large.

The *New Zealand Constitution Act 1852* was closely modelled on the structure of the British parliament and electoral system then in place. It conferred representative government on the colony and provided for a General Assembly consisting of an appointed Legislative Council, and a House of Representatives elected by qualified persons who were registered as electors. For New Zealand's earliest politicians, however, this represented little more than a necessary starting point and, whereas reform of the United Kingdom's electoral system was an almost inevitable corollary of franchise extension implemented only through inter-party agreement (Hanham, 1968:8; Butler, 1963:121–22), New Zealand's electoral law has been the subject of argument and controversy throughout much of the country's history.

Expanding the Franchise

The 1852 Act incorporated a very modest, and indeed liberal, property franchise. All males aged 21 years and over who met one of three criteria — ownership of land with a value of at least £50, leasing land with a minimum annual rental value of £10, or being a householder of a property with a rental value of £10 or more per annum in a town or £5 per annum in other localities — were eligible to register as electors and to vote in elections for the House of Representatives, provided they had owned, leased, or rented the property for a minimum specified period (*New Zealand Constitution Act, 1852*: ssVII & XLII).[3] Registration provisions closely followed the British model: electors formally claimed the right to be included on the register; these were published to give other citizens an opportunity to object; and Justices of the Peace adjudicated on those received, after which the confirmed roll, valid for one year, was published. In 1858, Registration Officers, the forerunner of today's Registrars of Electors, replaced resident magistrates as the preparers of electoral rolls. Registration was made compulsory for non-Maori in 1924 and for Maori in 1956.

The purpose of making the franchise dependent upon possession of property was to ensure that those who chose the representatives had a defined economic stake in the country. Provided electors met the property qualification, however, there was no restriction on the number of electorates in which they could register. Thus, wealthier electors were permitted to cast a vote in each electorate where they were registered. Herron has pointed out that since land was relatively cheap and there was plenty of it, property — and, therefore, the required property qualification — was not difficult to acquire (Herron, 1960: 36–38). Hence, from the earliest days of representative government, manhood suffrage was close to being universal. According to Frederick Weld, any sort of property test was almost useless in frontier countries like New Zealand, and New Zealand's first historian, A.S. Thomson, wrote that:

> [b]y general consent all settlers claiming the right of voting were permitted to register, and the franchise became universal. Men who influenced elections in England by brickbats were voters in New Zealand. (Thomson, 1859:II,208–09.)

It is little wonder, then, that in the 1850s one out of every five adult males was registered as an elector compared with only one in every thirty in Great Britain.

In 1860, the franchise was expanded to include male holders of miners' rights in designated goldfields, provided they were aged 21 years or older and had held a miners' right for at least three months. Although they did not necessarily own land, they were deemed to have a stake in the economic future of the country. This provision was replaced two years later by the *Miners' Representation Act*, which established separate representation for goldminers but did not rule out multiple registration by holders of a miners' right who were otherwise qualified to register in another electoral district. In 1879 the franchise was further widened to include all males aged 21 and over, although the continued presence of the property qualification meant that those who owned property in different parts of the country remained entitled to be registered as electors and vote in every electorate where they were qualified. Plural voting was finally abolished in 1889, and in 1893 residency was established as the sole criterion for registration as an elector.[4]

Although Maori who qualified under the provisions of the 1852 Act were able to register as electors, few did so in practice since most Maori land was held in communal ownership (Herron, 1960:32–33).[5] Towards the end of the 1860s land wars the franchise was extended to male Maori as of right through the establishment of separate representation. In 1867 four seats specifically reserved for Maori electors were created, and all Maori over the age of 21 years were eligible to register. Thus, universal manhood suffrage was granted to Maori some 12 years before it was conferred on non-Maori although the four seats allocated in no way reflected Maori population numbers.

New Zealand was the first nation state to accord the franchise to women[6] but this was not attained without a struggle extending over nearly thirty years prior to 1893. From the time of Mary Müller's pro-suffrage pamphlet in 1869, the agitation for female political emancipation gathered momentum to reach a peak in the early 1890s under the leadership of Kate Sheppard. Although the Liberal Government led by Seddon[7] was unsympathetic to the demands of the suffrage movement, there were sufficient legislators in both Houses favouring the move for it to pass into law shortly before the 1893 general election (Grimshaw, 1972). But while women had been granted the vote, another 26 years were to pass before they were permitted to stand as candidates for election, and a further 15 years was to elapse before the first woman MHR was elected.[8]

Votes of Equal Value

When Grey proclaimed the boundaries of electoral districts in 1853 he did so on the basis of the power vested in him by section 51 of the *Constitution Act 1852*. This required him to determine the number of districts, the number of members elected to represent each district, and that representation was broadly proportionate to the total population and its geographic distribution. Grey divided the country into 24 electorates represented by a total of 37 members, with each electorate having between one and three representatives. On a total population basis all six provinces fell within ±22 per cent of the mean. Variations in the population numbers of electoral districts within each province were, however, much larger, ranging from +122 per cent for Auckland's Southern Division to –68.1 per cent for Canterbury's Akaroa electoral district. Although the variations between the most populous and least populous electorates narrowed significantly over the next 25 years, a basic pattern had been established; less populous provinces were over-represented at the expense of the more populous ones and, within provinces, inequalities worked to the advantage of rural areas. Thus, primacy was given to the representation of communities, and an informal quota favouring the less densely populated districts was a feature of New Zealand's electoral system from the beginning. The votes of individuals were far from being equal in value.

Rapid population growth — the non-Maori population rose from approximately 34,000 in 1854 to over 625,000 in 1891 — and equally dramatic shifts in its distribution meant that regular revisions of electoral districts was necessary if the 1852 *Constitution Act's* insistence on reasonable equality was to be maintained. Until 1887 the House of Representatives undertook this exercise periodically, usually shortly before each general election but at shorter intervals when dramatic population influxes, such as those arising from the 1860s gold rushes, occurred. A variety of techniques was used — committees of politicians or the Committee of the Whole House were the most common — but most reviews were marked by acrimony and dissension as members sought to establish personal positions of advantage. At a time where frequent revisions to electoral district boundaries were imperative, parliament found itself totally unable to devise a procedure whereby politicians could undertake reapportionments in an atmosphere free from tension.

Interestingly, the automatic reapportionment of electoral districts by an independent authority had been first proposed as early as 1858. In that year Stafford's ministry introduced the Representation Apportionment Bill which, had it been enacted, would have left responsibility for determining the number and extent of electoral districts, and the number of members for each, with the Governor (*Bills Thrown Out*, 1858). The select committee which considered this bill (along with other electoral measures) rejected the proposal because, in its view, the "self adjusting system of apportionment ... is not required, and that any such change of apportionment ... ought to be provided by special enactment" (*AJHR*, 1858). Twenty years were to pass before the issue was raised again. In 1879, shortly before his Ministry fell, Sir George Grey introduced a bill to establish an independent five-member 'Representation

Board' in whom total responsibility for the regular division of the country into electoral districts would be vested. Although Grey's proposal was rejected by the Hall Government, it provided a model and a catalyst for the eventual establishment of an independent, politically neutral body to carry out this task.

The 1881 electoral redistribution, the first to adopt single-member electoral districts as the sole standard, brought the issue of political involvement to a head. Divisions among MHRs were so strained that 'party' and 'caucus' groupings were largely reformed as the issue was "... thrown on the floor of this House with ninety-one districts and a map to be scrambled over [and with] every man fighting over his own existence" (*NZPD*, 1881:205). Six years later, when another reapportionment was pressing, parliament established an independent, quasi-judicial Representation Commission armed with very specific and narrow terms of reference, to recast electoral boundaries following each five-yearly census. Although both the Commission's composition and the redistribution criteria it was required to follow have been modified from time to time since then, the principles of independence from direct political interference, impartiality, and the finality of its determinations, has stood the test of time for more than a century and, in more recent years, has provided a model for other countries.

The *Representation Act 1887* specified that the total population of all European electorates[9] must lie within ±750 of the electorate quota (calculated by dividing the country's total non-Maori population by the number of MHRs) although a nominal addition of 18 per cent — the 'country quota' — was to be added to the populations of designated special districts (McRobie, 1989:145).[10] The country quota (increased to 28 per cent in 1889) remained until its abolition 58 years later. It thus formally perpetuated the inequality of each vote's value as it sought to maintain a fair balance between the urban and rural sectors of society by offsetting an inbuilt advantage perceived to be enjoyed by the more compact urban electorates. Only after its abolition in 1945 could each person's vote be deemed, for all practical purposes, to have the same value.

Proposals for Expanding Representation

At an early stage parliament indicated its interest in making provision for the representation of special interests. The enfranchisement of mining interests and Maori has already been mentioned but other special interest groups were also considered for representation. A precedent had been established as early as 1853 when the Pensioner Settlements electoral district — a cluster of discontinuous frontier townships, originally established by Grey and whose residents (all former Imperial soldiers) had been granted a cottage and an acre of land in return for light military duties — was created. The 1858 select committee proposed extending this concept by recommending that "... in any readjustment of the representation of the Colony, regard, as far as possible, be had to the representation of minorities" (*AJHR*, 1858, F.1:3). It is doubtful, however, whether the mover, Hugh Carleton, the querulous MHR for the Bay of Islands electorate, intended this to be extended to Maori for, later in the committee's deliberations, he proposed, successfully, that the committee recommend that the franchise be extended to university graduates and members "of any of the learned professions ..." (ibid., 14–15).

Until the 1881 electoral redistribution parliamentary representation comprised a mix of single-member and multi-member electorates, although the proportion of members elected from a reducing number of multi-member districts declined steadily throughout this period.[11] Continuing concern for the adequate representation of minorities was evident in 1878 when Robert Stout, Attorney-General in the Grey Government, introduced an electoral bill which included a proposal to adopt a Limited Vote system for multi-member electorates. By seeking to restrict the maximum number of votes each person could cast in a multi-member district, Stout aimed to ensure that the minority viewpoint was represented where there was a close vote. His proposal was rendered redundant by the *Representation Act 1881* which made single-member electorates universal, and was not revived when New Zealand reintroduced multi-member electorates for the four largest cities between 1890 and 1905.

A desire to change the way that election results were determined was kept very much alive by a small handful of MHRs in the 1890s and early 1900s. In 1896 Seddon sponsored the Second Ballot Bill, the first of a succession of bills which sought to alter the way votes were turned into parliamentary seats by requiring a second election to be held where no candidate received more than 50 per cent of the total votes cast in the first election. Members rejected Seddon's proposal in both 1896 and 1897 — a decision that Seddon bemoaned because he feared that the Liberals would lose seats as a consequence of vote-splitting (*NZPD*, 99:700) — but this did not deter him from introducing it yet again in 1898. Thereafter the matter rested until raised by Sir Joseph Ward in 1905 (ibid., 132:8,10).

Politics lay at the heart of revived interest in the second ballot procedure. Since the mid-1890s successive elections had seen increasing numbers of candidates winning seats with fewer than 50 per cent of the votes cast — seven out of 80 in the 1899 election, 13 in 1902, and 16 in 1905. The Liberal Party had become so factionalised as a consequence of its individualism and indiscipline, that it faced seemingly insurmountable problems when it came to selecting candidates to contest elections. The second ballot procedure would, therefore, act as a form of primary election by compelling Liberal candidates to contest an electorate in the expectation that only one would advance where a second ballot was required. Although, when speaking to the bill, Ward stressed that it was based on "the very important principle that the majority should rule everything" (ibid., 144:574), in more pragmatic terms it meant that the Liberal Party's organisation could avoid having to choose between potential candidates before an election got under way (Hamer, 1988:309–10).

Whatever the reason, the outcome was not as the Liberals anticipated. In 1908 a second election was needed in 23 of the eighty electorates, and although the Liberal Party's total vote rose, it was returned with a reduced parliamentary majority (Burdon, 1965:3). In eight of the second ballot elections the initial result was reversed but the final parliamentary strengths of the parties differed little from the aggregate first ballot result (Hamer, 1988:132). Three years later the Liberal Party's parliamentary majority was practically wiped out and, as in the previous election, the second ballot made little difference to the final outcome. Thus, when the new Reform Government implemented its election promise to abolish the second ballot provisions there was little opposition (ibid., 335–40).

Another measure with similar intent was Robert McNab's Absolute Majority Bill which he introduced several times between 1896 and 1907 — in fact, it appeared with such regularity that, in 1905, he even referred to it as "an old friend" (*NZPD*, 132:57). It differed from the second ballot proposal to the extent that it did not require a second, run-off election. Instead, voters would be able to rank candidates in order of preference and, where required, votes would be redistributed successively from the lowest polling candidate to higher polling candidates until one candidate achieved an absolute majority of all votes cast. On several occasions McNab's bill was given a second reading, and once (in 1904) it even negotiated the Committee of the Whole House, but it never won sufficient support in the House of Representatives for it to be referred to the Legislative Council. Had McNab's bill passed into law, it would have pre-dated Australia's adoption of preferential voting by several years. Some years later, in the guise of the Preferential Voting Bill, it surfaced again, this time promoted by the Labour MHR, James McCombs; after narrowly retaining his seat in the 1925 election[12] McCombs promoted the concept of preferential voting for national elections. Parliament, however, remained unconvinced and the proposal died as the great depression intensified.

Perhaps the most persistent of all the proposed electoral reforms — certainly the one that politicians favouring electoral reform promoted most assiduously — was the proposal to replace the FPP electoral system with the

Single Transferable Vote (STV) first developed by Englishman, Thomas Hare[13] in 1857, and vigorously promoted by John Stuart Mill in his work *Considerations on Representative Government*. In both 1888 and 1889 T.W. Hislop introduced a Private Member's bill which proposed introducing STV and multi-member constituencies. His 1889 bill, substantially the more developed of the two, proposed that New Zealand should be divided into four electoral divisions with each division being further sub-divided into districts of convenient size but with each having a population equal to the New Zealand electorate quota or a multiple thereof (*NZPD*, 64:247). Clearly, Hislop wanted to create electoral districts of varying size, each of which would be centred on a community of interest, while, at the same time, preserving the principle of electoral equality.

Hislop's ideas were revived in 1896 by P.J. O'Regan when he introduced his Preferential Voting and Proportional Representation Bill. The main objective of his bill, O'Regan argued, was to give equal right to representation. FPP, he claimed, "... leaves large segments of the population unrepresented. ... Majorities must rule but that furnishes no reason against proportional representation." His proposal involved a modification of the Hare system of STV — "to adapt to the conditions peculiar to the Colony" — whereby 14 constituencies would each be assigned five members (*NZPD*, 94:501). The bill was defeated by 19 votes to 12 at its second reading. Undeterred, O'Regan resurrected the bill in each of the next three years, only to see it suffer the same fate.

O'Regan's defeat in the 1899 election gave the House only brief respite from considering bills promoting STV. In 1903, and again in 1904, George Fowlds introduced another Proportional Representation and Effective Voting Bill which bore a marked similarity to O'Regan's bills. It proposed a modified Hare system with six electorates centred on communities of interest. His stated aim was to achieve what he described as "[t]he ideal condition of a representative chamber ... a microscopic reproduction of the Colony generally". He countered opponents' criticisms that electorates would be large and that the voting system was complicated, by pointing out that the Hare system was already used in Hobart and Launceston, and that there was currently a bill before the Tasmanian Assembly for its introduction state-wide. Nevertheless, the House was largely unsympathetic: in 1903 his bill was, in Seddon's eloquent phrase, "put to sleep", and in 1904 it was defeated by 44 votes to 19 (ibid., 123:233; 127:452; 128:551–70).

The next time the House was asked to consider STV was in 1914 when Independent Liberal MHR, W.A. Veitch, tabled his Proportional Representation and Effective Voting Bill. Prefacing his remarks with the observation that the Reform Government was already committed to proportional representation through its decision to use STV to elect Legislative Councillors, Veitch contended that this voting method should have general application. His proposal, which was strongly supported by Labour's James McCombs, mirrored the proposals for an elected Legislative Council but included the abolition of both the country quota and separate Maori representation. Veitch justified the latter provision by arguing that separate representation for Maori,

> ... has operated greatly to the detriment of the natives ... if the Natives were distributed amongst the other electors and counted amongst them, and voted along with the Europeans in the ordinary way ... they would have an influence and a say in the election of quite a large number of honourable members. The effect of that, undoubtedly, would be that the welfare of the natives would be far better conserved and far more effectively defended in parliament than they are at the present time. (ibid., 169:314.)

Notwithstanding the eloquence of his plea, Veitch's bill was defeated by 28 votes to 27 at its second reading. One possible reason cited for its defeat was that the Chief Electoral Officer had visited Tasmania the previous year, and had reported that he saw difficulties in integrating the triennial local liquor licensing polls which were conducted within existing electorates, with the enlarged electorates that would be necessary if STV were to be adopted (McRobie, 1989:9–10). Equally, however, with the Reform Party just having won power there was little or no incentive for it to tamper with an electoral system that had proved beneficial.

With the sole exception of 1915, the Proportional Representation and Effective Representation Bill appeared on the order paper of the House of Representatives each year for the next eight years. It attracted little support, however, until 1919 when it was accorded a second reading. In 1921 two bills — one by Veitch, another by McCombs — were introduced. McCombs' bill is particularly interesting because it attempted to meet the objections which had been raised against the abolition of the country quota proposed in Veitch's bill by allowing the Representation Commission to reduce the number of members allocated to an electorate from a minimum of five to three where the country quota advantage could not otherwise be maintained. Neither progressed past the introductory stage and both were reintroduced in 1922. Then, Veitch's bill was struck out because it involved an appropriation while McCombs' bill remained low down on the order paper until it was discharged.

The next year the government endeavoured to pre-empt further attempts at electoral reform by circulating a draft Legislature Amendment Bill which proposed the compulsory registration of electors and preferential voting in rural electorates (*NZPD*, 202:704). The compulsory registration provisions were approved in 1924, but a revised, hybrid proposal for electoral reform — combining preferential voting in single-member rural electorates with multi-member electorates for the four main cities where representatives would be elected by proportional representation — won virtually no support and was soon abandoned (ibid., 203:681–85; 205:1075). This was to be the last serious attempt for more than sixty years to remodel New Zealand's existing electoral system to make it fairer to minority interests (RCES, 1986:A56). After the 1925 election there was little incentive for MHRs to pursue the reform path; the Reform Government, with 48.7 per cent of the votes and 71.3 per cent of the seats in the House of Representatives, had won a stunning victory while Labour, although its share of seats in the House dropped from 17 to 12, was elevated to the position of official Opposition. The modern, if still only embryo, two-party system was starting to emerge and neither Reform nor Labour, as the chief beneficiaries of the developing right–left cleavage, had cause to push for radical change.

Despite these setbacks the supporters of proportional representation had been able to secure the passage of the *Local Elections (Proportional Representation) Act 1914*. This Act, which was intended to be experimental, gave local authority councils the option of electing members by proportional representation. The only councils to accept the challenge were the Christchurch City Council, which used STV in its 1917, 1929, 1931 and 1933 elections, and the Woolston Borough (also in Christchurch) which adopted STV for its 1917 and 1919 elections. After 1933 no council sought to hold its elections under the authority of this act even though it remained on the statute book until repealed in 1966 as part of a periodic overhaul of the *Local Elections and Polls Act*.

Reforming the Legislative Council

New Zealand's Upper House, the Legislative Council, was established as an integral part of the General Assembly by the *Constitution Act 1852* which provided that its members would be appointed for life. Following the election of the Liberal Government led by Ballance in 1890, and the subsequent tussle between the two Houses, life appointments were replaced by term appointments of seven years with the right of reappointment (Jackson, 1972:136–53 *passim*).[14]

Despite this change, agitation for the replacement of the nominated Legislative Council by an elected body continued. In 1879 Sir George Grey had attempted to reform the Legislative Council with his Elective Legislative Council Bill, a measure that proposed the establishment of two electoral provinces, each of which would elect 12 European Councillors for a three-year term. Under Grey's proposal two Maori Councillors would also have been elected, one by North Island Maori and the other by South Island and Stewart Island Maori (*NZPD,* 33:255–60; Jackson, 1972:157–58). Twenty years later, Frederick Pirani, a man of strong left-wing liberal views (*DNZB,* 1993, 2:388–89) introduced his Elective Legislative Council Bill, a measure which closely reflected Grey's earlier proposal.[15] Although this initiative also foundered, its basic idea was resurrected three years later by another liberal, Henry Ell, who proposed a 40-Member Legislative Council, 38 European and two Maori, elected by simple plurality.[16] Under his plan, two European House of Representatives' electoral districts would be linked to elect one Councillor except in the four main cities where an adjoining electoral district would be grouped with each city electorate to return two Councillors. The two Maori Legislative Councillors would be elected from a single New Zealand wide electoral division (*Bills Thrown Out,* 1902).

Like Pirani before him, Ell failed to persuade his fellow MHRs to accept his proposal, but the notion of an elected Legislative Council remained alive. On no fewer than five occasions between 1904 and 1910, bills were introduced to transform the Legislative Council into an elective body. All were rejected but, in 1914, an amendment to the *Legislature Act 1908* established a 40-Member elected Legislative Council. The Act created four electoral divisions, two for each Island, with the North Island divisions each returning 11 Councillors and the South Island divisions each returning nine Councillors, all of whom were to be elected by STV (*Legislative Council Act, 1914*).[17] Before this new arrangement could be implemented, however, World War I intervened, and the price of the Liberal Party's membership of the wartime coalition was a indefinite postponement of the Act's operation. When, in 1920, the Legislative Council vigorously attacked its imminent implementation (during a debate on a bill involving minor technical changes) and passed a resolution opposing its operation by 23 votes to five, the government cancelled its proclamation bringing the Act into force. The Act was not, however, repealed and, in the words of one student of the Legislative Council, it "remained like a sword of Damocles suspended above the nominated upper house, available at will or whim to any succeeding government" (Jackson, 1972:176). The Legislative Council continued as an appointed chamber until it was finally abolished in 1950.

Proposals for Referendums and Popular Initiatives

Yet another issue promoting lively debate around the turn of the century was the push for legislation to make referendums an integral part of New Zealand's democratic process. Local option polls (effectively local referendums) had first been introduced in the early 1880s to allow residents to decide for themselves whether their local area should allow liquor to be sold within its boundaries. From 1893, electoral districts also served as liquor licensing districts, and every three years from then until 1946, all voters were given an opportunity to decide whether their electorate should be 'wet' or 'dry'.[18] This was viewed by a number of politicians as popular democracy at its best!

In 1893 E.J. O'Conor introduced the first of many bills designed to provide opportunities for electors to participate more directly in the development of their laws. O'Conor had chaired the House's 1891 Constitutional Reform Committee (*AJHR*, 1891:Sess. II, I.10) which had recommended that New Zealand adopt the Swiss practice whereby the Federal Assembly elected the Executive, and although that committee's terms of reference had restricted it to examining "the form and working of Executive Governments ..." with a view to recommending modifications to "the existing system of government in New Zealand as will diminish the evils of the present party system" (ibid., 1), his wider thinking was greatly influenced by the committee's study of the Swiss Federation's constitutional structure.

> It appears to me [he said when speaking during the bill's second reading] that the movement of opinion in this colony points to the conclusion that an increased power should be given to the electors of the colony to exercise a direct check upon our legislation. (*NZPD*, 80:564.)

His bill, modelled on the provisions of the Swiss constitution, provided for any bill or question to be referred to the electorate within six months if both Houses, or a three-fifths majority of either House, agreed to do so. All bills supported by a majority of voters would come into force once assent was given. In all other matters approved by a majority of voters, the Colonial Secretary would be required to introduce legislation incorporating the proposal into the House. Where a question was rejected, a delay of three years would be imposed before it could be revisited (ibid.). While O'Conor's proposal attracted some support from members, his bill was rejected by 33 votes to 20.

O'Conor lost his seat in the 1893 election but promotion of the referendum process was taken up by that indefatigable parliamentary reform advocate, P.J. O'Regan. The next year O'Regan introduced a modified version of O'Conor's bill which, if enacted, would have allowed the House of Representatives to specifically refer measures to the electorate which it had passed on two occasions, but which had twice been rejected by the Legislative Council (ibid.,

85:274). While provision was also included for both Houses to jointly refer specific matters to the electorate, O'Regan's bill was clearly designed to bypass what opponents of the reformed Legislative Council saw as obstructionist tactics. The House rejected the bill by 24 votes to 19. Undeterred, O'Regan renewed his efforts in 1895 when the bill passed its second reading by 28 votes to 14. It made no further progress, and was discharged later in the session (ibid., 87:642–44; 91:15).

The proposal to provide for referendums surfaced regularly over the next few years,[19] but made no further substantive progress. Frustration amongst its supporters was evident in a question Ell directed to the Premier in 1900. Seddon responded that the government intended "to introduce the Referendum Bill, and he hoped to see that bill yet on the Statute-book of the Colony" (*NZPD*, 112:67). A government sponsored bill duly appeared in 1901, was given its third reading in the House by 44 votes to 13, but was resoundingly rejected by 28 votes to 1 in the Legislative Council (ibid., 116:212ff, 266ff, 363ff, 393ff, 495–507; 117:174–75). Reintroduced again in each of the next four years; it twice passed through all its stages in the House of Representatives but was comprehensively voted down in the Legislative Council.[20] In 1905 Ell twice pressed Seddon to commit the government to passing a Referendum Bill that session; on the first occasion Seddon responded by advising that the previous year's bill would be reintroduced but, on the second occasion, he simply told Ell to "put a question on the order paper" (*NZPD*, 133:543; 134:611; 135:673). As Hamer (1988:46 & 285–99 *passim*) has noted, promises to refer questions to national referendums was one of Seddon's major devices for avoiding reaching decisions on controversial issues. Yet, while he professed to be willing to pass final responsibility for decision-making over to voters ('public opinion'), Seddon clearly banked on the Legislative Council's veto power to prevent the bill's final enactment while, at the same, time, avoiding public criticism that he, or his government, was the major obstacle to progress.

After Seddon's death, the new Premier, Sir Joseph Ward, declined to commit his government to promoting legislation providing for referendums. His response to yet another question from Ell was that "[i]n view of other, more important, work to be disposed of this session, it is not intended to introduce a Referendum Bill" (*NZPD*, 137:502). A new Premier with new priorities effectively killed all further initiatives in this area for a number of years.

A new form of referendum proposal, the popular initiative, first appeared in 1912 when John Payne introduced an Electoral Reform Bill, a measure that would have allowed electors to present a draft bill to the House of Representatives. This same bill also provided that a referendum could be held if the House failed to pass any draft bill presented to it by electors (ibid., 158:242).[21] A modified form, the Popular Initiatives and Referendum Bill, was promoted by James McCombs in 1914 which, if implemented, would have allowed 15 per cent of electors to petition for a referendum asking that a bill (presumably on any conceivable matter) be prepared and passed. Although McCombs reintroduced his bill several times during the next decade, it made no real impact, and after Labour reached the status of 'Official Opposition' following the 1925 election, it disappeared from the parliamentary arena until resurrected by Social Credit's Garry Knapp in the early 1980s.

Other Proposed Innovations

Two other early reform proposals warrant brief mention. Most noteworthy was the attempt to require Members of Parliament to elect the executive from among their number immediately after each general election. Modelled on the provisions of the Swiss Constitution and introduced by O'Conor, the Elective Executive Bill provided for the Executive to be chosen by exhaustive ballots until the specified number of members had attained majority support. Although never adopted, the idea was a persistent one, and a bill proposing that the Executive be elected was promoted by W.J. Steward nearly every year between 1893 and 1906. Steward's principal argument was that "as the people choose their representatives, so the representatives should choose the Executive Government" (ibid., 92:526–27), a point that struck a responsive chord among a good number of his colleagues. Although the bill was never given a second reading, the support it was accorded — 19 votes out of 51 cast in 1898, 16 out of 46 in 1899, and 22 out of 54 in 1906, for example — suggest that there was a significant amount of sympathy for its primary objective, that of distancing the Executive from the clutches of party. One interesting change of strategy occurred in 1902 when Steward — at the express invitation of Seddon who had indicated that this might make for an easier passage — promoted his idea in the form of an Elective Executive Referendum Bill. Once again, it appears as though Seddon was using promises of consulting public opinion as a means of avoiding a decision on the substantive issue. Similar proposals surfaced again briefly in 1909, 1911 and 1912 (when it was defeated by a solitary vote, 35 to 34), and was resurrected in another guise, the Election of Ministers and Party Government Reform Bill, promoted, without success, by Invercargill MHR, Josiah Hanan, intermittently between 1914 and 1925.

Another idea which won some support was a proposal that the Governor should be popularly elected instead of being appointed by the British government. First raised by John Joyce, MHR for Lyttelton, in 1887 (when it was defeated by 32 votes to 22), it was again put forward in 1895 when it was described as being modelled on the United States presidential elections (ibid., 87:161), although the election would be conducted under the provisions of the *Electoral Act 1893*. While neither this nor the elective executive proposal gained any real traction, both demonstrate clearly that ideas relating to electoral reform were regarded as being sufficiently important for them to be actively promoted by their advocates over a lengthy period of time.

An Innovative Society?

New Zealand's early experiments with electoral reform point to one clear conclusion: from the first years of responsible government (even earlier if the agitation of the Nelson and Wellington settlers is counted) a sizeable number of British migrant settlers were determined to participate actively in the decision-making processes of their new country. Certainly, from the time that elected politicians took over responsibility for the details of the electoral system from the Governor in 1858, many politicians were concerned to ensure that the representational values with which they were imbued were given every opportunity to take root in their new homeland. Democratic values such as electoral equality, universality, and participation were to the fore as successive generations of politicians strove to build a society incorporating these ideals. These were reflected in their early — and largely successful — efforts to widen the franchise, to prevent corrupt practices, or to minimise bribery and intimidation of voters by adopting the secret ballot mechanism. It is also highlighted in the various failed attempts to have both the Governor and Legislative Council elected by popular vote, by proposals to experiment with different ways of turning votes into parliamentary seats so that the final result more fairly reflected the views of voters, and the efforts that were made to broaden the democratic base by providing electors with a more direct input into decision-making through the mechanism of referendums.

In many, though not all, respects New Zealand was an innovator in the field of democratic practice. It was, for example, well ahead of Great Britain in its adoption of one-person-one-vote-one value, legislation targeting electoral corruption, removal of the details of reapportionments from direct political control, extending the franchise to include women, and experimenting with alternative methods of voting. On the other hand, at times it has followed Australia in, for example, adopting secret ballot and promoting electoral systems that were considered to result in fairer representation for voters.

Taken overall, these early electoral experiments resulted, predominantly, in cautious rather than radical reform. With few exceptions, changes were tightly controlled by politicians, particularly after the accession to power in 1890 of the Liberal Government when considerations of political advantage in the party sense began to emerge. Although a small number of committed politicians pressed cases for more radical change, their appeals went largely unheeded. For the most part, the development of New Zealand's electoral law was grounded in pragmatism and necessity resulting from the build-up of pressures that could no longer be ignored. It was not until the late 1980s that a full-scale public debate on possible changes to the electoral system occurred. The catalyst, a report by a Royal Commission, came at a time when voters' faith in their elected representatives was in steep decline and provided them with a unique opportunity to achieve what politicians of an earlier age had failed to do — establish an electoral system that converted votes into parliamentary seats in a way that was seen to be fairer and more representative of the public's mood.

Notes

1   In this chapter the term, Member of the House of Representatives (MHR) is used to distinguish them from Members of the Legislative Council (MLC), New Zealand's Upper House.

2   The adoption of the secret ballot in 1870 (two years before the United Kingdom) is a good example. The secret ballot was adopted by Victoria and South Australia in 1856. In 1858 the New Zealand government introduced a bill to regulate elections, including a proposal to adopt the secret ballot. The parliamentary select committee which examined the bill opposed its adoption because "secret voting is calculated to produce greater evils than those which it is intended to remedy", and the bill was defeated. See *AJHR*, 1858:3. In 1865 a further attempt was also rejected.

3   Electors must have owned or rented property for at least six months, or leased property for at least three years before they could register as electors. These qualifications also applied to Provincial Council elections.

4   The franchise age qualification was reduced to 20 years in 1969 and 18 years in 1974.

5   In 1853 there were approximately 100 Maori registered as electors.

6   The states of Wyoming and Utah in the United States granted the right to vote to women in 1869 and 1870 respectively, and the Isle of Man accorded the same right to women property-holders in 1880. Colorado granted women the right to vote in 1893 and South Australia did likewise in 1894.

7   In 1879 Seddon had said of the prospect of extending the franchise to women: "I hope honourable members will not allow any clause giving the ladies the franchise to be inserted in this bill. All domestic felicity would be destroyed once the ladies commenced to dabble in politics" (*NZH*, 1 November 1879).

8   Women were first able to stand in 1919 when feminist lawyer, Ellen Melville, stood as the Reform Party's candidate in the Eden electorate. The first woman MHR was

Elizabeth McCombs who was elected to represent Lyttelton in 1933 following the death of her husband MHR, James McCombs. There were, however, repeated attempts by supportive MHRs between 1894 and 1900 to amend the law to allow women to stand for election by deleting the word 'male' wherever it appeared in the Electoral Act and replacing it with the word 'person'.

9   The term 'European electorate' was dropped in favour of 'General electorate' in 1975.

10   The country quota was first formalised in 1881 when rural electorates were drawn so that they contained 25 per cent fewer people than town electorates.

11   In 1853, 54.2 per cent of electorates returned more than one member and 73.2 per cent of MHRs represented multi-member districts. After the 1870 redistribution the comparable figures were 8.3 per cent and 15.4 per cent respectively. The proportion of multi-member districts increased to 17.8 per cent (31.8 per cent of MHRs) in 1875 before multi-member electorates were abolished at the time of the 1881 redistribution.

12   Only after an election petition during which the key matter in dispute was the validity of ticks and crosses on the ballot paper.

13   Although Hare is generally credited with inventing STV, its discovery apparently owes much more to a Dane, C.G. Andrae, than to Hare (see McLean, 1996:215).

14   Appointments to the Legislative Council were made by the Governor on the advice of the Executive Council.

15   Pirani's bill proposed North Island and South Island electoral divisions, each of which would elect 17 European Councillors. Maori would elect three Maori Councillors from three electoral divisions, two in the North Island and one in the South Island. All Councillors would be elected for a five-year term. The total membership proposed (37) was the first to propose that the size of the Legislative Council should be half that of the House of Representatives.

16   Elections for the Legislative Council were to be conducted under the provisions of the *Electoral Act 1893.*

17   This Act subsequently was used as the model for the Second Chamber proposed by the Fourth National Government in 1991 (McRobie, 1993:248–53).

18   After the 1943 election, triennial Local Option polls were confined to licensing districts that were still 'dry'. Thereafter, as districts voted in favour of restoring liquor licenses, the Local Option poll ceased.

19   1896, 1898, 1899, and 1900.

20   Interestingly, the concept of popular referendums and initiatives was supported by Kate Sheppard in a speech titled 'Reform in Government' delivered to the National Council of Women at Napier in 1902. Her ideas contained in this address clearly owed a great deal to the Swiss model of government (*DNZB*, 2:459–61).

21   Interestingly, this bill also included a right of recall (whereby 40 per cent of electors could recall their MHR), and the abolition of the Second Ballot and country quota.

3 Labour Party Policy and Proportional Representation

All reformism is characterised by utopian strategy and tactical opportunism.
— Graffito written during French student revolt,1968.

The Radical Third Party Phase

Since its invention in the nineteenth century, proportional representation (PR) has come to be the favoured form of electoral system for non-homogeneous societies, particularly those with important social and economic cleavages. In those societies which have continued to maintain the simple plurality or First-past-the-post system (FPP), PR has tended to be favoured by third and minor parties, those parties which are, in effect, discriminated against by FPP. Why this should be so may readily be seen by the fact that under FPP it normally requires between 25–30 per cent of the vote before a third party begins to acquire seats in rough proportion to the votes cast. A party such as the New Zealand Party could win 12.3 per cent of the vote at the 1984 general election and yet fail to win a single seat. With PR, on the other hand, thresholds of 4-5 per cent are often introduced in order to keep smaller parties *out*.

In its early years the New Zealand Labour Party was a third party and like most third parties was a strong advocate of the principle of proportional representation. As early as 1905, even before the Labour Party formally came into existence, the Trades Councils were advocating the abolition of the upper house, and the introduction of proportional representation (Brown, 1962: 9–10). For socialist parties, any form of organisation which might be seen as limiting the expression of the people's will was seen as a form of vested interest, hence upper houses tended to be associated with the preservation of privilege, a hangover from aristocratic government, while PR, with the opportunities provided for upwardly mobile third parties, was viewed as a logical method of providing an alternative, more democratic, form of representation.

The councils were the prime movers in the formation of a Labour Party independent of the Liberals. The short-lived United Labour Party, formed in 1912, included proportional representation using the Single Transferable Vote (STV) among its policies in addition to the initiative, referendum and recall. And at the 1914 general election, proportional representation was among a number of matters which "unduly preoccupied" Labour candidates representing different facets of the movement (Gustafson, 1980:85).

Following the eventual formation of what is now the New Zealand Labour Party on 7 July 1916, the new party clearly inherited a number of planks, declaring in its platform for the 1919 general election that it stood for:

(a)   The securing of one vote one value by the adoption of proportional representation.
(b)   The enactment of the initiative, the referendum and the recall.
(c)   The abolition of the Legislative Council.
(d)   The removal of disabilities of women.
(e)   Full civil rights for State employees. (Harris & Levine, *et al.*,1994:138.)

Multi-member electorates were not an unfamiliar concept. A number had existed between 1854 and 1881, while at the four elections between 1893 and 1902 the major portions of the four main centres consisted of single electoral districts each returning three members, with each elector casting three votes. (Wilson, 1985:172 & 288). Thus, concepts such as proportional representation were less daunting than they might appear and discussion often occurred both inside and outside parliament, especially between 1890 and 1905. It was not even necessarily considered to be a radical plank. F.M.B. Fisher, a minister in the Massey Government from 1912 to 1915, had, for example, been a strong advocate of its use to elect the Legislative Council, while both Labour and Liberals were advocating its adoption at the 1919 general election (Brown, 1962:71). Both had a direct interest in its adoption but Labour's interest, as a third party seeking to become a major party, was the more pressing. Labour's leader, Harry Holland, pointed out shortly after the election, that despite the party's remarkable success, under proportional representation it would have won 18 or 19 seats instead of eight (ibid., 42).

Before the 1922 general election the party even flirted with the idea of coming to an arrangement with the Liberals not to oppose each other in a number of electorates. This would have helped to prevent vote-splitting, thereby helping to defeat the Reform Government. This, in turn, would have provided an opportunity to enact proportional representation. The proposal came to nothing because of a lack of trust in the Liberals, but Labour continued to emphasise the introduction of the principle as one of its planks in its 1922 manifesto, officially, to eliminate the possibility of minority government (ibid., 71-72).

This emphasis upon the need for a proportional representation electoral system continued at both the 1925 and 1928 general elections until, following the 1931 election and the formation of the Forbes (Coalition) Ministry, Labour was left as the second largest party and the official Opposition. This change of status was soon reflected in a change of policy. Realising that the possibility of enacting such a measure was coming nearer, in 1930 the Labour Party's annual conference had instructed the party's executive to make inquiries about its working in other countries. Following presentation of a special report in the following year the commitment to proportional representation was reaffirmed.

Despite the report, however, in a review of policy at the 1933 annual conference James Roberts of the Watersiders Union and president of the party 1936-50 (sometimes referred to as the 'uncrowned king of New Zealand'), and John A. Lee, the brilliant, independent-minded Labour MP who was to be expelled from the party in 1940, moved that proportional representation be deleted from the platform. Their motion was lost on procedural grounds, but in 1934 a formal remit along similar lines was presented to the conference. This time it was carried by an overwhelming majority: 60 to 24 (ibid., 170-72). On the verge of taking power for the first time, the principle was no longer seen as holding any advantage for a party which had succeeded in promoting itself from third to major party status under the existing electoral system. Indeed, to adopt PR at this juncture might be seen as more likely to hinder it in the implementation of its plans for the future.

Policy Moderation

Once Labour was established as one of the two major parties in a two party system, the attractiveness of PR as a means of electoral representation further receded. Party self-interest dictated allegiance to the FPP system. Why, then, in the 1980s did the party change its attitude, or, perhaps more accurately, why did the party help to bring about a situation in which a change to a proportional representation system became feasible?

In the 1940s the party was in government and clearly could only have viewed any change to the electoral system as likely to be detrimental to its interests. In the 1950s it was again returned to power, albeit narrowly and for one term only. In the thirty-five year period from 1949 to 1984, the party spent only six years in power, and it might be thought that this alone may have caused it to rethink its attitudes toward the electoral system. From the point of view of the politicians, however, the parliamentary party was never sufficiently far from power to cause it seriously to re-think its position.

It took the elections of 1978 and 1981 to begin to arouse public and party concern. At these elections, the Labour Party won a majority of votes, but the National Party won the majority of seats and hence became the government.

Even then, the concern of the party president (Jim Anderton), in particular, focused more on the drawing of the electoral boundaries than on changing the system.

Although, from time to time, remits (propositions) were introduced to the party conferences seeking a change in the electoral system this was hardly a popular issue with delegates. Despite the fact that the FPP system could disadvantage Labour, which had a tendency to pile up unnecessarily large majorities in urban electorates, while it continued to remain within reach of power the party appeared unlikely to favour PR.

Remits seeking a preferential system of voting for parliament were introduced in 1957 and 1958 but were rejected. Similarly remits introduced in 1973 and 1976 seeking, respectively, consideration of multi-member con-stituencies and the introduction of proportional representation were similarly rejected. It is only with the distorted election results in 1978 and 1981, together with the rise in influence within the party of new MP, Geoffrey Palmer, that the situation began to change. Palmer presented composite remits at the 1978 party conference advocating a Royal Commission on parliamentary and electoral reform, and although some of these were amended, the principle that a Royal Commission should be set up and that it should hear public submissions on electoral reform was carried.

A steady trickle of remits followed. In 1979, 1980, 1982, and 1984 remits were submitted seeking investigation of various forms of alternative electoral system including preferential voting, a type of Supplementary Member (SM), and STV, but, more frequently, 'proportional representation', although the particular form was unspecified.

To explain the change which occurred in the 1980s, therefore, it is necessary to take into account the impact of personalities upon politics — and one personality in particular. Throughout much of the post-war period the Labour Party had displayed scant interest in constitutional or electoral reform. Such interest as existed largely centred about the personalities of two lawyers, H.G.R. Mason who served as Attorney-General and Minister of Justice between 1935 and 1949 and again from 1957 to 1960; and Martyn Finlay, who held similar positions between 1972 and 1975; but this was largely confined to a limited interest in parliamentary procedural change.

By contrast, the election of Geoffrey Winston Russell Palmer, Professor of Law at Victoria University of Wellington, to parliament at a by-election in August 1979 did have an important impact, not only upon party policies but even more so upon policy outcomes. Palmer, who could have stood for either the Labour or National parties, joined the Labour Party in 1974 and was elected to its Policy Council in 1976. This enabled him to have an important influence.

Moreover, he proved to be a man of great enthusiasms who, once elected, was to have a meteoric rise, first to the position of Deputy Leader (in four years), then, to Leader and Prime Minister (in only ten years from the date of his first election).

But how was it that a party which for so long had become markedly disinterested, and thus conservative on constitutional and electoral concerns, could so rapidly change its stance? Important changes in the composition of the parliamentary party may have contributed. In the early 1960s, for example, the Parliamentary Labour Party was still predominantly 'blue-collar' in its origins (Forster, 1969:46) while by 1984 it had become predominantly professional (Jackson, 1987:77). Constitutional issues tended to be regarded as the province of lawyers and for many years Mason and Finlay were the only two lawyers in the Parliamentary Labour Party. Although Mason was in parliament for forty years (1926-66), Finlay had a broken career, being defeated in 1949 after serving only three years in the House and not gaining another seat until 1963, after which he served until 1978.

It was not that the party was suddenly captured by Palmer's enthusiasm but, as Skene (1987:73) has pointed out, he skilfully managed to sell his proposals as a contribution to the management of the economy by a more streamlined and efficient government. Given that there was little support for PR in the party at that time, a Royal Commission to inquire into the electoral system hardly posed a threat to the status quo, so his proposals were accepted without demur.

Moreover, from Palmer's viewpoint there was a remarkably happy conjuncture of circumstances. At the time that Palmer entered parliament, party leader Bill Rowling had felt himself dangerously exposed. By 1979, Rowling had lost two successive general elections, and although Labour nearly won in 1978, even gaining a majority of votes throughout the country at large, Rowling continued to be overshadowed by the aggressive personality of Prime Minister Robert Muldoon. This began to have a debilitating effect upon the morale of the party and, sensing himself under threat, Rowling began to withdraw from the established caucus figures and lean more heavily upon the new intake of MPs. With his election in 1979, Palmer gravitated towards MPs of this persuasion and gradually a small core of committed reformers began to coalesce. These included MPs such as John Terris (elected in 1978), Philip Woollaston, (elected in 1981 and particularly close to Palmer), as well as Richard Northey (elected in 1984), all of whom were to play important roles in the late 1980s.

Describing the struggle for control of the party in the 1970s and 1980s, former Labour Party president Margaret Wilson distinguished between the *élitists*, centred around finance expert Roger Douglas; the *populists* who centred about party president, Jim Anderton; and the *pragmatists* who included herself and people like Palmer (Wilson, 1989:27). Such a grouping, it might be thought, would have harmed Palmer's chances when, at the beginning of 1983, Rowling was replaced by David Lange as leader, thus bringing Wilson's *élitists* to power in the party. But Palmer, as a *pragmatist*, was seen as an ideal person to appoint to the deputy leadership as a balancing factor and as a means of maintaining the unity of the party. Because his interests could be seen as running parallel to, rather than competitive with, the immediate economic reforms of the new power group, his influence was in no way diminished and, as deputy leader with an outstanding capacity for hard work and a keen eye for matters of detail, he quickly became a virtually indispensable adjunct to the new leadership.

Another factor which tended to play into Palmer's hands was that, apart from economic and financial policies, before 1984, caucus apparently did not spend much time discussing the sort of issues in which he was interested. Although he had raised the issue at the 1978 party conference, he seems to have failed to persuade the party's Policy Council to examine alternative election systems before August 1979 when he was elected to parliament. As an MP, however, he acquired additional status and was able to write the 'Open Government' Labour Party policies for the 1981 election without let or hindrance, including the proposal for a Royal Commission to examine electoral reform.

The issues which tended to exercise Labour at this time were not matters concerned with proportional representation but those which bore more directly upon Labour's immediate situation. There was, for example, continuing concern about the four Maori seats, which the Third Labour Government had sought to place on a total population basis (the same as that for General, or non-Maori, electorates, thus allowing the number of seats to increase). The National Government which succeeded it had reversed this. Although the inequitable results of the 1978 general election (and later, the 1981 general election) which had seen National gain a majority of seats on a minority of the total vote was also a matter of considerable concern, the tendency was to mis-attribute this to the guile of the National Party Director-General (at the time, a member of the Representation Commission) rather than to the electoral system. In addition to these concerns, Labour was keen to establish a scheme for the state funding of political parties.

To these Palmer, in turn, was to add his own schemes for improving the efficiency of parliament. These included a Royal Commission to consider a broad range of matters relating to the electoral system, including an increase in the size and term of the House of Representatives; the criteria, membership, functions, and efficacy of the Representation Commission; the extent to which referendums should be used to determine controversial issues; whether they should be legislatively binding or not; the whole question of the level and application of limitations upon election expenses incurred by individuals and whether, or not, these should be extended to political parties.

Palmer was unequivocal about the fact that the majority should rule, but raised the question of what *kind* of majority that should be. He was unusual as a dedicated reformer as he was not a proponent of a particular form of electoral system. Palmer started from the standpoint that he was opposed to the degree of executive dominance exercised by the cabinet in New Zealand, and reached the conclusion that the only way change this was by some form of electoral reform, most probably some form proportional representation.

Initially, he appeared to favour the two-level system proposed by two Victoria University academics, Alley and Robinson (1971:2–8) in 1971. This was essentially what was to become known in New Zealand as the Supplementary Member system, a two-tier system not unlike a proposal put forward by the British for the German electoral system in 1946. In that case, the majority of seats were to continue to be allotted according to the FPP system and the balance according to the proportion of votes accumulated by unsuccessful candidates, or surplus to the requirement of successful candidates (Turner, 1983:34).

Under Robinson and Alley's proposal as presented in a submission to an Electoral Act Select Committee in 1974 (Palmer, 1979:155), a supplementary set of multi-member electorates was to be added to the existing single-member electorates. Additional members were to be elected on the basis of votes received by party lists in three regions, Southern, Central and Northern. Seats on these lists were to be allocated to parties in proportion to their share of the total vote in the three regions. The over-all effect would *not* be proportional, as it is in MMP, but semi-proportional. Third parties would have a much better chance of gaining some representation than under FPP, and the effect would, in all probability, serve to limit the executive dominance of the single majority party which had become a major concern to Palmer. In his book *Unbridled Power?* published in 1979, Palmer criticised the power of the executive and *inter alia* suggested adoption of this system (Palmer, 1979:156-7).

There is a direct line of development from Palmer's *Unbridled Power?* through the Labour Party 'Open Government' policy, devised for the 1981 and 1984 general elections, to the terms of reference established for the Royal Commission on the Electoral System established in 1985. The ultimate recommendation of the Royal Commission might have represented Palmer's broad hope but no doubt exceeded his expectations.[1] It is that 'sea-change', between the expectations that New Zealand might benefit from an element of proportional representation (such as SM) to the decision of the Royal

Commission to recommend the fully proportional MMP system, that helps to explain the inexplicable: that a government would voluntarily subscribe to the establishment of a commission with terms of reference broad enough, and personnel flexible enough, to bring down a verdict with which the government profoundly disagreed.

The key is Palmer. In the first edition of his book he discusses the problems with the existing system; considers such questions as the Representation Commission, electoral boundaries, Maori seats, and referendums, raising the possibility of a change to the voting system from First-past-the-post to a form of Supplementary Member system with 80 MPs elected by FPP and 40 by PR. These were the ideas embodied in the election manifesto in the 'Open Government' policy of 1981.

It was by no means clear at the outset that a fundamental reform of the electoral system was likely to occupy a prominent place on the agenda, or even that it would be on the agenda at all. Although Palmer gave prominence to the question in his book, there was certainly no question of a majority of MPs in caucus favouring PR, either then or later. The initiative for the Royal Commission was entirely that of Palmer. At best, he was supported by the small, loose minority group within caucus. Few MPs expected change and those that did anticipated, at most, a small additional proportional representation segment added to the existing arrangements, thereby allowing for an increased number of parliamentary seats and better representation of third parties.

Drafted by Palmer, and foreshadowed by his speech to the 1981 party conference, the Labour Party's 1981 official 'Open Government Policy' (NZLP, 1981:s.22) contained a wide range of proposals which foreshadowed the terms of reference of the future Royal Commission:

> Labour believes the time has come for an authoritative and exhaustive reappraisal of electoral law. There is considerable unease in the community concerning the way the system works. The next Labour Government will establish a Royal Commission of three persons to inquire into and report upon:
> (a)   defects which exist in the New Zealand procedures for electing Members of Parliament;
> (b)   the system of voting used and improvements which should be made;
> (c)   whether proportional representation or some other variant from the existing, first-past-the-post, system should be introduced;
> (d)   the method of fixing boundaries of Parliamentary seats;
> (e)   whether the life of Parliament should be increased from three to four years;
> (f)   whether increased use of referenda should be made in New Zealand to determine controversial issues;
> (g)   whether state funding of political parties should be introduced;

(h) any other questions relating to the electoral system which the Royal Commission may see fit to discuss.

This policy was substantially repeated in the 1984 manifesto, though without some of the detail and with electoral reform being downgraded from second in order of appearance in the 1981 version to last in 1984. References to 'community unease' at the working of the system were also dropped (Gomibuchi, 1995:50).

Labour and the Royal Commission

Because the main elements of this policy had already been aired at the 1981 general election it seems likely that Labour's Policy Committee, less enthusiastic about electoral reform than Palmer, took this second opportunity to moderate his viewpoint. In any case, the proposal for a Royal Commission, in itself, was hardly likely to be regarded as a strong or decisive policy, for this was the classic 'all care and no responsibility' type proposal by which an issue could be raised without firm commitment to change. At the same time, it is undeniable that the scope of the terms of reference provided for the Royal Commission was remarkably wide. The question of proportional representation or preferential voting was restored to its second ranking and the standard, catch-all, provision, "Any other question relating to the electoral system which you may see fit to inquire into, investigate, and report upon", acted as an open invitation to the Commission to range as widely as it pleased.

Even so, despite the fact that the Royal Commission had been handed a blank cheque there was little reason to believe that this would result in such a radical outcome. There is no evidence that there had been any substantial body of opinion, whether in the Labour Party or among the public at large, committed to the support of proportional representation. The party in its own submission to the Royal Commission declared quite unequivocally that:

> The party recognises that there is support by some sectors of the community for a system of proportional representation but believes that the advantages of plurality far outweigh those of proportional representation. (NZLP, 1985:10, quoted Gomibuchi,1995:51.)

This appears to be borne out by a National Research Bureau opinion survey held in August 1985 (*NZH*, 12 September 1985) when 48 per cent of respondents favoured the existing system; 31 per cent favoured PR; 12 per cent preferential voting; and 4 per cent the Second Ballot. Compared to a previous survey taken in 1982, support for the existing system had risen by 8 percentage points while support for PR had dropped 5 points. If anything, the trend appeared to be away from proportional representation, support for which may have been unduly inflated in 1982 by proximity to the 1978 and 1981 election results.

Palmer was not the usual type of New Zealand politician. He was a genuine and committed reformer who, as Deputy Prime Minister, Attorney-General and Minister of Justice, was ideally placed to pursue his enthusiasms, and few were prepared to deny him his particular pet schemes. Whether one wishes to regard Palmer as idealistic and politically naive, or as a crusading law professor in politics (Gomibuchi, 1995), it is clear that the possible political implications of what he was seeking to do were much more far-reaching and politically disruptive than seemed to be recognised by his colleagues at that time. As he correctly predicted on the release of the report: "I am quite sure it will not please all politicians" (*NZH,* 17 December 1986). Why was this?

The Prime Minister's Television Leaders' Debate 'Gaffe'

Certainly, there can be little doubt that the reaction of both the cabinet and caucus to the report of the Royal Commission, when it appeared in 1986, ranged from cool to hostile. The principles of proportional representation were not widely understood by MPs and there was no enthusiasm for coalition governments. On the other hand, what MPs of both major parties *did* understand was that the substantial reduction of the number of electorate seats involved in the adoption of MMP would cause extensive and unpredictable dislocation likely to affect them personally. Hence, all the indications were that the report of the Royal Commission would be quietly left to moulder on library shelves. That this did not happen is due to a number of factors: among the more important of these was the formation in 1986 of a small, but quite vociferous pressure group, the Electoral Reform Coalition (ERC).

What transformed the whole issue, however, was the Leaders' television debate held on 10 August 1987 in which Lange 'bequeathed' the country a new electoral system without meaning to. Faced by a question from a ERC spokesperson, Phil Saxby, who asked whether the Labour Party would allow a referendum to be conducted on the voting system as recommended by the Royal Commission, to most people's surprise and his colleagues' absolute astonishment, the Prime Minister replied:

There are aspects of unfairness which is why this Government supported the move to have the Royal Commission, and we will, in the next term, *refer* [emphasis added] that report to a parliamentary select committee, a referendum will thereafter be held. I believe that there will probably be a public acceptance of a four year term and a *modified* [emphasis added] form of proportional representation.

Asked what he meant by "a modified form of representation", Lange replied: "I think the German one is an example of it, I think that other forms of proportional representation, you can have not just the tail wagging the dog but the flea wagging the tail, and that would be crazy." The Leader of the Opposition, Jim Bolger, pointed out that this represented a "new policy" but failed to hammer home the real significance of Lange's statement at that point. Instead, he argued against the adoption of proportional representation. Surprisingly, despite this, Lange sought the moderator's attention in an attempt to score a further political point:

> I think it should be pointed out, that the referendum proposal for electoral law reform will *bind* the government. The referendum will determine the change, and the government will not have the capacity to reject it. Therein lies the difference between Mr Bolger's referendum and the Labour Government one. (TVNZ *Leaders' Question Time*, 10 August 1987.)

This declaration certainly helped give the Prime Minister a distinct psychological advantage although how it came about is obscure. It looked like a clever debating point. Palmer describes it as an accident due to Lange misreading his briefing notes (Palmer, 1992:178), despite the fact that Lange enjoyed a formidable reputation for absorbing large quantities of materials accurately at almost photographic speed. Lange himself attributed it to a mistake in his briefing notes:

> I think that our policy actually was to consider holding a referendum; in other words, avoid the issue... I said it was Labour's policy to hold a binding referendum...I thought this was our policy. It said so in black and white on a piece of paper in front of me. What happened was that there was a mistake in the notes. (*Press*, 16 September 1992.[2])

In a personal interview, however, the then head of the Prime Minister's Department, Dr John Henderson, has emphatically denied that there was any such mistake in the notes, a copy of which he retains (Henderson, 1995). Given that the Prime Minister returned to the matter in the Leaders' Debate in order to reinforce the *binding* nature of the referendum, thereby scoring a point off the Leader of the Opposition, it would have been surprising to find briefing notes so far astray and in such detail. And in an interview in 1994, Lange admitted that he had misread his notes claiming that: "I didn't misrepresent any detail of it all. I mean what I said about it was absolutely correct except that it was not policy, it was a proposal for policy" (Gomibuchi, 1995:53, fn.37).

Whatever the true cause, it is indisputable that no attempt was made to correct the misleading impression created by Lange's original statement. Indeed, writing to a Labour Party supporter 19 January 1988 the Prime Minister stated that:

> The Government has not reneged on my undertaking to hold a referendum on electoral reform; quite the opposite has occurred. Twice now the Cabinet has considered the matter of holding a referendum and in both cases it has noted the timetable necessary to hold such a referendum before the 1990 general election. It is inappropriate for Cabinet to do more than note the timetable at the present stage.

At the end of his letter, however, he states:

> After the Electoral Law Select Committee has reported back its findings and recommendations Cabinet will consider them. It is at this point when a decision will be made over whether to have a referendum and, if so, what topics will be addressed in the referendum. (Palmer, H.100:19 January 1988.)

'Noting' does not necessarily imply agreement. Lange appears to be accepting it as a personal undertaking.

That it was not part of the Labour Party's Official Policy Document had also become clear when the Official Policy Document finally appeared (bizarrely, only *after* the 1987 election had been held). Before the election Labour merely issued a 27 page booklet entitled *Labour's Plan for the Future* (NZLP, 1987a) which set out the main points of the Labour Party's 107 page policy document. A proposal for a referendum, and certainly not a binding referendum, was not included as one of the party's policy planks in either of these. *Labour's Plan for the Future* stated *inter alia* that:

> the Government will empower the Parliamentary Select Committee on Electoral Law (which represents all parties) ... to call for public submissions on the contents and recommendations of the Royal Commission report and on *alternative policies* [emphasis added] to respond to the issues in the report,

in short, a very limited commitment. The Official Policy Document included such generalities as — effective government, parliament and political parties; a system that is widely seen and felt to be fair, comprehensible and representative; with rights for all adult permanent residents to vote and have a real role in electing and influencing both central and local governments; effective Maori representation; and an appropriate term of Parliament.

Confusion Compounded

The Prime Minister had, in effect, let the genie out of the bottle, for the effect was to bring the whole issue back firmly onto the political agenda. The recommendation for a change of electoral system made by the Royal Commission was undoubtedly a political embarrassment, but politically it could, and should, have been contained. This should have been less difficult than appears in retrospect, for the years between 1984 and 1987 preceded the profound loss of faith in political parties. Ironically, if there had been quite strong contention from four political parties at the 1984 general election, by 1987 support for third parties had waned and not one of them was returned to parliament at the general election held in that year. Despite that, Lange's statement of what appeared to be policy now meant that more positive action was required.

Meanwhile, Lange's deputy, Palmer, had not been slow to exploit the loophole created by his leader's statement, endorsing, rather than correcting, Lange's incorrect television statement the next day. Surprised as he had been by Lange's announcement, he went on television. "... and backed him up. After that it was difficult for other people to deny the intention, so they had to keep quiet" (Palmer, 1992:178). Palmer further compounded the mistake just over two weeks later (*Press*, 26 August 1987) when he confirmed the *likelihood* of referendums, not only on the questions of proportional representation and a four year term but also, for good measure, on a Bill of Rights, the referendums to be held within 18 months or two years. Subsequently, he had to admit that "the position did not prevail and the Labour Party caucus refused to honour that part of his [Lange's] commitment" (Palmer, 1992:178). It appears at this juncture that both the Leader and Deputy Leader of the party were acting independently both of the party and of each other, although Lange was probably nearer to the party's thinking with his reference to "a modified form of proportional representation" — presumably SM, rather than MMP as supported by Palmer.

As a result of Lange's mistake and the Labour Government's decision not to publish the full policy document until after the election because, according to Palmer, the Government did not want to "confuse" the voters with a long list of policy promises (*Listener*, 16 April 1990), Labour's election policy was itself 'confused'. As was tradition, many members of the parliamentary party relied upon the Official Policy Document, but the electorate not only had a public undertaking from the Prime Minister to hold a binding referendum, but also the endorsement of that undertaking by the Deputy Prime Minister on the following day.

Lange had not accepted MMP, at least in the form recommended by the Royal Commission, but he had made it clear beyond any possible doubt that there would be a referendum on electoral law reform; that the referendum would "determine the change"; and that the government "will not have the capacity to reject it". Hence, in effect, Labour emerged from the election with two policies, both of which promised a Select Committee inquiry, but only one of which promised a referendum on the electoral system. Major difficulties were to follow from this.

When it finally appeared, the Labour Party's Official Policy Document promised merely to "encourage wide public debate on the matters raised" and to require the parliamentary Electoral Law Select Committee to "hear public submissions on the contents and recommendations of the Royal Commission report and on *alternative policies* [emphasis added] to respond to the issues in the report" (NZLP, 1987b:70).

Deputy Prime Minister Palmer's reiterated public support for his leader's statement, however, continued to stress the referendum. For Palmer, this was an opportunity to reconcile principle with interest, playing the role as the loyal deputy while at the same time advancing a cause that was close to his own heart. But what was the public to make of a situation in which a 'policy', later admitted to have been a 'mistake', was publicly affirmed by both Prime Minister and Deputy-Prime Minister?

The government itself was faced with a dilemma. What could it do to smother a public commitment to an issue about which it had serious doubts? No Opposition worth its salt, regardless of its own views, would allow a government to sideline such an issue, so active measures were called for. In these circumstances the next line of defence was further delay, plus obfuscation. When in doubt use a committee, a course already outlined by Lange in his Leaders' Debate statement. Parliament's Electoral Law Select Committee, chaired by a Labour backbencher, was the obvious vehicle for such a strategy. The 'peg' for further consideration of the issue was that, in presenting its report to the Governor-General, the Royal Commission had recommended that widespread public discussion and comment upon its suggestions needed to continue before any changes to the electoral system were made. The politicians, who had been deliberately excluded from membership of the Royal Commission, thus had an opportunity to reassert their control of the process.

The Select Committee was required to consider, *inter alia*, "All matters relating to the electoral system and related constitutional issues which may be referred to it". This now included "Public submissions on the Report of the Royal Commission on the Electoral System" (*AJHR*, 1988:5–7).

There can be no question that public discussion of so momentous a change was vital, but whether this required a laborious re-working of the Commission's report by a parliamentary select committee of self-interested MPs is another question. What is clear is the degree of back-tracking involved in referring the matter to a select committee. This is clearly indicated in the committee's report where it states that parliament had "acknowledged that further work should be done on the Report [of the Royal Commission] and its recommendations, including, *if it was agreed to,* [emphases added] the precise content of the referendum and how and when it would be undertaken". Apparently, the clear statement of intent made by the Prime Minister in the Leaders' Debate preceding the election counted for nought, presumably on the basis that the proposal did not appear in the party's election manifesto.

Clearly there was a promise to try to improve New Zealand's electoral system but, as far as the Labour Party was concerned, there was no formal commitment, whether in principle or practice, either to proportional representation or even to giving the public a choice in the matter at a referendum. That, however, was not clear to the public, which had accepted Lange's television statement as official policy.

Moreover, debate which seemed to support Lange's position had been taking place within the party organisation. In May 1987, following the issue of the Royal Commission's report, the Wellington Labour regional conference had supported a remit calling for a public debate on alternative electoral systems followed by a referendum. In the same month the Auckland Labour Party's regional conference had rejected both First-past-the-post and the Supplementary Member (SM). A major argument in favour of proportional representation was the need to combat the increasing tendency to focus on marginal seats by the party and opinion pollsters, largely ignoring safe seats. The conference believed that proportional representation would provide a more even spread of representation and equality of votes. However, reflecting the uncertainty within the party, at the 1987 Labour Party conference held after the election, a remit specifically proposing that a referendum on MMP be held in time to take effect by the 1990 election was defeated.

But for Lange's mistake the issue of a referendum on proportional representation might well have been effectively off Labour's agenda, despite the findings of the Royal Commission. In a political paradox bordering on the bizarre, Lange had, in effect, single-handedly firmly placed back on the political agenda an issue to which he was personally opposed. At the same time, the mistake gave an important fillip to the personal political agenda of Deputy Prime Minister Palmer. At the cabinet meeting held on 12 October 1987, chaired by Palmer in the absence of the Prime Minister, the cabinet was formally asked to note that the most appropriate time for a referendum was November 1989, as well as to note the following proposed timetable for electoral reform:

- October 1987: Electoral Law Select Committee calls for submissions on the Report of the Royal Commission.
- June 1988: Select Committee reports to parliament.
- July/August 1988: Consideration of the Select Committee report by caucus and cabinet.
- September 1988: Commencement of preparation of legislation.
- March 1989: Legislation introduced into the House.
- September 1989: Legislation passed by parliament.
- November 1989: Referendum held.

In addition it was formally proposed that the Minister of Justice be invited to present a further paper to cabinet following the report to the House of the Electoral Law Select Committee (Palmer, H.88: 9 October 1987). An annotation on the original draft — "This is one step at a time and commits us to very little" — appears to confirm suspicion that Palmer did not have support for full-scale reform for, by now, there was less readiness in the party to indulge the Deputy Prime Minister's enthusiasms as the potential political costs had become apparent.

Politicians Prevaricate

For much of the next three years the parliamentary party and government wrestled with the question of which 'policy' to follow. Should there be a referendum or not? If there was to be a referendum, what should it consist of? A four year term? An increased number of MPs? The electoral system? Or, possibly also, a Bill of Rights? Should it involve one or more of these? In the case of the four year term and, probably, a change to the electoral system, approval by either a 75 per cent majority of the House of Representatives or a majority of the valid votes cast at a referendum was mandatory, since this was required by section 189 of the *Electoral Act 1956*.

Labour's Electoral Law caucus committee members supported the idea of a referendum from which it would have been too embarrassing to try to escape. But a referendum on what? On the matter of choice to be presented there was no agreement whether it had to be a choice of electoral systems or whether the issue could be confined to a related matter such as the term of parliament. If, as promised by Prime Minister Lange and Deputy Prime Minister Palmer, there was to be a choice of electoral systems, then it seemed that it would have to be between at least three systems — FPP, SM and MMP. But apart from complicating technical factors, the key bodies involved —Labour's Electoral Law caucus committee, parliament's Electoral Law Select Committee, the Labour Party caucus and cabinet — all had attitudes which varied not only amongst themselves, but also over time, particularly as the 1990 general election approached.

The position was well summed up in the Electoral Law caucus committee in November 1987 by Philip Woollaston who believed that it was important to clarify the government's view after Lange's statement in the television Leaders' Debate. He pointed out that the government had *not* decided that a referendum would be held but it was *assumed* that one was likely to be needed. He also pointed out that although the 1987 Labour Party conference had rejected a specific proportional representation proposal, "that did not mean that the party was opposed to any electoral reform" (ibid., 17 November 1987). Equally, the cabinet once again sought to play down the issue by making it clear that although a paper on an electoral reform referendum had been noted on 12 October, no decision had been made on the nature of the issues to be voted on (*Dom.*, 3 November 1987). Thus, while a referendum on electoral reform remained a possibility, there was still no firm commitment, either by the Labour Party or the Labour Government, to any consideration of proportional representation or any other electoral system, despite Palmer's statement of 25 August 1987 about the likelihood of such events within 18 months or two years.

Meanwhile, overt opposition to change within the parliamentary party was growing. Third-ranked cabinet minister, Mike Moore, a firm supporter of First-past-the-post, now publicly criticised electoral reform, declaring in a tart dig at Geoffrey Palmer that it was "an academic exercise and a waste of time" (quoted in *NZPD*, 484:780). Other Labour members too, showed uneasiness, including former party president, Jim Anderton, who publicly stated his belief that MMP would be worse than the existing system (*DST*, 27 March 1988).

Under the New Zealand caucus system parliamentary select committees are regularly 'shadowed' by their relevant caucus committee. Almost invariably under FPP the government of the day had a majority of members on each parliamentary select committee, so the caucus committee frequently acted as a monitoring agent. There was also some overlap of personnel: in the case of electoral reform the chairperson of the Electoral Law caucus subcommittee, Richard Northey, a strong supporter of the Supplementary Member system, also chaired parliament's Electoral Law Select Committee and, at various stages, three other Labour MPs were also members of both the select and caucus committees. Other members of the caucus committee, not represented on the select committee, included Palmer and at least three other strong supporters of PR. Overall attitudes, tactics, and strategies were often agreed upon in advance at the Labour caucus committee to which members of the select committee frequently reported back.

By 1988, with the Electoral Law Select Committee due to report back to the House at the end of June, Labour's Electoral Law caucus committee was deeply involved in trying to untie what had become the 'gordian knot' arising from the Lange 'mistake'. Palmer, who had started out with a rather generalised preference for a proportional representation system had followed the deliberations of the Royal Commission closely, and by the time its report was published was a firm believer in MMP (Palmer, 1996). Well aware of the difficulties of persuading his colleagues, however, he believed that, apart from his personal preference for MMP, there were other alternatives to FPP. First, what he termed the 'Simple' Supplementary Member system — a two-tier system with the bulk of MPs continuing to be elected by the existing FPP system but with an additional number being elected by proportional representation — would see retention of the existing FPP seats with the addition of some 20–30 seats allotted on a proportional basis. Such a system would facilitate some representation of third and minor parties without being a fully proportional system. Unlike MMP, the party vote in the SM system applies *only* to the supplementary portion and does not determine the *overall* proportion of party strengths.

Secondly, there was a variation of SM, called the 'wasted vote.' As advocated by the British Hansard Society, it differed from the so-called 'Simple' system in the method of apportioning the supplementary seats. This involved adding up the total number of each party's votes that did not elect an MP, or which were above the figure needed to elect an MP where the party won an electorate, and were thus 'wasted'. Seats were apportioned according to each party's proportion of the total number of 'wasted' votes (Palmer, H.100:19 April 1988). Both remained as possibilities for, by May 1988, any expectations arising from the original Royal Commission report appear to have been scaled down. As Palmer explains it: "The only real way that it is possible to make progress in a situation like that is if you can get a strong Caucus Committee Report adopted by a Caucus" (Palmer, 1997). So, at an important meeting of the Electoral Law caucus committee held on 24 May, final recommendations were sought on a large number of electoral reform matters in order that they could be taken to caucus. The voting system was discussed with, according to the minutes, "... most members, including Geoffrey Palmer, favouring the Simple Supplementary System, while a few Members favour a[n] MMP system" (ibid., 24 May 1988). This appears to misrepresent Palmer's true position which, by this stage (as with his unentrenched Bill of Rights), seemed a classical example of 'half a loaf being better than none'. The Supplementary Member system was viewed as the system with the best chance of success, particularly as the Opposition was apparently undecided about its merits. The minutes of the committee noted that, "A key issue is their agreement. This could avoid the need for a referendum" (ibid.). Subsequently, Palmer argued: "I was not very keen on half-pie solutions, even though I had to go along with some of them for tactical reasons" (Palmer, 1997). One of the tactical reasons was that he wanted "to force some position out of the National Party" (ibid.). The Royal Commission, of course, had concluded that the Supplementary Member system "...does not go far enough in meeting the fundamental objections to the plurality system in respect of the relationship between seats and votes" (RCES,1986a:43).

Both the SM and MMP systems can work with either one or two vote arrangements. The committee also considered recommendations that whatever electoral system was adopted, each elector should have only *one* vote, and that separate Maori seats should be maintained on the basis of the number of electors who choose to go on the Maori roll. A further, unsuccessful, recommendation was for a fixed term of parliament — that is, if a four year parliamentary term was approved by referendum, elections to be held on the last Saturday in November could be entrenched in the *Electoral Act*. If a government was obliged to call an election before that it would still be obligatory to hold an election on the next entrenched date. Palmer queried the practicality of this.

In the following month, the committee duly resolved to support the retention of the single vote whatever voting system was adopted (Palmer, H.100:7 June 1988). Following this, and although aware that "it seemed unlikely that Caucus would accept MMP", the committee asked caucus to choose between MMP, SM and FPP, suggesting that any new system should be introduced for the 1990 and subsequent general elections. This would involve the new system becoming law in 1989. If the support of at least 75 per cent of all MPs (as required by the *Electoral Act 1956*) was not forthcoming, a referendum could be held in October or November 1989 (ibid., 21 June 1988).

With no decision forthcoming from caucus, at the cabinet meeting held 20 June Palmer presented a paper in which he recommended that cabinet endorse either MMP in a modified form, or SM; agree that the number of

Maori seats be related to the proportion of the total Maori population who register on the Maori roll; agree that the number of South Island seats should not be reduced; agree that the number of seats be increased by the addition of one list seat for every four constituency seats (subsequently amended to a total of 121) regardless of which system was adopted; and agree to a referendum on the extension of the term of parliament to four years (ibid., 15 June 1988).

In a memorandum accompanying his cabinet submission, Palmer admitted that whatever the theoretical advantages of the pure form of MMP (60 list MPs and 60 constituency MPs) as recommended by the Royal Commission, that proposal did "not seem to have sufficient support". Hence, he proposed a modified form of MMP which bore all the marks of a compromise between the supporters of the Supplementary Member and MMP systems. The proposal was to alter the ratio of constituency to list seats; the existing 97 constituency seats were to be retained, at least initially, and an additional 24 new list seats created. This looked remarkably like the Supplementary Member system except that, under MMP, the party vote would continue to determine the *overall* outcome. Both systems would use one vote only to determine both constituency and list outcomes.

From the viewpoint of MPs, this modified system would have had the advantage of retaining all the existing FPP seats, thus minimising disruption. It could, however, have led to difficult problems with what the Germans term the *uberhängmandate* or 'overhang'. Assuming that the major parties found their strength in the electorate seats and third parties fared best in the list seats, as occurs in Germany, there is always the possibility that one, or more, of the major parties can win more electorate seats than its share of the party vote entitles it to. Under MMP, such extra seats are retained by the party, or parties, winning them for the life of that parliament and the size of parliament is increased accordingly. Under such a proposal the enlarged parliament advocated by the Labour Party might well have become further enlarged on a more or less regular basis. In other words the work of the Royal Commission was in danger of being heavily 'watered down' in order to reach an acceptable agreement. Fortunately, cabinet did not adopt either system as policy, choosing instead to defer the matter, apparently indefinitely, with no specific date set for further consideration. Seemingly only Palmer and Russell Marshall spoke in favour of *any* form of proportional representation. Senior ministers opposed to any form of PR included Helen Clark, Jonathan Hunt, Lange, Moore, Peter Tapsell and Bob Tizard. Richard Prebble, while not adamantly opposed, did not favour Palmer's paper. Michael Bassett did not speak but was another "most hostile" to any change (Bassett, 1996).

Following the failure of cabinet to accept either the modified form of

MMP or SM, the political centre of gravity on the issue moved back to caucus, and Richard Northey, chairperson of the Electoral Law caucus committee, undertook to circulate more information to caucus on the relative merits of the FPP, MMP and SM electoral systems. Lange is reported to have said of his energetic Finance Minister, Roger Douglas, that "like rust, Roger never sleeps". The same might well have been said of Geoffrey Palmer, although his activities tended to be more subtle, low-key, and behind the scenes. The fact that the 20 June cabinet meeting constituted a rebuff to his plans may be deduced from the fact that he now shifted the emphasis of his activity back to caucus.

Under instructions from Palmer "that it was now appropriate for the committee to report to Caucus on major issues" (Palmer, H.100:21 June 1988), the caucus committee prepared its recommendations for the referendum questions at meetings held on 21 June, and 5, 12, and 19 July 1988. At the 21 June meeting Northey urged his committee to support SM as "it seemed unlikely that Caucus would accept MMP", but eventually he moved that caucus be asked to choose between FPP, SM and MMP, and that any new system be introduced for 1990 and subsequent elections.

On 7 July, caucus decided to retain the existing FPP system and not to seek to increase the number of MPs. Northey, characteristically, brought a mass of paper to the caucus which was not numbered properly and resulted in confusion. While he sorted it out, caucus went on with other business. When, after a long discussion, a vote was eventually taken, the issue was clearly lost on a show of hands.

Nevertheless, at a meeting held on 12 July to finalise the draft response for caucus on chapters 2 and 4 of the Royal Commission's report, the caucus committee recommended that there should be an indicative or 'straw' referendum in October or November 1989. This referendum could express a view for or against the government giving "further consideration" to a partly or wholly proportional system such as MMP or SM. The suggested shape of this referendum on the voting system would take the form of linked questions asking whether the voter preferred the existing plurality system, or a changed voting system involving some degree of proportional representation? If a majority were to favour change, which of two alternative systems — Supplementary Member System or Mixed Member Proportional system — was preferred? The Labour Party would then give 'serious consideration' to the outcome of the referendum in determining the electoral section of its policy manifesto for 1990. One can only attribute such a weak series of recommendations to frustration. Northey adjured the government to "take the outcome of the referenda very seriously", admitting at the same time that the possibility of not achieving a majority was "not so crucial" (ibid., 12 July 1988).

The unreality of this proposal may, however, be gauged from the fact that it was recommended that the referendum on electoral reform be held in conjunction with a referendum on the term of parliament which was to be binding (ibid.). Thus the referendum on the term of parliament was to be binding while the 'promised' binding referendum on the electoral system was to be essentially a 'straw' vote designed to influence a party manifesto in which, by this time, the public were likely to have little faith.

Nevertheless, Palmer ensured that the issue of reform of the electoral system was back on the caucus agenda for the meeting on the 14 July. At that meeting he berated his caucus colleagues for not coming to grips with the Royal Commission's report, and accused them of self-interest on the issue. Despite his strictures, the issue was deferred and did not arise again until the caucus of 11 August, after the budget and other problems had been cleared away. This was a smallish caucus with 49 MPs present. At the meeting a motion to enable Northey to negotiate terms with the Electoral Law Select Committee on the holding of a referendum was passed. At the same time, however, in a delaying move, an amendment proposed by Hunt, that no change be contemplated until the 1993 general election, was also carried (Bassett, 1996).

Palmer maintains that, at this point, opinion about reform in caucus was divided, with cabinet being more opposed to change than caucus. He stressed that:

> It was quite impossible to gain consensus in either the Caucus or the Cabinet on the subject of electoral reform. It was simply too threatening to too many people. It was threatening to senior politicians because they would have to learn new skills about how to ascend the heights of politics, and these may be unknown ... So far as those at the less influential end of politics were concerned, these tended to be people who knew about how to win a First-Past-the-Post election in a particular seat. Anything new tended to be run through the very detailed experience of what they did know ... It is vital to understand in respect to the Cabinet that I was probably the only person in it who was an unqualified supporter of what the Royal Commission had recommended. (Palmer, 1997.)

Thus it is clear that, although still haunted by Lange's 1987 promise, by mid 1988 the balance of opinion in both the Labour caucus and cabinet was against any change in the electoral system. As a result caucus relitigated the issue in September. This time, by a majority, it rejected change, and the idea of any form of referendum on the proportional representation issue (Gomibuchi, 1995:61).

With the way forward in caucus blocked, the reform supporters, Northey in particular, shifted the emphasis to the parliamentary Electoral Law Select Committee but this, too, was destined to fail. By 1989 Northey was conceding that the idea of an indicative referendum "is now dead" (Palmer, CH95/3/ 372:20 April 1989). This appeared to settle the matter once and for all. It was the type of outcome which political analysis would have led us to expect. Whether judged in terms of the self-interest of MPs, the two major political parties, or, in broader terms, the political uncertainties likely to result from such a radical change, few governments might be expected to embrace such an outcome unless under very strong pressure indeed. Accordingly, the Royal Commission's recommendations, even watered down and substantially modified, had failed to win approval. The limited changes contained in the second recommendation of the Electoral Law Select Committee for a referendum only if an increase in the number of MPs was accepted, were also cast aside. Despite the Prime Minister's public promise of a referendum, the government had side-stepped and ultimately reneged on the issue except in relation to the term of parliament. It is hardly surprising, therefore, that the original architect of the policy for electoral change, Geoffrey Palmer, was prepared to concede defeat despite his seemingly unquenchable enthusiasm. Speaking at the Labour Party's regional conference at Timaru, he said that although he regretted the government's decision against debating proportional representation, he accepted the decision and would not make waves. He declared that the issue was "effectively dead for the immediate future," but that it might be revisited "in another 20 years time" (*Press,* 17 April 1989).

Publication of the government's decision led to a spate of criticism. Correspondents criticised Palmer, particularly, for suggesting that there was not enough public support for reform. Some typical comments were:

> Your promise of a referendum on a 4 year term is simply adding insult to injury. It is certain to fail as the public want more control over government, not less. **(Palmer, CH95/3/372:25 April 1989.)**

> [I]t is irrelevant now whether the Labour Party's pre-election statements concerned 'investigating having a referendum' or actually having one. Many people ... consider the 'election promise' was to *hold* a referendum. (ibid., 17 April 1989.)

But the most cogent criticism of all came from an editorial under the heading 'Broken Promises' in *The Dominion* newspaper of 18 April 1989. It is worth quoting excerpts at some length:

> In August 1987 Prime Minister David Lange gave his word that Labour would hold a referendum on proportional representation and a four year parliamentary term ... and the results would be binding.

There was nothing equivocal in the promise. It was not subject to further party, caucus, cabinet, or parliamentary debate... "The people would determine any change and the government would not have the capacity to reject it," Mr Lange said.

The Prime Minister has broken his word, and he didn't even front up to the public to tell them. A broken promise is just that, and there is no elegant way to explain it away. All that Mr Palmer succeeded in doing was to dig the Government further into the mire.

His first excuse was that the party, the caucus and the select committee all turned the idea down. So what? Mr Lange promised a referendum, not a head count among politicians who have a vested interest in preserving the status quo.

He [Palmer] argued that he got very few letters on the issue, there was no public pressure for change.

The 1986 Royal Commission attracted 804 submissions on the issue, 61 per cent of them favouring proportional representation. The Royal Commission on the Electoral System recommended proportional representation. The Electoral Reform Coalition has lobbied tirelessly. What would it take to convince the Government — postcards from the Mongrel Mob, mass demonstrations by Rotary Clubs? If there wasn't enough public pressure for a referendum then on what basis did Labour promise one in the first place?

The editorial also tartly pointed out that the government did not wait for public support before introducing a surtax on superannuation, closing 534 post offices, or selling Air New Zealand!

Conclusion

How was it, therefore, that with most of the senior members of his own party opposed, with the Opposition firmly opposed, and even the main champion of change, Palmer, conceding defeat, that the issue could be revived within months rather than years, and ultimate success achieved in less than five years? It seemed that an opportunity to quit itself of this increasingly embarrassing issue had presented itself in August 1989, when David Lange was replaced as leader. It had been Lange's personal 'contribution' to the 1987 televised leaders' debate which had placed the issue firmly back on the political agenda. Ironically, however, any attempt to walk away from the question was undermined at the outset by the fact that his replacement was the main proponent of the reform, Geoffrey Palmer. Although Palmer, as leader, was too preoccupied with other concerns to advance the matter further, the party continued to be plagued by an issue which had become a political embarrassment of its own making.

In September 1989, after Palmer had become Prime Minister, the full Annual Labour Party Conference passed a remit this time endorsing a referendum on the PR principle which, in turn, was to constitute grounds for yet again raising the issue in caucus as the government was required to respond. So, although reform seemed to be a lost cause, it would not go away as an issue, and the small group of PR supporters in caucus, in particular, maintained its efforts to keep the matter on the political agenda. Against it were key figures from opposite sides of the cabinet spectrum, such as Mike Moore (the next leader), and Helen Clark (deputy to both Palmer and Moore) who, together with senior members, Jonathan Hunt and Michael Bassett, were united in intransigent opposition to such a change. It looked like deadlock. Thus the parliamentary party had continued its evasive tactics and, despite now having a leader known to support the principle, in December caucus once again rejected the proposal, albeit narrowly this time (Gomibuchi, 1995:63).

One contributory factor was the labyrinthine nature of the Labour organisation. This meant that there were numerous ways in which matters could, repeatedly, be placed back on the agenda. As we shall see later, Labour backbencher (and parliament's Deputy Speaker) again resuscitated the issue when he successfully introduced his Private Members' Proportional Representation Indicative Referendum Bill in May 1990. The party organisation, extensively alienated from its own government on economic grounds, had adopted an ambivalent attitude, keen to preserve the party but also reflecting the widespread public distrust of professional politicians.

And so, often by inadvertent and tortuous means, the government had reluctantly dragged itself back almost to the position to which Prime Minister Lange had publicly committed it in 1987. Both major parties had now become irretrievably committed to a position to which the leadership of each (following the resignation of Palmer) was resolutely opposed. This time, however, National was proposing a *binding* referendum and Labour an *indicative* form. Such are the idiosyncrasies of party politics.

The answer to the question of why a major political party, in power as government, should seek to change the electoral system which served to elect it, is that one has to distinguish between appearance and reality. There is no question that Geoffrey Palmer was a genuine crusader, but that does not explain why the party and government originally went along with his schemes. There are two possible explanations and they are not mutually incompatible. One is that when the original decision was taken by the party to advocate the setting up of a Royal Commission to consider the question of electoral reform, this was only one of the matters for consideration, and not necessarily the most important. For most MPs a Royal Commission involved no firm commitment to proceed on any particular aspect of policy and so it all seemed harmless enough. Even if proposals were made for a change of electoral system there was no reason to suppose that this was likely to be radical.

The second explanation is that the cabinet misjudged its judge. There was a failure to recognise on the part of a majority of cabinet that Justice John Wallace was an open-minded rational man, likely to follow logical arguments wherever they led. Palmer, of course, recognised this, which is why he wanted Wallace, but it seems doubtful that many of the cabinet shared his insight. If they had, the Commission's terms of reference would have been more tightly drawn; as it was, not only was the chairman liberal (in the sense of open-minded) but so too were the terms of reference. And so the Royal Commission was virtually given carte blanche by a cabinet, most of whom had failed to give full consideration to the possible consequences of their action. This was a case of the 'Petrouchka' syndrome where, from the viewpoint of most Labour politicians, the government had created a puppet which had assumed a life of its own and become a political monster.

In defence of the then government, it might be argued that other matters were more pressing. The Royal Commission was to consider a number of issues of direct interest to the party such as the number of MPs; the Representation Commission which it believed needed reform; the nature and basis of Maori representation; the term of parliament; use of referenda; election expenses, donations to parties and, above all, the question of state funding of political parties. Few were anticipating radical outcomes. The proposal for a Royal Commission, therefore, had the advantage of combining what were anticipated to be specific objectives, with the advantage of helping to satiate the reforming constitutional zeal of the deputy leader.

Even when the Commission's report was published and it was found to have 'bolted' (although not on Palmer) there were fall-back positions. The most obvious was to select the parts from the report in which the government was both interested and in agreement, and leave the rest to moulder on library shelves, a not unprecedented fate for such documents. The decision to refer the report to parliament's Electoral Law Select Committee was intended to be one way of doing this. It was a calculated political act which acquired added significance as a result of the potential damage arising from the leader's mistake on television. For most Labour MPs, the Royal Commission's recommendation of MMP was unacceptable with, or without, a referendum.

By the time the Labour Government was defeated in 1990, no one had the result they wanted. Palmer came nearest, but at no stage did he receive the unequivocal support of a majority of his colleagues for fundamental change to the existing electoral system. As he expressed it subsequently, "The greatest disappointment that I had in politics was not being able to get the 1986 Report of the Royal Commission on the Electoral System adopted as policy by the government" (Palmer, 1992:177).

It is one of the great ironies of New Zealand's electoral history that, despite the departure of failed electoral reform advocate, Geoffrey Palmer, from parliament following his replacement as Prime Minister, the anti-reform leaderships of both major parties were committed to a referendum which neither really wanted. Both remained complacent, however, believing that MMP would, be defeated at a popular referendum.

Notes

1   Although Palmer became a firm supporter of MMP once the Royal Commission reported, his previous lack of commitment to any particular form of PR is shown by a letter dated 17 April 1984 in response to H.W. van der Beck where he stated that: "I do not believe it would be practicable to elect half the MPs one way and the other half the other [way]…" (Palmer, CH95/3/372).

2   Ironically, Lange's comments were made during an address on 'ethics in politics'.

4   The National Party and Constitutional Reform

> All conservatism is based on the idea that if you leave things alone you leave
> them as they are. But you do not. If you leave a thing alone you leave it to a
> torrent of change.
>
> — G.K. Chesterton, *Orthodoxy*, 1908.

How is that a right-of-centre conservative party could become the instrument of such a radical change to the electoral system as the replacement of the long-established Westminster-model majoritarian system by the introduction of a continental European system of proportional representation? How is that a party which had seen the problems a Labour Government had created for itself by the unguarded promise of a popular referendum on the question of the electoral system could repeat the mistake? How is that a party which, unlike Labour, contained no highly placed proponent of proportional representation, could become committed to a policy, the outcome of which it resolutely opposed? And lastly, having made the mistake of a commitment to a popular referendum, why did it fail so miserably to defend the existing system?

First, it is necessary to decide what *sort* of conservative party the National Party represents. There is a variety of forms of conservatism. The connecting thread is that they tend to be anti-doctrine, anti-political theories. The five most distinctive forms are Reactionary, Natural, Pragmatic, Liberal reformists, and Radical conservatives.

Reactionary Conservatism attempts to prevent change and then seeks to undo it once it has taken place. With a heavy reliance upon institutions and dogma, the tendency is to regard the state as an organic development which should be tampered with as little as possible. Although New Zealand's dependence upon its British inheritance is great, it is difficult to sustain the concept of organic state development in a new, pioneering society such as New Zealand clearly was. Accordingly, apart from a handful of homesick emigres, there has been little of this form of conservatism in New Zealand.

Natural Conservatism tends to be expressed in terms of support for the status quo. Thus Natural Conservatives tend to oppose all change until after it has taken place. Unlike Reactionary Conservatives, they quickly adapt and come to accept change once made. Elements of this type of conservatism have been quite numerous in New Zealand, but a more notable strain has been empirical, or pragmatic, conservatism. Pragmatic Conservatives differ from Natural Conservatives in that they are prepared, if necessary, to act as the agents of change. In reacting to pressure they are prepared to make changes if, and when, the pressure is strong enough to persuade them to do so.

Even more common are the Liberal Reformists. Liberal Reformists are conservatives who accept change quite readily provided that this leads to practical improvements and is not merely based upon principle. This is essentially another aspect of Pragmatic Conservatism. To these, in recent times, have to be added the Radical Conservative. This stems partly from 'Thatcherism' in the United Kingdom where Mrs Thatcher was leader of the Conservative Party. In New Zealand, conservative minister and writer, Simon Upton, believes that 'Radical Liberal' is the more appropriate term for the policies adopted by Finance minister Ruth Richardson. Philosophically that may be so, but politically the most widely understood term is Radical Conservative and this can be justified on the ground that although its adherents *are* largely driven by principle — economic principle — they qualify as conservative on the grounds that the key principle is opposition to state intervention.

Although New Zealand has become well acquainted with Radical Conservatism in recent times, it has been the preserve of individuals rather than political parties, with neither Labour nor National ever completely captured by it. Thus the dominant strain of conservatism which has tended to characterise the National Party has been a mixture of Pragmatic Conservatism and Liberal Reformism. This combines the ability to adapt to change, whether brought about by others or forced upon it by public pressure, together with an open-minded approach to change provided that it is driven by practice rather than theory. This does not mean that such conservatives lack principle. Rather, underpinning principles tend to be expressed in terms of values. In this sense conservatives tend to stress such things as individualism and self-reliance, incentives, the importance of the family, and the rule of law. While these aspects continue to exist in New Zealand conservatism generally, there has also been a strong injection of community values. What used to be touted as equality in New Zealand is today essentially a sense of equity, summed up in the expression of giving everyone a 'fair go'.

Hence the key individual values are always qualified by social considerations — concern for the less fortunate, not just as a safety net, but as the *opportunity* to better oneself and one's family through employment, education, and welfare. Although the balance has shifted in recent years to a heavier weighting upon what might be regarded as the more traditional conservative individualistic values, and the levels at which such supports have been available have been scaled down, a strong sense of community values continues to persist.

The National Party was formed in 1936, primarily to unite all those opposed to the advance of what it saw as socialism, in the shape of the new Labour Government. Although considerable effort was expended in making the party internally democratic, the original objectives which it adopted made no specific reference to the principles of democracy, or even (as added later) the rule of law. It was never, however, a wholly Reactionary Conservative party; *inter alia*, it stood, for example, for a "policy of progressive and humanitarian legislation" (Gustafson, 1986:9).

Examples of its Pragmatic Conservatism include the welfare state, originally fiercely opposed, but then accepted until its continuance began to be undermined in the radical Labour reforms of Rogernomics.[1] The Rogernomics reforms, in turn, were adopted and, indeed, furthered by National. Another example, was the banning of nuclear weapons and ships from New Zealand, a Labour policy fiercely opposed until its widespread popularity became apparent, and then embraced in active opposition to French nuclear tests in the Pacific in 1995. These are the hallmarks of the Pragmatic Conservative.

The Second Chamber Issue

There appears to have been little interest in issues often regarded as fundamental to conservative parties such as constitutional and institutional matters (apart from loyalty to the monarch and the form of the party organisation itself) until 1941 when the leader of the party, Sidney Holland, first questioned the role and effectiveness of the Labour dominated second chamber, the Legislative Council, leading ultimately to the abolition of the Council in 1950. This, in turn, led to a debate, which has continued on and off ever since, about the need for a replacement or adequate alternative arrangements. A more short-lived concern was added in 1946 when the then Labour Government unilaterally changed the electoral rules. The third phase occurred from between 1981 and 1993 when the second chamber issue re-emerged only to disappear again after the 1993 electoral referendum.

The abolition of the Legislative Council and its consequences thus serve to provide useful insights from a number of different aspects into the nature of the National Party as a conservative party. It is an axiom of political science that left-wing political parties are inclined to abolish second chambers while conservative parties defend them. The National Party showed itself to be an important exception to this principle when it abolished the Legislative Council in 1950. This action reveals much, not only about the type of conservatism adopted by the party but the attitudes of individual members, a large number of whom remained convinced bicameralists. In this sense, it is not without a certain irony that 40 years later, National Party leader, Jim Bolger, waged an unsuccessful personal campaign in favour of restoring an upper house.

But, above all, the abolition issue is a prime example of the mixture of pragmatic conservatism and liberal reformism which has characterised the party. There was certainly no pressure on the party to deal with the largely moribund Legislative Council, nor were there any Liberal Reformism principles of parliamentarianism involved. Rather, here was a party which became willing to initiate a major constitutional change for tactical political advantage.

When Holland first raised the issue in 1941 the Legislative Council, stuffed with Labour appointees, was clearly an ineffective institution which was being maintained by a party which had a long tradition of opposition to second chambers. The opportunity to make political capital was just too tempting to resist. Yet initially, Holland was cautious, making an 'end or mend' speech in which he suggested that the Legislative Council should *either* be made a more useful body *or* wiped out altogether. In its existing form he regarded it as an extravagance.

The issue also recurred in the National Party manifesto for the 1943 general election when a proposal to "reduce the number of seats" was coupled with a proposal to devote any savings made to reward underpaid members of the House of Representatives (Jackson, 1972:184). There can be little doubt that Holland personally favoured abolition, and that the abolition policy, when it finally emerged, was leader-driven and received only reluctant support from many in his party. It is significant that, despite constant harrying from the Opposition, at no stage did Holland or the party ever commit itself unequivocally to the principle of unicameralism. Holland's Private Member's Legislative Council Abolition Bill, introduced in 1947, was once more primarily politically motivated.

Surprisingly little thought appears to have been given to consequences or alternatives. As Holland said of his bill "there is nothing much in it other than the short title" (*NZPD*, 277:129). The Labour Government, with a majority of 42 to 38, had three members openly in favour of abolition, and the government was unquestionably embarrassed when the bill was only narrowly defeated.

Equally, however, there were problems within the National Party in this curious reversal of role. It is a safe assumption that National Party members of whatever stripe objected to the Labour dominated Legislative Council of the day, but most favoured reform rather than abolition in the liberal reformist tradition, remaining staunch supporters of the bicameral principle. True, there were some senior members of the Opposition in addition to Holland who, by implication, favoured unicameralism but these were the exception. Most favoured caution and preferred reform. The degree to which they were prepared to temper their preferences and support the leader's initiative is, however, revealing.

The staunchest of the reformers, R.M Algie, had justified his support for Holland's Private Member's Bill in 1947 on the ground that, while many would have preferred reform, procedurally it was not possible to pass a Private Member's Bill with that purpose without the agreement of the government of the day. This was the case because, under the Standing Orders of the House, an appropriation of public funds was required to be recommended by a message from the Governor-General who acts, of course, only on the advice of ministers. The transparency of Algie's excuse, however, was revealed in 1950 when, with the party in government, Standing Orders were no longer a limitation, but the abolition proposal went ahead. This time the bicameralists had to be content with Holland's promise to set up another Select Committee to search for a suitable alternative *after* the Legislative Council had been abolished.

Following abolition, when the Constitutional Reform Committee chaired by Algie submitted its report recommending the creation of a Senate of 32 members, it was reported that Holland, asked by a journalist what he was going to do with the report responded: "I'm going to take it home, I'm going to bore a hole through the top left hand corner, and I'm going to put a piece of string in it and take it up and hang it in the outhouse" (Gustafson, 1986:59).

It is noteworthy that, throughout the whole process of abolition, Holland revelled in the simplicity of his approach. He brushed aside complicating questions such as the consideration of possible reform, abolition, or questions of a referendum on the issue — the latter an issue which was to cause such problems for the Fourth Labour Government over the possibility of changing the electoral system. Holland had effectively rail-roaded the 1948 Joint Constitutional Reform Committee (of both Houses) set up by the First Labour Government, thereby largely ignoring a valuable body of relevant information, and he completely avoided the likely consequences of abolition, such as the question of compensation for redundant Councillors or constitutional matters.

Holland's personal view is well summed up in the statement that he made when introducing his Private Member's Bill in 1947: " ... our proposition is. this: that firstly, we should abolish the Legislative Council and then run along without one and see what need there is in the future, if any, for a Legislative Council" (Jackson,1972:187). Such a position is far removed from the conservative who resists change and seeks limitations upon the popular will. His colleague, and later Prime Minister, Jack Marshall, described him as:

> ... an organisation man rather than an ideas man; a manager rather than a director
> ... His political philosophy could be written on the back of an envelope and

sometimes was. He stood for the freedom and independence of the individual citizen, and for the competitive private-enterprise economy. He supported progressive and humanitarian social policies, but at the same time was opposed to high taxation. He favoured a strong line on national defence within the framework of the British Empire. Within those limits he was a pragmatist who tried to find practical, flexible answers to the problems of government. (Marshall, 1983:253–254.)

Others in the party were more conscious of the constitutional, as distinct from the political, consequences. Lawyer Oswald Mazengarb, was one of the 'suicide squad' of new Legislative Councillors appointed by Holland to ensure that his abolition bill passed in the upper house. He suggested a "Constitutional Rights and Privileges Protection Act", re-enacting those provisions of the *Constitution Act 1852* previously safeguarded, to cover such matters as the appointment of a Governor-General; the composition of the legislature; the power of the Governor-General to dissolve parliament; the necessity for an oath of allegiance; the manner in which money was to be voted for the purposes of the Crown and the maintenance of customs and law of the Maori people. Re-enactment, Mazengarb believed, might also extend to other provisions of the constitutional law for which there was general agreement. Examples given were: the electoral laws; independence of the judiciary; right of access to the Supreme Court (now High Court) and other provisions inherent in the administration of justice. In addition, he sought a Constitutional or State Council which was to be a nominated body undertaking the type of work carried out by a Law Revision or Statutes Revision committee rather than a law-making body in the fuller sense of that term (*NZPD*, 289:89-90).

Again, this appears to have been an individual effort, very cautious in the circumstances and lacking any real innovative ideas. Yet, few other constructive suggestions were forthcoming. Opinion in the parliamentary party appeared to be divided. On the one hand there were those who believed that the adoption of the *Statute of Westminster* in 1947 meant that it was no longer possible to adopt an effective written constitution, even if there was the will, because of the Diceyian contention that one parliament was unable to bind a successor. Under this doctrine any constitutional restraint adopted could be readily discarded by a successor parliament. On the other hand there was the view put by Clifton Webb, Attorney-General and Minister of Justice in the first Holland Ministry: "I think one characteristic that marks out the people of British communities is that they can be trusted to take the right course in a crisis." Webb believed that the British system of justice, "... has bred into the community an ethical code which, as I say, enables us to approach all problems in a constitutional way" (*NZPD*,

289:620). In practical terms this meant, as Stanley Goosman, another senior member of the party, summed it up: "So long as we maintain democracy in the country, and so long as the people have the right of a free vote, the only second chamber we need, and which we have got, is the people outside" (ibid., 628). The conservative view which traditionally had viewed second chambers as a necessary check upon popular excess, now saw the popular will itself as the safeguard, using an argument familiar to later generations "There is no alternative and I defy anyone to find one" (ibid., 627).

In one sense abolition of the second chamber was presented in Natural Conservative terms. Because of the manifest ineffectiveness of the Legislative Council, it was claimed that, for all practical purposes, New Zealand had become a single chamber system long before abolition and that, in effect, this was merely recognition of a change that had already taken place. Lawyer Jack Watts, another minister in the Holland Government, declared that:

> In New Zealand at the present time we have in fact a single chamber system... . Our present single chamber works well and provides all the checks and balances that are necessary to a government attempting to carry out its policy... . Our system of elections every three years is one of checks, one of balances... . (ibid., 707-8.)

This then is a very basic form of conservatism which characterised the National party. There appears to have been scant interest in constitutional principle, the acid test being what worked at the time and the political advantage, or disadvantage, inherent in change. No doubt this type of approach had been conditioned by New Zealand's recent political history. Before 1935, conservatives entertained genuine fears of the 'socialist' threat represented by Labour. After 14 years of Labour Government, however, despite the political rhetoric, conservative fears had lessened. New Zealand had entered the two-party era where governmental change and overall moderation was accepted as a fact of life. The distance between the two parties was no longer what it had been and National with its object of standing for progressive and humanitarian legislation could, with Labour, derive a certain shared inherited pride in the pioneering social legislation of the Liberals at the turn of the century. This was a practical, working democracy which paid little heed to theoretical or legal principles qua principles. Certainly, not all conservatives shared this view and many lawyers in particular became very concerned at the lack of formal constitutional safeguards, particularly following the use of tough strike-breaking tactics and draconian emergency powers by the National Party Government during the 1951 waterfront strike. Unease, expressed, in particular, as a need to restore a second chamber, was vented at National Party annual conferences by the rank and file. Meanwhile, however, attention had turned to the enactment of a new electoral statute.

The *Electoral Act 1956*

In 1945, with its political support waning, the First Labour Government had made a number of significant changes to the electoral laws, some of which were overdue, but which, overall, were calculated to favour the government's fortunes. It unilaterally abolished the country quota, first introduced in 1881 but which, by 1945, had become anachronistic. The country quota discriminated in favour of rural based parties by giving rural electorates an additional weighting of population and hence votes. Since 1889 this weighting had been set at 28 per cent. With the development of the two-party system since 1935, the quota had clearly favoured the National Party. At the same time the government unilaterally changed the basis for electoral computation from *total* non-Maori population to *adult* non-Maori population, and reduced the tolerance allowed in the size of electorates to 500 adults above, or below, the average. In addition, the merging of the North and South Island Representation Commissions, had the effect of increasing the number of unofficial members to four, at which point they outnumbered the official members (McRobie, 1989:95). Most of these were moves which were widely seen as helping to secure the return of the government in the following year.

The election of a National Government in 1949 — despite these changes — promptly led to a restoration of total population as a basis for electoral computation and an increase in the tolerance for electorate quotas to ±7½ per cent. Although no attempt was made to restore the Country Quota, this self-interested tampering with the basis of the electoral system by successive governments, coupled with the abolition of the Legislative Council, raised serious concerns about the adequacy of New Zealand's constitutional arrangements.

In particular, the issue was taken up by J.R. (Jack) Marshall, Attorney-General and Minister of Justice in the second Holland and first Holyoake ministries, who was Minister in Charge of the Electoral Department. Although more interested in constitutional matters than most of his colleagues, Marshall saw his task in practical terms, seeking: "To ensure that governments could not, in future, influence the shape of electorates to their own advantage [and] ensure that future governments would not change the basic electoral laws..." (*NZPD*, 310:2839).

The 1956 *Electoral Act*, for which he was responsible, represented a practical compromise between the interests of the two major political parties. Total non-Maori population was retained, favouring National, while the low tolerance figure to which the Representation Commission was to work in drawing electoral boundaries was fixed at ±5 per cent which was believed to favour Labour. The National Government did, however, bring a new element into constitutional thinking when it introduced the concept of entrenched sections.

The original United Kingdom *Constitution Act 1852* had, of course, originally been largely entrenched. The *New Zealand Constitution (Amendment) Act 1857*, for example, conferred power to amend all but twenty-one sections of the original Act, and fifteen sections remained entrenched until full powers of amendment were conferred on the New Zealand parliament in 1947. This form of entrenchment was, however, vested in the Westminster parliament and outside New Zealand's immediate control.

The new form of entrenchment introduced by the *Electoral Act 1956* meant that certain key sections of the Act were not to be amended or repealed except by a vote of 75 per cent of all Members of Parliament, or by a simple majority of the votes cast at a nation-wide referendum. Providing for a referendum as one means of approving constitutional change was also an innovation for New Zealand; another was the section adopted for entrenching these provisions. Again adopting the Diceyian view that a parliament could not bind its successors, the entrenching section (s.189) was not itself entrenched, with the result that any government could remove that restrictive section by a mere majority vote. It was thus a 'moral' entrenchment binding succeeding governments as a matter of honour rather than strict legal requirement.

Many years later, at a time when voter support for a third party had increased substantially, Marshall raised the question of the adequacy of the FPP system which he had in effect entrenched. He concluded, somewhat pessimistically, that:

> This has led to a questioning of the democratic validity of our present entrenched system of one person with only one vote, and an interest in one or other of the alternatives, which might more accurately represent the will of the majority. It is unlikely that a 75 per cent majority of parliament could be found to bring about any change; a referendum might, provided the Government of the day took the initiative, but that too is unlikely. (Marshall,1983:248.)

Other Reforms

Such problems, however, were for the future. In 1956, although the Social

Credit Political League was attracting political support, it showed little sign of winning seats in parliament and there was little or no interest in the merits of proportional representation. Rather, talk of constitutional safeguards continued to focus on the second chamber issue for a time before taking other forms. In 1957 a number of influential business and professional men (including National Party members) banded together to form a 'Constitutional Society for the Preservation of Economic Freedom and Justice in New Zealand' (later known simply as the 'Constitutional Society'). This body concentrated at first upon the need for a written constitution, but later also came to advocate the need for a new second chamber.

Meanwhile, a smaller 'Legislature Reform League' was also founded, dedicated primarily to the re-establishment of a second chamber. A leading promoter of the League was a Wellington lawyer, D.J. Riddiford, who was elected as a National Party MP in 1960, and other National Party members also played a prominent role. Yet, the party itself was divided on the issue. At the 1957 National Party conference, for example, 110 delegates voted in favour of a second chamber with 119 against (Jackson 1972:205). Shortly before the 1960 general election the Constitutional Society organised a petition to parliament praying for a written constitution and a second chamber. The petition raised 11,525 signatures in a very short time with a further 2007 too late to be included (ibid., 207).

K.J. Holyoake, Holland's successor as leader of the party, was reputed to be one of the bicameralists in the party. He favoured a second chamber 'in principle'. And, in 1960, a committee of the Dominion Council, the governing body of the party, declared itself in favour of a nominated upper house broadly similar to that proposed by the 1950–52 Constitutional Reform Committee (known as the Algie Committee). This, however, was rejected by the party conference which preferred the introduction of a written constitution and a Bill of Rights on the Canadian model.

Already alert to the views of its supporters and potential supporters, the National Party included a wide range of proposals obviously designed to alleviate the pressures in its 1960 general election manifesto. Many of these seemed designed to distract attention from the central issues of a second chamber and written constitution. The possibilities of a written constitution and a Bill of Rights were merely to be *investigated*.

With the return of National to power in 1960, pressures for it to undertake more positive remedial constitutional measures were stepped up. Despite continued pressure, however, National soon made it clear in the absence of any apparent widespread public support that it was unlikely that an upper house would be restored "in the foreseeable future" (*NZPD*, 342:1149). Similarly, the idea of a Bill of Rights and a written constitution was also rejected, with the government favouring instead the establishment of a Broadcasting Corporation and an Ombudsman. Once again, both represented practical responses to practical problems. Subsequently, the size of the unicameral House of Representatives was allowed to increase slowly in order to prevent any further reduction in the representation of the South Island, while a series of Standing Orders Committees brought about a number of important changes, particularly in the role of parliamentary select committees, which have come to play an increasingly important role. Yet, surprisingly, no serious attempt was made following the abolition of the Legislative Council to review the adequacy of New Zealand's institutional arrangements as a unicameral state.

The possibilities of greater National Party involvement in constitutional matters seemed likely to be enhanced when Marshall succeeded Holyoake as leader of the National Party in 1972. Gustafson (1986:86) comments that: "Unlike Holyoake, who was a pragmatic, intuitive conservative, Marshall had a clearly defined, intellectual grasp of English liberalism." Gustafson goes on to describe how Marshall became the National Party's philosophical conscience wanting to go:

> ...beyond Holland's and Holyoake's simple belief in the freedom of the individual, the dislike of bureaucratic government, a wish to lower taxes, and the desire to provide opportunities for farmers and businessmen... (ibid., 87.)

Marshall's liberalism emphasised personal liberty under the rule of law together with a sufficient degree of economic security largely through a property-owning democracy by, "... the encouragement of small businesses; the control of land aggregation; the settlement of individual farmers on their own farms; and the establishment of every family in a home of its own" (ibid.). The 1973 National Party conference had a liberal bias but, in parliament, Marshall failed to counter the ascendancy of new Labour Prime Minister Norman Kirk, and was replaced by R.D. Muldoon in 1974.

Unalloyed Pragmatism

Muldoon was another Pragmatic Conservative in the stamp of Holland and Holyoake, a man who owed his position to the fact that he could win elections, and who had little concern for constitutional niceties. He believed, "[t]hat human values are more important than material values...[and] That the individual does not exist for the State — rather the State for the individual"

(Muldoon, 1974:28). Beyond that he freely admitted that:

> My approach to politics has tended to be pragmatic as I believe that New Zealand is unique and that theories and policies that originate in the major industrial countries will not necessarily work in an affluent European-type country which relies for its wealth on a narrow range of vulnerable agricultural products supplemented by import substitution and limited export from our manufacturing industries. (ibid., 31.)

Hence, it is perhaps not altogether surprising that, for a western-type democracy, New Zealand under Muldoon became one of the most regulated regimes outside the Eastern bloc. As Jesson (1988:31) aptly summed it up:

> Muldoon was very much the traditionalist in social and foreign policy areas where his attitudes were right-wing and authoritarian, and interventionist in his economic policies which were the culmination of New Zealand's history of state capitalism.

Nevertheless, even under the Muldoon administration some changes were taking place. As a result of a major debacle when the electoral rolls were computerised for the 1978 general election, a select committee of the House was set up in August 1979 to review various aspects of the electoral law. Necessarily, most of the work of this committee was concerned with administration of the law but its terms of reference included the following:

> Whether the present form of parliamentary representation (that is, single member electorates with the candidate securing more valid votes than any other candidate being elected) should be retained, and if not, what form should be substituted. (*AJHR*, 1980:4.)

It might be thought that this term of reference was included to achieve the support of Social Credit leader Bruce Beetham who, in 1977, had collected some 40,000 signatures in his campaign for proportional representation. Beetham, however, suggests that proportional representation was not, in practice, an issue for the committee (Beetham, 1993). Similarly, according to J.K. McLay who, as Minister of Justice, was also at that time the minister in charge of the electoral office:

> The term of reference in question was simply designed to ensure that, as the Committee proceeded with its work (and as interested parties made submissions), the opportunity was available, if required, to address that issue. (McLay, 1993.)

Like Palmer in the Labour Party, McLay did not hold a brief for any particular alternative form of electoral system, but he was less committed to reform, merely regarding FPP as not being "set in stone". Nevertheless, the committee, in its second report (*AJHR*, 1981), did display some interest in the matter, and reported that of 23 submissions seeking a modification of, or alternative to, the existing electoral system, 15 favoured proportional representation. It found that the main reasons for supporting PR in the 1920s, when it had been advocated previously, had been to provide minority parties with better representation; as a means of avoiding frequent boundary changes; and as a response to overseas influence at a time when several overseas countries were moving to PR.

The committee gave some consideration to the Second Ballot; Preferential Voting; List and STV proportional systems as possible alternatives but decided that the case for replacing the existing position was "not sufficiently strong" (ibid., 48). By a majority, it failed to support the setting up of a Royal Commission to carry out a detailed investigation, devoting itself instead to its principal task of addressing issues relating to the electoral rolls.

Meanwhile, the undue dominance that Sir Robert Muldoon had achieved by holding the offices of both Prime Minister and Minister of Finance led to renewed concerns within the party. These came to a head over the constitutional crisis following the defeat of the government at the 1984 snap general election. Muldoon's successor as party leader, deputy leader Jim McLay — like an earlier leader, John Marshall — was, as we have seen, a lawyer and a liberal, particularly so on social and moral issues. He is another example of the Liberal Reformist strain in the National Party. But he differed from Marshall in that he placed a greater emphasis upon the role of the free market. However, like Marshall, McLay's tenure of office was cut short when he was replaced by J.B. Bolger, a Catholic farmer who was conservative on moral issues and more interventionist on economic issues, but who otherwise was to prove deeply steeped in the Pragmatic Conservative tradition that has been characteristic of so many National Party leaders.

Tending to be slow to move, even to the point of obstinacy, and sometimes appearing to close off his options, once he moved Bolger was decisive. Moreover, he also represented something more. Despite his earlier record, in the first term of his government between 1990 and 1993 he was prepared to risk acute unpopularity and strong opposition by supporting a continuation of the Roger Douglas market-economics reforms and the implementation of far-reaching reforms in industrial relations even though we was not a Radical Conservative himself. He also attracted further unpopularity within his own party by raising the issue of republicanism. Bolger, in this sense, served to represent the growing complexity of party ideology in New Zealand at the end of the twentieth century.

In relation to the introduction of MMP, the attitude of both Bolger and his party epitomised the pure strain of pragmatism. In theory, National should have seriously considered the introduction of a form of proportional representation in order to enhance representation at the time that the Legislative Council was abolished in 1950, but this was never raised as a serious option. Indeed, National as a party never displayed any serious interest in introducing an alternative form of electoral system to FPP. Although some of the younger, newer MPs (1990–93) supported a change, four of the five National Party divisions, and the various branches which made submissions to the 1986 Royal Commission, overwhelmingly supported FPP. The rare dissentients, such as the Selwyn Young Nationals, tended to favour a form of Supplementary Member (*Press*, 26 September 1985). The leadership of the party, in particular, remained resolutely opposed until after the result of the 1993 referendum.

Following the release of the Report of the Royal Commission in 1986, Bolger was reported as saying that the Commission had not identified enough defects in the present system to justify such a radical departure from the Westminster model and that the recommendations would turn the political system on its head. He believed that it would lead to the appointment of members, "... owing allegiance only to their party and not to a constituency which comprises people of all political views and persuasions" (*Press*, 17 December 1986). Coalition governments would "render meaningless political manifestos prior to an election"; a party with approximately 10 per cent of the vote might "substantially dominate the political arena"; "[i]n seeking to accommodate the views of the minority, as the Royal Commission clearly did, we must make certain that the minority are not put in a position of dictating to the majority" (Bolger, 1987).

Bolger repeatedly defended the existing system as simple, accountable, producing a clear result, minimising fringe politics and avoiding the transfer of too much power to minorities. However, recognising growing public concern, in 1988 he conceded what had been starkly obvious since 1950, that New Zealand:

> ...is now unique among Western nations, in that it has no written constitution, Bill of rights or an upper house of Parliament ... and that citizens' rights in constitutional systems without such structures ... [a]re vulnerable to abuse by executive government. (Bolger, 1988.)

This did not mean that he supported Geoffrey Palmer's attempts to enact a Bill of Rights. Rather, Bolger looked for alternative strategies, in particular, to finesse the perceived threat of a proportional representation system posed by the Royal Commission. Just as abolition had been largely a personal policy espoused by leader Sidney Holland, so restoration of a second chamber was predominantly a personal policy driven by party leader Jim Bolger.

Deputy leader Don McKinnon also assumed (probably correctly at that time) that the case made by the Royal Commission was not an accurate reflection of the current state of public opinion, and that if reform was supported, then it should not be as radical as that proposed unless the existing system could actually be discredited. If people wanted proportional representation, he believed, it should be through the medium of a second chamber able to highlight minority points of view. He also thought that the likely intervals before the successful formation of a coalition government could only lead to greater power passing into the hands of the bureaucracy (*Press*, 31 August 1987).

National in Opposition, 1988–90

National used the three years following its 1987 defeat to develop what it believed was an acceptable public stance on electoral reform. Never a supporter of MMP, Jim Bolger became a persistent advocate of the re-establishment of a second chamber (Bolger,1988). His view was that the core problem was the abuse of executive power (an oft-expressed position adopted by opposition MPs), particularly the parliamentary process that allowed legislation to be passed swiftly and without appropriate consultation. Bolger saw this as a much more important question than the issue of electoral fairness, although he did acknowledge that this was a matter of concern to others, and he believed that the Royal Commission had failed to consider seriously the reintroduction of a second chamber as a reform option. His stance brought accusations from his colleagues, both in public and in private, that he was trying to force his preferred option on people. Bolger responded to his critics by acknowledging that electoral reform was of significant public concern and that there were a range of options in addition to a second chamber that should be explored. According to McCully, who chaired National's caucus committee on electoral reform throughout this period, Bolger also believed that electors' desire for change could be channelled toward a particular outcome and that there was no particular reason for MMP to be that preferred outcome.

It is clear, even from the Electoral Law Select Committee's 1988 report, that National had a very different agenda for electoral reform. There it assiduously but unsuccessfully promoted Bolger's preference for the re-introduction of a second chamber (*AJHR*, 1988:133; Palmer, H.100, 22 August

1988)[2] and opposed any extension to the parliamentary term, unless accompanied by "adequate constitutional checks on executive power". It also opposed any change to the existing arrangements for Maori representation unless Maori agreed to changes or a better alternative was proposed, and any increase in the size of the House of Representatives. It did, however, propose that an indicative referendum be held towards the end of 1989 to ascertain public opinion on an integrated package involving:

(a) a three or four year parliamentary term;
(b) whether the number of Members of Parliament should be increased; and if so
(c) whether this increase is elected on a plurality or SM basis; or
(d) whether a Senate should be established. (*AJHR*, 1988:60.)

The entire thrust of National's case was that the concerns giving rise to the proposed reforms could best be met by the creation of an elected second chamber to review legislation.

Even though the Labour Government had decided against holding the referendum it had promised, National's leadership seems to have concluded that the issue of electoral reform was unlikely to disappear. The problem facing Bolger was finding a way whereby the debate could be controlled to produce an outcome acceptable to his party. While a number in his caucus believed that the First-past-the-post electoral system should continue, most accepted that it was no longer a credible option so, in April 1990, Bolger referred the question to the caucus committee responsible for constitutional matters and invited it to make recommendations to the full caucus on what commitments to electoral reform should be included in the party's 1990 election manifesto.

The committee, chaired by McCully and including a number of the party's senior MPs— Bolger, Bill Birch, Winston Peters, Doug Graham, Robin Gray, and Muldoon — spent some months developing the party's policy. From the outset it was obvious that, since a number of its members were known to have personal agendas they wished to promote, the committee would be difficult to control. As the then secretary to the committee dryly observed:

...Muldoon was against any reform, Peters only wanted referenda, Birch wanted parliamentary/standing orders reform, and Bolger wanted a Second Chamber. Nobody on the committee actually wanted MMP! (Eagleson, 1997a.)

The committee canvassed opinion widely. It invited submissions from the party organisation and the public on a second chamber, reform of the House of Representatives and/or the electoral system, the use of the referendum process, and the need for a Bill of Rights and a written constitution. In all, over 350 submissions were received. In addition, a forum on electoral reform issues was held at the National Party's annual conference in July 1990. The outcome of these deliberations were two manifesto commitments: a binding referendum on electoral reform issues, and legislation to provide for indicative citizens' initiated referendums (CIR) to be held on specific questions where at least 10 per cent of registered electors endorsed the petition within one year.

National did not commit itself to any particular form of alternative electoral system; as set out in its manifesto, the referendum would be used "to determine what reform or reforms will be made", and would include questions on how MPs should be elected and whether a second chamber should be established. Even the commitment to a binding referendum was less than fulsome; the result would be regarded as binding if a majority of those voting supported a specific reform, but if no absolute majority existed the result would be regarded as indicative only and the government would "give it weight relative to the support expressed", whatever that meant! National also committed itself to hold the referendum before the end of 1992 so that, if a majority of electors voted for a change, it could be in place in time for the 1993 general election.

Although Bolger was known to be a long-time supporter of the bicameral system, the fact that he emphasised constitutional issues publicly at the time that he did suggests that whatever the leader's personal beliefs may have been, tactical political considerations remained of outstanding importance. Whether he lacked the crusading drive of Holland, or whether it was because he encountered greater difficulty in selling the concept of a second chamber involving more parliamentarians compared to Holland's task of abolishing an existing Legislative Council packed with Labour nominees, is a moot point. By now, the party as a whole appears to have had even less interest in the possibilities of bicameralism than its predecessors had had in the possibilities of abolition. Whatever the cause, little enthusiasm was evidenced for the idea either within or outside the party, even when it was offered as a partial solution to the problems of Maori representation.

And so, by election year 1990, Bolger was reported as favouring a binding referendum likely to include options for some form of PR in addition to his own preferred choice of a second chamber (*Press*, 11 April 1990). It would appear, however, that this was, to some extent at least, 'policy-making on the hoof', for he not only made it clear that his statement was subject to clearance by his party, but was also reported as saying that a National Party committee was *not* considering electoral reform at that time — less than six months before the general election.

Why then, this apparently sudden commitment? Probably, the main factor was the pending introduction into the House of Labour MP John Terris's Private Member's Bill. For example, it was reported in March 1990 that about one-third of the 56-strong Labour Party caucus were likely to support the bill as well as up to a dozen National Party MPs (*Dom.*, 13 March 1990). Although there was no guarantee that the bill would proceed, once again the issue was being given prominence on the political agenda. Sensing the change in public mood, and aware that the Labour Government might yet take up the bill itself, the National Party Opposition leader could well have seen political advantages in pre-empting the issue.

Not unlike Prime Minister Lange before the 1987 general election, the leader was announcing policy without party approval, although in this case subsequent approval was forthcoming from the National Party's policy committee, which he chaired. Politically, the effect was to partly outflank Labour on an issue that had originally been its own. Clearly National did not favour proportional representation, but it was prepared to reflect public dissatisfaction with the results of the existing system because this greatly discomfited the Labour Government, now led by Geoffrey Palmer, the main proponent of PR.

The electoral reform policy eventually announced by National on 11 September 1990 duly contained a firm promise to:

> Provide for a binding referendum to be held on electoral law matters prior to the end of 1992, including questions on the method of electing the House of Representatives, whether a Second Chamber should be introduced and, if so, how it would be elected.

The party admitted in its manifesto commitment that:

> ...the current 'first past the post' electoral system no longer enjoys universal acceptance among the public.
> Disillusionment with the political process generally has led to growing support for alternatives. The use of proportional representation to elect members of the House of Representatives is advocated by some, although there is little agreement as to which form of proportional representation is preferred. (NZNP, 1990.)

It seemed a carefully judged exercise. The policy was deliberately vague. After adopting Terris's bill, Labour was offering a clear-cut choice between the existing FPP system and MMP with an indicative referendum to be held in 1991. National promised a binding referendum to be held in 1992 on "the method of electing the House of Representatives". As the *New Zealand Herald* pointed out at the time: "That could mean a one-sided test of support for the existing method with no alternative specified, or a multi-choice poll in which the public is invited to choose from a smorgasbord of electoral techniques." If the latter was to be the case the paper noted that:

> In that event, the small print of the policy would become quite cynical. It promises that a referendum result will be binding on a National Administration "if a majority supports a specific reform". National well knows that an electorate presented with multiple choices can be practically guaranteed to produce no absolute majority for anything. (*NZH*, 13 September 1990).

The referendum proposal has to be seen as part of a series of commitments by National to restore public confidence in the electoral process. These were wider than the electoral system, embracing the second chamber issue, citizens' initiated referendums, and reform of parliament's standing orders. Above all, however, the election issue stressed by National was 'integrity' in government, to be achieved by electing National, which promised to implement the promises it had made and consult with a wide range of New Zealanders along the way. National's commitment to a referendum on the electoral system therefore needs to be seen in terms of the two-party electoral competition. It cannot be taken as a desire by the party, or even an influential group within it, to change the electoral system; quite the contrary, the policy was vague and so hedged about with qualifications, that it attracted little attention at the time.

As Prime Minister in the approach to the referendum, Bolger emphasised that formally: "The National party is taking no stance on the proportional representation question", but showed little hesitation in expressing his own view, claiming that:

> Proportional representation means that small single-issue groups — including some considered socially abhorrent, such as race-hate groups — will be represented in parliament... . Proportional representation would mean that voters would have no real idea for what or for whom they were voting at general election, because it's the deals that are made after the election that determine policy and determine who leads the country... . Proportional representation is the politics of closed doors,and the smoke-filled rooms of political wheelers, dealers, brokers and pork barrelers... . And it is a system in which the public has far less influence than it does today. (Bolger, 1992.)

The limitations of PR (actual and alleged), with a heavy emphasis upon the problems of government in Italy and Israel, were themes continually heard through to the referendums held in 1992 and 1993. Senior National Party MP

John Falloon, for example, claimed that in West Germany, minor parties and factional groups such as the farm lobby had effectively "been bought" by major parties seeking political office. He believed that this served to maintain the European Common Agricultural Policy, reading some significance into the fact that the United Kingdom, the one country to oppose the policy, was the only country without PR! (*TH*, 20 June 1990).

Third and minor parties, whether weak or influential, were presented as a problem, as bodies likely to wield a disproportionate influence beyond their numbers. Paradoxically, however, the proposition that such parties might substantially dominate the political arena, presented as a potential threat, began to appear in an advantageous light to many of the electorate who increasingly viewed it as a means of limiting the power of an overpowerful executive rather than diluting the doctrine of the mandate, a doctrine which they had learned to distrust anyway.

In the 1960s Holyoake had delighted in referring to the National Party as "a broad spectrum party" to mark it off from what he regarded as a sectional Labour Party. In 1992 and 1993, two National Party MPs in particular — cabinet minister Simon Upton and backbencher Tony Ryall — made a point of publicly defending the existing FPP system. Upton stressed the bi-partisan nature of his views, not hesitating to quote Labour Party Deputy Leader, Helen Clark, with approval, and referring to *both* National and Labour as broad spectrum parties, and claiming that such parties were part of New Zealand's British inheritance:

> Unlike many continental countries, ours is not a society in which political parties are defensive groupings based around the preservation of an ethical, religious or regional identity. Contrary to the suggestion of some that we're fractionating as a society, I still believe the 3.5 million of us have more in common than not. It's a view that makes party politics less important. (*Dom.*, 30 August 1993.)

In Upton's view, two broad spectrum major parties, each 'in-house coalitions' based upon a broad general consensus throughout the country at large, left no effective room for third parties. (It also means, of course, that under the two party system there was no room for a truly conservative party, and perhaps the terms 'right' and 'left' of centre — wherever the 'centre' may be at any given time — is perhaps as good a description as any.) He queried the inexperience of the Royal Commission members in the *practice* of politics (ibid., 15 November 1993), claiming that their view of the importance of party may have been true in the 1960s but no longer held for the 1990s (ibid., 28 September 1992), and stressed the direct accountability of the First-past-the-post system (ibid., 15 November 1993). Upton believed that FPP provided the basis for consensus whereas MMP was, in effect, about recognising the "Balkanisation of loyalties and values" (ibid., 28 September 1992). Conceding that for a time at least, the old coalitions had fractured, he had to admit that "... whatever that outcome, the major parties have a serious identity crisis to confront. They are the shells of old coalitions" (ibid., 28 September 1992).

In one sense that was a key problem facing defenders of the existing system: it was not just the problem of executive dominance (which had been the main concern of Palmer) but how the obviously so necessary party realignment could be achieved under the existing system. To that, there was no real answer at that time other than Upton's suggestion of relaxing the parliamentary whip (ibid., 30 August 1993), an impracticable solution.

Thus, the National Government found itself in a difficult position. Apart from some individual exceptions, mainly among some of the newer, younger National MPs, it was known to oppose the introduction of proportional representation. Yet the adoption of a public stance in opposition to reform seemed simply to fuel support for it, such was the lack of public faith in politicians. Following the issue of the Report of the Royal Commission on the Electoral System there had appeared to be a need for the party to develop some positive constitutional or electoral proposals if the system of proportional representation proposed by the Commission was to be challenged effectively. But, beyond a proposal for citizens' initiated referendums and another review of parliamentary standing orders, the best that it could offer, apparently, was the restoration of an upper house. Although there was little public or political support for such a proposal, the government had nevertheless offered it as a possible option at the time of the 1990 general election and provision for the creation of a Senate was included in the Electoral Reform Bill introduced into the House by the Bolger Government on 15 December 1992.

Following the 1992 referendum, where a majority voted in favour of a change to the voting system and indicated a preference for MMP, this bill provided for a second two-part referendum, to be held in 1993, which would ask:

(a) whether voters favoured retaining FPP or supported MMP; and

(b) whether or not voters supported the creation of a Senate

It was proposed that if a majority of voters favoured both the retention of the FPP system and the creation of a Senate then the Senate Bill would come into effect but, if the MMP system were favoured, the Electoral Act providing for MMP would come into effect and a Senate would not be created.

Reporting back to the House, the Electoral Law Select Committee recommended, however, that the Senate Bill be removed from the Electoral Reform Bill and deferred until after it was decided at the 1993 referendum whether, or not, to retain FPP (*NZPD*, 536:16729). Thus the question of the Senate was not included in the referendum, and following the success of MMP at the 1993 referendum the separate Senate Bill was subsequently discharged.

This was only one of a number of significant changes recommended by the Electoral Law Select Committee at this time. The electoral threshold was set at 5 per cent instead of 4 per cent as recommended by the Royal Commission; separate Maori representation was retained and the number of Maori seats allowed to increase according to the number of electors opting for the Maori rolls; the recommendations of the 1988 Select Committee, which had rejected the regulation of party candidate selection methods by law, was reversed, permitting challenge to their fairness in the courts. In addition, it also recommended a select committee review of the electoral reform process after 1 April 2000 if MMP was endorsed by a majority of the electorate (*AJHR*, 1993c:11).

In retrospect, the National Government's resistance to MMP was remarkably weak. Why was this? As explained by one cabinet minister who declines to be named, with the economic problems that the country continued to face at that time the "government just had so much on its plate", by 1991 the cabinet was "wrung out ... dealing 18 hours a day with economic matters", and often meeting from 10.30am until 6.30pm, either in full cabinet or in cabinet committees. As a result, most cabinet ministers "never got their minds around it properly" — a situation remarkably similar to that immediately after Labour came to power in 1984.

Beyond that, there was the question of whether the new National Government had any alternative but to implement its referendum policy. Performing badly in the public opinion polls, and having executed a U-turn on one of its major 1990 policy planks — removal of the superannuation surcharge introduced by the Labour Government in 1985 (Richardson, 1996) — the government was in no position to break another promise. So the policy rolled on by default with a government unable to drop it, but with little time to devote to it.

A major problem faced by the leaderships of the major parties, both of whom were firmly opposed to MMP, was the fact that their opposition was interpreted as political self-interest and the case for change merely strengthened. Frequent discussions did, in fact, take place across party lines, particularly by those opposed to change (Upton, 1996a). Yet despite support for, or opposition to, change expressed by MPs as individuals, both major parties were forced to resort to a 'hands-off' policy. For example, Acting Prime Minister Don McKinnon, a supporter of FPP who was "not convinced that proportional representation is the answer for New Zealand", nevertheless declared that the Government would not take sides on electoral reform, its priority being to ensure that adequate information on the alternatives was available (*Press*, 18 May 93). Similarly, the next month, Labour Party General Secretary, Tony Timms, said that his party would not take sides in the run-up to the referendum although Labour now believed that change was inevitable (*NBR*, 5 June 1993).

Given the continued strength of public disaffection with a system in which one major party with unpopular economic policies had been replaced by another continuing to implement similar unpopular policies, it proved difficult to produce any distractive alternatives with appeal. Economic and policy issues were the potent factors. As far as the general public was concerned both major parties failed to reflect popular discontent. Thus, National's second chamber gambit failed miserably, and while the concept of citizens' initiated referendums enjoyed some popular appeal, it was seen as ancillary to, rather than a substitute for, changing the electoral system.

It also has to be remembered that the 1993 referendum was held at the same time as the general election, despite the unprecedented, exaggerated, majority of seats which National had won in 1990 (for some, in itself an indictment of the FPP electoral system). Rather than seeking to fight an unpopular cause, National's priority was the return of the government. While promising popular resolution of the issue at referendum, both major parties had placed themselves in a position where they were unable to campaign effectively without further damaging themselves politically. The way was thus left open for third parties and the Electoral Reform Coalition to capitalise on the mistakes that both major parties had made during the campaign for change.

If the National Party and National Government failed to defend the status quo, so too did most of its natural allies. There was opposition to electoral reform from leaders of the larger corporations but smaller businesses were more divided. The Employers Federation, for example, failed to adopt a position on MMP.

By holding two separate referendums, time was provided for a hoped-for swing-back in public opinion in favour of the status quo. Although this form was technically necessary to avoid any legal ambiguity under the terms of the *Electoral Act 1956*, the double referendum process appeared more complex and protracted, reinforcing popular perceptions that the government was attempting to stall the issue. So, not only did the major parties fail to wage an effective campaign against MMP, delay also failed to work to their advantage.

Citizens' Initiated Referendums (CIR)

In assessing the role of the National Party in this process it has to be borne in mind that the proposal for the referendums on the electoral system was not the only promise made by that party which might be regarded as uncharacteristic. It needs also to be seen alongside the less publicised but related proposal to introduce citizens' initiated referendums, another example of the unusual nature of the New Zealand National Party's conservatism. It is understandable that a conservative party would favour a second chamber; indeed, the surprise is rather that the National Party for so long failed to do so. There is little in the conservative credo, however, which would prepare us for the National Party's support for such a radical proposal as its *Citizens Initiated Referenda* legislation. That said, there are hints to be gleaned in the history of the party, in particular the statement by Stanley Goosman quoted earlier that "the only second chamber we need, and which we have got, is the people outside".

For this type of pragmatic conservatism the role of the 'people outside' is viewed as a support, rather than a threat. Traditionally, conservative parties tended to be cadre rather than mass parties but the National Party was unusual among this company by building up a large mass membership from the outset. Thus, despite a declining membership, by the 1980s the party, which in 1936 had omitted reference to democracy or the rule of law in its objectives, had adopted the following article in its constitution: "To maintain within New Zealand our time honoured system of open democratic government based on the principles of freedom, tolerance and justice" (Harris & Levine, et al., 1994:133).

The party faced the fact that in the 1980s popular scepticism about the role of government had reached probably unprecedented heights. The traditional political party mandate system appeared to have broken down. Parties were making promises which they were unable to keep. With the ideological role reversals epitomised by the Muldoon Government and its immediate successor, the Fourth Labour Government, the extent of the political changes taking place might be compared to fundamental shifts in moral attitudes to which the public were also having to adapt.

The basic issue for many was that of democratic control over elected governments. New Zealand was a country long accustomed to regular triennial elections in which two main parties, each usually within reach of power, competed for the people's votes by offering as broad a range of inducements to vote for them as they could muster. Many of the promises contained in the manifestos were implemented as part of the party's 'mandate' when elected to government, and parties were thus seen as fulfilling their promises.

While the political system was primarily engaged in distributing benefits (of whatever sort) this system worked adequately. Once, however, a flagging economy and the increasing burdens of the welfare state led to the need for a reversal of this process, the system effectively broke down. The political parties, unable or unwilling to attempt to market themselves on the basis of scarcities, continued to promise more than they could hope to deliver. Hence, the search for alternative modes of control.

The National Party was fundamentally opposed to a number of recommendations made by the Royal Commission on the Electoral System. The question of a citizens' initiated referendum, which had been rejected by the Commission, was more contentious. The issue was one that had been promoted for some time by various small, mainly right-wing, pressure groups. The avowed object of such groups was to express concern with the prevailing system of party politics and to advocate greater direct democracy to counter it (Spoonley, 1987:115–116). A total of 10 groups are listed by Gobbi (1992: 180–1), most of which, but not all, were right-wing. A number of these appeared to have links with the right-wing organisation, the League of Rights. Voters' Policy Associations had originated in Australia after 1964 in association with the Australian League of Rights.

One of the earliest such groups was the Voters' Association of New Zealand. Formed in Tauranga (Winston Peters' electorate from 1984 on) in 1981 as "a non-party political organisation", it was designed to represent the true interests of all voters regardless of their political ideologies or allegiances. One of the founders, R.H. Miskin, stated that voters were:

> ... frustrated by the primitive electoral system imposed upon the voters, and alarmed at the consequent non-democratic functioning of the New Zealand parliament. They are disillusioned with political party politics. (*NZ First,* 1 June 1981.)

J. Stewart-Menzies, another founder member and a former founding member of the League of Rights in New Zealand in 1970–71, was reported as saying that the main objective was simply to put pressure on Members of Parliament to work in the interests of the electors and to ensure they were more accountable to the people (ibid.). *New Zealand First*, a publication of the New Zealand League of Rights, also based in Tauranga, reported and commented favourably upon the foundation and objectives of the Voters' Association.[3]

It was, however, a group called Voters' Voice which was most prominently associated with the CIR proposal. In the case of this group the promotion and introduction into New Zealand of CIR was the sole objective and it stood for the principle of direct democracy. Voters' Voice, too, had one of its two main bases in Tauranga. The issue attracted the attention of the New Zealand Superannuitants Federation, known as 'Grey Power', which passed a resolution in favour of CIR, largely because of its dissatisfaction with both major parties over the question of superannuation surtax. Once again, Winston Peters was involved, this time as a champion of the superannuitants' cause.

Accordingly, the issue surfaced at National Party conferences. In 1989 there were a number of remits at divisional conferences, and it was also discussed both at the 53rd annual conference and at the party's five divisional conferences in May 1990. At the divisional conferences the proposition was energetically supported by the then National MP for Tauranga, Winston Peters. Graeme Lee (Minister of Internal Affairs 1990–93), was another personally strongly in favour of CIR. In the same year Philip Burdon, a senior member of the Opposition, sent out 30,000 letters canvassing his blue ribbon constituency and subsequently reported that:

> ... the majority, almost without exception, considered that changes had to be made in the present form of parliamentary representation — the First-past-the-post system. However, most revealing was the high level of support for citizens-initiated referenda as a discipline that could by-pass the perceived abrogation of absolute power by the government of the day during its term of office. (*NZPD*, 510:4167.)

Despite that, both the leader of the party, Jim Bolger, and party president, John Collinge, were reported as opposed to the principle (*Press*, 6 July 1990). Serious problems arose when remits for the discussion of electoral reform, including CIR, were not included in the programme for the 1990 Annual Conference, despite being discussed at a number of that year's divisional conferences. Bolger was reported as saying that the issue deserved the calm, mature reflection of MPs rather than the 'emotional' debate of delegates (*Dom.*, 6 July 1990). His reported preference was for a citizens-initiated debate to be held in parliament if there were sufficient signatories on a petition reported to parliament (*NZPD*, 510:4160). Like his earlier upper house proposal, however, this too failed to win support.

Meanwhile, following its success as a remit in 1989, the issue had been passed on to the National Party caucus committee on Electoral and Parliamentary Reform (*Press*, 6 July 1990). A majority of the submissions received by this committee favoured a direct democracy system that included the popular referendum and the legislative initiative (Gobbi, 1992:181). The chairman of the committee, Murray McCully, who had spent three weeks in the USA largely devoted to studying the referendum process there, did not help matters by publicly stating — shortly before the 1990 National Party election year conference — that the caucus committee was unlikely to support the introduction of CIR. He believed that lobby groups could see it as a means of avoiding the legislative stages of scrutiny, avoiding the select committee process, scrutiny of officials, and government priorities in a normal budget round. "Vested interests," he believed, "see it as a wonderful mechanism for quickly promoting a point of view in to law" (*TDN*, 16 July 1990).

McCully pointed out that the rate for a professional firm to get the requisite signatures for a referendum in California was US $700,000, and that the California state legislature had control of less than 20 per cent of its own budget. "Referendums," he believed, "are too blunt an instrument to make law with." At the same time he conceded that they were a good vehicle for communicating a public view on an issue, thus drawing a clear distinction between indicative and binding referendums. Conscious of the strong view coming forward that cabinet had too much power, McCully's own preferred remedy (like Upton's) was a relaxation of the parliamentary whipping system which, he believed, would greatly improve the balance of power (ibid.). Such solutions, while theoretically true, ignored the fact that it was never in a party's self-interest to implement this type of measure, and it was party self-interest which was at the heart of many of the problems with New Zealand's parliamentary system.

Such was the outcry about the projected non-discussion of CIR and electoral reform at the 1990 National Party Annual Conference, that the leadership was forced to back down and resort to the traditional practice when under pressure of allowing a two-hour debate on the issues. The caucus committee also finally recommended in favour of a manifesto commitment to establish a system of non-binding referendums on any issue of public concern. The committee recommended that to qualify for a referendum, a petition signed by 10 per cent or more of eligible voters must be presented to parliament, and a government would then be required to hold a referendum within 12 months. Accordingly, the National Party became committed to the principle of the referendum and included a proposal for introduction of the CIR in its 1990 election manifesto, once again despite the reservations of its leadership.

Under the heading 'Improving New Zealand's Democracy' the policy objective was stated to be: "... to reform the electoral and parliamentary system to provide members of the public with more opportunities to influence the decisions of government." One means of achieving this was to: "... [e]stablish a procedure whereby non-binding referenda can be held on any issue that attains the signatures of 10 per cent of eligible voters on a petition seeking such a referendum." An information sheet issued at the 55th Annual conference in 1991 anticipated that the necessary legislation would be passed by the end of 1991, and implied that it might be viewed as a distraction from the appeal of MMP: "This will ensure that Citizens' Initiated Referenda (as a check in the hands of the people) can be included in the status quo option when the public vote on other reform options."

Before the 1990 general election, CIR clearly had a tactical appeal to the National Party while, more generally, it appears to have been seen in terms of a need to respond to public concerns rather than as a useful policy in its own right. As with the referendum on MMP, the approach of a majority of National MPs was one of grudging acceptance rather than support. The Labour Government still had not fulfilled its promise, made before the 1987 election, to hold a referendum on the electoral system. A manifesto commitment by National, not only to hold such a referendum but also to introduce a system of citizens' initiated referendums, could be seen as fulfilling a dual purpose. On the one hand, Labour's apparent duplicity would be underscored, and on the other the proposal enabled National to offer a positive policy alternative in response to public concerns which could be seen as less disruptive than the introduction of a PR electoral system. It would also be a useful supplement to the less saleable proposals for a second chamber or the Supplementary Member electoral system.

Speaking after the election, in December 1991, the then President of the National Party, John Collinge, emphasised the link between public disillusionment with politics; the large number of undecided voters, which he put as high as 33 per cent at times; and the call for citizens' initiated referendums (Collinge, 1992:80). He also indicated how the radicalism of CIR proposals (as called for by the Voters' Voice organisation, for example) might be tempered. The Voters' Voice demands called for referendums passed by a majority to be *binding* upon a government. Although now approving the principle of referendums in general terms, Collinge still appeared luke-warm on the principle of CIR. While approving the use of government-initiated referendums he firmly rejected the idea that any referendum should be binding on a government, believing that:

> Referendums are arguably too blunt an instrument to be used as a legislative process. Instead, initiative referendums should be used as means of guiding and persuading an elected government on appropriate issues. (ibid., 82.)

Support for CIR at this time also came from another largely unexpected source. In 1992 the influential Business Roundtable commissioned CS First Boston New Zealand Ltd to prepare *An Analysis of Proposals for Constitutional Change in New Zealand* (Brook-Cowen, et al., 1992). This report pointed out, *inter alia*, that the referendum and initiative are substitutes for political parties; and that the existence of such substitutes reduces monopoly power and hence the power of parties. It provided some reassurance for those who might be worried by the radicalism of the proposal, arguing that "... referenda increase the influence of the median voter and reduce the influence of special interests" (ibid., 5:10), a proposition likely to appeal to National Party supporters.

The report also endorsed the principle of the Citizens Initiated Referenda Bill and echoed other critics in expressing the belief that the 10 per cent of eligible voters required for a successful petition was too high. Not all systems use a percentage figure and, as a gross figure (approximately 215,000 electors at the time the report was prepared) this was significantly higher than many other states with much larger populations, such as Switzerland or many of the U.S. states. For example, the State of California, a heavy user of such referendums, required approximately 525,000 signatures, rather more than twice the New Zealand requirement, from a population over eight times larger. The report advocated that the 10 per cent requirement for signatures from electors for a successful referendum petition be reduced to 5 per cent (ibid., 5:22). It endorsed the non-binding character of the referendum, but advocated an additional binding 'protest', or legislative referendum capable, within 90 days, of nullifying a bill passed by parliament, unless overridden by a 'super-majority' of the House.

The government chose not to adopt these suggestions, but this positive reaction no doubt served to further strengthen its resolve that it had judged the policy correctly in the sense that, not unlike the Labour Government's proposal for a Royal Commission in 1984, CIR would be unlikely to pose real problems.

The bill eventually enacted by the National Government in 1993 was, therefore, a cautious measure. It provided that the new system of citizens' initiated referendums would be non-binding on a government, and that there should be a steep qualifying requirement of 10 per cent of valid signatures from eligible voters. These provisions, it was widely believed at the time, would largely neuter the proposal. Despite the pressures for it, CIR attracted surprisingly little attention as a policy proposal, but once implemented as law, pressure group response was immediate despite the hurdle involved. The result was that it rapidly became clear just how ill the measure sat with its National Government originators.[4]

Conclusion

It is ironic that the period from 1984 to 1993, which saw both major political parties abandon the habits of a lifetime and implement economic policies which they deemed to be necessary rather than popular, saw such a loss of faith in the two-party system. Judged in a longer term perspective, that was atypical. Despite that, CIR and MMP in many ways seem to sum up the National Party approach to constitutional and electoral matters. Whether abolishing old, redundant institutions, or introducing new ideas, the party does not appear to have been unduly influenced by principle. All too often the determining criterion has been electoral advantage, although there are always MPs committed to a cause for its own sake. Traditionally, the party has been stronger in reacting to short-term clear political need than in formulating longer term solutions.

In the case of CIR, although MPs and cabinet ministers refuse to be quoted directly on the issue, it seems clear that because the proposal was for a non-binding system, neither cabinet nor caucus took it particularly seriously. In recent years we have also seen examples of the typical conservative tendency to propose a lesser change in an attempt to frustrate a greater. All such moves tend to take place, if not wholly in isolation, then seriatim. There seems to have been little interest in trying to assess the overall picture or how the various aspects of change might relate to one another, whether in providing fair representation for the various groups which make up our society or in providing the type of limitations upon executive government considered as normal by other democratic states.

A high official of the National Party who declines to be named has argued that the National Party simply misjudged the MMP issue:

> Generally the issues seem to have been taken rather casually and the pre-election policy promotion as being without risk to the status quo. In other words, a political mistake... . I remain incredulous that the German system *was inflicted upon us* (emphasis added) — in a state of sublime ignorance, but driven by antagonism to politicians.

Thus, Governor Lord Glasgow was correct when, as long ago as 1893, he complained that, "There are no conservatives in this Country: everybody has more or less advanced political views..." (quoted Jackson, 1972:150).

New Zealand has no tradition of Reactionary Conservatism, but the National Party, at different times, has succeeded in representing strains of all three of the other aspects of conservatism. The Holland years of the 1940s and 1950s witnessed an admixture of Pragmatic Conservatism and Liberal Reformism with the proviso that Liberal Reformism was interpreted in terms of change motivated by political advantage rather than practical improvements for their own sake. The Holyoake and Muldoon years represented almost pure Pragmatic Conservatism; while the 1970s and 1980s saw two short-lived shifts of emphasis to Liberal Reformism, but with different interpretations, by Marshall and McLay.

The second half of the 1980s and the 1990s, under the leadership of Jim Bolger, witnessed almost bewildering mixtures of Pragmatic Conservatism and Radical Conservatism. It is tempting to argue that the common thread — as in most large modern parties — is the desire for power. But the emphasis upon structural economic reform under Labour between 1984 and 1990, continued and furthered under National with the Radical Conservative policies of Finance Minister Ruth Richardson from 1990 to 1993, have clearly been exceptions to this, with Labour badly defeated in 1990 and National only narrowly avoiding loss of power in 1993. In 1996 the President of the National Party, Geoff Thompson claimed that:

> We regard ourselves as moderate conservatives, supporting traditional institutions of our society, but generally promoting individual opportunity with the underpinning of State provision of social services. (Thompson, 1996.)

But even as a current view, one must wonder about the degree of support for the "traditional institutions of our society". Overall, if we take into account the various pressures to which politicians are exposed — political, economic, social, ethnic, cultural, external and bureaucratic — National is what it has long seemed to be, middle of the road, moderately conservative, and sometimes surprisingly pragmatic.

Notes

1   A free-trading, market-led economy named after its principal architect, Roger Douglas, Minister of Finance (1984–88) in the Fourth Labour Government.

2   In response to National's advocacy of a Senate, Labour resolved "that this committee is not interested in an Upper House".

3   New Zealand First was also the title chosen for the party formed by Winston Peters in July 1993 following his split from National.

4   Despite 18 proposals for CIR having been approved by the end of 1997 only one — initiated by the New Zealand Professional Firefighters Union — has so far managed to reach the statutory minimum number of signatures (10 per cent of registered electors) to force a poll. The question posed was: "Should the number of professional firefighters employed full-time in the New Zealand Fire Service be reduced below the number employed on 1 January 1995?" Essentially an industrial relations matter (it should properly have been placed before the Employment Court), its overwhelmingly one-sided result — in a 27.0 per cent turnout, 87.8 per cent voted 'no'— highlighted the potential abuse of the CIR provisions. The Minister of Internal Affairs, Warren Cooper, attacked both the referendum and the professional Firefighters, arguing that "industrial relations should not be conducted by referendum" (*Press*, 24 May 1995). The Minister of Justice (Doug Graham) also criticised the strategy, declaring it a 'useless' poll, and warning that: "If people act irresponsibly and put up silly referendums, then we are going to have to take a look at changing the Act" (*NBR*, 2 June 1995).

5 The Royal Commission: Recommendations and Consequences

Royal Commissions have a funny track record in New Zealand.
A lot of people put them up and nothing much comes of them
so they are not seen as inevitably the way to go.
— David Lange (quoted Gomibuchi), 1994:71.

Royal Commissions and Commissions of Inquiry fall broadly into two types — commissions designed to investigate, to ascertain *facts*, particularly after a serious accident or similar occurrence, and commissions designed to assist in *policy* formation (Easton, 1994:241). It is a common belief among politicians that Royal Commissions with *policy* concerns are set up by a government, either for the purposes of delay or to provide a government with the answers that it requires. Certainly, politicians usually have no liking for letting a policy issue pass out of their hands. It has long been pointed out that "there are a number of ways in which a government may impose a positive or negative influence on the commission process" (Simpson, 1978:26) The outcome can usually be influenced, if not determined, by the nature of the terms of reference which are set and the personnel who are selected to serve on the commission, especially the selection of the chairperson. These are matters decided by the government. As suggested over 60 years ago:

> The statesman who nominates the commission can almost always determine the course that it is going to take, since he will have a pretty good knowledge beforehand of the minds of the experts whom he puts on it, while, of course, avoiding any appearance of 'packing' his team. (Dibelius, quoted Easton, 1994:243.)

The time allowed for deliberations, the financial support granted, together with the levels and expertise of the staff appointed, may also have an important bearing on the eventual outcome. This should not be taken to imply that all commissions are loaded exercises because a number of different variables are involved. For example, the degree of commitment to a policy by any particular government may vary; the particular personnel sought by a government to

95

serve on a commission may not always be available; some governments are more directional in their activities than others, while the balance between seeking indirect government influence and credibility is always a delicate one likely to be upset.

Occasionally a Royal Commission, or Commission of Inquiry, does the unexpected when outcomes do not follow a government's optimum desired path. Various reasons may account for this. Closely defined terms of reference may create frustration; a commission may become overwhelmed by the load of evidence adduced; given the vagaries of human nature, the evidence before them and/or the persuasiveness of their fellow commissioners, commissioners may shift their attitudes; or a commission may simply get the bit between its teeth and 'bolt', interpreting its orders of reference in terms of what they will bear rather than following a literal interpretation. Previous examples of where commissions have exceeded the expectations of the governments that set them up have included the Royal Commission on Compensation and Rehabilitation in respect of personal injury in New Zealand, chaired by Justice Woodhouse (1966–67) and the Royal Commission to Inquire into the Crash on Mt Erebus, Antarctica, of a DC-10 Aircraft Operated by Air New Zealand Limited (1981), by Justice Mahon.

Frequently, Royal Commissions produce a more or less expected result. 'Blank cheque' inquiries of whatever sort are a rare species because there is always the potential for political embarrassment arising from their reports. In this regard, it is not without interest that a young lawyer who assisted Justice Woodhouse in an Australian Committee of Inquiry on Rehabilitation and Compensation was the person who was to be largely responsible for setting up the Royal Commission on the Electoral System in New Zealand in 1985. That young lawyer was Geoffrey Palmer.

Given the obvious political embarrassment which was to follow publication of the report of the Royal Commission on the Electoral System in 1986, a number of questions must be asked: did the Commission exceed the expectations which governed the terms on which it was set up, and, if so, how and why? Was the result a matter of accident or design? And why the recommendation in favour of the German-style Mixed Member Proportional (MMP) system, not found anywhere outside West Germany at that time, rather than the system most commonly used in English-speaking countries (including neighbouring Tasmania and the Australian Federal Senate), the Single Transferable Vote (STV)?

In trying to decide whether the findings of the Royal Commission were occasioned by accident or design, it is necessary to ask at the outset, if by design, whose design? Why was a Royal Commission established in the first instance? Clearly, it was in fulfilment of an election promise, but why the promise?

As we have seen, the proposal to use the device of a Royal Commission to reappraise the electoral law of the country first appeared in the Labour Party policy for the 1981 general election where it was suggested that, "There is considerable unease in the community concerning the way the system works". The 1984 'Open Government' policy was a modification of this initial formal proposal offered in 1981. The successful candidature of Geoffrey Palmer at a by-election in August 1979 was an important related factor. As we have already seen, using Palmer's expertise, at the general election of 1981 Labour proposed a Royal Commission of three persons to inquire into and report upon a range of constitutional and electoral issues.

This was a timely and attractive package, so that although Labour failed to win the 1981 general election, the ground was already established for the setting up of a Royal Commission complete with a broad outline of its likely terms of reference. Hence, the origins of the policy may be traced back to a conjuncture of circumstances. Palmer became an MP in a by-election at a time of growing public unease, and his election to parliament had not only provided him with a public vehicle for his interests, but also ensured that the Labour Party had a broader policy agenda. If there is a design to be detected in the origins of the introduction of MMP into New Zealand, it may be said to have originated with the work of Palmer. Although Palmer did not advocate MMP as such, it was largely through his influence that the proposal for a Royal Commission to examine the possibility of the introduction of proportional representation was included in election manifestos in 1981 and 1984.

As we have seen, a proposal for a Royal Commission does not involve any binding commitment to act upon the advice which is forthcoming. Certainly, if the question had been raised while Labour was still a third party there would have been little doubt about the answer. But, if we ask — in whose political interest was it to alter the electoral system in the mid 1980s? — the answer is much less clear-cut. Undoubtedly, unease had existed since the 1978 general election when a National Government had been returned on a minority of the total vote in the country as a whole, and the administration of the first computerised enrolment at a general election had left grounds for criticism, and this unease was compounded when National was re-elected in 1981 on a minority of the total vote, albeit a small minority. Current political experience was obviously important. On the other hand, the Royal Commission was set up following the 1984 election in which Labour had won 59.8 per cent of the parliamentary seats on the basis of 42.9 per cent of the total vote. In a simple statistical sense this result, too, was inequitable, but it did succeed in clearly demonstrating that the First-past-the-post (FPP) electoral system, with its propensity to exaggerate parliamentary majorities of seats, also worked in Labour's favour even though National had proved to be the main beneficiary of such exaggerations since 1945.

Despite two major and two substantial third parties competing in the 1984 general election, only one third party, Social Credit, succeeded in winning any seats — two out of 95. There was no widespread discontent amongst Labour members or supporters with the electoral system as such; discontent had mainly focused about the role of the Representation Commission during the 1977 electoral redistribution.[1] Despite the appearance of the New Zealand Party, there was no fractionalisation of political parties at the parliamentary level, and welling public discontent with the political system generally, which was to become such a feature of the 1990s, had hardly developed at this stage.

The party likely to have benefited most from the use of a proportional system at the 1984 general election would have been the New Zealand Party which won 12.3 per cent of the votes and no seats. Although it is possible that, if the New Zealand Party had won 12.3 per cent of the seats in a PR election, there would have been a coalition with Labour, it cannot be assumed that acceptable coalition terms would have been found. So what was in it for Labour?

Equally, it is necessary to ask why would politicians allow such a potentially important issue to get out of their grasp? On the principle of kicking away the ladder which brought it to power, fundamental electoral change, far from being a priority, is unlikely to be attractive to any government in power, unless it seems likely to perpetuate its chances of remaining in office, or in the unlikely event that it suffers from an unprecedented rush of altruism to the head.

But there is frequently a gap between theory and practice. Governments are made up of individual ministers and, as the Fourth Labour Government was to amply demonstrate, there are circumstances in which particular, determined, ministers can exercise a disproportionate influence. So, when the new government took office on 26 July 1984, Geoffrey Palmer — now Deputy Prime Minister, Attorney-General, and Minister of Justice (the last-mentioned portfolio including responsibility for electoral matters) — moved with great speed to implement the 'Open Government' section of the manifesto. A draft Bill of Rights was published, the Royal Commission was established just over six months after coming to power, and important parliamentary reforms were completed within a year despite the economic and constitutional crisis which marked Labour's accession to power.

Clearly, the intention was to strike while the iron was hot, while other ministers were busily occupied dealing with the economic crisis or mastering their new responsibilities, and while the faintest hints of the euphoria of victory lingered on in the form of an indulgent tolerance. Under most circumstances it might have been expected that the government would keep a close eye on the question of a change to the electoral system in particular, if only because it was a move charged with such potentially far-reaching consequences.

Given the nature of the constitutional, economic, and foreign policy crises which New Zealand encountered at this time, few would have expected that an analysis of the electoral system would be an urgent priority. Why, then, did Palmer's colleagues agree to act with such impressive promptitude? For those members of cabinet and caucus who considered the question seriously at this time, a change of electoral system was not even the central feature of the 'Open Government' policy; Labour MPs were much more interested in the question of state funding of political parties.

It is also necessary to bear in mind that only two members of the government (Roger Douglas and Bob Tizard) had had any previous experience of government office. Even the Prime Minister, David Lange, was remarkably lacking in any form of executive experience. To this has to be added the enthusiasm, drive, and weight, of Palmer, as Deputy Prime Minister, for 'his' project. Constitutional matters had never been mainstream interests in the Labour Party, so the Royal Commission idea was regarded as useful at best and relatively harmless at worst. Moreover, it has to be recognised that, initially at least, his parliamentary colleagues indulged Palmer.

Third ranked cabinet member, Mike Moore, stated that there was little opposition because it was hard to turn down the Deputy Prime Minister; potential opponents were "so busy enjoying their own areas" that they were not "keeping the overview"; and because electoral reform was still regarded as a minor issue and given a very low priority (Gomibuchi, 1995:71). Moore's statement brings into perspective the point which is so easily overlooked in retrospect: that, for most Labour MPs, electoral reform was a minor issue forming only one part of a seven point plan for 'open government'. Indeed, it is fair to say that virtually no one, in or out of parliament, expected major change and certainly not radical change on the scale later recommended by the Royal Commission. A modification of the existing FPP system along the lines of the Supplementary Member system would have been the maximum change expected and few expected even that. Prime Minister Lange, for example, declared:

Mostly governments like to use Royal Commissions on sort of development of policy type Royal Commissions. They really do want to know where they are going to go to... . I mean I know what I wanted, but to have a sort of 'refined' First-past-the-post — I didn't ever want an MMP system. But to be honest I didn't know anything about an MMP system. (Lange,1994.)

Thus, Palmer appears to have encountered surprisingly little opposition, on the basis that this was a broad manifesto commitment in which the consideration of PR was only one proposal. The device of a Royal Commission was not seen as committing the government to anything specific. From the point of view of most of Palmer's colleagues little of real substance was at stake, certainly not at that stage. The cynic might well have concluded, therefore, that this was likely to be another example of where such bodies are resorted to either to delay action or to provide a government with a justification for what it already intended to do. In the case of the Royal Commission on the Electoral System, however, the nine wide-ranging terms of reference were almost too broad. There were several potentially controversial issues capable of rivalling, or overshadowing, any anticipated recommendations about change to the electoral system. The result was not to be the usual form of Royal Commission. As David Lange, with the benefit of hindsight, put it:

> [w]e were endorsing a Commission to establish something that we did not know what the answer was. We were not using it to give credibility to a course we wanted. We were resting on the edge...and having to depend, for our political future, on *their* assessment of what was good for New Zealand not *our* assessment of what was good for New Zealand... . (Gomibuchi, 1995:72.)

If, then, it was Palmer's design, at least in broad outline, what was the form of that design? In the case of reform of parliament the outline was clear enough, particularly with the reform of the select committee system along lines charted by the earlier Westminster reforms. But for the electoral system there was no immediate precedent to call upon. New Zealand was embarking upon an unusual and highly innovative track.

While Palmer was not likely to encounter serious opposition to his plans for parliamentary reform generally, there was little support in his own party, or in the Opposition, for any major change to the electoral system as distinct from a readiness to concede the desirability of a discussion. Even Palmer himself was not a PR zealot. His main interest centred on the relative roles of parliament and the executive rather than on electoral systems as such. He may have believed that an element of PR was necessary to correct the worst flaws of the FPP system but that did not necessarily mean that he was an advocate of a fully-fledged PR system, or any particular electoral system.

Nevertheless, from Palmer's viewpoint, there was a need to 'sell' the idea of some form of electoral reform, not just to the country but also to his own party. In this sense, it was not just that any change required careful and concentrated consideration, both in determining the best type of alternative and its likely consequences, but also that a positive recommendation from an important public, authoritative, body was necessary to give such a policy the 'legs' that it required. As ex-Prime Minister Lange expressed it later:

> I'm quite sure Geoffrey wanted proportional representation. He knew about things like MMP, he knew STV. But Geoffrey wanted proportional representation, and also he wanted the authority inherent in the Royal Commission of distinguished, non-partisan people to deliver it. (Lange, 1994.)

In this sense, then, the terms of reference and composition of the Royal Commission had a particular importance.

Composition

The size of the Commission, which had been set at three in the 1981 and 1984 manifestos, proved to be more difficult to finalise, being closely tied in with the question of composition. In such matters the question of chairmanship is crucial, and Palmer made, what was for his purposes, an inspired choice.

As early as 2 October 1984, John Wallace, then Human Rights Commissioner and a judge of the High Court, was approached, on Palmer's behalf, by the Secretary of Justice about the possibility of chairing the Commission. Wallace indicated that he was "keen to accept" but was concerned about the consequential staffing arrangements at the Human Rights Commission (Palmer, H.39:2 October 1984).

The choice of a lawyer (frequently a High Court judge) to chair commissions has become virtually axiomatic in New Zealand since 1936. It has been pointed out that of all the commissions appointed between 1909 and 1934 (both Royal, and Commissions of Inquiry), approximately half the chairmen were drawn from legal backgrounds, but that since 1936, "a mere 7 per cent of chairmen have been drawn from occupations other than law" (Simpson, 1978:29).

The appointment of a judge is intended to be seen as a means of ensuring impartiality. However, judges may range in their views from those of a liberal outlook to hidebound conservatives. In general, judges might be expected to be conservative in outlook to varying degrees. As chairpersons of Royal

Commissions they may be weak, or strong; efficient or inefficient; ready to interpret terms of reference literally, or to explore what interpretations they can be made to bear; they may be expert in seeking out areas that merit inquiry, or, as Simpson puts it "through ... limited perceptions, fail to understand the importance of particular matters" (Simpson, 1978:27). In the case of Justice Wallace, Palmer clearly chose a judge in whom he had personal confidence, a factor of considerable significance. It is, perhaps, a testimony to Palmer's standing with the cabinet that Wallace's appointment was not seriously questioned. Subsequently, however, several cabinet ministers clearly felt betrayed by the Royal Commission's report, construing what Palmer saw as open-mindedness, as weakness.

Because it was clear that the Commission would require someone with technical expertise, a former Government Statistician, John Darwin, was also sounded out about his availability for membership by the Secretary of Justice at the same time as Wallace (Palmer, H.39:2 October 1984). Darwin had the advantage of having served on the Representation Commission as an Official Member in 1983. He had also had a close understanding of the census process and afforded the Commission useful quantitative skills. Wallace, who had not met Darwin, believed that someone like him with "real mathematical and statistical knowledge is required" in relation to the proportional representation question (Palmer, H.39:5 November 1984).

With Palmer's approval, Wallace spoke to Sir Thaddeus McCarthy (a former Royal Commission chairperson) to gain his advice on chairing Royal Commissions, and also sounded out other possible appointees, including law professor Kenneth Keith, political science professor Richard Mulgan, President of the Labour Party and senior law lecturer Margaret Wilson, and historian Judith Bassett. His inquiries showed that Keith and Mulgan were interested. He reported that, "[o]ther names suggested to me by the people whom you agreed I might approach" included Alison Quentin-Baxter (Barrister, and well-known constitutional expert); former Law Professor and constitutional expert, Colin Aikman; and three political scientists with expertise in electoral matters, Nigel Roberts, Professor Robert Chapman and Professor John Roberts. At the same time he noted: "I am aware from my discussions with you that the Commission should have members able to represent both women's and the Maori viewpoints" (ibid.).

The opinions of government officials and MPs were also solicited. At a meeting held on 3 October 1984 officials were asked if they had considered further names for membership of the Royal Commission. Three names raised at this time as possible Maori representatives were all male. Palmer decided to talk to the Minister of Maori Affairs, Koro Wetere, about further names and at the same time asked Ann Hercus, Minister of Women's Affairs, to submit names if the Maori nominees continued to be all male (ibid., 3 October 1984).

In addition, a memorandum dated 21 November was issued by Palmer inviting members of the party caucus to submit names of possible appointees. Some 19 names were submitted including five academics; three former Labour MPs; and two Maori (Palmer, H.39). Of the names originally sounded out, or suggested, three also appeared in the caucus nominations: Darwin, Mulgan, and Professor Robert Chapman, two of whom (Darwin and Mulgan) were ultimately appointed (Gomibuchi, 1995:74).

In seeking to ensure that the whole exercise was kept at a level above party political considerations Palmer, together with Wallace, also consulted the then Leader of the Opposition, Jim McLay, about the composition of the Commission. McLay had, in fact, written to Palmer as early as 15 August, when the Royal Commission was no more than a manifesto commitment. He expressed the hope that it would be non-partisan, and offered full co-operation (Palmer, H.39:15 August 1984). *Inter alia*, McLay's idea of 'non-partisan' seemed to be that each of the three political parties with seats in parliament at that time — Labour, National and Social Credit — should all be represented by political appointees, bringing the overall size of the Commission to seven members.

The 'politicisation' of the Commission, at least in part, appears to have been seriously considered. Palmer maintains that he came under "quite a lot of pressure" to put former politicians on it (Palmer, 1997). A number of alternative appointments were looked at, including former National Government ministers, Brian Talboys and John Marshall. Palmer resisted such pressures because it seemed to him that: "They would have been opposed to anything that threatened perpetuation of the two-party system" (ibid.). The problem facing Palmer and Wallace was the classical dilemma of how to constitute a body which would avoid the self-interested views of political parties and yet produce a report which would prove either broadly acceptable, or at least appear to be so patently reasonable as to make it difficult to reject.

Apart from the question of the Commission's overall size (the larger the body the more difficult to reach an agreed, effective, solution), there were difficulties about which political parties should be represented. It is arguable, for example, that if Social Credit were the only third party to qualify for representation, it could have been readily outgunned by the two major parties. Moreover, Social Credit, despite winning two parliamentary seats at the 1984 general election, won only 7.6 per cent of the vote, compared with the New Zealand Party which won 12.3 per cent but no seats. Which, therefore, qualified for representation, Social Credit, the New Zealand Party, or both?

Palmer avoided the problem by reverting to an earlier 1984 proposal for a chairperson plus five members. The one-plus-five formula had originally been suggested by Wallace in his preliminary comments on the possibility of chairing the Royal Commission (Palmer, H.39:5 November 1984). The proposal was motivated by a wish to ensure the membership of Professors Ken Keith and Richard Mulgan, both of whom could only serve part-time. It was this arrangement that accounts for the increased size of the Commission compared to the original manifesto commitment. Thus, the eventual recommendation forwarded by Palmer for cabinet approval consisted of six names: Wallace (Chairman); Alison Quentin-Baxter; Darwin; Keith; Mulgan and Whetu-marama Wereta, a research officer (ibid., 5 February 1985).

Palmer had deliberately sought to ensure that no MPs, or former MPs, were included. This was intended to encourage more radical solutions, and he had to fight strenuously for such an outcome (Palmer, 1996). All his nominations were approved by cabinet with the exception of Alison Quentin-Baxter. It is not clear why this was so. Quentin-Baxter was not among the original group of suggestions by Wallace but had survived the various scrutinies. The budget for the Commission had already been approved by the Minister of Finance, and the size agreed as necessary for the work-load envisaged. Certainly, there was some overlap in the sense that both Keith and Quentin-Baxter were constitutional lawyers, but Keith's appointment was only part-time. Quentin-Baxter's omission at the last minute was then, surprising. Overall, however, as Gomibuchi (1995:73–74) has pointed out:

> What was interesting is that all the final Royal Commission members except for Whetumarama Wereta were already mentioned in Wallace's recommendation.

Wereta, originally proposed amongst the caucus nominations by Minister of Customs, Margaret Shields, served to rectify the glaring gap caused by the lack of representatives of Maori, or women, once Quentin-Baxter was omitted. Thus the final composition of the Royal Commission included a judge; a statistician; a constitutional lawyer, a political scientist and a Maori. Structurally, it appeared well-balanced. That, however, is not sufficient in itself to guarantee a fair, or balanced, outcome. Much can depend upon the views of the members and, particularly, whether they are radically or conservatively inclined.

Clearly, Wallace worked well with Palmer from the outset, playing an important role in helping to select the Commission's personnel. He was of a broadly liberal persuasion, and open-minded, with no commitment to PR or any pretensions to a detailed knowledge of electoral systems. Like Palmer himself, there is no evidence that he had any strong views in favour of, or more importantly, *against* any particular form of electoral system at this stage.

Keith, a former colleague of Palmer in the Law Department at the Victoria University of Wellington and close personal friend, shared many interests. Again, however, there is no prior indication of any strong views that Keith may have had on the question. John Darwin too, a former Public Service Department head, does not appear to have been associated with any political party or to have any recorded preferences about types of electoral system. His main qualification appears to have been his previous membership of the 1983 Representation Commission, together with his knowledge of the census process and his skills as a statistician.

Whetu Wereta's appointment did lead to some criticism. A former senior research officer in the Department of Internal Affairs, she had been a member of the New Zealand delegation to the World Population Conference, Bucharest, in 1974 and had led the New Zealand delegation to another population conference in Bangkok in 1975. She also had statistical skills. But her appointment was criticised by the Leader of the Opposition on the grounds that she was, or had been, an active member of the Labour Party, while the Commission was intended to be non-partisan. Palmer confirmed that his preference was for a commission on which no member should have political links but, in justifying her appointment, said, "that was my aim but it was not able to be achieved... She was easily the best qualified person I could find and so I persuaded my colleagues that she should be appointed" (*Press*, 22 February 1985).

It may be significant that three of the successful nominees were *all* included among the caucus nominations by cabinet minister Margaret Shields. They were the only caucus nominations to survive. Shields has admitted that Palmer approached her prior to the official invitation to other caucus members, but she had also known both Darwin and Wereta when all three had worked at the Department of Statistics (Gomibuchi, 1995:77fn).

One person who had expressed definite views before being appointed to the Royal Commission was Mulgan, a supporter of the First-past-the-post electoral system. In the first (1984) edition of his book, *Democracy and Power in New Zealand*, Mulgan outlined a model based upon the First-past-the-post system and, in what appeared to be a direct tilt at Palmer's view as expressed in *Unbridled Power?* stated that:

> Domination of parliament by one party is ... not necessarily the perversion of democracy or the negation of people's rights which it is often said to be, particularly by those who take the account of parliament given in constitutional law as a literal account of how parliament ought to function. (Mulgan, 1984:78.)

Mulgan also believed that the effects of PR, particularly where coalitions were formed, were not all that they were claimed to be:

> Where coalition governments are created by a process of bargaining between the parties after a government has been elected, the function of making and unmaking governments is to a certain extent removed from the electors and returned to parliament with consequent loss of power by the people. Increasing the independent power of parliament, in this case by giving MPs more opportunity to make and unmake governments, is not necessarily a change towards more democracy. (ibid., 77.)

Clearly Palmer was familiar with Mulgan's work: some years earlier, in a review article in the journal *Political Science*, Mulgan had directly criticised Palmer's views,[2] arguing that:

> his theory finds no room for political parties as legitimate parts of the constitution ... [and] ... If governments were made or unmade by shifting coalitions of individual MPs, then the right of the electorate to choose a government must be weakened. (Mulgan, 1980:173-74.)

Whether we should regard Mulgan as the token FPP supporter or not is, however, a moot point. In a marginal annotation on Wallace's original letter to him, Palmer noted, "Not perceived to be neutral" (Palmer, H.39:5 November 1984), a comment presumably related to his views on electoral systems. None of the appointees appeared to have any strong commitment to PR. There was a degree of liberal outlook and open-mindedness which signalled that some might be open to persuasion but there is no evidence to show that any of them approached their task determined to change the electoral system, which was, after all, just one part of their brief. It is difficult to divide them into supporters of FPP or supporters of change. Even in the case of Mulgan, his degree of commitment to FPP was found to be wanting for, during the course of the Commission's deliberations, he switched sides. He showed that he was prepared to support the Commission's preference for MMP even though he did not become fully committed to that cause until after the 1990 general election and the final breakdown of the mandate and caucus system on which his support for FPP had been based (Mulgan, 1992:530-31). Still later, he wrote that:

> ... single-party governments, in their extreme Westminster form, have failed as mechanisms of democratic accountability. The reason, however, is not intrinsic to single-party government itself or of the Westminster system in general ... . Provided that single-party governments and their immediate advisers accepted

the values of accountability to political parties and of consultation with sectional interests, and provided the parties themselves had the numbers and resources over their parliamentary leaders, the two-party system was able to deliver effective and accountable government. (Mulgan, 1995:95.)

Unfortunately, politicians, especially professional politicians, are not given to self-denying ordinances. It is arguable that even in the 1980s when he was writing, Mulgan's view had already become unduly idealistic and dated.

Mulgan was essentially an exponent of party politics, believing that, "[t]he main function of parliament is ... to provide a public forum for party competition" (1984:36). It follows that he opposed the Single Transferable Vote system which placed emphasis upon the individual candidates at the expense of party, but he came to favour MMP because it has the effect of *strengthening* the role of party. This eased his change of support from FPP to MMP, but by no means met all the objections that he had raised in his book. The Commission apparently took decisions by general agreement and it seems clear that Mulgan exercised a degree of influence, particularly in gaining acceptance of the importance of political parties. Ultimately, this commitment was to prove stronger than his commitment to FPP which he saw merely as a means of facilitating strong party government. Another important influence may well have been the work of one of the research assistants, Lewis Holden, who produced some excellent research reports on the strengths and weaknesses of the West German electoral system.

The Commission was also impressed with the merits of the STV system. Certainly, at the outset, if a fully proportional electoral system was to be considered, it might be thought that STV, as the only PR system favoured in the British Commonwealth, would be the leading contender. Although there was no single STV advocate comparable to Mulgan and his initial support for FPP, Whetu Wereta, for whom the eventual decision in favour of MMP involving abolition of the separate Maori seats must have been extraordinarily difficult, initially appears to have been inclined towards STV, a position supported by a strong submission from the Ratana Church. Paul Harris, the other research assistant, also produced important research reports on STV. Both Harris and Holden made important contributions, not only in drafting research reports, but also in the internal discussions of the Commission. The role of researchers in helping to influence outcomes is frequently overlooked but can be an important factor. Harris may well have personally favoured STV but was studiously professional in his presentations. Another influential piece of work was the specially commissioned History of Maori Representation by Professor M.P.K. Sorrenson, an historian at the University of Auckland. This was particularly important in bringing to the Commission's notice the extent to which the Maori race had become politically marginalised. Overall, therefore, if there was a bias in the appointments to the Royal Commission it was a bias *against* strong commitment to FPP and towards open-mindedness. This meant that the Commissioners lacked any particular allegiance to the existing system and that a final recommendation of some alternative form was always possible, if far from assured.

The Commission was certainly not constituted in a manner that Prime Minister Lange regarded as the usual practice. This was to propose terms of reference in line with party policy and then to appoint commissioners who could be relied upon to present a report broadly in line with policy. Because of the uncertainties implicit in Palmer's proposals, Jonathan Hunt, Minister of State and Leader of the House, challenged its proposed membership in cabinet, something that was rarely done. He was unsuccessful (Hunt, 1996a).

Bearing in mind that he was more interested in the limitation of executive power than in any specific form of electoral system, the outcome, regardless of the usual practice, did give Palmer what *he* wanted. The crucial determinant in the composition of the Royal Commission was that Palmer was more idealist than politician, and that he chose as chairperson a judge who liked to establish principles and work logically from them. Lacking any confirmed PR supporters, the Commission's composition presented a difficult target to attack, except on grounds of uncertainty of outcome. Moreover, we have to remember that, *at that time,* a recommendation for radical reform of the electoral system seemed an unlikely prospect. Few would have anticipated anything more than a recommendation in favour of modifying FPP with the Supplementary Member system (SM), an add-on, semi-proportional system. An 'enlightened' Royal Commission might be thought more likely to look with favour upon the other, more pressing issues such as state funding of political parties, increasing the size of the House, extension of Maori representation, and modification of the composition of the Representation Commission. Hence, whatever uncertainties may have plagued individual members, neither cabinet nor caucus appeared willing to take a stand on grounds that the composition of the Royal Commission was too liberal, or too academic.

Terms of Reference

In establishing such a Commission three considerations are uppermost: the terms of reference; the size; the selection of chairperson, and personnel. For all practical purposes the terms of reference had already been largely set in the election policy, with the Commission's nine formal terms merely adding more specificity. At first, 12 terms of reference were suggested, and initially this led to some confusion. As Justice Wallace commented to Palmer (Palmer, H.39:5 November 1984), he was originally under the impression that the Commission related mainly to electoral machinery matters and the question of PR, but the projected inquiry appeared "vast in scope", including, for example, PR, the number of MPs, the parliamentary term, Maori seats, and the use of referendums, each of which could form the basis for a full inquiry. This was obviously too large a task for a Commission of the suggested size of three to complete in 18 months — the suggested time span. Wallace wondered if the scope of the inquiry could be narrowed, perhaps separating parliamentary and electoral matters, although he appreciated that was not what Palmer wanted. He also wondered whether the related question of an upper chamber had been omitted deliberately (inviting the annotation 'Yes' from Palmer).

Palmer met with Wallace on 18 December when the possibility of narrowing the terms of reference was discussed. On the following day the Secretary of Justice proposed that three of the existing terms — those concerning possible changes to voter qualification and registration; possible changes to the existing system of voting (such as the marking of voting papers); and disputes over the outcome of elections such as election petitions — could be dropped. In the event the Commission finally found time to deal with these topics anyway. Accordingly, the terms of reference came to be focused more upon the structure of representation than on the conduct of elections. The main exception was the question of election expenses and state funding of political parties. On this the Secretary of Justice commented diplomatically:

> However, as that item is of some topical interest because of the recent Australian experience, I assume you [Palmer] would wish to see it dealt with in the Royal Commission report. (Palmer, H.39:19 December 1984.)

Thus, the Commission finally had nine terms of reference, although these were still remarkably wide-ranging:

1. Whether any changes to the law and practice governing the conduct of Parliamentary elections are necessary or desirable:
2. Whether the existing system of Parliamentary representation (whereby in respect of each electoral district the candidate with the highest number of votes is elected as the Member of Parliament for that district) should continue or whether all or a specified number or proportion of Members of Parliament should be elected under an alternative system or alternative systems, such

as proportional representation or preferential voting:

3.   Whether the number of members of Parliament should be increased, and, if so, how many additional Members of Parliament there should be:

4.   Whether the existing formulae and procedures for determining the number and boundaries of electoral districts should be changed and, in particular,—

   (a)   Whether the redistribution of electoral districts should be based on total population or adult population:

   (b)   Whether the allowance of five per cent by which the population of an electoral district may vary from the quota should be changed:

   (c)   Whether the membership and functions of the Representation Commission and the time limits and procedures governing its functions should be changed:

   (d)   The feasibility of some form of appeal from decisions of the Representation Commission:

5.   The nature and basis of Maori representation in Parliament:

6.   The term of Parliament:

7.   To what extent referenda should be used to determine controversial issues, the appropriateness of provisions governing the conduct of referenda, and whether referenda should be legislatively binding:

8.   Whether the present limits on election expenses are appropriate and whether any limits on such expenses should be extended to political parties and to the amount of individual or total donations candidates or parties receive and whether such expenses should be defrayed wholly or in part by State grants and the conditions, if any, which should apply to such grants:

9.   Any other question relating to the electoral system which you may see fit to inquire into, investigate, and report upon. (RCES, 1986a:xiii–xiv.)

One side aspect of these arrangements which ultimately proved of some significance was the question of travel. Wallace noted at the outset that he agreed with Palmer "that it is not desirable for Commissions to travel around the world", no doubt reflecting a widespread public suspicion of political junketing, but went on to suggest that he was troubled about deciding on the merits of proportional representation without studying the practical aspects at greater depth. He believed that if PR proved desirable, there was a need for one or two people, "not necessarily members of the Commission", to examine it (Palmer, H.39: 5 November 1984). Given the significance of the Commission's subsequent experience, particularly in Eire and West Germany, which played an important part in the final outcome, this was sound counsel. The fact that Palmer had apparently put less weight upon such considerations may reflect one of two influences. His first consideration may have well been to keep costs down in order to ensure a favourable Treasury report. At the same time, he may genuinely have believed that overseas travel was less important, envisaging the Commission recommending the Supplementary Member (SM) electoral system for which there was no exact counterpart to study at that stage. Less inhibited by the possibilities of political constraints and thus more wide-ranging in his approach, Wallace was, perhaps, more conscious of the need to review a range of overseas practical experience. Hindsight suggests that but for travel overseas and first-hand experience of the West German system, it is unlikely that the Commission would have recommended MMP for New Zealand.

Programme

This raises the question of why an apparently open-minded Commission which might have been expected to stress the deficiencies of FPP and possibly favour SM as means of helping to remedy these — or, perhaps if it wanted to be really radical, to favour STV — not only found against FPP, but finally espoused the wholly unfamiliar system of MMP as the preferred alternative?

As we have seen, the terms of reference under which the Commission was set up required it, *inter alia*, to report upon:

> Whether the existing system of Parliamentary representation...should continue or whether all or a specified number or proportion of Members of Parliament should be elected under an alternative system or alternative systems, such as proportional representation or preferential voting. (RCES, 1986a:xiii.)

In seeking to fulfil this requirement, the Royal Commission adopted ten criteria against which to test the existing plurality system and other possible systems. These were:
(a) Fairness between political parties;
(b) Effective representation of minority and special interest groups;
(c) Effective Maori representation;
(d) Political integration;
(e) Effective representation of constituents;
(f) Effective voter participation;
(g) Effective government;
(h) Effective Parliament;
(i) Effective parties;
(j) Legitimacy. (RCES, 1986a:11–12.)
Although it was careful to state that not all the criteria were of equal weight,

and that no system would adequately meet all ten criteria, an overseas electoral expert, Arend Lijphart, was of the view that they show that the Commission was firmly committed to the principle of proportionality, suggesting that, "It is not surprising that, measured in terms of these yardsticks, the plurality single-member district system does not fare well" (Lijphart, 1987:98). Much depends upon the weight that each criterion is given but, certainly, FPP does not fare well. The FPP system, as it evolved originally, was geared to the election of individuals and local communities, not political parties. It consisted, in effect, of a series of mini-elections held in each electorate. Thus, while each of these mini-elections might yield a fair result, with the entry of political parties into the equation the sum of these elections did not necessarily produce a fair result nationally. Considerable distortion was likely to ensue, a fact recognised by the Royal Commission.

Once, therefore, political parties are recognised as an integral feature of the political system, the disproportional results produced by FPP are in conflict with the first criterion, fairness between political parties, and amount to what the Commission regards as "a major deficiency in our present system" (RCES, 1986a:16). Beyond this, effective representation of minorities, and particularly the Maori minority whose separate system of representation with plurality was also regarded as "seriously deficient," was given considerable weight by the Commission, even to the extent of being viewed as a threat to political integration (RCES, 1986a:20).

There is a certain irony in this. Although every member of the Commission had a hand in drafting the criteria — what was included, what was excluded, and their ordering — the final list of ten criteria almost certainly owed much to the work of political scientist Mulgan. The implicit assumptions, particularly those relating to political parties, and the ranking of the criteria, accord closely with Mulgan's published views. Yet those views favoured FPP, not PR. How, then, can the apparent disparity be explained? Probably by the fact that, not unlike most of the politicians that had set it up, the Commission at this stage viewed its contribution to reform of the electoral system as likely to involve a modification of the existing FPP system rather than its replacement. Thus the ten criteria would also have fitted a semi-PR, add-on type system like SM.

Of the ten criteria applied, FPP failed to achieve the Commission's unqualified support on any one. Even the apparent strengths of the system, such as "Effective Representation of Constituents," receives only grudging support. Significantly, the one criterion for which the FPP comes closest to receiving a clean bill of health is that of 'Effective Government'. The Commission also found that FPP did encourage the development of effective political parties and, while not encouraging a good balance between diverse groups or enabling parties to protect their MPs in marginal seats, did encourage party unity and the formulation of policy.

Although literally true, there is the question of whether parties can be considered effective in the broader sense when they lose the faith and support of the voters. It was, after all, the failure of political parties to keep their election promises which was to be a major factor in the public loss of confidence in the electoral system, although this failure was not so obvious at the time that the Royal Commission was deliberating. What *was* obvious, particularly following the 1984 general election, was the extent to which FPP, in effect, discriminated so heavily against the development of third parties.

SM scored much better against the ten criteria than FPP (RCES, 1986a: 38-43) but, while keeping it under consideration, the Commission decided that, apart from the novelty of the system at that time, it did "not go far enough in meeting the fundamental objections to the plurality system in respect of the relationship between seats and votes". Later however, because of differing views amongst the commissioners over the merits of STV, it was agreed that if there were not to be a change to MMP, SM would be the next choice (RCES,1986a:64). Once the Commission began to move beyond the SM system, it opened up possibilities not seriously considered by most politicians and unlikely to prove acceptable to the general public at that time.

The most widely adopted PR system within the Commonwealth is the Single Transferable Vote system (STV), also known (in Australia) as the Hare-Clark system. This was adopted by Tasmania as early as 1907, Malta and Eire in 1921, and for elections to the Australian Commonwealth Senate in 1949. In the event that the Commission might recommend a fully proportional electoral system, STV, a preferential rather than List form of PR, seemed the most probable outcome. Indeed, it is clear from the Royal Commission's report that it received close attention and support.

Despite being a mixed system, using single member constituencies as well as party lists, MMP is fundamentally a system which places the emphasis heavily upon political parties. By contrast, STV is essentially a constituency based system although, unlike the plurality system, these are much larger multi-member constituencies. Given the animus against the two major political parties which was to develop *after* the Report of the Royal Commission was published, had the report been written later the Commission might have been tempted to place a different emphasis on its criteria. As it was, ranked against plurality and STV on the ten criteria adopted at the outset, MMP was placed first on no less than seven counts — effective Maori representation; effective voter participation; effective parliament; effective parties and legitimacy — albeit narrowly in several instances. MMP and STV were ranked equal on two counts, political integration and effective representation of constituents. Plurality was ranked first on only one criterion. The advantage conceded was that of effective government, and even this was only conceded with evident reluctance.

Overall, the Commission viewed MMP as "clearly superior" to STV and to plurality. In particular, MMP was seen as likely to be more closely proportional and thus likely to be fairer to small parties (because it was more party-based). An added advantage was that it retained single member constituencies, the latter reason being an important selling point. However, for many, and obviously for the Commission too, there was a danger that the final report would become little more than an academic exercise.

Experience

Lijphart (1987:98) has suggested that the Royal Commission had its own agenda:

> The Commission's strong preference for proportional election results — and hence PR — might make one suspect that PR's effect of undermining the Westminster system is merely an unintended by-product. That is not the case; on the contrary, the Commission fully and explicitly intended such a shift away from the existing Westminster rules and institutions.

In practice, the process was more subtle and complex than that statement infers. There can be little doubt that Justice Wallace had no personal axe to grind, and went to great lengths to consider all points of view. It is arguable, however, that his very open-minded qualities were precisely those necessary to produce the result that ensued. A more closed-minded, less sensitive, less carefully logical person might well have presided over a very different outcome. In particular, once committed to the cause, Wallace and the other members of the Commission undoubtedly did follow through relentlessly to their radical conclusions.

At the same time the Commission made a commendable attempt to solicit as wide a variety of views as possible, advertising, not only in the press but also on television, and arranging for poster displays in all post offices; soliciting opinions from various organisations, groups and individuals; holding public hearings in three metropolitan centres for the convenience of those wishing to make a personal appearance in support of their submissions; and arranging five *hui* (gathering) to be held on marae in order to effectively tap Maori opinion. Lastly, it made what turned out to be a very important visit to the Federal

Republic of Germany, Eire, Australia, Canada and the United Kingdom.

Of the 804 written submissions received, the Commission reported that 65 per cent referred to the method of voting at parliamentary elections; of these, 61 per cent favoured a change to some form of PR and only 10 per cent favoured retention of the existing plurality system (RCES, 1986a:27). This may well be more a reflection of the degree of motivation and organisation of those promoting change than an accurate reflection of opinion throughout the country at the time. For example, opinion polls included in the Commission's report show a range of results which approximate to a 50:50 split (RCES, 1986a:27-8).

Because the Commission included no MPs, it made a particular effort to hear the views of a range of current and past MPs, together with groups of MPs selected by each of the three political parties represented in the House of Representatives and the Maori MPs. Neither of the major parties favoured radical change; only the Democrats (formerly Social Credit) sought a proportional system. Not a single party submission favoured the German-type MMP system and only a handful of the more general submissions mentioned it. The Women's Electoral Lobby, for example, was attracted to the system with its two votes but failed to support it "because it would mean increasing the number of Members of Parliament ... that was something we didn't favour" (RCES, 1986e:451).

Some of the other submissions were more influential. In particular, Philip Saxby, who subsequently founded the Electoral Reform Coalition, was commended by the chairman for producing an "excellent submission ... You have produced all the major arguments in favour of the West German system very succinctly" (ibid., 1986d:26). Another important submission came from Louis Erhler of Wellington who had been resident in West Germany for the previous 7 1/2 years. Moreover, as noted earlier, the Commission was well-served by its research officers who had produced detailed appreciations of the West German and STV systems (RCES, 1986f:9.2). So if, more widely, the perception and understanding of the German system by the general public and MPs was virtually nil at this time, the possibilities of the system were apparent to the Commission almost from the outset.

Over 40 per cent of the submissions received referred to Maori representation, a matter of particular concern to the Commission. The Labour Party submission supported continuation of the existing system with the number of seats varying according to the numbers opting for the Maori electoral roll. During its term (1972-75) the Third Labour Government had amended the *Electoral Act 1956* to this effect but the succeeding National Party government had promptly returned the situation to the status quo ante (McRobie, 1989:18).[3]

Both the Democratic Party and the Maori Mana Motuhake Party supported STV. The Democrats saw this as enabling the abolition of separate seats while Mana Motuhake recommended that there should be two separate multi-member Maori electorates within an STV system. There was, in fact, a clear division along racial lines, with the overwhelming majority of non-Maori submissions supporting abolition of separate representation, while, with the exception of one oral presentation, all the Maori submissions were in favour of continuation.

At least 40 Maori groups and individuals made written submissions, and all but six of those who wanted to present their submissions personally were heard on one of the five marae visited, along with many other oral submissions (RCES,1986a:85-86). As the Commission pointed out, almost all the Maori submissions were based upon the assumption that the existing FPP system would continue (ibid., 85). A major concern of the Maori submissions was well summed up at a hui organised by the New Zealand Maori Council and held at Turangawaewae Marae where those present opposed linking the word "abolition" with the concept of Maori representation and expressed a unanimous belief that the number of separate Maori seats should be increased (RCES, 1986c:2:18 June 1985). The main impact of the submissions was to convince the Commission of the depth of critical feeling about the way in which parliament operated (RCES 1986a:25) rather than to advance any particular positive solutions. It seems that the Commission failed to follow this up by probing possible Maori preferences for a form of representation under PR.

Not that the Commission was without ideas of its own. Sorrenson's "History of Maori Representation in Parliament" (RCES, 1986a:App.A), together with Professor Robert Chapman's annex, "Voting in the Maori Political Sub-System, 1935-1984" (ibid., App.B:83–108), had served to show how politically marginalised Maori had become, and was an important factor in causing the Commission to favour the possibility of a system which offered a common electoral roll. A common roll would have the effect of unlocking the isolation of Maori interests which, the Commission believed, the system of separate seats under FPP had induced.

But, as the Commission pointed out (RCES,1986a:99), a common roll was likely to have different effects under different electoral systems. STV has a common roll but is based upon local multi-member constituencies. The evidence of population distribution available to the Commission showed that STV with, say, five member constituencies, would be unlikely to provide many opportunities for Maori to reach the necessary quotas (ibid., 52; Harris, 1996a).

MMP, too, was not without similar disadvantages, but the German system did provide for small national groups by lowering the threshold in specified cases. Such a provision could be applied to 'Maori parties' and possibly other ethnic groups in the future (RCES,1986a:101). This, together with the opportunities offered by list nominations, led the Commission to believe that the German system would prove more adaptable to New Zealand circumstances. The major concern, however, was to ensure that Maori were on the same roll as Pakeha and thus in a better position to influence pakeha thinking. Such findings were important in leading the Commission to the conclusion that MMP would offer the prospect of a better solution for Maori than either FPP with separate Maori seats, or STV with a common roll.

The Commission believed that continued Maori representation would be assured even with the abolition of the Maori seats. Such representation, however, was not necessarily representation of Maori by Maori. Even though the Commission admitted that abolition of the Maori seats could conceivably result in no Maori being elected, it still believed that the advantages of a common roll would outweigh any disadvantages. For a race which hitherto had been marginalised politically, such an act of faith was always too much to expect, and the proposal received little or no support. Moreover, the concept of a 'Maori party,' to be given favourable treatment in relation to the threshold, raised important definitional and other practical difficulties. Despite good intentions, the Commission's recommendations on the question of Maori representation were among the least satisfactory of its outcomes, as is shown by the eventual adoption of MMP combined with retention of the separate Maori seats.

Apart from the issue of Maori representation, the positive conclusions reached by the Commission appear to have owed more to investigation, discussion and experience than to submissions. As it pursued its task, the inequities of the FPP system were more tellingly revealed and the commissioners clearly became more convinced of the need for change. But change could still mean either a lesser reform, with a modification of FPP, or a major reform, with the adoption of a fully proportional system such as the STV or MMP. The SM system also continued to remain in contention. What then caused the Commission to pass over SM, and favour MMP over STV? What caused it to bring what most would have regarded as an 'alien' system, MMP, into such serious contention? Perhaps the single most valuable experience of the commissioners was the trip to investigate how a number of different electoral systems operated in practice. This was not due simply to what they discovered about how STV and the West German electoral system worked in practice, but arose from the group interaction which developed. This was the longest continuous time that the Commission spent together as a group. As Mulgan explains:

The trip was important not only for what we saw and heard but also because we were together for a month — the only time — and knew that we would have to begin writing as soon as we got back. Hence the discussion was very intense. (Mulgan, 1996a.)

If, when it left New Zealand in March 1986, there were trends in the Commission's thought, by the time it returned the die had been effectively cast. In March and April 1986 the commissioners visited Canada, the Federal Republic of Germany, Eire and the United Kingdom. Later, it also visited Australia. Australia and Canada were mainly of importance for administrative issues such as state funding of political parties, voter registration, and various technicalities associated with the running of a general election, although a Supplementary Member system had been proposed for Canada by the Task Force on Canadian Unity in 1979 (RCES,1986a:33).

Two countries clearly had a marked impact on the thinking about the type of electoral system best suited to New Zealand. Those countries were West Germany and Eire. The Commission and its researchers had thoroughly investigated the literature on STV and MMP in particular before they commenced their travels. They knew that STV could produce distorted results, as in the case of Malta in 1981; that it fostered intra-party competition; and, in the case of Ireland, not only intra-party competition but also what is often regarded as an over-concentration on constituent needs (RCES,1986a:48 & 54); but direct discussions with participants was a powerful reinforcement. In Eire, politicians have twice tried to rid themselves of STV only to be rebuffed by the public in referendums.

During its visit to Eire the practical problems associated with STV, particularly those relating to proportionality for small parties; complaints of excessive localism; political log-rolling by MPs; the fragmenting effect of the system; and the difficulties of developing national policies; were all clearly revealed. Perhaps even more important, given the emphasis placed by the Commission on the importance of the role of political parties, STV is regarded as antipathetic to strong party cohesion. Although strong party cohesion is often decried by the public there is no doubt that the Commission regarded it as an essential feature of a stable democratic system.

West Germany, on the other hand, provided a first-hand introduction to a modern system, then the only one of its type. The Commission found that although West Germany had had coalition governments since 1949, those governments had been extremely stable with only two early elections and three changes of government between 1949 and 1986. Irish governments had proved less durable with three elections in three months in 1981–82, as minor parties and independents withdrew their support from the government. On the other hand, the Commission found that, as in most other European proportional systems, governments have demonstrated their ability to act decisively when that has proved necessary (RCES,1986a:58).

The Commission was also influenced by two German political scientists, Professors Dieter Nohlen and Klaus von Beyme. These academics stressed the need, in terms of systems, to decide between a majoritarian system, however modified it might be (such as SM), and a fully proportional system such as MMP. They stressed that, in effect, there was no satisfactory middle-ground. That is a contestable issue, but such was the impact of the overseas tour that all the commissioners came to accept the West German type system as the front-runner, leaving them divided over the relative merits of STV and SM for the second place (RCES,1986a:64). The German tour also has to be seen against the background of the original criteria. As the Royal Commission report points out:

> ...for New Zealand, MMP is clearly superior. It is fairer to supporters of significant *political parties* and likely to provide more *effective representation of Maori* and other *minority and special interest groups*. It is likely to provide a more *effective Parliament* and also has advantages in terms of *voter participation* and *legitimacy*. (RCES,1986a:63.)

There is no doubt that MMP does favour political parties much more than STV, but while STV puts the emphasis more upon individual candidates it is by no means clear that MMP necessarily encourages greater voter participation or legitimacy.

Several of the other propositions advanced by the Royal Commission are also disputable. Clearly MMP was not seen, least of all by Maori, as offering them "effective representation". From a Maori viewpoint the Commission's genuine desire to have both races on the same electoral roll in order to avoid the marginalisation of Maori was, however well-intended, an essentially Pakeha majority viewpoint. And the contorted arrangement proposed by the Royal Commission under which 'Maori' parties would not be required to achieve its proposed 4 per cent threshold, although based upon a German precedent, was further evidence of this. Similarly, it is arguable whether MMP would provide better representation for minority and special interest groups, or have advantages over STV in terms of voter participation and legitimacy. It is not even clear that it would provide a more 'effective Parliament'.

One clear advantage, not mentioned by the Commission, that MMP did have was that it appeared to have more respectable antecedents. Despite some lack of understanding of it by German voters, arising from the confusion caused by the so-called *Zweitstimme* (second ballot) being more important than *Erststimme* (first ballot) — serious enough to be described as a "fault in the electoral law" by Unkelbach (quoted Kaase, 1983:164) — the system has succeeded in providing a remarkably stable governmental system in Germany and is widely regarded as a successful modern electoral system. Despite a long pedigree, dating from 1855 in Denmark and 1857 in Britain, STV, on the other hand, was only notably in use in Eire, Malta, Tasmania and the Australian Senate.

The Advantages and Disadvantages of MMP

Mixed Member Proportional was the term devised by the Royal Commission to describe the type of system used in the Federal Republic of Germany, a mixed, or additional member (AMS) type electoral system. The arguments in support of it (largely based upon the German system) as presented by the Commission's research officer, Lewis Holden, were:

- High degree of proportionality,
- Minor parties discouraged,
- Encourages consensus decision-making,
- High turn-outs,
- Retains single member constituencies —
  * Allows parties to appoint women, experts, or minorities,
  * Flexibility — possible to endorse or oppose a candidate while still registering support for the party,
- Few 'wasted' votes, even in 'safe' constituencies —
  * Able candidates in marginal electorates can be retained, despite adverse swings, because of the list system,
  * Allows parties to have representation in areas where they cannot win single member seats,
  * Can be used to free-up cabinet members from electorate duties,
- Coalition government is a more attractive option to moderates within each major party than to more extreme factions,
- The threshold provides near proportionality for strong parties but a plurality effect for weaker parties,
- The limited number of parties (and hence coalition options) contributes to stability and encourages moderate policies.
  (RCES, 1986f:85/9,85/27,85/28 & 86/7.)

The threshold requires some explanation. Proportional representation provides seats in proportion to votes cast. As an electoral system type, MMP is *highly* proportional, and it can be so effective that it may be desirable to take measures to *reduce* the degree of proportionality in order to prevent undue fractionalisation of the number of political parties represented in parliament. Such measure can be achieved by means of redistributing constituencies; by changes in procedure for the allocation of 'remainder' seats in party lists; or, above all, by the introduction of 'thresholds'.

Thresholds, used in West Germany from 1956 on; Sweden 1971; Spain 1977 and more recently Israel, are designed to winnow out the smaller political parties. In other words to introduce a deliberate element of *disproportionality* in representation in order to maintain a degree of executive stability in parliament. The Royal Commission originally recommended that the threshold be set at 4 per cent for New Zealand, although the subsequent report of the Electoral Law Select Committee favoured 5 per cent as in West Germany (*AJHR,* 1988:15).

The arguments against MMP cited by Lewis Holden were:

- A substantial increase in the number of seats required or there would be a marked increase in the size of electorate seats (a particular problem in rural areas),
- Potential for manipulation, especially with coalition deals,
- Successful minor parties could attain undue power,
- Parties not voters would determine governments,
- Party lists offer considerable influence to parties, e.g. candidates rejected by the electorates could be 'elected' by the party list,
- Complexity of the system with the confusion of two ballots,
- By-elections discarded [under the German system],
- Two classes of MP may develop with list MPs treated as inferior,
- The system merely a means of disguising a party list system,
- Government change may not take place at general elections,
- No guarantee that the most popular party will gain even a share of government.

Finally, in May 1986, Holden warned that, "Popular wisdom suggests that list systems of proportional representation are unlikely to find favour in Westminster democracies in selecting representatives".

At the same time, even after the Commission's visit to Germany, Wallace was writing to a friend there:

It would take too long for me to give a summary of my own reactions to the German system. In any case I have not formed definite opinions about some aspects of it. It seems a fairly bureaucratic system in the sense that parties are

heavily supported by the taxpayers, almost as extensions of the public service...
Whatever the basic reasons for the German system being the way it is, there are
fundamental matters for us to sort out in the possible application of a similar
system in New Zealand with its different history and traditions. (RCES, 1986c:4,
14 May 1986.)

At this stage — like the New Zealand public subsequently — it seems that the
Royal Commission was clearer about its dislike of FPP that it was about which
system should replace it.

The Report and Outcome

As we have seen, despite the fact that the Royal Commission had been set up
in fulfilment of a manifesto pledge, there had been little expectation that the
government, any government elected under FPP, would be likely to change the
electoral system substantially. As recently as 1975 a parliamentary select
committee, when considering the possibilities of multi-member electorates,
had found no advantage in proportional representation or preferential voting
and rejected a West German type system.

Nevertheless, the Commission had, in effect, produced the result that
Palmer had hoped for, despite the fact that, as Wallace affirms unequivocally,
"Palmer never expressed any views to me on his own position" (Wallace, 1996).
The problem, however, was that Palmer represented minority opinion within
his party, and the Commission's report met with a predictably hostile reception
at the hands of both cabinet and caucus. It was one thing to indulge Geoffrey
Palmer and his constitutional interests but quite another matter when it resulted
in a political hot-potato, such as this report, being dropped in their laps, all,
from a politician's point of view, quite unnecessarily.

Criticisms within Palmer's own party varied. Backbench MP Larry
Sutherland, for example, described the submissions as originating largely from
the middle-class and academics. He claimed that ordinary people preferred a
quick, clean, clear-cut choice when voting (*DST*, 27 March 1988), while former
Labour Party president Jim Anderton claimed that MMP was worse than "the
present system" (ibid.). Later, as leader of a smaller party, Anderton was to
recant this view.

The Labour Government was obviously embarrassed by the report, some
of the key recommendations of which it had no intention of implementing, at
least in the form recommended. Jonathan Hunt has stated that the cabinet
"poured scorn" on the MMP recommendation in particular (Hunt 1996a). The

then Leader of the Opposition, Jim Bolger, believed that the recommendations made by the Royal Commission would turn the political system on its head (*NZH*, 17 December 1986).

Despite the fact that, in many ways, this read like an excellent academic report, even academic commentators were pessimistic about the recommendations for the change to the electoral system. Boston (1987:112), for example, regarded the chances of PR being introduced as 'poor', although Lijphart, while equally pessimistic, added a prescient caveat: "Short of a voters' revolt against the two strongest parties, the adoption of PR appears to be very unlikely" (1987:103). At that stage of course, there was little indication of the voters' revolt which was to characterise the 1990s. The power to legislate for change, or not to change, was in the hands of the two major parties, and it was clearly not in their interests to make fundamental, rather than cosmetic, changes. Thus, unless they mishandled the situation or could be pressured to act, radical change of the type advocated by the Commission seemed highly unlikely.

The effective significance of the Royal Commission at a crucial time, therefore, was that its findings provided a necessary focus. A body free of MPs was seen as reasonably impartial. It is a fair assumption that the commissioners themselves did not expect any radical change to follow from their recommendations in the short-term. They were aware that they were running ahead of public opinion. What they sought to do was to establish a blueprint for an electoral system, almost in an academic rather than a practical political sense. Such an outcome may well have fulfilled the expectations of its original promoter, Geoffrey Palmer, but the report obviously came as a sharp shock to the government as a whole.

The Royal Commission's report had not only had the effect of helping to place the principle of electoral reform conspicuously before the public, if not on the political agenda, it had also resolved an important problem of confusion. Hitherto, while the degree of dissatisfaction with the existing political situation had been growing there had been no agreement about a solution or about any particular electoral system to replace FPP. PR seemed to offer a confusing myriad of often complex alternatives. Opponents of the system had been able to range widely over a variety of different PR systems in order to illustrate the disadvantages of change, with Italy always being a favourite example, despite the fact that many of these systems had little in common apart from the fact that they were proportional. By recommending MMP the Royal Commission had not only focused on a specific system for discussion but had chosen one which manifestly did not appear to suffer from many of the problems associated with the some of the more notorious examples of PR. However much politicians subsequently might seek to obscure the issue by introducing alternative systems into the debate, whether modifications of the existing system, such as the Supplementary Member and Preferential Vote systems, or other PR systems such as the Single Transferable Vote, once the Royal Commission after careful consideration had recommended the MMP system, this became the effective marker around which supporters of proportional representation could, and did, rally. The work of the Royal Commission had ensured that when dissatisfaction with the existing system reached a high enough level, the alternative MMP system, now firmly implanted in the public's consciousness, could be seen as an agreed acceptable alternative.

Notes

1   A new redistribution had been carried out in 1983 which, while eliminating National's parliamentary majority on paper, actually made it slightly more difficult for Labour to win a working parliamentary majority (McRobie, 1984:14–16).

2   In turn, Palmer had reviewed Mulgan's book, *Democracy and Power in New Zealand* (*Listener*, 14 July 1984).

3   In 1993, National conceded that if separate Maori representation were retained, the number of constituency seats would need to reflect Maori population numbers.

6   Political Obfuscation

> Politics is the art of preventing people from taking part in affairs
> which properly concern them.
>
> — Paul Valéry (French journalist), 1943.

If there is one thing that stands out, above all else, in New Zealand's seven-year debate on electoral reform it is the failure of MPs on both sides of the political divide to control the direction of that debate. Several times, particularly during the second half of the 1980s, politicians had the opportunity to rebottle the genie let loose by the Royal Commission's report. That they failed to do so was the result of divisions within each caucus, the inability of Geoffrey Palmer (then Deputy Prime Minister and Minister of Justice) to persuade his caucus to adopt as policy the minimalist reform proposed by the Labour majority on the parliamentary select committee on the electoral law, and the National Opposition's determination to cover every base in its quest to win the 1990 general election. As a result, indecision was the order of the day and this gave the pro-MMP Electoral Reform Coalition (ERC), at this time the only significant lobby group, a window of opportunity that enabled it to keep the issue before the public. Seven years and three referendums later New Zealand electors determined that, regardless of the views of politicians, the country should adopt substantially the electoral system proposed by the Royal Commission.

Reform Revisited, 1990: the Terris and Anderton Bills

In theory, one might have expected that the Labour Government's decision not to proceed with its promised referendum would have effectively killed debate on the Royal Commission's proposal to adopt MMP. At the very least it appeared that the government had regained the initiative in the debate and that, henceforth, it would work to retain control, thus ensuring that any changes made to the electoral system would be acceptable to the great majority of MPs. The reality, however, was very different. Fundamental philosophical disagreements existed over electoral reform and many other policy issues. Leadership tensions were present between Lange and his deputy, Palmer, and, later, between Palmer and his deputy, Clark. The result was a deeply divided Labour caucus (Terris, 1996).[1]

Between mid-1989 and the 1990 election, a number of attempts were made by individual MPs to keep the issue of electoral reform alive. Shortly after the government had announced its decision, Northey attempted to renew pressure on the government by advocating that the Electoral Law caucus committee support a "favourable consideration" recommendation for a petition seeking a referendum on PR in 1989 because it believed that a referendum should be held "to keep faith with the electors" (Palmer, 1989:22 June 1989). Clearly, it would have been highly embarrassing for the government if the select committee (by a government majority) had made such a recommendation (ibid.).[2] The petition was eventually referred to the government "for consideration", the lowest level of endorsement available to a select committee (*AJHR,* 1990:29).

Under the FPP system, few Private Members' bills were enacted in the New Zealand parliament unless taken up by the government of the day, but they did serve a useful purpose by drawing attention to an issue, or helping to keep it on the political agenda. Thus it was, in May 1990, two such bills, seeking referendums on electoral reform, were proposed. John Terris, Deputy Speaker and Labour MP for Western Hutt, had won sufficient caucus support to guarantee that his Proportional Representation Indicative Referendum Bill would be introduced. (He was ably supported by other members of the Labour Electoral Law caucus committee such as Bill Dillon, Northey, Ralph Maxwell and Woollaston, and also, no doubt, he enjoyed the personal support of Prime Minister, Geoffrey Palmer.) Jim Anderton's Mixed Member Proportional Representation Bill, on the other hand, fell at the first hurdle. The primary objective of both bills was to maintain pressure on the government to keep its 1987 promise.

Terris's bill proposed that a non-binding referendum should be held in conjunction with the 1990 general election to determine whether electors favoured changing to a more proportional electoral system and, if a majority supported the 'change' option, a second referendum would be held to allow electors to choose an alternative electoral system they preferred. The bill's introduction was supported by 49 votes to 19 and referred to the Electoral Law Select Committee (*NZPD,* 507:1614–21 & 1870–83).

By specifying a binding referendum between First-past-the-post and MMP — essentially the Royal Commission's recommendation — to be held in conjunction with the 1990 election, Anderton's Bill went much further. He freely acknowledged that his aim was to tie the next parliament's hands to the extent that if the electorate voted in favour of MMP it would automatically become law and any reversal would require the passage of repealing legislation — which, clearly, would fly in the face of public opinion. Anderton's MMP proposal was closely modelled on that recommended by the Royal Commission but proposed the retention of the four separate Maori electorate seats (because "[n]ot enough consensus exists to change the Maori seats or their role in parliament at the present time") and a reduction in the number of list seats to 56. This Bill, however, won little support and its introduction was denied by 53 votes to nine (ibid., 1883–85).[3]

For Terris, who had called for "serious study and work to resolve such issues as proportional representation ..." in his maiden speech in 1979 (*NZPD*, 422:345), the main objective was to secure a referendum because he was convinced that Labour's failure to honour its 1987 undertaking would be used by its opponents to undermine the government's credibility in the 1990 election campaign. Nevertheless, even though he had a close association with Electoral Reform Coalition's (ERC) secretary, Phil Saxby (who was also chairperson of Terris's electorate committee), he deliberately decided to keep his distance from Saxby on this issue to avoid being categorised as 'a PR loony'.[4] Even so, while he was able to attract considerable support and encouragement across party lines (Terris, 1996),[5] he encountered repeated obstruction within Labour's caucus. Between February and May 1990 his bill kept being pushed to the bottom of the caucus agenda because, according to Terris, there was "a lack of willingness on the part of the leadership to even entertain the idea", and the divisions within the caucus meant that much of the discussion took place outside the caucus room. According to caucus rules Labour MPs are required to, "... first discuss the Bill in Caucus, and seek its approval. The timing of the introduction will be decided by the Whips in consultation with the Leader" (Harris & Levine, *et al.*, 1994:137). It was only after he had indicated that he proposed exercising the right, open to all MPs, to introduce his bill regardless of whether caucus had given its approval, were its contents discussed (Terris, 1996; Gomibuchi, 1995:64).[6] When caucus finally did so, it agreed that the bill (by then with the Electoral Law Select Committee) should be amended and adopted as a government measure, and that a referendum on PR should be held during 1991 (Palmer, 1990:CAB[90] M 27/33, 27 July 1990).

Caucus's approval displayed yet another of its shifts on the issue. At this stage it may well have decided that the bill would prove to be a useful lightning rod, focusing attention away from official party policies and, once again, because its chances of success were so limited, it did not constitute any real commitment. But caucus may have had only a limited option. Further, it would have put the party in a very bad light if it were seen publicly to have opposed the introduction of a Private Member's bill introduced by one of its own MPs in fulfilment of a commitment given by the party's then leader immediately prior to the 1987 general election.

Following an inconclusive meeting of caucus on 12 July 1990 when the issue was again discussed, the chairperson of the Electoral Law Select Committee, Richard Northey, was reported as saying that his committee now faced two options, either to report the bill knowing that it would not reach a final vote before the general election, or leave it for the next parliament. Yet again, however, unpredictability reigned, for on 19 July, caucus decided to support the Terris bill subject to certain amendments. In particular, it wished to change the date on which the legislation was to come into effect, with the result that a referendum on the electoral system would be held sometime in 1991 and not at the general election. It also wished to substitute a choice between FPP and MMP specifically rather than Terris's proposal for a choice between FPP and PR. It was proposed that these amendments to the Terris bill should be effected at the select committee stage and that, after amendment, the bill would be adopted by the government and passed before the end of the session.

Meanwhile, and with the election only a few months away, the government had already acknowledged the increasing intensity of the public discussion by examining ways whereby it might once again assume control of the debate. In May, Palmer had placed a number of options before the government, which agreed that an indicative referendum should be held on the Royal Commission's recommendations "in conjunction with the next local body elections" (ibid., CAB[90] M 16/37, 21 May 90), although Palmer himself appears to have been opposed to its indicative nature (ibid., 18 July 1990). At the same meeting the government agreed that any referendum should be preceded by a programme of public education on the pros and cons of PR (to be prepared by the Department of Justice) and that a bill to provide for PR should be introduced before parliament was dissolved prior to the election.[7] Although the Terris bill was still with the select committee, government discussions had progressed to the point where it agreed that an indicative referendum on MMP should be held with the 1992 local authority elections (ibid., CAB[90] M 26/40, 6 August 1990),[8] only to rescind this decision the following week and replace it with a resolution favouring a stand-alone indicative referendum involving a straight choice between FPP and MMP, to be held in October 1991 (ibid., CAB[90] M 27/33, 13 August 1990).[9]

When, only a few days before parliament was dissolved, the Proportional Representation Indicative Referendum Bill was reported back, there was clearly insufficient time for arrangements for a referendum to be held in conjunction with the general election. Palmer, however, announced that an indicative referendum had been adopted as government policy: "...it has been agreed to by government and the government caucus, and it is the government's policy to hold a referendum on a mixed member proportional representation system before October 1991..." (*NZPD*, 510:4165).[10] And, when Labour's 1990 election manifesto was released, the party publicly committed itself unambiguously to allowing electors to decide the future of the country's electoral system:

> Labour has given full consideration to proportional representation and has decided to hold an indicative referendum on whether they prefer the current system or MMP. ... Labour will conduct a referendum on the mixed member proportional system (MMP) of electing MPs. MMP was the method recommended by the Royal Commission on the Electoral System. (NZLP, 1990:101.)

Terris believed an indicative referendum was a necessary transitional step to allow those MPs who did have some enthusiasm for reform to argue that electoral reform should be debated outside the framework of a general election campaign and that the electorate should be given an opportunity to express its view. As he observed during the parliamentary debate on Anderton's bill, the principal question to be established was whether or not electors wanted change: if the government was to go about the process sensibly and responsibly "...it is important to be fully consultative" (NZPD, 508:2183). Once introduced, however, the issue built up its own momentum; its proximity to the 1990 general election provided an opportunity for the ERC and the public to put additional pressure on MPs and candidates and this, in turn, placed added pressure on the incoming National Government. There can be little doubt that, although highly unlikely to become law, both proposals contributed significantly to the inability of both Labour and National to return the genie to the bottle and screw the cap on tightly.

The National Government and First Steps to Electoral Reform, 1990–91

Once in power, the National Government had little choice other than to move towards implementing its promise of allowing voters to determine the future shape of New Zealand's electoral system. To have recanted would have resulted in it being damned by the electorate as Labour had been before it. Nevertheless, the realities of office soon persuaded it to modify its election pledge by committing itself to a two-stage process — an indicative referendum covering a range of electoral reform issues to be held before the end of 1992 and, depending on the outcome of that referendum, a binding referendum in conjunction with the 1993 general election. Wishful thinking, perhaps, but some at least hoped against hope that the indicative referendum would endorse the status quo. Supporters of electoral reform, on the other hand, opposed this change in policy because it meant that the implementation of any reform agreed to by voters could not be introduced until the 1996 general election at the earliest.

There are several reasons which help explain why the National Government adopted this solution. First, within weeks of taking office, it had broken its promise to repeal the superannuation surtax. Bolger regarded this as a major catastrophe and, according to Richardson (1996), he was absolutely resolute in his insistence that his government would honour all of its other 1990 election commitments. He believed that he had given a solemn undertaking to the electorate that it would be given an opportunity to express its views on electoral reform and he was not prepared to retract because to do so would have meant that his integrity would be seen to be no greater than Lange's.

Perhaps even more important, however, was the advice given by officials in the Department of Justice, advice not available to National when it developed its policy while in opposition. The Department argued that it would not be possible to deal with proposals for reforming the electoral system in a single referendum unless the issue was reduced to a simple choice between FPP and MMP. If the electoral system was to be the subject of a binding referendum, section 189 of the *Electoral Act 1956* — which required that amendment to any of six specified clauses had to be approved by at least 75 per cent of all MPs or by a majority of valid votes cast in a referendum — must be adhered to and this required that any proposal for change must be quite specific.[11]

In the context of the electoral reform debate, two of the six entrenched provisions[12] were crucial. Section 16(1) of the 1956 *Electoral Act* fixed the number of South Island General electorates at 25 and section 106 defined the way in which voters were required to mark their ballot papers. If either provision was to be altered, the procedure set out in section 189(2) had to be met, and that meant that any proposed changes must first be drafted as amendments to that Act. Thus, if any proposed new electoral system involved amending the number of South Island General electoral districts (or abolished electoral districts altogether) the precise details would first have to be established in legal form. Similarly, if a different method of casting a vote—for example, preferential voting (where voters numbered each candidate in order of preference) or a two vote system (such as that proposed for MMP)—were to be introduced these, too, could only be achieved by following the procedure laid down in section 189(2).

Apparently Winston Peters, in particular, was most unhappy with the

Department's advice, but although officials were instructed to re-examine the issues involved, their response was the same: if the government was intent on pursuing its desire to test public support for several different proposals for electoral reform it could only be done through an indicative referendum. A binding referendum involving a change to the 1956 *Electoral Act* would require parliament to establish a clear choice between alternatives. In the end the government accepted the Department's advice and modified its campaign promise to one of holding an indicative referendum before the end of 1992 and, depending on the outcome, holding a second, binding referendum in conjunction with the 1993 general election.

This decision represented a major U-turn for the government and resulted in accusations that it, too, was reneging on its election promise. Doug Graham, in his capacity as Minister of Justice, assumed responsibility for persuading the electorate that the new strategy was the appropriate one in the circumstances. By repeatedly emphasising the complexity of the options involved, and stressing that he wanted to give electors time to develop an understanding of them before they were faced with making their final decision, he was largely effective in defusing public suspicion about the government's motives for altering its pre-election promise.

Acting on the advice of his officials, Graham invited Professor Colin Hughes of the University of Queensland, to visit Wellington in May 1991 to meet with himself and his officials. While there, Hughes also spent a day with National's Electoral Law caucus committee, sharing his thoughts on a number of issues that were concerning it: generally, how should a referendum be arranged and, more specifically, how many questions could reasonably be put to voters, and how should a programme of electoral reform incorporating public education be sequenced. Hughes gained the distinct impression that neither the Minister nor his department wished to be seen to be pushing political self-interest, although Graham appeared to have a "fairly firm set of ideas" about what he wanted to achieve (Hughes, 1996). Over the next few months Hughes was involved in New Zealand's electoral reform process as a consultant in the earliest stages of planning for the indicative referendum.

Why the preference for Hughes? Why did Graham and his officials not seek expert advice from suitably qualified New Zealand academics? As the recently retired Australian Chief Electoral Officer and a leading Australian academic, Hughes was recognised as having an extensive knowledge of both the theoretical and practical aspects of democratic choice through elections. Hughes, himself, believes that the government was convinced that no New Zealand political scientist with the necessary expertise was completely neutral. Eagleson's view was that the government sought external advice from an international expert because "overseas experts have a different perspective" (Eagleson, 1997b). Regardless, Hughes wondered whether he was invited to provide a stamp of approval for a course of action already largely determined: "... perhaps I was invited so that they could say that they had run it (the government's proposal) past me and I had approved. They appeared more concerned to not be seen as 'pulling a fast one' than being genuine seekers after knowledge" (Hughes, 1996).

Following his May 1991 visit, Hughes was asked to comment on the proposed voting paper, and in December 1991 he was contracted to review a draft paper, prepared by the Department of Justice and based on the Royal Commission's report, which described different electoral system options (see *AJHR*, 1991:11–17). Although Graham subsequently claimed that "... expert material on the nature of the electoral reform options has been prepared by Professor Hughes of Queensland" (Graham, 1992), it is clear that Hughes's role was largely confined to modifying the text in a number of minor ways. Perhaps one of his most significant comments was that any public presentation of the various options should be ordered from the most to the least familiar (Hughes, 1991). As we will see later, however, the legislation authorising the indicative referendum specified that the order the options appeared on the voting paper was to be determined by lot. Hughes's involvement ended with the completion of this review and all subsequent development of the proposal to be placed before the electorate took place in New Zealand (Hughes, 1996).

By late 1991 the government's policy position had been clearly established and incorporated into the Electoral Poll Bill, subsequently renamed the *Electoral Referendum Act 1991*. As introduced, it provided for an indicative referendum before the end of September 1992. Voters were to be asked to vote on whether the FPP electoral system should be changed and, regardless of their response to this question, a second question asked which one of three alternative voting systems—Preferential Voting, MMP, or Supplementary Member—they preferred. The order that the reform options appeared on the voting paper would be decided by lot. Provision was also made for a second, binding referendum, pitting FPP against the reform option receiving most support in the indicative referendum, to take place if a majority of votes cast favoured changing the electoral system. The option of a second chamber was omitted but the government indicated that it intended legislating for a referendum to be held on this issue at the same time as the 1993 general election (*NZPD*, 521:2689).

Although the Electoral Law Select Committee made a number of changes to the bill, it rejected many submissions, mainly because they did not accord with the government's expressed policy of allowing voters to choose from more than one reform option. For example, a number of submissions proposed a single binding referendum involving a direct choice between FPP and MMP. Some wanted the referendum timetable shortened to enable both the indicative and binding referendums to be held during 1992 so that any changes approved by the electorate could apply from the 1993 election. The committee also rejected a proposal that each reform option should be described in detail in the bill on the grounds that this material, which would be characterised by "generality and abstraction", would be more appropriately dealt with in the public education campaign to be funded by the government. A suggestion that the outcome of the referendum should be determined using proportional representation was also rejected. The committee did, however, accept a number of points made in the public submissions. As introduced, the bill required that electors vote on both questions (although how this would be guaranteed, or what would happen to voting papers which did not express an opinion on both questions was never made clear); the committee accepted the argument that this could lead to strategic voting and recommended that voters should not be required to express an opinion on which reform option they preferred. In this way, the committee believed, the referendum would more accurately measure support for the present system. The Single Transferable Vote system (STV) was added to the list of reform options, and the Local Government Association's concern that the timing of the referendum might conflict with the local authority elections due to be held, for the most part by postal ballot, in the three weeks leading up to 9 October was acknowledged by the committee which recommended that the referendum be held on 19 September, just before the commencement of the three week local authority voting period. The select committee, however, rejected a proposal that the referendum be held by postal ballot because "...[T]his would be an inadequate way of dealing with such a significant and sensitive issue" (*AJHR,* 1991b:4–8). The government accepted the select committee's recommendations and parliament passed the bill through its remaining stages in December 1991, thus setting the scene for the first of two referendums on electoral reform.

Why did the government ultimately go along with the inclusion of no fewer than four reform options? Clearly, its policy, coupled with advice from the Department of Justice, precluded a simple referendum such as that proposed by the Royal Commission (RCES, 1986:65), and the Prime Minister's strong preference for an Upper House opened up the possibility of making the indicative referendum a wide-ranging one. In the end, three of the four options chosen for inclusion were ones that had found favour, to varying degrees, with the Royal Commission. Thus MMP, the Royal Commission's recommended system, stood alongside the Supplementary Member system recommended by the majority of the Electoral Law Select Committee chaired by Richard Northey, and STV which the Royal Commission regarded as a serious alternative although it was unanimous in preferring MMP as better meeting the range of criteria it used to assess different electoral systems (ibid., 64).[13] The inclusion of Preferential Voting is, however, largely inexplicable: the Royal Commission had dismissed it as representing only a slight improvement on the existing simple plurality system (ibid., 31), and it had only minimal support amongst politicians. The most likely explanation is that to have eliminated the Preferential Voting option from consideration would, in Graham's eyes at least, have deprived the public of an adequate range of choice (*NZPD*, 521:6288).

What were the government's motives for setting up what was, to many, an unnecessarily complicated referendum? Cynics suggested that National deliberately set out to make the referendum questions as complex as possible in order to improve the chances of First-past-the-post surviving the onslaught from electoral reform advocates. Those of a more pragmatic persuasion, however, reasoned that if MMP was to be adopted, it should be done only after the most intense public scrutiny. The truth probably lies somewhere between but it seems highly unlikely that the National caucus, as a group, intentionally embarked on a strategy aimed at torpedoing the demand for electoral reform. Although not a supporter of MMP, the Minister of Justice accepted that electoral reform was a major issue for the government. There can be little doubt that he was committed to ensuring that the integrity of the referendum process would not be questioned, and that the government could not be accused of trying to force its own preference on the electorate in an attempt to undermine its choice. During the bill's Second Reading debate Graham indicated that the government would not promote any particular voting option, and that it would be over to the public to debate the issues involved and make their own judgments about the relative merits of each electoral system (*NZPD,* 521:6288).[14] This comment did no more than recognise the inevitable—that the government caucus had, like its Labour predecessor, been totally unable to reach an agreed position on the electoral reform question.

1992: Politicians Attempt to Shape Public Opinion

Although parliament formally approved the shape of the 1992 referendum, deep divisions remained within both the National and Labour caucuses. Table 6.1, which summarises the assessed preferences of all MPs in the 1990–93 parliament by party (*NBR*, 24 July 1992), illustrates the sharp cleavages that existed in the months prior to the 1992 referendum. The presence of markedly divergent views made it impossible for either caucus to resort to its accustomed practice of resolving differences through debate until a clear majority position emerged and, consequently, most discussions between MPs on electoral reform took place outside, rather than within, the caucus room, including, at times, discussions across party lines. Because the caucuses of both major parties were, to all intents, rudderless and unable to give any direction to their members, the issue of electoral reform became one for MPs to respond to as individuals. Only the three minor party MPs (two of whom had been elected as National MPs in 1990) were unanimous in their support of MMP; they realised that only a fully proportional electoral system presented them with any sort of a lifeline to a political future.

**Table 6.1   1992 Electoral Referendum Options
Assessed Support for each Option by MPs[15]**

	FPP	MMP	SM	STV	PV	Totals
National	49	9	4	1	2	65
Labour	20	4	2	2	1	29
NewLabour		1				1
Liberal		2				2
Totals	69	16	6	3	3	97

Source: NBR, 24 July 1992

Efforts by some MPs to persuade the public to reject electoral reform intensified during the early months of 1992. In January, Helen Clark (*NZH*, 4 January 1992) and Simon Upton (ibid., 8 January 1992) both published articles in which they advocated parliamentary rather than electoral reform as the solution to the political system's perceived ills, and further articles by pro-FPP MPs appeared later in the year (see McRobie, 1993:128–31, 158–60). Many also took the opportunity afforded by speaking engagements to opinion-making groups to advance the case for retaining First-past-the-post (ibid., 131–33, 154–58).

The most concerted attempt to organise a campaign in support of the status quo came, however, with the launching of the cross-party Campaign for First-Past-the-Post (CFPP) in June 1992 (*Dom.*, 22 June 1992). Records are sparse, but the impetus appears to have come from discussions between Helen Clark, Simon Upton, and others opposed to MMP, shortly after the Tamaki by-election in February 1992. By the time of its launch its supporters included Graham Latimer (chair of the New Zealand Maori Council and a former senior National Party official), Ross Armstrong (National Party activist and CFPP convenor), Lee Burdon (chair of the National Party's Canterbury-Westland Division), Sir Robert Jones (founder of the New Zealand Party in 1983), Bill Jefferies (Minister of Justice in the Fourth Labour government), Gary Taylor (a Labour Party activist), Neville Young (a former National Party president), Michael Barnett (Chief Executive, Auckland Chamber of Commerce), Geoff Atkinson (chair, Mobil New Zealand), Michael Fay (a Merchant Banker), and lobby groups such as the Employers Federation, the Auckland and Canterbury Chambers of Commerce, and the Business Roundtable (ibid., 153–54,160–66; Brook-Cowen, 1992). At least one National Party Division appears to have been involved: leaked confidential party documents indicated that the Wellington Division was "looking to influence opinion in the public's perception (of electoral reform). ... We feel that there should be an attempt to discredit this right now. ... Money has been set aside to use for publicity purposes in opposition to (MMP)" (*NZH*, 21 February 1992). There was, however, no concerted attempt by MPs who supported FPP to organise a caucus to promote the status quo; there was simply no willingness to do so because they recognised that, in the electorate's eyes, politicians, particularly those who openly supported FPP, were not to be trusted.

The campaign aimed to promote the case for First-past-the-post before the electorate in order to "even up the debate", and encourage people to recognise the strengths of FPP and the risks that were involved in adopting proportional representation, especially the MMP version proposed by the Royal Commission. According to Verna Smith (1996), the campaign's designated spokesperson, the primary objective was not to discredit MMP *per se* (although attempts were made to do so through stressing the dominance of "party" in the formation of party lists, and the greatly enlarged electorates), but to provide electors with sufficient information to enable them to make an informed decision on an extremely complex issue. CFPP campaigners also sought to put a positive slant on their case by arguing that reforming the way parliament and the executive operated would alleviate the public's concerns (McRobie 1993:112–115).

The organisational structure of the CFPP appears to have been minimal and limited to a small ginger group of four or five people, each with access to personal networks which provided some (though, by all accounts, minimal) financial support, and sometimes created opportunities for speaking engagements. While Smith recalled that considerable planning and discussion took place before the campaign was publicly launched, others involved are not as certain. Helen Clark admits only to "occasional conversations" with FPP supporters, and on the Monday following the referendum she was reported as saying that she had "never particularly wanted to be involved in this thing at all" (*NZH*, 21 September 1992). Another FPP supporter, Jonathan Hunt, observed that there was no willingness on the part of pro-FPP MPs to organise a caucus in support of the status quo, and he noted that many MPs were reluctant to publicly attack party colleagues who held a different position on electoral reform (Hunt, 1996). Evidence of the looseness of the campaign's organisational structure also comes from Hunt, who identified Terry Dunleavy as a key figure, whereas Smith did not recall him having been involved. What is clear is that its founders failed in their efforts to mobilise nationwide support behind a concerted campaign opposing change to FPP. In the short time available to them they simply lacked the necessary human or financial resources needed to compete with the pro-MMP campaigners who had been moulding public opinion for more than five years and, in the end, they had to rest content that they had at least tried to put the other side of the argument before the electorate.

Although Clark accepted that a campaign in favour of retaining FPP was bound to be criticised as a last-ditch attempt by vested interests to preserve the status quo (*Press*, 20 June 1992), neither she nor anyone else appears to have been prepared for the level of personal attack which came from the supporters of MMP. Both she and Hunt described their experience as among the most unpleasant they had ever been involved in during their political careers; every time supporters of FPP spoke up they were denounced as "self-serving", a charge that could equally be levelled at MPs—particularly those representing recently-formed parties—who supported MMP. In the final analysis, however, the campaign failed because electors felt let-down by successive governments and had little interest in considering arguments against changing the electoral system, particularly those advanced by MPs.

In July 1992, although nearly seven out of every ten MPs supported FPP (Table 6.1), most avoided any open association with the CFPP, largely because they believed that any organised support for First-past-the-post by MPs would simply encourage people to vote in favour of change. Within their own electorates, though, many exhorted voters to support the existing electoral system, and some actively campaigned nationally. The Prime Minister, for example, made clear his view with several impassioned pleas to voters to support FPP. At a press conference in late July he said, "I don't believe we can improve upon the First-past-the-post system with all its strengths and weaknesses" (ibid., 28 July 1992), and at the National Party's annual conference a couple of weeks later he implored electors to

> [D]efend your right to elect your own MP. ... The only reason the smaller parties want proportional representation is because they want to deal in the back room;

to deal themselves into government because they will never get there by popular vote.

FPP, he contended, was the only electoral system that could give strong clear and accountable government. Proportional representation meant more politicians, more politics and minority parties dictating to larger ones (ibid., 10 August 1992). It was all to no avail. As many supporters of the simple plurality electoral system had already concluded, any intervention by politicians in support of the status quo would be counter-productive.

Politicians Debate Electoral Reform: The *Electoral Act 1993*

There can be no doubt whatsoever that MPs were shocked at the extent of voter support, both for a change to the electoral system and for MMP as the preferred option in the indicative referendum. Although most had expected that a majority of those voting would support the change option, many believed that the margin would not be great, and that following mature reflection, and with 1992 non-voters (a majority of whom, they believed, would support FPP) turning out for the 1993 general election, the status quo would win through. Although only verbal assurances had been given, the overwhelming vote in favour of change ensured that the government would not renege on this undertaking. It meant, too, that politicians were faced with responsibility for determining the details of an electoral system that stood a very real prospect of being endorsed by electors in the binding referendum.

The Department of Justice anticipated that the indicative referendum would favour change and that MMP would be the preferred option so, some two months before the referendum, officials began preparing a draft Electoral Reform Bill based closely on the Royal Commission's MMP model and its associated administrative features. The early start was regarded as essential if the bill was to be introduced into parliament before the House rose for the 1992 Christmas recess. If it failed to make that deadline there was a very real prospect that the detailed structure of MMP might not be enacted in time for the binding referendum to be held with the 1993 general election. While not attempting to pre-empt or pre-judge cabinet's eventual decision, this draft included provision for an Electoral Commission, the registration of parties, a ballot paper (modelled on that used in the 1990 general election) which would be physically divided by poll clerks before being handed to voters, and details of the Senate option (Moore, 1996).[16]

Even before the final result of the indicative referendum had been declared,

Graham moved to set the legislative process in motion. Early in the week following the referendum a meeting was held in Graham's office, attended by McCully (chair of parliament's Electoral Law Select Committee), David Oughton and Bill Moore (Justice Department), and Eagleson (Director of the National Party's Research Unit), where the content of the bill was discussed (ibid.). Three weeks later, cabinet made its formal decision. The Minute of the cabinet meeting on 12 October 1992 is instructive because it sets out the framework within which the Electoral Reform Bill was developed. Under the heading "Proposals for Electoral Reform Bill", cabinet:

- a. approved the inclusion in the Electoral Reform Bill of the essential features of the system of mixed member proportional (MMP) recommended by the Royal Commission on the Electoral System ...;
- b. agreed that no provision in the Electoral Reform Bill (as introduced) shall be made for:
  - i. an Electoral Commission; or
  - ii. rules governing the selection of political party candidates; or
  - iii. State funding of political parties; or
  - iv. additional restrictions regarding election expenses by political parties; or
  - v. additional requirements for the reporting of political donations;
- c. agreed that provision be made for a system of registration of political parties by the Chief Electoral Officer, but without any restrictions as to the content of party rules;
- d. i. agreed that the Electoral Reform Bill should be introduced by 15 December 1992 at the latest and passed by 1 July 1993;
  - ii. noted that the constituent measures in that Bill which enable MMP and the Senate will come into force or be deemed to be repealed, as the case may require, depending on the outcome of the binding referendum ...;
- e. agreed that no changes will be made by the Electoral Reform Bill to the provisions of the *Electoral Act 1956* relating to the number or composition of Maori seats under the present first-past-the-post electoral system, unless there is prior agreement with or support from the Maori people. (CAB[92]795, **12 October 1992**.)[17]

Prior to the indicative referendum the Prime Minister and the Minister of Justice had both stated that if a majority of voters supported the adoption of a new electoral system in principle the government would scrupulously follow the Royal Commission's recommendations for the option receiving most support. Shortly after the referendum, however, Bolger asserted that his government had always said that it would use the Royal Commission's recommendations "*as the basis* for the form of MMP introduced to parliament" (*Press*, 22 October 1992; emphasis added). Cabinet's 12 October decision suggests that the government, at least, was still intent on modifying the Royal Commission's proposed structure, particularly those aspects — candidate selection, election expenses, and disclosure of political donations — where long-standing party practices might be compromised. The government also resolutely refused to bow to pressure, notably from NewLabour leader, Jim Anderton and the Electoral Reform Coalition, to hold the binding referendum before the 1993 general election so that the next parliament could be elected using MMP (*NZH*, 8 October 1992).[18]

As introduced, the Electoral Reform Bill comprised three segments: statutory authority to hold the binding referendum, details of the MMP electoral system as determined by the government, and the structure and functions of the proposed Senate. In his introductory remarks Graham identified two issues as requiring attention—the fairness of the electoral system (and whether a new method of electing the House of Representatives should be adopted), and whether there needed to be greater constraints on the Executive (and, if so, was the establishment of a Second Chamber the best means of achieving this). He was at pains to stress that the Senate option would come into effect only if First-past-the-post won majority support *and* voters also accorded majority support to the Senate proposal, and that while the Royal Commission's core recommendations were included "without modification", the government had determined that its "subsidiary recommendations...involving major issues of policy" would not be addressed. Thus "extraneous and contentious matters," such as the rules governing the selection of list candidates (a matter he described as "irrelevant to voters"), state funding of parties, restrictions on parties' election expenses and disclosure of political donations, were not included. On the future of Maori representation Graham indicated that while the government had accepted the Royal Commission's recommendation that separate Maori representation in the House of Representatives should be abolished, it had an open mind on whether there should be separate Maori representation in the proposed Senate (*NZPD*, 532:13157–13163).

One aspect of the bill which was to cause considerable consternation in the following months was the government's decision not to make any changes to the existing First-past-the-post electoral system. This decision meant that the number of MPs in the two competing electoral systems would differ, and that, whereas under MMP, separate Maori representation would disappear, separate seats would continue if FPP were retained. Although the government left the way clear for changes to the structure of the FPP electoral system at some future point, the supporters of MMP believed that the binding referendum would be weighted in favour of the status quo (*Press*, 16 December 1992).

In the 1990–93 parliament select committees, all with government majorities, normally comprised an odd number of MPs. Before the Electoral Law Select Committee met to consider the Electoral Reform Bill the government, albeit reluctantly, accepted a proposal from the Labour Opposition to reconstitute the committee so that it had equal numbers of Government and Opposition MPs (*NZH*, 25 September 1992). As reconstituted, this committee included five government MPs (McCully, Christine Fletcher, Jeff Grant, Marie Hasler, and Tony Ryall), four Labour MPs (David Caygill, Pete Hodgson, Whetu Tirikatene-Sullivan, and Judith Tizard) and one minor party representative (Jim Anderton, NewLabour). According to the *National Business Review's* assessment (24 July 1992), McCully, Ryall, Tirikatene-Sullivan and Tizard were supporters of FPP, Anderton and Fletcher supported MMP, Caygill and Hasler had favoured STV, Hodgson had preferred the Supplementary Member system, while Grant had favoured the Preferential Voting system.[19] Since, however, the committee was confined to examining the government's detailed proposals for an MMP electoral system, members were required to put their personal preferences to one side and work towards developing a Bill that commanded broad public support. When the Bill was reported back in July 1993, members were effusive in their praise at the manner in which the select committee had risen above partisan preferences to produce what the chairperson described as "a fair, robust, and workable system of mixed-member proportional representation (MMP) for New Zealand".

> ...[M]embers of the committee, [he continued] decided that they had a duty to the House and, indeed, to the country, to forge a consensus that would enable us to fashion a workable and consistent model of an MMP system, acceptable in all its key components to the majority. In that respect the Bill has seen quite an unprecedented level of consultation by select committee members with their parliamentary colleagues, (*NZPD*, 536:16729.)

a view that was endorsed by others involved in the select committee deliberations.

The committee, which received over 400 written and more than 150 oral submissions, identified six major issues concerning the public: the proposed abolition of separate Maori representation; the differing number of MPs proposed for the FPP and MMP electoral systems; the absence of any rules governing the selection of party list candidates; 'open' as opposed to 'closed', and 'national' as opposed to 'regional', party lists; the omission of an independent supervisory body as proposed by the Royal Commission, and the proposed Senate (*AJHR*, 1993:4–10). In addition, there were some lesser issues (for example, the number of financial members a party would need before being eligible for registration, the 4 per cent threshold and its application to parties representing minority ethnic interests, voter registration procedures, and the state funding of political parties) addressed by the committee.

The question of continued separate Maori representation is dealt with in detail elsewhere in this book. Suffice to say that the select committee received a great many submissions, from non-Maori as well as Maori, urging retention until such time as Maori themselves decided that they should be abolished. The committee heeded these pleas and recommended that not only should separate representation be retained, but that the number of Maori constituencies should, in future, be determined in the same way that the number of General electorates had been calculated since 1967. The adoption of this recommendation meant that in future the number of Maori constituency seats could rise or fall depending on the number of Maori choosing to register on the Maori roll. Thus the future of separate Maori representation was placed fairly and squarely in Maori hands. As quid pro quo, the Royal Commission's proposal that the party vote threshold should be waived for parties representing primarily Maori interests (which had been incorporated into the original bill) was removed.

A recurring theme from just over one-half the submissions received was that it was unfair to pit the proposed 120 seat MMP electoral system against the existing FPP electoral system with its 99 MPs. Most advocated that the number of MPs should be the same for both systems — either 120 or 100 — and some submissions even suggested that a further referendum should be held to determine the final number of parliamentary seats (ELSC, 1993a). Although a small number within National's caucus — notably Winston Peters and Michael Laws — argued strongly for the maximum number of MPs to be set at 100, the vast majority came down firmly in favour of the larger ceiling. Its provincial centre and rural MPs, in particular, were apprehensive about the task of representing what, to them, were likely to be unduly large electorates. Self-interest was also apparent as MPs realised that their parties were likely to face serious and potentially destructive management problems unless there were sufficient list seats to accommodate most incumbent MPs who failed to gain selection for a winnable constituency seat.[20] For their part, members of the Royal Commission who appeared before the select committee were adamant "that irrespective of what system was in place ... Parliament would be better served by increasing the number of members to 120" (*AJHR*, 1993:7).[21]

Why, then, did the select committee not recommend that the number of seats should be increased to 120 even if First-past-the-post was retained? Put simply, the committee's terms of reference restricted it to considering the proposed MMP structure; it had no authority to widen its investigation to encompass the existing electoral system enshrined in the 1956 *Electoral Act*. Thus, when the committee reported that it supported 120 MPs under an MMP electoral system, politicians were accused of creating a deliberate bias by weighting the referendum in favour of the existing FPP electoral system (*Dom.*, 23 July 1993).[22]

The absence of any requirement for registered parties to use democratic procedures when selecting candidates also drew much critical comment, not least from members of the Royal Commission who appeared before the select committee. In their written submission (ELSC, 1993a:EL/93/126)[23] they criticised the absence of any provision requiring the democratic selection of candidates. While they conceded that parties were likely to adopt democratic methods, they argued that it was "vital" that rules safeguarding the democratic principle in candidate selection be included in the bill: "It is ... of importance under any system to ensure that candidates are chosen democratically. This is, however, particularly so in relation to the list vote under MMP." Their plea was supported by Christine Fletcher whose earlier experience with candidate selection had convinced her that there needed to be some form of monitoring of party rules and processes to make sure that democratic standards were observed (*Press*, 18 March 1993). On the strength of this and other submissions, the committee recommended that democratic provisions governing candidate selection should be included in the bill. It therefore proposed that candidates would be deemed to be democratically selected if selected by direct ballot of all financial members, or chosen by delegates elected by financial members, or by a combination of these methods (*Electoral Act 1993*:s.71) — procedures that reflected the requirements for candidate selection already included in the constitutions of both the Labour and National parties!

Why was this provision not included in the original bill? Two explanations are possible. Perhaps departmental officials did not consider it to be important, but since work on drafting the bill began well before the referendum and closely followed the Royal Commission's prescription, this seems unlikely. A more likely explanation is that this was a deliberate strategy designed to prevent the establishment of an Electoral Commission with wide-ranging powers. According to Caygill (1997), it was no accident that when the select committee conceded a limited version of the proposed "democratic requirement" with respect to party rules, it did so without widening the Electoral Commission's jurisdiction, and the cabinet's 12 October directive was deliberately worded to achieve this objective. Even then, a number of the options considered by the select committee were considered to be "too prescriptive" (McCully, 1996). As the committee noted in its report to parliament, its final recommendation reflected the Royal Commission's view although it differed from its detail by shifting responsibility for determining the appropriateness of each party's rules from the Electoral Commission (as proposed by the Royal Commission) to the courts (*AJHR*, 1993:7).

MMP is a fully proportional electoral system based on the primacy of political parties. Having concluded that MMP was the best alternative electoral system for New Zealand, the Royal Commission was faced with recommending the type of party list that would best fit its core recommendation. After considerable discussion of 'open' versus 'closed', and 'national' versus 'regional' lists it concluded that closed national party lists should be an integral element of its proposed electoral system, and that the party vote should be the sole determinant of each qualifying party's share of parliamentary seats. For an electorate used to choosing their MPs on the basis that they represented clearly delineated geographic areas, this was a largely foreign concept, even though modern elections were essentially contests between competing parties.

Although most submissions which referred to the provision for party lists supported the concept of nationwide closed lists as proposed by the Royal Commission (ELSC 1993b), the select committee still spent a great deal of time debating whether party lists should be 'open' or 'closed', and whether 'regional' lists would be preferable to 'nationwide' party lists. Several reports to the committee from the Department of Justice make it clear that officials were opposed to any deviation from the closed nationwide list proposal set out in the government's bill for a number of reasons: open regional lists were substantially more complex, both legislatively and administratively (ibid., 1993c), open nationwide lists would involve lengthy ballot papers, an excessive degree of voter knowledge, extensive delays in the allocation of seats, and would represent "a radical departure" from the Royal Commission's recommendations (ibid., 1993d), and the experience of Australian Senate elections suggested that open lists were likely to result in a significant increase in the number of informal votes cast (ibid., 1993e).[24] The committee finally decided that this was a matter that could be left over for reconsideration at a later date, perhaps after the first two MMP elections, and no substantive changes were made to the original proposal (*AJHR*, 1993:8).

Why, when most of those making submissions appeared to accept the concept of closed nationwide lists, did the select committee spend so much time debating whether party lists should be nationwide or regional, open or closed? It seems that committee members were sharply divided over the alternatives. While McCully and Ryall were known to have supported the Royal Commission's recommendation for closed nationwide lists, partly because they believed that open regional lists could lead to excessive regionalism (*NZPD*, 536:16733), Caygill, Hodgson, and Anderton all favoured some form of open regional list.[25] It is also possible that both major party caucuses examined the different options from a perspective of future political advantage. There appears to have been a genuine fear, particularly amongst longer-serving Labour MPs, that their party would not be able to survive as a major one if MMP was adopted (Dunne, 1996). Caygill and Hodgson, both of whom were opposed to closed lists, tried hard, but without success, to persuade their caucus colleagues to support open regional lists because they believed that it might engender greater confidence amongst electors that MPs were not endeavouring to shore up their own positions. Anderton also came round to promoting open regional lists, and both he and Hodgson sought to revive the issue during the bill's committee stage. However, even though there was some sympathy for their arguments, the Labour caucus remained sharply divided (Caygill 1996). In the National caucus, however, Graham and McCully argued strongly that MMP was about representing parties on a nationwide basis and, since open and/or regional lists contradicted this concept, acceptance of closed national lists was the only viable option (McCully, 1996; Eagleson, 1997b).[26] Further, many National Party MPs were of the view that any departure from the Royal Commission's key recommendations would be regarded by the electorate as a further breach of trust. Faced with these arguments they decided finally not to deviate from the Royal Commission's proposal.

In its report the Royal Commission envisaged an electoral system that could be seen to function independently of the government of the day. It therefore recommended that New Zealand establish an electoral commission to supervise the legal and administrative arrangements relating to elections (including the work of the Representation Commission), provide advice to the Minister and the parliamentary select committee responsible for electoral matters, and promote public knowledge about electoral and parliamentary matters. The rationale for this recommendation was that it would strengthen the independence of electoral administration from governments and enhance public confidence in the integrity of the electoral system (RCES, 1986:271–75).

As we have seen, however, the National Government specifically excluded any reference to an Electoral Commission in its instructions to the Department of Justice. That this was purely a political decision is obvious from a report to the select committee prepared by the Department:

> In the event that the committee decides to establish an Electoral Commission the committee should note that drafting instructions for an Electoral Commission (based on the recommendations of the Royal Commission) were prepared by the department during the preparation of this Bill. (ELSC, 1993f.)

Why, then, did the select committee go against cabinet's original directive to the Department of Justice and recommend the establishment of an Electoral Commission? Clearly, with over one-third of the 437 written submissions supporting the establishment of some form of supervisory body, the select committee was faced with a significant public demand. A number of the submissions suggested that the functions of such a body should include: supervising the provisions relating to the democratic selection of candidates; overseeing the work of the Representation Commission, undertaking the allocation of state funding to political parties in respect of election broadcasting, and promoting public education on electoral and parliamentary matters (*AJHR*, 1993:9). Faced with this level of demand the select committee could do little other than to at least give serious consideration to recommending the establishment of an Electoral Commission.

Within the select committee there was some support, principally from National MP Christine Fletcher, and only minimal opposition to the establishment of some kind of supervisory body. Even so, few, if any, wanted a body with power to supervise party finances, or with more than the bare minimum authority to scrutinise party memberships for party registration purposes. Nor was there much enthusiasm amongst departmental officials for an independent commission with a similar structure and powers to the Australian Electoral Commission;[27] they were not against the establishment of a commission with minimal powers but were opposed to any significant divesting of the department's existing responsibilities in the electoral arena. Caygill believes that a crucial element of New Zealand's electoral system, the point where it departs from the Australian model, is its level of political input.

> There is absolutely no way that most members of the select committee were going to sacrifice our representation on the Representation Commission. ... We had a very clear understanding that while we were keen for the allocation of broadcasting funding to be handed over to the commission, that would mean a change in the membership of the commission. We didn't put that in our report but the members who were there in 1993 understood that perfectly well. If the functions of the commission had been any wider than were agreed at that time, the membership of the commission would have come out differently. We would have looked at some kind of semi-political appointment but with extensive rights of consultation. We would never have ended up with the essentially apolitical body we have if its functions were to go beyond the straightforward registration of parties and publicity. (Caygill, 1996.)

This view, coupled with cabinet's original brief to the Department of Justice, makes it clear that while select committee members were prepared to accede to public pressure for the inclusion of some supervisory body, most were not willing to recommend the establishment of an independent body with wide-ranging powers for fear that parties' freedom of manoeuvre might be inhibited. Thus, when the committee's report was presented, it included a recommendation favouring the establishment of an Electoral Commission whose authority would be limited to the registration of political parties, public education and information campaigns to promote increased public awareness of the electoral system, and to considering and reporting on electoral matters referred to it by the Minister of Justice or House of Representatives (*AJHR*, 1993:9).

Although the Electoral Reform Bill incorporated the government's 1990 election manifesto commitment to provide for the establishment of a Senate as an alternative to reforming the electoral system, it won very little public support. Both the Electoral Reform Coalition (ERC) and the Campaign for Better Government (CBG) believed that it distracted from the referendum's primary purpose and was likely to confuse the public (*Press*, 29 May 93). Given this, and recognising that by including the Senate option in the referendum its complexity would be increased, the select committee suggested to the government that the House of Representatives authorise it to hold over the Senate option for later study should the FPP electoral system be endorsed by a majority of voters in the binding referendum. Parliamentary authority was formally granted at the beginning of June (*AJHR*, 1993:8–9). Even Bolger chose not to fight for his preferred option! (*Dom.*, 25 May 93.)

A large number of other, relatively minor and mostly technical, changes were also made to the bill before it was reported back to the House of Representatives. The most important of these reflected the committee's concern for the possible fragmentation of parliamentary representation across a number of parties. As a result, the 4 per cent threshold proposed by the Royal Commission (and included in the original bill) was raised from 4 to 5 per cent of the party vote. Similarly, since separate Maori representation was incorporated into the revised bill, the Royal Commission's proposal (also included in the original bill) to waive the threshold in respect of "parties primarily representing Maori interests" (RCES, 1986:44) was abandoned, and the criterion for parties to qualify for registration was raised from 200 to 500 financial members. The wording of the referendum questions was also altered to make clear that the choice facing electors was between FPP as set out in the *Electoral Act 1956* and MMP as set out in the *Electoral Act 1993*. This change was important in order to make it clear that the referendum was fully consistent with the provisions of section 189(2)(b) of the 1956 Act, which required that any amendment involving an entrenched provision must be approved by a majority of those voting (*AJHR*, 1993:10). Finally, in response to a number of submissions, the committee included an additional provision requiring a parliamentary select committee to review specified aspects of the *Electoral Act 1993* — the provisions for the regular redistribution of electoral districts and Maori representation, along with a more general consideration of whether there should be a further referendum on any changes that the committee might propose — following the second MMP election (ibid., 10–11).

Because neither major party had been able to reach an agreed position, there was a great deal more discussion between committee members and their caucus colleagues than is normally the case. In an interview in July 1996 Caygill observed that of all the select committees he had been involved with during his 18 years in parliament, the committee dealing with the Electoral Reform Bill involved more personal interaction between it and the caucus than any other because all MPs, and their caucuses, were "desperately interested" in keeping abreast of developments. Consequently he reported to the Labour caucus formally on a number of occasions and held many informal discussions throughout the deliberations process (*NZPD*, 536:16731; Caygill, 1996). We can be sure that a similar process occurred on the government's side of the House.

It is fair to conclude that the many changes made to the original bill represented a genuine attempt by committee members from all parties to develop a robust and broadly acceptable MMP structure. As a number of members noted, the committee had not necessarily achieved "the objective of producing the best possible form of MMP" but the result was a bill developed "on the basis of what is reasonable" (ibid.). Even though the committee had the bill before it for seven months, its complexity, and the differing views of individual members, meant that it was always going to be under some pressure. Eventually, it was forced to concede that there were some issues that might require revisiting at a later date. As it was, when the bill was finally reported back in the third week of July 1993, only four months, at most, remained before the referendum was scheduled to be held.

The Final Act: The So-called 'Shirtcliffe Amendment'

Although the Electoral Reform Bill was reported back with a large measure of agreement, some aspects were still the subject of debate that did not respect party lines. Fletcher (National) moved a series of amendments designed to strengthen the powers of the Electoral Commission; Hodgson (Labour) and Anderton (NewLabour/Alliance) both endeavoured to persuade parliament to replace closed nationwide lists with open regional lists; Anderton also moved to set the number of MPs at 100 (a proposal that was supported by Helen Clark who also contended that if the number of MPs remained at 120, there should be between 70 and 80 constituency seats so that electorates did not become too unwieldy [*EP*, 6 August 1993]), and to vest responsibility for electoral redistribution and the allocation of state funding for election broadcasts with the Electoral Commission; Peters (New Zealand First) wanted the number of electorates reduced to 40; and Tirikatene-Sullivan (Labour) endeavoured to have the number of dedicated Maori electorates set at a minimum of four and to have specific reference to the Treaty of Waitangi included in the bill's Long Title (*NZPD*, 537: 17221–35).

None of these proposed amendments was successful. Although both major parties withdrew the 'whip' for the committee stages, thus allowing MPs with strong views on particular clauses to cross the floor with impunity, the government whips confirmed that the passage of the entire bill would be subject to the whip. Thus, while the changes proposed by the select committee were accepted by the government for incorporation into the legislation, proposed amendments not endorsed by the select committee stood no realistic chance of success. The bill, as amended by the select committee, was given its third reading on 5 August and signed into law on 17 August 1993.

In the days before the debate on the select committee's recommended amendments took place, a last-ditch attempt was made to raise the threshold of support required for the bill to finally pass into law. Peter Shirtcliffe, chairman of Telecom Corporation, had instituted a private crusade in support of First-past-the-post in April 1993 and, as his campaign gained momentum, he began promoting the view that the referendum result should not be binding unless the proposal to change to MMP was supported by a majority of registered electors, not simply a majority of those who actually voted (*NZH*, 20 May 93).

Shirtcliffe expanded on his argument in a late submission to the select committee: the proposal to change to MMP was, he said, of such vital importance to the country's political and economic future that it was neither appropriate nor constitutionally desirable to make such a change without the support of "a true majority of registered electors". Citing the provisions of the *Licensing Act 1910* (which had required a three-fifths majority of valid votes before prohibition could be adopted) and a recently conducted opinion poll (*NBR*, 23 April 1993) which showed that 57 per cent of respondents believed that a change should only be made if it was supported by a majority of all voters, Shirtcliffe insisted that "[F]undamental changes demand a clear-cut demonstration of support. ... There must be a higher level of responsibility and public support to ensure the result truly reflects the majority view of the people" (ELSC, 1993a:EL93/166).

Reaction to Shirtcliffe's suggestion was predictable. Anderton, for example, accused him of patronising voters and of seeking to make it more difficult for MMP to be adopted while Caygill asked why the referendum should be biased in favour of First-past-the-post. People, he said, would be aggrieved if MMP won a majority of the votes cast but failed to reach the threshold that Shirtcliffe proposed. Although, predictably, support came from the Campaign for Better Government (headed by Shirtcliffe), the Business Roundtable, and a small number of individuals, one of whom wrote that "Parliament should have the courage, the will, and the determination to insist that a majority of all registered voters will be required" before MMP passes fully into law (*Dom.*, 9 July 1993), the select committee showed no real interest in Shirtcliffe's arguments which were quickly dismissed (Moore, 1997). The select committee avoided making any recommendation on the grounds that, since Shirtcliffe's proposal to raise the threshold required for the legislation to win acceptance had been received well after the deadline for submissions had passed, it would have been "quite unfair and inappropriate (to those who had already prepared their submissions) for the committee to recommend any such new initiative" (*NZPD*, 1993, 536:16730). This did not, however, preclude any individual politician or group of MPs from promoting the idea in the parliament.

Over the next two months Shirtcliffe campaigned assiduously in an effort to persuade MPs and the public that the referendum acceptance threshold should be raised. Advertisements pressed the argument that "[A] fundamental change to our constitution is too important to be decided by a minority" (*DST*, 11 July 1993). Shirtcliffe, who believed that the issue could be resolved by persuading parliament to amend the bill when it returned from the select committee by including a requirement for the support of a majority of registered electors, invested a considerable amount of time lobbying MPs and political parties — and anyone who, he believed, might be able to exert influence in favour of his proposal — in the weeks before the bill was reported back (*Press*, 12 July 1993; Shirtcliffe, 1996). Throughout, his argument was driven by his belief that this was a constitutional issue, not a political one (CBG, 1993b, 22 July 1993). He even persuaded one or two MPs to 'count heads' for him and about 10 days before the crucial committee stage of the bill he was told that "it looked as though he might have the numbers" (Shirtcliffe, 1996). On 24 July, *The Press* reported intensive lobbying around parliament and that MMP proponents feared that an attempt might be made "by at least two senior MPs" to move "the so-called Shirtcliffe amendment".[28] The Electoral Reform Coalition responded tersely:

> If this were to happen it would destroy any remaining shred of confidence in our political system. It would be seen as a deliberate abuse of political power by those who stand to gain from keeping the present electoral system intact. (*Press*, 24 July 1993.)

In the end, however, no amendment surfaced. Although the news media reported that intense back-room lobbying was being carried out (*NZH*, 27 July 1993), the proposal quickly ran into "a storm of flak" as opposing camps prepared for a bruising encounter; MPs known to support Shirtcliffe's proposal argued that electoral reform was too important an issue to be decided by a simple majority, while their opponents contended that it would be wrong "to change the rules half way through the game" (*NBR*, 30 July 1993). One pro-MMP MP went so far as to allege that it was no more than "a device to derail MMP — a trick, a last-ditch attempt by the status quo people to retain the status quo" (ibid.), while another called it a campaign to sabotage the referendum (*Dom.*, 24 July 1993).

Why did those who supported the inclusion of a higher threshold draw back? Shirtcliffe believes that former Prime Minister Geoffrey Palmer's intervention may have been decisive. In describing the proposal as a "constitutional obscenity" (*NZH*, 24 July 1993), Palmer argued that:

> Section 189 (of the 1956 *Electoral Act*) is not a reserved provision. It is not entrenched. It never was. But it was passed by a 75 per cent majority. To change it should require the same majority. As a matter of law it looks as though the provision could be repealed by a simple majority. The only reason Section 189 itself is not legally entrenched is that legal opinion thirty years ago was that double entrenchment was not legally effective because one parliament could not bind its successors. That is not the state of legal opinion now. But the 'moral' entrenchment which was agreed upon in 1956 has been followed ever since without question. (*Dom.*, 4 August 1993.)[29]

Palmer's view was supported by F.M. Brookfield, Professor of Law at the University of Auckland, who argued that "the rules for running referendums were, by convention, entrenched. This meant that it would take 75 percent support in parliament or another referendum to change the rules" (*Dom.*, 27 July 1993). Not everyone, however, agreed: Auckland lawyer, Guy Chapman, disputed that section 189 of the *Electoral Act 1956* had any relevance; it was "far-fetched, desperate and contorted stuff", arguing that it was unfair that under the 'majority of valid votes' provision, registered electors who did not vote would effectively be treated as having supported MMP (ibid., 3 August 1993). Electoral Reform Coalition spokesperson, Rod Donald, highlighted the circularity of this argument by counter-arguing that under the 'majority of registered electors' proposal, electors who did not vote would be treated as supporting the status quo (ibid., 4 August 1993).

There can be little doubt that Palmer, a committed electoral reformer and an acknowledged authority in the field of constitutional law, intervened at this point in a conscious effort to derail any possible attempt by supporters of the 'Shirtcliffe Amendment' from formally introducing the proposal and to frighten off those MPs who were wavering in favour of its inclusion in the Act. Certainly, activists within the Electoral Reform Coalition were thankful for his timely intervention because, by their own admission, they did not handle the possible introduction of such an amendment at all well.

There are, however, other, perhaps more compelling, explanations. Anticipating the possibility that an MP, or group of MPs, might seek to propose a new clause incorporating the substance of the 'Shirtcliffe Amendment', Clerk of the House of Representatives, David McGee, prepared a draft opinion to guide the Speaker. McGee pointed out that in 1991 the Electoral Law Select Committee had accepted that any binding referendum involving electoral reform had to "spell out the details of the alternative electoral system ..." (*AJHR*, 1993:5). Since the bill before the House proposed that the final say on whether New Zealand adopted a new electoral system rested with registered electors, the provisions of section 189(2)(a) did not apply. However, the House could not

> ...by a simple majority, ...pass a proposal handing over the decision on the repeal of an entrenched provision to the electors and require the electors to make that decision effective by a different standard to that set out in section 189(2)(b). ... To satisfy section 189 in such circumstances Parliament must first have passed legislation amending section 189(2)(b).

McGee also pointed out that since section 189 of the *Electoral Act 1956* was not itself a reserved provision, the way was clear for the House to amend it by a simple majority. This would require a separate piece of legislation amending section 189 to be passed by the House and receive the Royal assent *before* the Electoral Reform Bill was passed: "The proper course, if this is what the House desires, is first to change the law" (McGee, 1993). Alternatively, any proposed amendment to Part I of the Electoral Reform Bill,[30] in so far as it related to the requirements for the referendum proposal to be carried by the electorate, would need to comply with the section 189(2)(a) of the 1956 *Electoral Act* (that is, be passed by a 75 per cent majority of Members, which it could not conceivably obtain).

In effect, McGee proposed advising the House that openness, transparency, and some delay were essential; if it wished to raise the threshold for the binding referendum, parliament would first have to amend section 189(2)(b) of the 1956 *Electoral Act* to require that a majority of registered electors support any proposal to alter the electoral system before any proposal could be deemed to be carried. When faced with this opinion, supporters of the 'Shirtcliffe Amendment' realised that if they took this course, not only would they face delay, but electors would be alerted to a last-ditch attempt to place a significant obstacle in the path of change. Given the pro-FPP MPs' 1992 experience, the near certainty that massive public opposition and odium would be heaped upon them ultimately discouraged those who had contemplated attempting changing the rules at the eleventh hour from inserting a higher threshold of approval.

A third significant factor appears to have been the obduracy of the Prime Minister, Jim Bolger. According to Ruth Richardson (1996), when the prospect of setting a higher threshold was raised at cabinet, admittedly at a very late stage,[31] Bolger "got very angry, very obstructive, and tried to block it off the cabinet agenda. He simply dug his toes in". Even when he was lobbied by a number of influential businessmen, he simply refused to countenance any late attempt to tilt the playing field towards the status quo. Finally, he told cabinet that his government could not go into the general election after having been seen to tamper with the referendum process. His determination to honour what he regarded as the substantive commitment made in the party's 1990 election manifesto lay at the heart of his decision. This instinctive reaction thus made it impossible in practical terms for the government to support raising the threshold (Richardson, 1996).

Richardson believes that overall the issue was finely balanced. She concedes that Bolger managed to win the support of a majority of cabinet for his stance, and the government caucus was divided so that the proponents could not be sure of winning majority support in that arena. The bottom line, then, was that the supporters of the 'Shirtcliffe Amendment' could not guarantee that they had sufficient support to carry the day. Even if they had had the numbers and chose to force the issue, this would have involved individual decisions that would have undoubtedly incurred Bolger's wrath, something that National Party MPs, at least, were loathe to do.

As noted earlier, Shirtcliffe believed that he may have had sufficient support from MPs to carry the day. He believes that he was defeated, not by the proposal itself but by its timing, which had all the hallmarks of a last-ditch effort to prevent change. The anticipated political consequences to incumbent MPs were very real, and most of those who were opposed to MMP, either collectively or individually, had long since reached the conclusion that supporting the 'Shirtcliffe Amendment' would virtually guarantee that MMP would be endorsed.

Others close to the scene of the action are not so sure that there was majority support for the proposal. Jonathan Hunt (1996) says that it was "never a starter", that although discussions were held, the absence of the party whip meant that success was unlikely. Michael Cullen (1996) believes that although, initially, a good number of MPs were attracted to the idea, ultimately it was not a practical proposition because it would have been seen as another belated attempt to try to secure a particular result and would have hurt those who supported it both politically and electorally. Caygill (1996) believes that it was raised too close to the final decisions on the content of the bill and, since there was insufficient support, those who did favour a change were not prepared to push the issue to the bitter end.

One thing is very clear: even if the proposal had merit, it came far too late. To the public, many of whom watched with dismay, it had all the appearance of a desperate, last-ditch effort to bolster support for the status quo. The fact that it was attempted belatedly inevitably raised questions about its legitimacy. Shirtcliffe's argument that proposed changes to a country's electoral system is a constitutional question, not a political one, has merit but any consideration of the merits or otherwise of any proposed changes should have taken place well beyond the heat of the immediate debate. Then, and only then, can basic principles be debated rationally and with minimal emotion.

Conclusion

One cannot escape the conclusion that the major political parties and many individual politicians were primarily responsible for what most of them came to regard as a most unfortunate referendum decision. Had Lange not re-opened the question during the 1987 election campaign, and had Palmer and Northey been able to persuade their caucus colleagues that moderate reform would leave the major parties in control, the final outcome might well have been very different. As it finally transpired, attempts by both Labour and National Governments to work their way through a labyrinth of, at times, contradictory commitments while, at the same time, striving to minimise the impact of electoral change on both themselves and the electoral system, did little more than increase the suspicions of large numbers of electors that their politicians were primarily concerned with preserving a system of representation that they were familiar with and understood.

As a number of those interviewed confirmed, the caucuses of both parties remained sharply divided. Neither caucus was, therefore, able to provide a coherent lead to its members and, in a number of instances, party discipline and cohesion — a core characteristic of New Zealand's two-party system between the 1930s and 1980s — broke down. As a consequence, many discussions centring on electoral reform took place outside the more controlled atmosphere of the caucus room, and frequently occurred across party lines.

There can be little doubt, too, that there was a marked cleavage between the more experienced and newer MPs in the 1990–93 parliament. As Table 6.2 illustrates MPs who were elected prior to the 1987 election were three times less likely to favour replacing the FPP electoral system with some other form than MPs who were first elected in 1987 or 1990.

Table 6.2   Support for Electoral Change by Length of Time as an MP

	Elected before 1987	Elected 1987 & 1990
Support Status Quo	34	35
Support Change	7	21

Source: NBR, 24 July 1992

In 1956 the then Minister of Justice, Jack Marshall, described the Electoral Bill then before parliament as:

> ... a major advance in the progress of democratic government in New Zealand. ... The Bill is a genuine, and I believe, successful attempt to place the structure of the law above and beyond the influence of Government and party. ... the effect of these reserved sections is not in their legal force to bind future Parliaments but in their moral force as representing the unanimous view of Parliament. (*NZPD*, 1956, 310:2839.)

He concluded the third reading debate by remarking:

> ... What we are doing has a moral sanction rather than a legal one, but to the extent that these provisions are unanimously supported by both sides of the House, and to the extent that they will be universally accepted by the people, they acquire a force which subsequent Parliaments will, I believe, respect, and which subsequent Parliaments will attempt to repeal or amend at their peril; against the will of the people. (ibid., 2852.)

In the light of the belated moves towards increasing the level of electoral support required before the *Electoral Act 1993* was carried, Marshall's comments are worth recalling. Although section 189 of the 1956 *Electoral Act* was not, itself, entrenched, the passage of time, and the respect past parliaments had accorded it, finally convinced those MPs who wanted to raise the hurdle, that it would be inappropriate to do so at a late stage in the public debate.

Marshall's 'moral sanction' had stood the test of time, and when it was openly and covertly challenged it proved robust enough to hold the line against those who wished to change it for possible political gain. Although, in one sense, the constitutional superiority of New Zealand's electoral law has been strengthened, this appears to have occurred by chance rather than by design. Contrary to Palmer's view (*Dom.*, 4 August 1993), there does not appear to be any convention that would have prevented section 189 of the *Electoral Act 1956* from being amended by a simple majority. Those MPs who toyed with proposing the 'Shirtcliffe Amendment' did not consider themselves to be under any legal or moral constraint about amending section 189 in this way. Their difficulty was a political one — the proposed amendment had emerged altogether too late to allow them to act without incurring political opprobrium.

By the time the *Electoral Act 1993* and its companion, the 1993 *Electoral Referendum Act*, were signed into law, many MPs were probably resigned to the fact that the 1993 general election would be the last to be held under the First-past-the-post electoral system. While the electoral reform debate continued for a further three months, politicians prepared themselves to fight the next general election. Few engaged in the final stages of that debate; they had had their opportunity to influence the direction of events but had largely failed. It was now over to electors to pass their collective judgment on the MMP electoral system recommended by the Royal Commission seven years earlier.

Notes

1   Terris recalled a number of incidents that indicated that Palmer's consistent support for PR came to be used as a weapon against him by those who wanted him replaced (and who wanted to replace him) as leader.

2   Appended to this copy is a handwritten note from one of Palmer's secretaries stating "This is pretty much Richard re-litigating! I think he has to be told he's lost this round". Palmer responded: "Easier said than done. I'm in sympathy with it (i.e. the suggestion) though." Northey believes that his initial recommendation had been to try for a "very favourable consideration" recommendation in another attempt at getting around caucus opposition (Northey, 1996).

3   It is worth noting that Anderton was a very recent convert to proportional representation and to the Royal Commission's MMP recommendation. In April 1987 he responded to a challenge to explain why he opposed proportional representation with: "... In countries where proportional representation is the basis of the electoral system, we find not the tyranny of the majority, which can be bad enough, but the tyranny of the minority which is surely worse. It is, in these instances, not the overwhelming majority of votes which determines who wins or loses an election but a small percentage — sometimes as small as 5 per cent — which decides who governs and who does not. And these decisions are not made in public or on the campaign trail of a general election but

behind closed doors in 'smoke-filled rooms' where the political trade-offs are made. ... Is this the kind of government we want in New Zealand? I hope not. It is neither 'democratic' nor representative, and on many occasions not very tolerant either" (*Press*, 6 April 1987).

4   ERC leaders acknowledge that they were unaware that Terris was working on the Bill until Saxby 'saw something on Terris's desk'. This was regarded by the ERC as a stroke of luck and they supported him as far as possible (Saxby, 1996; Donald, 1996).

5   Terris cited Braybrooke, Dillon, Maxwell, Northey, and Woollaston (Labour), Graham and Peters (National), and Knapp (Democrat) among the MPs who encouraged him. The Bill was developed from a draft of Northey's. As a close friend of Helen Clark (who was "absolutely opposed") Northey felt that he could not promote the Bill himself.

6   According to Northey (1996), the mood of caucus changed as public pressure grew, to the point where it accepted that it was inevitable that Terris would introduce his Bill.

7   Palmer wrote to Terris to advise that he did not support the two-stage process, preferring that whenever a referendum is held ("sooner rather than later") it should be specifically on MMP as proposed by the Royal Commission. In the same letter Palmer floated the idea that if MMP were rejected the way might be open for further referendums on the other options canvassed by the Royal Commission. On 23 July 1990 Palmer wrote to the Minister of Justice, Bill Jefferies, to indicate that the Terris Bill, as amended by the Select Committee, would be adopted by the Government and passed before the end of the parliamentary session.

8   Subsequent to this decision Palmer was asked what form the question included in the Terris Bill was to take. Palmer's handwritten note is instructive: it records that he had discussed the question with Woollaston and was happy if the select committee 'fudged it' by making some reference to the Royal Commission's recommendation but not in any specific form. (Note dated 14 August 1990.)

9   At this meeting costings of various alternative referendums were tabled. An indicative referendum held in conjunction with the 1990 general election was estimated to cost $200,000; a stand-alone referendum held about March 1991, c.$11 million, but a postal ballot at the same time would cost between c.$5.1 million (if centralised) and c.$7.1 million (if held on an electorate basis); if held between August and October 1991, the estimated cost would range from c.$7 million (postal – electorate basis) through c.$9.1 million (postal – centralised) to c.$12.6 million for a stand-alone referendum; and if it were held in conjunction with the 1992 local authority elections, the estimated cost would be between c.$7 million and c.$8.5 million (Palmer to Jefferies, nd but between 6 and 13 August 1990).

10   After the 1990 election the National Government sought to kill the Bill by refusing to make an appropriation but most Labour MPs wanted the debate to proceed so that they could be seen to have some integrity in the matter after the experience of 1987–90. Eventually, after considerable behind scenes negotiations, the Government agreed to recommend an appropriation on the understanding that the Bill would then be struck out. Ultimately, the Government consented to the Bill being referred back to the Electoral Law Select Committee to be considered along with other electoral law matters (*NZPD*, 512:163).

11   Labour had been given similar advice in 1988 (Palmer, H., 100:14 June 1988).

12   The entrenched provisions are: the maximum length of the parliamentary term, the composition of the Representation Commission, the terms of reference governing the Representation Commission's deliberations, the maximum population variation between electorates, the minimum voting age and the method of voting.

13   Paragraph 2.183 of the report suggests that there was some disagreement among commissioners as to whether STV should be ahead or after SM and FPP.

14   According to Peter Dunne (1996), in late 1991 the Labour caucus decided that it would honour the outcome of the referendum but would not take a position on what that outcome should be. As a group, Labour's Extra-parliamentary Party was much more pro-MMP than the Labour Party caucus, and it pressured the party to openly support MMP.

15   In some cases, where MPs had not publicly stated their views, preferences were assessed from their public comments. The *NBR*'s classification of MPs' preferences does not appear to be completely accurate; there were, for example three Labour MPs (Caygill, Dunne and Wilde) who openly supported STV in the weeks before the 1992 referendum. Of the 19 MPs supporting MMP, only three (Anderton, Ross Meurant, and Peters) had entered parliament before the 1990 election.

16   The 1990 referendum asked voters whether the parliamentary term should be extended to four years. For details of the Senate option, see McRobie, 1993:248–53.

17   Moore (1996) indicated that the decision not to include an Electoral Commission in the bill was taken at the initial meeting held in the Minister's office.

18   Labour front bench MP, Richard Prebble, called on the Labour Party to adopt all of the Royal Commission's recommendations "as a fair and balanced package". Labour Party leader, Mike Moore, was, however, decidedly unenthusiastic (*NZH*, 12 October 1992).

19   The 15 temporary replacements on the committee were also divided in their support, with nine assessed as having supported FPP and six having supported MMP prior to the 1992 referendum.

20   Apart from eight sitting MPs who broke with their parties after the 1993 election, only five MPs (four Labour, one National) failed to win a seat in the first MMP parliament.

21   During his submission to the select committee, Wallace made it clear that the bill, as introduced, did not reflect the Royal Commission's thinking. He told the committee that, "the firm view we do express is that having differing number of seats for the two systems, in the light of what we know about public opinion, will be likely to skew the result" (*Press*, 18 March 1993). When the bill was reported back to parliament, Wallace was reported as describing the select committee's decision to accept the difference in the number of MPs in the two electoral systems as "unfortunate" and restated his view that there should be 120 MPs regardless of whichever system was finally endorsed (*Dom.*, 24 July 1993).

22   Peters, by this time the leader (and sole MP) of a minor party, accused supporters of FPP of deliberately trying to derail MMP by endorsing an uneven contest between the two electoral systems.

23   This was the only issue that the commissioners addressed in writing. Other comments about the bill were made in response to questions by committee members. The commissioners who appeared before the committee were John Wallace, Richard Mulgan, John Darwin and Kenneth Keith.

24   It should be noted that the form of STV used to elect the Australian Senate permits voters to indicate their preferred party, thus leaving it to that party to determine both the order in which its own candidates will be elected and the order of preference that other parties (and, therefore, their candidates) are counted.

25   Caygill was reported as saying (*Press*, 10 April 1993): "That (i.e. closed lists) comes close to saying that the voters cannot be trusted ... but we can trust the parties." His personal preference was for an MMP system in which electors exercised a constituency vote only, with the allocation of list seats determined by each party's share of that vote. He recognised, however, that this was not achievable but he thought that he might be able to achieve agreement that party proportionality would be determined through the constituency vote with a second, party vote enabling voters to approve or alter the rank-order of their preferred party's list candidates (Caygill, 1997).

26   Caygill (1996) believes that had the government caucus come down in favour of open lists, the Labour caucus would have accepted the shift.

27   The Australian Electoral Commission's wide-ranging powers include: (1) considering and reporting to the Minister in charge of the *Commonwealth Electoral Act* on matters referred to it by the Minister or on its own initiative; (2) promoting public awareness of electoral and parliamentary matters; (3) providing information and advice on electoral matters to the parliament, the Government, Departments of States and other Commonwealth authorities; (4) promoting and conducting research into electoral and related matters, and (5) it "...may do all things necessary or convenient to be done for or in connection with the performance of its functions".

28   MPs reported as being in favour of the Shirtcliffe Amendment were Max Bradford, Hamish Hancock, Graham Reeves, Clem Simich, Ruth Richardson (all National), Helen Clark, and Jonathan Hunt (Labour). Those opposed were listed as Doug Graham, Bruce Cliffe, Christine Fletcher, Michael Laws, Nick Smith, Peter McCardle (all National), and David Caygill and Pete Hodgson (Labour).

29   In 1988, in response to a question as to whether proposed changes to the electoral system could be implemented by a simple parliamentary majority, the Secretary of Justice (David Oughton) had advised that: "The question for consideration, therefore, may not be whether the government of the day is legally bound by s.189 if it introduces changes to the electoral system which ... do not directly affect the entrenched provisions. ... (T)he more important question is whether the understanding reached in 1956 regarding major changes to the Act, and since observed as a matter of constitutional convention, obliges a government to obtain broad political and public support before such changes are made. The answer to the latter question would appear to be 'yes'." (Palmer, H., 100: 13 May 88). See also Joseph (1993:118–19), and RCES (1986: 287–92).

30   This bill was divided into the Electoral Referendum Bill (No.2) and the Electoral Bill at the conclusion of the committee stage. Part I, which was renamed the Electoral Referendum Bill, established the legal machinery for the binding referendum.

31   Apparently the matter invariably came up as an oral item. Richardson is critical of the Minister of Justice, Doug Graham, for failing to alert the cabinet to the full range of options available as he was bound to do.

7 The Campaign for Electoral Reform

We must educate our masters.
— Robert Lowe, Viscount Sherbrooke, 1867.[1]

Although the Royal Commission did not generally favour the use of referendums as a means of resolving questions of important public interest (RCES., 1986a:175–76), it specifically excluded matters involving constitutional change from this caveat on the grounds that "basic changes to the constitutional framework of government should be matters of broad agreement, and should not be decided by a Government itself constituted in accordance with that framework" (ibid., 176) Thus, its recommendation that MMP should be adopted (ibid., 64) was qualified by a second recommendation that this should not occur until the public had indicated its support for the proposed change through a referendum. The commission believed that it was essential that there was "... a period of public consideration of this report during which the advantages and disadvantages of change may be discussed and debated" (ibid., 65), before the electorate was asked to pass its judgment.

For most New Zealanders, who do not pretend to have even a passing interest in matters involving the country's constitutional framework, the suggestion that they should debate the advantages and disadvantages of an electoral system that lay well beyond their range of experience was a tall order. For nearly 150 years electors had chosen their governments through the First-past-the-post electoral system inherited from Great Britain, an electoral system that usually resulted in a clear-cut result and installed a government that could be held accountable for its actions at the next general election. They were now being asked to come to terms with an electoral system based on a foreign (ie. non-Anglo-Saxon) model involving two votes, and where the election result was unlikely to be clear on election night. They were also being asked to make a quantum leap in understanding the principles of coalition governments where it would be rare for a single party to win sufficient parliamentary seats to be able to form a government on its own.

The Royal Commission was right to insist that public education and discussion should precede any final decision. The core problem facing the community, however, was how such a debate on what was an extremely

160

complex question might be stimulated. As we have already seen, neither major political party was keen to engage in a public debate. Had it not been for the efforts of a tiny group of political activists, the Royal Commission's report might have suffered the fate of a number of previous reports — gathering dust among the plethora of parliamentary papers until unearthed by some assiduous researcher well into the future. That this did not happen is attributable, at least in part, to the formation of the Electoral Reform Coalition (ERC), a lobby group dedicated to promoting public awareness of, and support for, the Royal Commission's central recommendations and, much later, to the emergence of the Campaign for Better Government (CBG) which endeavoured, albeit belatedly, to promote the case for retaining the existing FPP electoral system. It is to the groups that stimulated the public debate on the pros and cons of changing from first-past-the-post to MMP that we now turn.

Precursors

As we saw in chapter 2, New Zealand has not been averse to experimenting from time to time with its constitutional and electoral structure. It is somewhat surprising, therefore, to note that the half century from the mid-1930s to the mid-1980s stands out as a period of substantial electoral stability with the only significant development being a major consolidation of the country's electoral law in 1956.[2] In large measure, this stability may be attributed to the almost total dominance — in parliamentary terms — of two political parties, Labour and National. Between 1935 and 1993 Labour and National together won 1494 of the 1516 seats contested.[3] The undoubted advantage enjoyed by the two major parties meant that their MPs had little incentive to question the appropriateness of First-past-the-post.

Yet, the halcyon years of strict two-party politics, when the winning party won more than half the total popular votes cast and a majority of the parliamentary seats, spanned only the 1946, 1949, and 1951 elections. This cosy arrangement began to break down in 1954 when the Social Credit Political League (formed the previous year) contested all 80 constituencies, won 11.2 per cent of the total vote but failed to win any parliamentary seats. Since then, no party has won a majority of the valid votes cast even though single party governments remained the order of the day.

Table 7.1 highlights a central characteristic of the First-past-the-post electoral system as it has operated in New Zealand — the almost invariable inflation of the parliamentary representation of the winning party at the expense of all other parties. Although, as the table shows, the winning party's vote (regardless of party) share declined steadily during the period under review, its share of parliamentary seats actually increased over the period. Also shown is a substantial rise in voter support for minor parties and independent candidates coupled with their almost total failure to win more than minimal parliamentary representation. It is a well documented characteristic of single member electoral systems that minor parties do not win representation proportionate to their overall electoral support particularly where that support is evenly but thinly spread (Duverger, 1964:321–22).

Table 7.1   Average Votes (%) and Average Number of Seats for Winning Party, and for all Third and Minor Parties Combined, 1940s–1990s (by decade)

	Decade						Average
Average of —	1940s	1950s	1960s	1970s	1980s	1990s	1943-93
Winning party's vote (%)	50.3	48.8	45.9	45.3	43.3	41.5	46.1
Winning party's seats (%)	55.8	56.7	55.8	60.6	56.4	59.8	57.3
Minor parties' vote (%)	3.8	6.5	10.9	14.3	17.1	23.7	12.0
Minor parties' seats (%)	0.0	0.0	0.3	0.4	1.4	2.6	1.3

Also, as we have already seen, third and minor parties are almost invariably the leading advocates for changing electoral systems that are weighted against them. Nevertheless, the demand for change to New Zealand's electoral system to make it fairer to smaller parties did not re-emerge until some time after Social Credit's arrival as a serious third party. True, Social Credit's 1954 election manifesto included a long-term objective to introduce preferential voting as "the only system whereby the true wishes of the electorate can be made effective" (Harris & Levine, 1994:153–54),[4] but it was not until 1972 (after the party had won, and then lost, its first parliamentary seat) that it included a promise to introduce proportional representation when it became the government. Thereafter the Single Transferable Vote (STV) form of proportional representation was a standard feature of Social Credit[5] election manifestoes, and was joined in 1978 by promotion of a proposal for citizens' initiated referendums (CIR) and, three years later, a promise to make greater use of referendums. By 1990 the party's policy had developed to the point where it committed itself to the MMP form of proportional representation ("so that power rests with the people, not politicians"), **citizens'** initiated referendums,[6] and the right of recall. It was, however, opposed to the re-establishment of an Upper House as proposed by National.

In 1972, a new party, Values, emerged shortly before the general election. Its first manifesto declared that "[t]he Values Party believes that there is an urgent need for reform of parliament in order to make it a more effective and relevant body". Its proposals were wide-ranging and substantially in advance of other parties at the time: open government, freedom of information, possible increased use of referendums, some form of youth representation in parliament, limitation of the length of time a person could be an MP, and increasing the number of MPs to 120 (Harris & Levine, 1994:166–67). This last proposal envisaged a form of supplementary member representation with slightly over one-quarter of MPs being elected by proportional representation (cf. Alley & Robinson, 1971:2–8). Values returned to this theme in its 1978 and 1981 manifestoes when it advocated the adoption of full proportional representation "so that the number of MPs each party had in the House reflected the number of votes that party received nationally". First-past-the-post was seen as "unjust" — more than 200,000 New Zealanders who voted for Social Credit or Values in 1975 were denied parliamentary representation — while proportional representation was held to be "fairer, more stable and less divisive".

Since the inherent unfairness of FPP electoral systems penalises smaller parties, it is natural that they should be to the forefront as advocates of change to an electoral system that would give them a significantly better chance of winning parliamentary representation. Although Social Credit and Values were the first parties in fifty years to promote electoral reform, most other new parties adopted proportional representation as a goal when they were formed. The NewLabour and Christian Heritage parties, both of which were established after the release of the Royal Commission's report, are good examples;[7] a notable exception is the New Zealand Party established in 1983.

A number of individuals also helped keep the cause of electoral change before the public, albeit intermittently, through letters to newspapers and petitions to parliament throughout this period. In the early 1970s a number of submissions suggesting modifications to, or replacement of, FPP were made to the Electoral Act Select Committee, including STV and two forms of the Supplementary Member (SM) system incorporating both a constituency and a party vote. Predictably, the select committee rejected all alternatives to FPP. It rejected STV because electors,

... would face far too complex a task in deciding the relative merits of the various candidates. Further, any system of proportional representation or preferential voting leads to unreasonable delays before the final result is determined. ... The electoral system should be designed so that the result of the election should be speedily obtained.

Its assessment of the proposal to adopt some form of Supplementary Member, semi-proportional electoral system was even more damning: while it might provide some slight representation for minor parties,

> ... the proposal would provide candidates who were successful or influential enough to get the 'top' positions on the 'party' lists with more or less permanent seats in Parliament. But this means that the real electors are no longer the voters, but the party officials who decide the order on the list. This gives them far too much power. (*AJHR*, 1975:8–9.)

This attitude was also very much in evidence when, in 1977, a Social Credit organised petition containing 40,790 signatures, requested the adoption of a proportional representation system of election to the House of Representatives. The select committee which considered it declined to make any recommendation (ibid., 1977:7). Clearly, MPs were not of a mind to take seriously any suggestion that New Zealand's electoral system should be modified in a way that might diminish the power and position of the two major parties. Their attitude might best be summed up by the comment of one major party activist shortly after the Royal Commission's report had been published: "I support the present electoral system. I mightn't like what the present government is doing but I support their right to do it. When our turn comes we'll be able to implement our polices without obstruction."[8]

A small number of MPs also contributed to keeping the debate alive, if not vibrant. We have already noted that John Terris, Labour MP for Western Hutt, referred to the need to consider some form of proportional representation in his maiden speech in 1979. Bruce Beetham did likewise when he entered parliament following the Rangitikei by-election in 1978, and Geoffrey Palmer promoted the concept after his election in 1979. In 1980, too, Gerald Wall, Labour MP for Porirua sought to introduce a Private Member's Bill which, if passed would have reintroduced the Second Ballot.[9] His aim was to ensure that every MP was elected with the support of an absolute majority of voters (*NZPD*, 346:5818–24). That none of these efforts was successful is testimony both to the dominance of the Labour and National parliamentary parties and the absence of any persistent and strong public demand for the electoral system to be modified to allow smaller parties to achieve more than nominal parliamentary representation at best. This latter condition was met only after the Royal Commission's report was released.

The Electoral Reform Coalition — A Pro-MMP Lobby

Origins and development

In 1985 a number of small, independent, and highly localised groups, dedicated to the cause of electoral reform existed in different parts of the country. In the context of the promotion of electoral reform over the next decade the most significant were those in Taranaki and Nelson, where remnants of local Values Party branches (both of which favoured STV) had established electoral reform associations, and Wellington, where the Women's Electoral Lobby (WEL) actively promoted electoral reform ideas. Each of these groups made submissions to the Royal Commission in support of the introduction of some form of proportional representation although none specified any particular form.

Also, in 1985 a small band of Labour Party activists, convened by Philip Saxby, chair of John Terris's Western Hutt Labour Electorate Committee, prepared a submission to the Royal Commission on the Electoral System. The content of this submission (RCES, 1986c, 4:687) makes it abundantly clear that Saxby, at least, had made an extremely thorough study of the Additional Member electoral system (AMS) introduced into the Federal Republic of Germany in 1949. The submission closely followed the West German model in proposing the adoption of a new, proportional electoral system in which half (or more) of the MPs would be elected by simple plurality in single member electorates with the balance of MPs being drawn from party lists. The retention of single member constituencies, the submission contended, would provide a bridge with the existing First-past-the-post electoral system. Further parallels with the West German electoral system were clearly evident: the submission proposed that each elector should have two votes, an electorate vote and a party vote, with the latter being used to allocate list seats on a regional basis. The submission also expressed a clear preference for the West German model over STV because "it was more truly proportional". While it is difficult to determine with any certainty the degree to which the commission was influenced by Saxby's submission, there can be no doubt it ultimately received a favourable reception from commissioners.

The Electoral Reform Coalition (ERC) was not set up until nearly a year later — after the Royal Commission had completed its public hearings but some six months before it presented its report. Early in 1986 Louis Erhler, New Zealand born but of Swiss descent, contacted people who had made submissions to the Royal Commission supporting change. His enthusiasm provided an initial catalyst; another was provided by Geoffrey Debnam, a political scientist teaching at Victoria University who arranged for Erhler and

Saxby to meet. In May, some 400 letters inviting people to attend the foundation meeting of the coalition were sent out, and at a meeting held at Victoria University of Wellington on 14 June 1986, a steering committee, comprising Saxby, Erhler, Bob Stephenson (a Democrat activist), and B.H. Paton, was set up. There is, however, no evidence of any concerted activity by this group in the months between its establishment and the publication of the Royal Commission's report in December 1986.

The release of the Commission's report provided the stimulus for greatly increased activity. In January 1987, John Taplin, an executive member of the Proportional Representation Society of Australia, toured New Zealand promoting the STV form of proportional representation. His visit further stimulated interest in electoral reform and resulted in the formation of ERC branches in Auckland, Wellington, Christchurch and Nelson, and, shortly thereafter, in Taranaki, Hamilton, the Hawkes Bay, and Dunedin. In March 1987 the ERC held its first conference, and in June the New Zealand Council, (addressed by both Geoffrey Palmer and British MP, Austin Mitchell) was established. At this meeting the ERC Executive resolved to support the adoption of proportional representation, promote the public understanding of MMP, and support a campaign for a referendum on proportional representation as recommended by the Royal Commission.

Over the ensuing months the coalition's membership and organisation expanded rapidly outside its Wellington base; by the middle of 1987 it had penetrated the greater part of the country and had a mailing list of just under 1,000 sympathisers. Its founders were quickly joined by, among others, Louise Ryan (Wellington Branch, WEL); Rod Donald, and Wayne Hennessey (LERN[10]), Lowell Manning (Policy Committee Convenor, Democratic Party); university teachers Graham Bush (Auckland) and David Round (Canterbury); and Values or former Values Party activists, Janet Roborgh and Gill and Peter Winter (all Taranaki), and Patrick McGrath (Nelson).[11] Former Prime Minister and architect of the *Electoral Act 1956*, Sir John Marshall, Sir Charles Bennett (a former president of the Labour Party), Angela Foulkes (Vice-president of the NZ Council of Trade Unions), and, later, former National MP Michael Minogue, all accepted appointment as patrons. ERC also enjoyed the tacit support of a number of Labour MPs, among them Geoffrey Palmer, John Terris, Russell Marshall and Philip Woollaston. Although activity varied across the country, by mid-1992 there were 22 branches (ERC, 1992c), and a year later ERC chairman, Colin Clark, claimed that the coalition had 26 branches and "hundreds of activists throughout the country" (*Dom.*, 26 June 1993). In addition, it had developed a network of contacts which penetrated a significant number of smaller population centres (ERC, 1993f).[12] Thus, by the time of the binding referendum in November 1993, the Electoral Reform Coalition had extended its campaign throughout the length and breadth of New Zealand.

Objectives

Throughout its seven-year campaign the Electoral Reform Coalition promoted itself as a non-profit society solely dedicated to achieving a better voting system. According to its published brochures it was not linked to any political party or business interest — it aimed to be multi-party, and wanted to involve a wide range of organisations, including trade unions and Maori groups, under its umbrella (ibid., Saxby, 1996). In 1988, for example, it told the Electoral Law Select Committee that its aim was "... to have the present voting system replaced with more fair and democratic procedures governed by the principle of proportionality" (ELSC, 1988a). By 1991 its objectives had been expanded and refined to include:

- promoting a wider understanding of voting systems and informing the public about proportional representation in general and MMP in particular;
- lobbying parliament to implement the main recommendations of the Royal Commission;
- promoting the view that any referendum should be a "fair and simple choice" between MMP and First-past-the-post; and
- arguing the case that future parliaments should be elected by a proportional representation system "in which each vote is of equal value" (ERC, 1991b).[13]

In a letter to Graham Bush, written in December 1992, Helena Catt, lecturer in politics at the University of Auckland, noted that the:

> ERC was created to press for the implementation of the findings of the Royal Commission in relation to the voting system (with the one and long-standing exception of the Maori seats). It is crucial that the Royal Commission's report remains the credible document on the matter. If we start to deviate on this issue then others may start to tinker with other vital aspects of MMP— this is something we must fight hard to avoid. (ERC, 1992d.)

The single-mindedness of purpose demonstrated here was crucial in ERC's ultimate success in achieving its primary objective. Without such dedication and commitment on the part of both its leaders and supporters the coalition may well have failed in its efforts to have the Royal Commission's key recommendation adopted.

What is noteworthy is the fact that, by the end of March 1987, the embryo ERC organisation had, with the sole exception of the proposal to abolish separate Maori representation, accepted the main thrust of the Royal Commission's report. Although, on the surface, it appears that the coalition's decision to endorse the Royal Commission's report was taken in haste in order to provide a concrete platform on which to build a coherent campaign for change, Saxby is adamant that its arguments and recommendations were worked through very carefully, a view that is supported by a number of others involved. There were a number of PR advocates present at the March 1987 ERC meeting — notably some members of the Democratic Party — who were reluctant to abandon their party's STV platform so, according to Donald, those present agreed to promote proportional representation, but not necessarily MMP as recommended by the Royal Commission. Saxby's view is that the ERC never actually adopted the MMP electoral system and kept the door open so that MPs could propose some alternative and, to them, more acceptable form of proportional representation should they wish to do so. He believes that had MPs decided to support STV or some other PR system, this would have been endorsed by the ERC (Saxby 1996; Donald, 1997).[14] Be that as it may, the key element of the ERC's campaign — indeed its whole rationale for its existence — was to secure change to some form of PR. The Royal Commission's report, and its MMP recommendation, thus became the vehicle by which this goal might be achieved, and by 1990 opinion within ERC had crystallised to the point where MMP was seen as the only truly viable option to be promoted.

The ERC's case for a new electoral system

As we noted earlier, apart from rejecting the proposed abolition of separate Maori representation, the ERC wasted little time in accepting and promoting the MMP electoral system recommended by the Royal Commission. Throughout its lengthy campaign it stuck close by the arguments put forward in the commission's report — in fact, for many members and supporters, the report, subtitled 'Towards a Better Democracy', became the bible to be referred to whenever questions arose or statements by MMP supporters were challenged.

ERC spokespeople argued their case for the adoption of MMP on the basis that it was the unanimous recommendation of a Royal Commission established by the government of New Zealand to "investigate and report" on the country's FPP electoral system. Taking its lead from the report, it promoted the argument that MMP was the fairest and most proportional of the different electoral systems canvassed by the commission; it was an electoral system that would make constituency MPs more accountable because they would be elected independently of parties; it would encourage government to operate "by co-operation, not confrontation"; it would reduce the power of the executive; it would provide fairer representation for all groups; and, using West Germany as its example, it stressed that strong and stable government would result (ERC, 1992a).

At its 1992 annual general meeting, held shortly after the indicative referendum, the ERC again endorsed the broad structure of MMP as outlined in the Commission's report. It rejected the 'best losers' concept proposed by the British Hansard Society (Hansard Society, 1976:37–40) as an alternative to the two-vote system proposed by the Commission, endorsed a parliament of 120 MPs (although members conceded that MMP would work satisfactorily with 100 MPs and they were concerned that the possibility of an MMP system being pitted against a First-past-the-post system with 99 MPs would not be fair), endorsed the commission's 50:50 ratio of constituency to list seats, and supported the proposed 10 per cent tolerance allowed when constituency boundaries were required to be redrawn (ERC, 1992b). The near total adoption of the Royal Commission's report and recommendations gave the ERC's campaign a stamp of authority that was difficult to rebut.

Structure and organisation

Throughout, the ERC's organisational structure was something of a contradiction. In one sense it was extraordinarily centralised, with its activities planned and directed by a small group of Wellington-based activists. On another level, however, it was a highly decentralised and largely informal grouping — similar to the earlier Halt All Racist Tours (HART) and anti-Security Intelligence Service (SIS) coalition organisations of the 1970s and early 1980s. ERC branches enjoyed a high degree of autonomy and were free to follow different strategies when promoting MMP, including authority to appoint their own spokespersons to promote ERC's case to the public (ERC, 1993c). Thus, while a national policy existed, individual branches could disagree with it and, although this was not encouraged, individual branches did, at times, promote different views. In 1993, for example, the nine branches which made submissions to the Electoral Law Select Committee revealed opposing views on some issues. A major item of discord occurred when the Auckland branch, which wanted the coalition to adopt a policy to fix the maximum number of MPs at 100, sought to use the opportunity afforded by the submission process to press its case (ELSC, 1993b:118). Saxby concedes that a major priority was to ensure that the coalition's national spokespeople were totally co-ordinated and that they did not promote contradictory positions through speaking out of turn.

Between 1987 and 1993 ERC had four chairpersons, David Round, a University of Canterbury law lecturer (1987–88), Brigette Hicks-Willer (1988–90), Lowell Manning, (1990–91), and Colin Clark, recently retired General Secretary of the Public Service Association (1991–94). Clark was the most publicly prominent. He brought several key attributes to the ERC organisation; in his previous employment he had developed a high public profile, vast experience as a public speaker, a considerable ability in handling a range of media, and strong organisational and administrative skills. These, combined with a strong commitment to MMP and his availability to devote the considerable time needed to promoting the ERC cause, made him an ideal chairperson during the period spanning the 1992 and 1993 campaigns for electoral change. According to Donald, Clark was recruited because he was seen as an acceptable and credible front-person — one who, it was anticipated, would have a broad appeal to the mainstream New Zealand and particularly to the trade union movement (Donald, 1996; Saxby, 1996).

Only one attempt appears to have been made to develop a more formal and coherent structure. During Manning's term as president steps were taken to broaden the coalition's base by forming a grouping to be known as the Campaign for Proportional Representation (CPR). The origins of this idea are not clear; both Manning and Rod Donald (ERC's South Island vice-chairperson, 1989–94) claim responsibility. Regardless, both believed that an umbrella organisation was needed to pull in other organisations which were sympathetic to the cause of electoral reform but reluctant, or perhaps even apprehensive, about becoming associated with what some regarded as a fringe group, and others a Labour Party front. Manning's view was that while networks were an important means of disseminating information and encouraging debate at the grassroots level, their amorphous nature meant that ERC lacked the cohesion and discipline necessary for a nationwide campaign. Although the CPR sent an open letter signed by leaders of eleven constituent groups to the Minister of Justice, Douglas Graham, in July 1991 (CPR, 1991[15]), both Saxby and Donald are adamant that it never amounted to more than a declaration of support for electoral reform by a range of groups and organisations, and that the less formal ERC (itself a component of CPR) remained the spearhead of the campaign for electoral reform. While Manning concedes that the leadership of the movement for reform remained with ERC, he argues that CPR was instrumental in expanding the number of groups compared with the number linked with ERC prior to the formation of CPR. He believes, for example, that the CPR initiative was instrumental in securing the involvement of the Alliance,[16] thus providing the ERC with the foot-soldiers that ERC had hitherto lacked, and that both organisations complemented one another, with ERC devising the strategies and preparing campaign materials, and the CPR providing the troops who fanned out across the country to spread the ERC message (Manning, 1996).[17]

What does seem seems clear is that the ERC in general, and Saxby in particular, were suspicious of Manning's motives. In September 1991 Saxby told Helena Catt that Manning:

> ... sees himself as the spokesperson for 'one of the most broadly-based organisations seen in New Zealand politics'. I think it is not appropriate for the CPR, which is at most a Wellington co-ordinating committee to make such claims and to try to get agreement from 11 separate parties and groups for a detailed submission. (ERC, 1991c.)[18]

Shortly thereafter, he wrote to Manning:

> As you know, the CPR is not a[n] organisation in its own right. It is a campaign initiated by the ERC which other groups have joined at our invitation. ... Your proposals to form CPR into an umbrella group do not, at this stage, have the support of the ERC. (ibid., 1991d.)

ERC leaders apparently also feared a possible backlash against their organisation because some media regarded the CPR as "a wing of the third party alliance" (ibid., 1991e). Although Manning claimed that the presence of CPR ensured that the campaign for electoral reform was effectively promoted at the grassroots level, the CPR itself was not a highly visible player in the overall campaign to persuade the electorate to support electoral reform; the ERC kept the CPR at a discreet distance and, by 1992, had firmly established itself in the mind of the public as *the* authority on MMP.

As it developed, the ERC broadened its base. Its 1991 constitution allowed for both individual and group memberships, the latter as affiliates although none ever formally joined in this category. The need for as broad a base as possible was well recognised, and efforts were made to attract representatives from all political parties, trade unions and those without any known partisan affiliation (Saxby, 1996). In an interview, Donald described it as "an odd mix" — predominantly individuals with different backgrounds — of Labour, Democrat, and Socialist Unity Party activists, along with former Values Party members, trade unionists, members of the Federation of University Women,

Women's Electoral Lobby, and, later, people with experience in organising protest campaigns with environmental and similar organisations (Donald, 1996).[19] Two months before the 1993 referendum, the ERC could boast active support from the Council of Trade Unions (CTU), Public Service Association (PSA), Post Primary Teachers Association (PPTA), the Peace Movement, the Environmental and Conservation Organisation (ECO), the Communications and Energy Workers' Union, the New Zealand University Students Association, and the Alliance and Christian Heritage parties (ERC, 1993c; *Press*, 6 October 1993).[20]

According to its 1991 constitution, ERCs governing body comprised an executive made up of representatives of approved branches (one delegate for every 20 members to a maximum of 10 delegates), approved affiliates (one delegate each), plus the management committee and patrons. The constitution granted it wide powers of printing, publishing and selling literature promoting ERC objectives; purchasing property; employing staff; providing educational services; determining policy; appointing the management committee; approving branches and affiliates; suspending or dismissing branches or affiliates where appropriate; setting subscriptions; convening special general meetings of any branch; and ruling on disputes. Apart from its promotional activities and the appointment of a management committee, the powers entrusted to it do not appear to have been used to any extent. What is clear, however, is that the heart of ERC's organisation was its 10 member executive committee which exercised the powers of the ERC council between council meetings, and had total authority to further ERC's objectives within the limits delegated to it by the council although regular consultation with branches was required. In the final analysis, it was this centralised feature of ERC's organisational structure that drove the coalition's campaign throughout the critical years between 1990 and 1993.

Despite the provision in its 1991 constitution, ERC appears never to have embraced the structure of a formal coalition. There were, however, a number of groups and organisations which informally lent their support. Probably the most significant was the Social Credit/Democratic Party which, as we have seen, had kept the cause of electoral reform before the electorate during the 1970s. The founders of ERC, however, did not want their organisation to be seen as a wing of the Democratic Party so it kept a low profile, its members joining ERC as individuals. Saxby was wary of its long-standing commitment to STV and regarded it as an 'ally' rather than a coalition partner (Saxby, 1996; Manning, 1996). This did not, however, dissuade the ERC management committee from seeking financial and personnel support from the Democratic Party's Auckland branch (ERC, 1989c). For their part, the Democrats made an internal policy decision to give their full support to the Royal Commission's recommendations as an interim measure even though the party's long-term goal remained the adoption of STV. It saw the commission's report as providing a window of opportunity and did not want to be left on the sideline. According to Manning, it was an easy decision to get through because party members accepted it as practical politics (Manning, 1996).

As the 1993 referendum approached, support for the ERC campaign emerged from several other quarters. Two are worth mentioning. Between August and October the *New Zealand Listener* published articles unashamedly promoting MMP to its readers,[21] and at the beginning of the week leading up to the referendum the Public Affairs Unit of the New Zealand Anglican Church endorsed MMP on the grounds that it would serve citizens' interests better than First-past-the-post because a more consultative approach to political decision-making would result. In a side-swipe at the opponents of change it argued that the Campaign for Better Government offered no change to the status quo and no guarantee that there would be any improvement to the existing political system (*Dom.*, 1 November 1993).[22] Although not formally associated with ERC, support of this kind was openly welcomed by the ERC campaigners.

Campaign strategies

In its earliest days, ERC concentrated on promoting the idea of holding a referendum as proposed by the Royal Commission. A basic leaflet setting out the arguments for change was prepared,[23] along with placards, posters and bumper stickers, all promoting electoral reform slogans and focusing on the single theme that FPP meant wasted votes which could be avoided by changing to MMP.[24] Members of the ERC who were activists within the Labour Party also sought to bring pressure to bear on the Lange Labour government by promoting resolutions supporting electoral reform through Labour Party conferences (Saxby, 1996).[25] Public petitions calling on the government to hold a referendum on proportional representation before the end of 1989 were also organised through ERC activists.

Coalition members remained highly optimistic that a referendum would be held during 1989. According to a newsletter to ERC convenors dated 5 December 1988, the select committee's report was understood "to contain recommendations for referendums on PR and a four year term". Their misplaced confidence was based on the belief that "select committees tell governments what the governments have decided what they would like to hear". There was, however, a note of concern about a possible proposal to increase the membership of the House of Representatives to 120: "The purpose of this seems to be to feed off the anti-politician feelings of the public in angling the proposal towards a 'No Vote'." If this does eventuate, ERC should "go on to the attack on this ...." (ERC, 1988a).

When, three days later, the select committee tabled its report (*AJHR,* 1988), the ERC criticised its recommendations[26] as "a repudiation of the Labour government's leadership" (ERC, 1988b), and in his report to convenors dated 13 December, Saxby wrote that the referendum recommended by the Electoral Law Select Committee "... is the one nobody has asked for! It is clearly a betrayal of the promise to hold a referendum on proportional representation." Further, since any increase in the size of parliament was opposed by the National Party opposition, "it is almost certain that there will be no referendum on the voting system next year" (ERC, 1988c).

ERC's response to the select committee's report was swift. The national executive met on 10 December and resolved to continue campaigning for the public's right to choose the voting system. It rejected the select committee's proposal for a referendum on the Supplementary Member (SM) system, condemned its rejection of the public's right to choose, restated its support for MMP as a fair and democratic voting system, and opposed any extension of the parliamentary term until parliament was "elected by a democratic voting system in which each vote counts equally" (ibid.). As Saxby later observed, the select committee's report 'died a horrible death' because there was no public support for holding a referendum on an SM system, although one ERC branch argued that the coalition should push for a referendum on SM because it "might be the best we'll ever get so let's take it!" (Saxby, 1996).

In 1989 the ERC regrouped to reinvigorate its campaign for electoral reform. Its goal now shifted towards the longer-term task of increasing public awareness of the case for reform, to act as a focus for public pressure on parliament, and to lobby MPs and groups to support proportional representation. During 1989 most activity focused on gathering signatures for a number of smaller, localised petitions calling for a referendum in 1989 rather than a single nationwide petition because the ERC leaders believed that this strategy would facilitate a rapid and comprehensive coverage, and demonstrate widespread local support. In his report to convenors in March 1989, Saxby noted that this would probably be the last major effort for 1989 but " ... please have faith that there will be a cumulative effect ... even if 1989 seems a disappointment at present" (ERC, 1989d). Its campaign received a further setback in April 1989 when Palmer announced that no referendum would be held. In the end only two petitions were presented to parliament and neither was particularly well supported (*AJHR,* 1990:29–30). Nevertheless, the coalition continued to chip away, and in a somewhat bizarre attempt to raise public awareness and support for electoral reform after Labour's decision not to proceed, it proposed holding "a referendum on PR ... independently of the government, in 20 electorates on election day 1990". Saxby conceded that such a move would need to be well organised because "[i]f the referendum is a flop, the ERC will almost certainly fold up" (ERC, 1990a). Ultimately, and with not inconsiderable relief, this proposal was dropped; manifesto promises made by all parties had rendered it unnecessary, and the ERC had experienced major difficulties, both in securing a sufficient number of activists to staff the proposed referendum tables (many MMP activists were also political party activists) and in obtaining sites that were located sufficiently close to polling places to allow voters to make the connection between the two events.

A major turning point for the ERC came with the 1990 commitments of both the Labour and National parties that a referendum on electoral reform would be held prior to the 1993 election. ERC activists threw themselves with renewed enthusiasm into the task of promoting the case for electoral reform to a public that they believed was now much more receptive — a subjective judgment based on their perception of a growing disenchantment with and alienation from politicians amongst ordinary New Zealanders. The ERC's goal was to promote the idea that the promised referendum should be held sufficiently early for the result to be implemented in time for the next election in 1993, that MMP was ERC's (and the Royal Commission's) preferred option, and that the proposed referendum should provide a clear-cut choice between FPP and MMP. It sought to achieve this through a multi-faceted programme involving media releases, letter-writing, lobbying MPs, demonstrations in the grounds of parliament, submissions to the Electoral Law Select Committee considering the Electoral Poll Bill, and a nationwide petition which, when presented in August 1991, contained c.35,000 signatures (ERC, 1991a). In the period prior to the 1992 indicative referendum ERC members actively promoted the change option and support for MMP as the preferred alternative to the existing FPP electoral system. The overwhelming voter support for change, and for MMP, in the 1992 referendum convinced them that, with the continued promotion of MMP, electoral change would be effected.

Between 1987 and the early months of 1993 the ERC experienced little opposition to its campaign to promote the case for electoral reform in general and MMP in particular. Following the 1992 referendum, however, and with the government committed to a binding referendum in 1993, support for FPP began to gain momentum and, particularly after the Campaign for Better Government (CBG) was established, the ERC found itself facing an unexpected onslaught from supporters of the status quo. While it continued to press what it saw as the positive benefits of adopting MMP, the ERC was forced to adopt a much stronger reactive mode as it fought to turn back this challenge. Its spokespeople, for example, found themselves having to respond to newspaper articles supporting FPP which appeared in the months before the referendum, and to reply to the flood of press releases and statements originating with defenders of the status quo.

In the months leading up to the 1993 referendum, and in the face of public opinion polls which revealed a significant decline of support for MMP, ERC strategists were forced to review their tactics. According to Clark, although the coalition had hitherto adopted a restrained and reasoned approach to the public debate, the shift in public opinion meant that the ERC had not only to promote the merits of MMP but it also had to be "more scathing about FPP" (*Dom.*, 6 September 1993). Similar advice was given by TV3 political reporter, Sean Plunkett, who advised ERC to be more 'pro-active' and reply to any unfavourable comment, and to blitz the media with 'real news' press releases. In reporting this to ERC campaigners, Saxby advised that "TV3 is willing to promote MMP/ERC, but TVNZ was not interested in a story on how different ERC is from CBG" (ERC, 1993c).

Not all of ERC's publicity, however, was negative. Buoyed by the results of the indicative referendum, ERC's 1992 annual general meeting identified five issues it believed would be critical to its ultimate success — the total number of parliamentary seats, the retention of separate Maori representation, party lists, the registration and funding of political parties, and democratic candidate selection processes. Concerted efforts were made at this meeting to ensure that all ERC members supported clear and detailed policy positions on the shape of MMP before the coalition prepared its submission to the Electoral Law Select Committee (ibid., 1992b). In February 1993, author and MMP advocate, Philip Temple, who had recently returned from a visit to Germany, published a lengthy article supporting MMP in the *New Zealand Listener*.[27] Other positive promotional strategies included a 'pseudo' telephone survey which sought to shape public opinion in favour of MMP,[28] and establishing a range of support groups under the banner of 'New Zealanders for MMP' (ibid., 1993c).[29]

About two months before the 1993 referendum Kevin Hackwell and Nicky Hager, veterans of the Peace and Environmental Research and Peace Movement Aotearoa groups, both of whom were very experienced in organising protest campaigns, joined Danna Glendenning (WEL) and Stephen Russell (ERC's office manager), in the final campaign thrust. Hackwell prepared a report for the coalition's executive in which he identified a number of strategies including: target ERC's audience (for example, listeners to commercial radio's Pam

Corkery, not those who listened to non-commercial radio's *Morning Report*), cease trying to educate electors about MMP (rather, assure them that MMP 'is the right thing to vote for'), make messages simple and emotional (focus on the concept of 'fairness' and 'if politicians don't like it, MMP must be good'), and attack the credibility of CBG ('no more than a front for the wealthy'). (ERC, 1993c.) The entire thrust of the final two months of campaigning was to create strong MMP product recognition. It no longer mattered whether or not electors understood the detail of MMP; what was important was that they were constantly reminded that this was the electoral system unanimously recommended by the Royal Commission and that most politicians were opposed to it. It is clear that ERC was able to marshall significant resources when it was under pressure and Hackwell's proposed strategy demonstrated a high level of organisation and sophistication. In the final month, especially in the two weeks prior to the election, the ERC used every means within its relatively meagre resources to persuade electors to hold fast against what was clearly a very expensive campaign waged by supporters of the status quo.

Financing the campaigns

Public campaigns designed to bring about change to existing structural frameworks usually require substantial financial resources if the core message is to be embedded in the public's psyche. Although, over time, ERC developed an extensive network of supporters across the country, at no stage did its income — overwhelmingly from donations — allow it the luxury of promoting its case for change without constraint. The over-riding story of the ERC's finances is one of endemic cash shortages and hand-to-mouth existence. From the ERC's point of view, it was indeed fortunate that serious opposition to its campaign did not emerge until a matter of months before the 1993 binding referendum.

During its first years the ERC depended heavily on donations and regular pledged commitments from supporters and extensive voluntary efforts by a small group of dedicated and single-minded individuals.[30] Until 1992 the organisation spent between $8,000 and $10,000 annually on its campaign to build public support for MMP (Saxby, 1996). It is clear, however, that its income seldom matched its expenditure. Although, in its first two years, it raised c.$20,000 (ERC, 1989b) this was insufficient to cover the costs of promoting its argument. In December 1988, for example, Saxby reported that the ERC had a deficit of $1,100, and in February 1989 he told convenors that the current newsletter could not be printed "until we are more secure financially" (ERC, 1989a). He also expressed his disappointment and concern that only a small number of supporters appeared willing to support the ERC's activities through a regular financial commitment by pointing out that regular financial donations from the Auckland area totalled a mere $70, all of which came from Values or former Values Party supporters. "It seems to me", he wrote, "that if the Democrats cannot match that, we might as well fold up ..." (ibid.). Despite this plea, there is little sign of any subsequent improvement; an undated sheet included in the ERC's files shows that in 1991/92, automatic contributions totalling a mere $270 a year were received from 15 supporters.

As the referendums drew closer the ERC's financial demands grew substantially. In 1992 the ERC spent c.$26,000 in promoting its cause, an amount augmented by contributions from the Alliance which included the costs of the large public billboards erected throughout the country (Saxby, 1996; Donald, 1996). Although it had budgeted for an income of c.$41,000 in 1993 (ERC, 1993b), when confronted by the CBG campaign, its expenditure rose to over $300,000, most of which was incurred in the final few weeks before the referendum. It seems clear that the ERC had never intended to mount a major advertising campaign but felt forced to do so when successive public opinion polls revealed a rapid closing of the gap between supporters and opponents of electoral reform. A successful appeal for funds to "better put the case for MMP" (ERC, 1993f) enabled it to launch a last-minute advertising campaign on radio, television and print media aimed at countering the CBG's saturation publicity blitz. This appeal to supporters, and a wider public appeal launched at the beginning of the final week, saw money pour in, most of it in small donations (Saxby, 1996; Donald, 1996).[31] In this final week, the ERC spent c.$75,000 on television advertisements (*NZH*, 3 November 1993; *Dom.*, 3 November 1993)[32] and a further c.$35,000 for radio advertisements. Nevertheless, despite the success of this last minute appeal, when the dust had finally settled, the ERC's finances were in deficit by between $20,000 and $30,000.

The level of concern shown by ERC spokespeople at the speed that the gap between the two options was closing is clear from their comments. Without doubt, they genuinely feared that the financial resources they believed the CBG had at its disposal might result in defeat for the supporters of change. Donald described the CBG campaign as "the establishment versus the rest" (*Listener,* 9 November 1993). In justifying the ERC's last-minute decision to advertise on television, Clark said,

> We did not have the money but we felt we had no choice. The gap in the polls was closing. The anti-MMP lobby had launched a massive propaganda onslaught against MMP on television and radio, and with full page advertisements [in newspapers]. Our supporters were pressing us to counter the onslaught. (*NZH,* 9 November 1993.)

Since the ERC had publicly stated that its income during 1993 was only c. $50,000 (*Listener,* 11 September 1993), its success in raising sufficient money to mount a last-ditch campaign is indicative of the commitment many New Zealanders had to electoral change. As Donald (1996) said, "a donation was a statement about a commitment". At the critical point when the chips were down, the sleeping supporters of MMP swung in behind the campaigners for change. Whether or not this demonstration of support was critical to the outcome must, however, remain an open question.

ERC and the politicians

Throughout its seven-year campaign, ERC maintained pressure on MPs. Many of its members inherently distrusted MPs' promises, particularly whenever senior government MPs publicly opposed proportional representation. After a lengthy statement by third ranking Minister, Mike Moore, outlining his opposition to any change in the electoral system was published (*EP*, 20 October 1987), Saxby wrote to Palmer urging the government not to "retreat from its undertaking to hold a binding referendum on the voting system. ...in the end the public is entitled to vote on the electoral system and approve a change or not. Please hold firm to the promise of a binding referendum" (Palmer, H.88: 1 November 1987). Other examples are ERC's public endorsement of Terris's bill in 1990 (ERC, 1990b), repeated calls for parties to keep their promises to hold a binding referendum *before* the 1990 (and, later the 1993) general election, criticism of the length of time it took the select committee to report the results of its deliberations to parliament, and concern that the delayed referendum debate would be swamped by the election campaign. "The public", said Clark, "can be excused for thinking this delay is deliberate" (*NZH*, 14 June 1993; *Press*, 14 June 1993).

When Bolger announced that the bill setting out the form of MMP would follow the Royal Commission's report, including a proposal for the state funding of political parties (*NZH*, 22 September 1992), Clark complained that this was incompatible with any pretence of fairness unless parallel provisions were also included in the *Electoral Act 1956*. It indicated, he said, a "continuation of this programme of fear-mongering and red-herring raising" (ibid.). This was a theme that was to continue throughout the next year. When, for example, the Electoral Reform Bill was reported back to parliament with no change to the original proposal for an MMP parliament to have 120 seats against 99 for a parliament elected by First-past-the-post, ERC supporters claimed that this was a deliberate strategy to create an uneven playing field: "The government", Clark said, "has deliberately decided to do its damnedest to sabotage the referendum on MMP (because the public will be hostile to more MPs)" (*Press,* 23 July 1993).[33] The coalition also voiced its concern at the possible composition of the select committee charged with developing the MMP legislation. Fear was expressed that the major parties would dominate the committee and try to make MMP unpalatable to the electorate in the hope that it would be rejected. As we have already seen, however, the membership of the select committee included supporters of a number of different electoral options; nevertheless the ERC's well-publicised concerns may well have been a well-timed pre-emptive strike to ensure that the committee listened carefully to the views of the public.

The Campaign for Better Government — An Anti-MMP Lobby

Origins

On Sunday 25 April 1993[34] a full-page advertisement appeared in the nationally circulating *Sunday Star* attacking MMP. Inserted by Peter Shirtcliffe, chairman of Telecom, New Zealand's largest company, it focused on the fact that the number of seats won by each party represented in parliament would be determined by its share of the party vote. "These seats", continued the advertisement, "would not be filled by candidates fairly elected, but by professional politicians chosen by the party hierarchy from a list over which we, as mere voters, have no control". Shirtcliffe announced that since MMP was likely to create even greater problems than the existing First-past-the-post electoral system, he intended "to initiate a campaign for better government within the present system". The following day he expanded on his reasons for publishing the advertisement: so far, he said, no informed debate had taken place; many who voted for MMP in 1992 had done so because they wanted to signal their discontent with the behaviour of successive governments; and he was concerned at the lack of control voters would have over list MPs (*EP*, 26 April 1993). He claimed that the advertisement was not politically motivated; it was, he said, a means of "testing of the waters" to gauge the public's response.

Reaction from the pro-MMP lobby was predictable. Colin Clark (ERC) angrily retorted that the advertisement was "factually wrong"[35] and amounted to scare-mongering; newly Independent MP, Winston Peters, claimed that it "confirmed a campaign of misinformation by some in big business and politics who wanted to protect their privileges" (*Press*, 26 April 1993); NewLabour MP, Jim Anderton, condemned Shirtcliffe's initiative as "an example of the establishment using its substantial wealth to discredit the MMP option" (*Dom.*,

27 April 1993); while Victoria University academic, Jonathan Boston, claimed that Shirtcliffe had done a grave disservice to the public's understanding of MMP: "[o]n a major constitutional question we have a senior business person spending substantial sums of money misleading the public" (ibid.) These criticisms set the tone for much of the ensuing public debate.

What were Shirtcliffe's motives for taking the steps he did? Was his campaign a 'front for big business' which may have been becoming increasingly wary of the impact that any change to the electoral system might have upon their ability to influence government decision-making? According to Ruth Richardson, although Shirtcliffe had been a member of the Business Roundtable, he was never a central figure nor power broker in that organisation (Richardson, 1996). While this was not an impediment preventing him from fronting a big business campaign to oppose MMP on behalf of the Business Roundtable, there is no hard evidence to support this proposition. Shirtcliffe's own explanation is that he became increasingly concerned after the 1992 indicative referendum about whether electors really understood what MMP entailed (Shirtcliffe, 1996)[36] and during the 1992/93 Christmas vacation period he asked people he met to assess how well they understood the proposed MMP electoral system. Predictably, perhaps because the final shape of the new system was still far from clear, by far the majority of responses he received indicated little or no knowledge. In the light of this evidence, and an apparent unwillingness by anyone else to publicise the case against MMP, he decided to become involved. According to a report in *The Dominion* newspaper two days after the advertisement appeared, the springboard for action was a meeting called by Shirtcliffe the previous February — described much later as a high-powered business cocktail party held at his private residence (*Listener*, 11 September 1993) — to canvass the possibility of mounting a campaign in opposition to MMP (*Dom.*, 27 April 1993). Although Shirtcliffe has denied that any meeting to explore the possibility of mounting an anti-MMP campaign took place (*NZH*, 22 May 93; *Listener*, 11 September 1993), the available evidence suggests that he did meet with several people, including businessman Michael Fay, politicians Bill Birch, Simon Upton and Tony Ryall, and Peter Cullinane, chief executive of the international advertising agency, Saatchi and Saatchi. According to Cullinane, who admits to being present, Shirtcliffe's campaign did not originate at this meeting but rather in a subsequent approach by Shirtcliffe to his company (*Listener*, 11 September 1993). Nevertheless, it is inconceivable that, at some point during this gathering, discussion did not turn to the question of how the pro-MMP lobby's campaign might be halted and, since politicians had been badly burnt through their association with the Campaign for First-past-the-post the previous year, some consideration was not given to setting up a structure to oppose MMP from which MPs could distance themselves.

Why did Shirtcliffe deliberately initiate his campaign through a nationwide full-page advertisement which personally cost him around $20,000? There is little doubt that the basis of his opposition to MMP was his concern that it would be endorsed by default if no one was prepared to promote an alternative argument. According to Shirtcliffe, his first advertisement, which focused on recent changes to Italian electoral law, was deliberately controversial and designed to generate news. It was not expected to change individuals' views; rather, he realised that the Italian law change provided him with a marketing opportunity and a means to launch his campaign in a spectacular way.

Three weeks later, Shirtcliffe inserted a second full-page advertisement in which he outlined five objections to MMP: a 20 per cent increase in the number of MPs; weaker direct links between MP and constituents; lack of local accountability to local electors by party list MPs; the inevitability of coalition governments which, in turn, would place disproportionate power in the hands of small parties; and governments that would still not be kept in check. At the same time he formally announced that he would launch the Campaign for Better Government (CBG), with an office and staff to promote an alternative to MMP. An appeal for donations and volunteer assistance followed: "Please show your support. The issue is far too important to be left to politicians" (*DST,* 16 May 93). When asked if big business would be involved Shirtcliffe replied: "Either people will rally to the cause or not. If they do they will be transparently clear" (*NZH,* 15 May 93). In response to another question, he said: "The truth is I've already received a large number of donations and offers of support, all from individuals, and this will more than cover the next phase of the campaign" (*Dom.,* 15 May 93). The real issue, argued Shirtcliffe, was which of the two options — FPP or MMP, would give New Zealand better government (CBG, 1993b:14 May 93). He was in no doubt as to what the answer should be.

The CBG's case against MMP

The nub of the CBG's case against the adoption of MMP was, at first, overwhelmingly negative. MMP, it argued, would result in an increased number of MPs and therefore additional costs to taxpayers. Second, larger electorates would greatly increase the workload of constituency MPs, especially those representing rural areas, and, as a direct consequence, substantially reduce their effectiveness — local areas would lose local representation. Third, since political parties would determine the shape of party lists, list MPs would be answerable only to their party and electors would thus effectively be denied their right to choose nearly half of their MPs — this, claimed the advertisement, was undemocratic. Fourth, coalition governments would result in small parties holding the balance of power. Fifth, the economy would react adversely to coalition governments. All of these disadvantages, the CBG contended, would increase the power of political parties at the expense of electors. Nor would there necessarily be an improvement in the performance of the political system; less accountability was likely to result in a continuation of broken promises, and it was doubtful if the public's trust and confidence in its MPs and the political system would improve (CBG, 1993a, 1993b; *Canterbury Digest*, 1993:26; *NZH*, 23 October 1993). It also claimed that Maori spokespeople had stated that FPP gave better representation for Maori because "if Maori did not fit into a party they would be effectively barred" (CBG, 1993b:21 October 1993), and that there was no guarantee that MMP would be good for women because parties would continue to control the candidate selection process — a changed political culture was required (ibid., 24 August 1993).

In its first issue of *Referendum Review* (1993a:1) the CBG claimed that the Electoral Reform Coalition had "consistently failed" to explain how improvements to the political system would result from the adoption of MMP: "MMP won't change MPs, won't make them more honest, won't stop them from breaking promises." The third issue asked: "Why should we trust the political parties any more than we do now?... Once having gained the power to appoint Members of Parliament the 'king makers' of the political parties will have no trouble in gerrymandering the system to suit themselves" (ibid.). Predictably, these attacks prompted the advocates of MMP to challenge the CBG to detail how it would bring about an improvement in the political process. Shirtcliffe responded by announcing that the CBG would propose a plan for reforming parliament (*Press*, 10 July 1993). The effect of this was to force the CBG to inject positive proposals for reforming the existing electoral system into the public debate.

Leaders and supporters

Many times during the months before the 1993 referendum, questions were asked about Shirtcliffe's role and motives. By his own admission, his interests were in business, not politics, which he described as " ... a grubby business. Neither I nor my family would have been involved in any campaign if the country had opted for any of the other alternatives [included in the 1992 referendum]. I wouldn't have taken any notice of the campaign in 1993 had it not been for MMP" (Shirtcliffe, 1996). Clearly, then, he was galvanised into action by the dominance of political parties which, he believed, would result from the adoption of MMP. It seems clear, however, that Shirtcliffe accepted the leadership role only reluctantly after it became clear that no one else was likely to do so; several times he spoke with Owen Jennings, immediate past president of Federated Farmers, about the disadvantages he saw, both for himself and his business connections, and the personal costs of his association with the campaign (Nicolle, 1996; Tate, 1996; Jennings, 1996).

Once committed, Shirtcliffe devoted a great deal of his time to the campaign. According to CBG staff members, Brian Nicolle and Priscilla Tate, he was very much the driving force (ibid.).[37] Jennings, who joined the campaign after it was well under way and became a key figure, confirmed that the CBG was very much a Shirtcliffe campaign: "Peter ran it very much from his desk although Brian [Nicolle] had a good deal of authority in terms of the mechanics" (Jennings, 1996). Tate cautioned that Mrs Margaret Shirtcliffe should not be ignored: "[s]he has a fine brain and was just as dedicated." Nor should the contribution of their daughter, Janet Shirtcliffe, be overlooked; she became a key part of the campaign from July onwards and is credited with expanding CBG's support base, especially amongst women and younger voters (Tate, 1996).

Since time was of the essence, the CBG set out to attract prominent citizens to its campaign. In addition to Shirtcliffe and Jennings (whom Shirtcliffe described as "dedicated, committed, articulate, politically experienced, and a tower of strength"[38]), its spokespersons included Rob McLagan, Chief Executive of Federated Farmers; Fleming Jensen, a Danish veterinary surgeon who had lived in New Zealand since 1965; John Jensen, professor of History at the University of Waikato; Auckland lawyers, David and Patricia Schnauer; and Terry Dunleavy, an Auckland journalist and Executive Officer of the New Zealand Wine Institute. The Schnauers and Dunleavy were openly National Party supporters,[39] while John Jensen had been an office bearer in both the Labour and National parties. The CBG also worked to broaden its base, both geographically and demographically, and to this end designated a number of spokespersons representing special interest groups — among them Greg Harford, an Auckland university student; Belinda Lee-Hope, a film and television production executive; Hilary Bennett, an Auckland housewife with a nursing background, who was associated with Defensive Driving, the AIDS Foundation, Life Education, and the New Zealand Education Foundation; and Aubrey Stancliff of Christchurch, a commercial artist.

Expertise in the field of electoral systems was also tapped. Most New Zealand political scientists were either supporters of MMP or adopted a strictly neutral stance but Associate Professor G.A. Wood, of the University of Otago, an open supporter of First-past-the-post, acted as an adviser to the campaign. Two more prominent experts were, however, overseas academics, Malcolm Mackerras, senior lecturer in Politics at the Defence Force Academy, University of New South Wales at Duntroon, and Ludger Kühnhardt, Director of Political Science at Freiburg University in Germany.

Described by the CBG's publicity machine as "a leading international commentator", Mackerras was approached by Nicolle in June 1993 and invited to assist in putting the CBG's case for FPP to the New Zealand electorate. Mackerras, a long time opponent of MMP who, in 1988, had said that the Royal Commission's recommendation was "so radical that it has virtually no prospect of popular endorsement at a referendum" (*NZH,* 18 May 1988), and who, following the indicative referendum, had condemned MMP as "a ratbag scheme ... utterly out of sync with the experience of parliaments in the Anglo-American world" (*Press*, 2 January 1993), accepted this invitation with alacrity! (Mackerras, 1996.) In August, at the CBG's invitation, he visited New Zealand where he addressed meetings, and was interviewed on radio talkback programmes and television, to put the case against MMP. His other main contribution was to clarify specific debating points when asked to do so by Shirtcliffe or Nicolle (ibid.). Nicolle believes that by raising its public profile and generating fierce debate, Mackerras made a significant contribution to the CBG campaign: "Everywhere he went he created a media feast for the week he was in New Zealand" (Nicolle, 1996).

Kühnhardt's contribution was as welcome as it was unexpected. On honeymoon in New Zealand during the early stages of the government-funded public education campaign, he was recruited by the CBG after he had spoken out against MMP. His opposition stemmed from his view that MMP produced professional politicians who were not accountable to the electorate while FPP provided strong opposition and, therefore, governability and accountability. He claimed that there was a demand in Germany for a more majoritarian electoral system that would provide clear-cut governments with a mandate to act (*Press*, 9 September 1993; *Dom.*, 11 September 1993). As one of a tiny handful of persons currently in New Zealand with extensive, first-hand experience of the German electoral system on which MMP had been modelled, Kühnhardt was able to support the CBG's case against MMP with an air of authority.

The CBG also tried to recruit British MP, Brian Gould (a New Zealander), who had been a member of the British Labour Party's working party on electoral reform. Although Gould was in New Zealand before the referendum, personal factors prevented him from entering into the public debate. At a late stage the former German Chancellor, Helmut Schmidt, who had been publicly very critical of MMP, was invited to support the CBG's campaign. Although he declined, Schmidt's key criticisms of the German electoral system were translated and circulated as widely as possible (Nicolle, 1996). Former Prime Minister, David Lange, was also approached to lend his support but, although opposed to MMP, declined to do so (Tate, 1996).[40]

Others to publicly support the CBG's campaign came mainly from the business community — the chief executive of Countrywide Bank warned of the dangers of coalitions (*Press*, 2 June 1993), as did Guy Chapman, a partner in a leading New Zealand law firm (*Dom.*, 9 July 1993). Leading businessman, Sir Robertson Stewart, argued that New Zealand needed strong, decisive government if it was to prosper (*Listener*, 11 September 1993). The most sustained support, however, came from the Business Roundtable which had, the previous year, commissioned a report (Brook-Cowen, *et. al.*, 1992) that concluded that MMP would increase policy uncertainty without any strong presumption that the adoption of MMP would result in any overall improvement in the political system (*NZH,* 22 May 93). In the following months the Roundtable's executive director, Roger Kerr, peppered the media with the Roundtable's defence of the First-past-the-post electoral system (*Press*, 23 June 1993; *Ind.*, 23 July 1993). Throughout its entire campaign, however — and despite Shirtcliffe's repeated denials — the CBG was hampered by the strong public perception that it was nothing more than a front for big business. David Lange perhaps encapsulated the public's view of the CBG when he damned its leaders as "the worst people in the world …. They represent the very people who were involved in the relationship between government and business which so angered the public and caused the demand for electoral reform in the first place" (*Listener*, 11 September 1993). This perceived association with 'big business' hung like a millstone around the CBG's neck throughout its entire campaign.

Tate, however, hastened to point out that the CBG also received considerable support from what she described as "the smaller business community who put their cheques in the mail". She also noted that the CBG experienced no difficulty in filling its allocation of audience seats for Television New Zealand's *Counterpoint* current affairs programmes which examined the electoral referendum issues (Tate, 1996).

Organisational structure

The response to his initial advertisement persuaded Shirtcliffe to put his campaign on to a broader footing. He announced his intention to do so in mid-May, and by early June the national office — essentially an information centre with the stated aim of improving public awareness and understanding of alternatives for electoral reform — had been established with Nicolle at the helm. Nicolle and Tate were employed full-time from late May. As the campaign developed three more paid part-time staff, augmented by volunteers, were appointed. Networks of supporters were developed in many parts of the country, with centres in Wellington, Hamilton, Nelson, Christchurch, and Invercargill, and spokespersons were appointed encompassing a range of activities, including business, law, farming, journalism, academia, science, the arts and homemakers. Brian Talboys, Deputy Prime Minister in the Muldoon Government from 1975 to 1981, was appointed patron, and former MP, Richard Harrison, added his support. Nevertheless, and while Shirtcliffe disputes it, the CBG was very much centred on Auckland; he did concede, however, that Auckland, as the 'biggest market', demanded a great deal of attention and effort (Nicolle, 1996; Tate, 1996; Shirtcliffe, 1996).

Throughout the entire campaign, the CBG was a largely amorphous organisation. It had no formal meetings, kept no minutes, and retained few records of value. There was, Shirtcliffe argues, insufficient time to devote to strategy meetings; what was needed was a decisionmaker on the run. The CBG was, according to Tate, 'a real business structure' where Shirtcliffe made the key decisions and Nicolle and Tate, as the executive officers, implemented them. Shirtcliffe admits to substantial toll and facsimile bills arising from his daily contacts with the CBG office located in Auckland, although his business interests meant that he was frequently in that city.

Shirtcliffe appointed Nicolle (whom he knew to be a supporter of the post-1984 economic direction) as campaign manager of CBG before the end of May. A Labour Party activist between 1977 and 1990, a strong supporter of Roger Douglas and co-founder of the Backbone Club, Nicolle was an experienced political campaigner, particularly at the grass-roots level. He agreed to become involved in the campaign "out of a concern that political parties had too much power and would have even more under the MMP system" (Nicolle, 1996; *NZH*, 28 May 1993). Tate also brought a background in Labour Party politics, including the Backbone Club, as well as involvement in a wide range of community activities. They, along with Shirtcliffe and, later, Jennings, were the lynchpins of the CBG organisation.

Nicolle confirms the highly centralised nature of the organisation. He accepted responsibility for controlling and directing the campaign from an Auckland base because it was essential that everything that the CBG did and said was absolutely accurate, that all publicity was properly signed off, and that spokespeople located in different parts of the country spoke with a single voice. Centralisation was extreme: for example, media releases were drafted in Auckland and sent to spokespeople who duly released them as their own.

Campaign strategies

From the outset Shirtcliffe's primary objective was to persuade electors to buy his product (FPP) rather than MMP, the product of his competitor (Shirtcliffe, 1996). The recent changes to Italy's electoral system had provided him with a window of opportunity to get his campaign off the ground. Although his first advertisement was roundly criticised as inaccurate and misleading — and was found to be so by the Advertising Standards Complaints Board following a formal complaint from the ERC (*Press*, 27 April & 25 June 1993; *Dom.*, 27 April & 7 May 1993; *NZH*, 25 & 26 June 1993[41]) — he is convinced that it 'worked brilliantly' because it was deliberately designed to create news, not alter electors' opinions. However, when no immediate reaction was forthcoming (it was, after all, Anzac Day) he drew attention to it by distributing a media release to key people. This had the desired effect of focusing attention on the advertisement and making it a newsworthy item. Pointing to a drop in support for MMP of nine percentage points between early April and early May, and a corresponding increase of four percentage points for FPP, Shirtcliffe believes that in terms of coverage per dollar spent, it was highly effective in achieving his initial objective of developing an organised support base (Shirtcliffe, 1996; *Press*, 6 May 1993).[42] At the end of the first week in May he announced that he had been overwhelmed by the initial public response to his initiative. A second full-page advertisement was published in mid-May and this, too, brought a huge response. Shirtcliffe realised that he had to move quickly if he was to maintain the initial momentum he had generated. Nicolle was therefore instructed to move out into the community, generating news wherever he went — an extension of the marketing strategy that lay at the heart of Shirtcliffe's entire campaign.

Given its goal of undermining the credibility of the proposed MMP electoral system, much of the CBG's early campaigning strategy was essentially negative in character. In many respects it replicated the referendum campaign strategies developed to a fine art in California —direct mail, letter-writing campaigns, market research, a paid radio talkback programme,[43] and overwhelmingly negative television advertisements. For example, its spokespeople latched on to the desertions of Alliance candidates, Terry Heffernan and Gilbert Myles, to the newly-formed New Zealand First Party (CBG, 1993:30 June,14 & 16 July 1993; *Press*, 26 July 1993) and the selection of a former National Cabinet Minister, Ian Shearer, as a New Zealand First candidate (*Press*, 28 July 1993) as examples of instability and the kind of political backroom dealing that was likely to result from the increased power MMP gave to parties. Shirtcliffe also publicly supported the Governor-General's questioning of the consequences of MMP and defended her right to do so (ibid.). Later in the public debate, the CBG damned an ERC promise to campaign for a 100-seat parliament as "reek[ing] of desperation ... opportunistic ... incoherent ... [and a] last minute play to sweeten MMP" (CBG, 1993b:3 October 1993) and latched on to the Proportional Representation Society of Australia's declaration of opposition to MMP on the grounds that its closed party lists were unacceptable (ibid., 21 October 1993). The CBG's overriding strategy was to seek to portray the ERC and the Alliance "... as small factional interests ... [who] clearly do not make for effective government" (ibid., 13 July 1993).

To a large extent this strategy appears to have been determined as a result of a confidential report prepared by UMR-Insight Research in April 1993. Although Shirtcliffe disavowed any direct knowledge of the report — he said that he had not commissioned it although "where his advisers draw their inspiration from is their business" (*Dom.*, 10 July 1993; *Listener*, 11 September 1993) — *The Independent* which first broke the story, described it as providing a blueprint of how to manage an anti-MMP advertising campaign through targeting "the least educated and most gullible" sector of the electorate, raising the stakes by providing "easily digestible, alarming material", warning electors of the consequences of MMP, and focusing on MMP's economic and societal impact (*Ind.*, 9 July 1993). Each stage of the CBG campaign closely followed this prescription and was particularly noticeable in its 'crying baby' and 'paper bags' television advertisements.

The CBG contracted UMR-Insight Research to carry out a limited amount of survey research, principally to measure the impact its campaign was making and to indicate where it might be refined. By early July, poll data suggested that the campaign should project a more positive message. As a result, Shirtcliffe announced that he proposed developing a plan for reforming parliament. "I want", he declared, "to get together a package of ideas that we can discuss as a community that would reinvigorate confidence in the FPP system" (*Press*, 10 July 1993; CBG, 1993b:20 July 1993). On 1 August, CBG announced the appointment of an advisory council, headed by Owen Jennings and including a number of what it described as "mainstream credible Kiwis",[44] whose task would be to consult with New Zealanders across the country and recommend "a more constructive and effective political system" (CBG, 1993b:1 August 1993; *Press*, 2 August 1993). Suggestions the CBG identified as likely to improve the governmental process were smaller cabinets, a minimum of three months between the introduction of legislation and its final passage into law, greater use of referendums,[45] improved candidate selection processes, higher quality politicians, increased delegation of responsibilities to local government, improvements in the efficiency of the Public Service, and greater independence for select committees (CBG, 1993a:2).[46] Although its proposals attracted some attention, by the middle of September the CBG had abandoned its goal of securing the agreement of the major parties to overhauling the parliamentary environment and reduced to two its list of reforms — an independent Speaker elected by 75 per cent of all MPs, and the establishment of a parliamentary commission which would suggest reforms to parliament (*Dom.*, 16 September 1993).[47] According to Jennings, the original list was altogether too long!

Nevertheless, it was the negative aspects of the CBG's campaign that stood out above all else. Jennings believes that a constructive campaign designed to defend First-past-the-post was an impossibility because many of those involved had varying levels of discomforture with FPP, although a number of its supporters joined because they took the view that the problem was fundamentally one relating to the operation of the whole parliamentary system (Jennings, 1996). There is evidence that at least some of those who were actively involved in the CBG's campaign were unhappy with its predominantly negative approach but they found it difficult to campaign positively to retain the existing electoral system in the face of the huge level of public cynicism then existing (Tate, 1996). In the end, it had to accept defeat but it did feel that New Zealanders had been alerted to difficulties likely to arise if MMP were adopted; encouraged to look beyond simply using the referendum to punish politicians; and to find solutions to the perceived deficiencies in the present political system.

Financing the campaign

Throughout the months leading up to the referendum repeated allegations continued to be made by the pro-MMP lobby that the CBG's campaign was funded by big business for big business. This claim appears to have been based on the fact that Shirtcliffe, Chairman of Telecom New Zealand (previously a State-owned Enterprise but, since 1991, a private company largely owned by two United States' telecommunication companies), and Jennings were its two most prominent spokespeople. Both Nicolle and Jennings were adamant that the CBG was supported by many ordinary New Zealanders, and Tate noted that the small business community gave good financial support. Nevertheless, it is clear that the CBG saw the business community as its main support base,[48] and its decision to approach this group paid — according to the CBG's leaders — handsome dividends, although Nicolle stated that in the early stages of its campaign business support was only lukewarm. The turning point came following publication of a full-page advertisement centred around a Garrick Tremain cartoon showing Gilbert Myles 'jumping ship' from the Alliance to the just formed New Zealand First Party (*Press,* 26 July 1993).[49] According to

Nicolle, support flooded in as people began to realise that this was the kind of political environment that might result from the adoption of MMP (Nicolle, 1996; Tate, 1996; Jennings, 1996).

To this day the CBG's budget has remained a closely guarded secret. When asked, Nicolle said that the CBG's budget was "not relevant" to the MMP debate (*NZH*, 3 November 1993), and in an interview published in the *New Zealand Listener* (11 September 1993) Shirtcliffe said "That's nobody's business". Shirtcliffe did, however, admit that the CBG had received a small number of four-figure personal donations, although the average donation from business "would be something under that". Donations, he said, had come from a wide range of people outside the business community, as the appeal for donations included in the first newspaper advertisements generated a huge response. The same article claimed that the CBG campaign was enthusiastically supported by the Employers Federation, Business Roundtable and Chambers of Commerce: "[m]oney is sluicing into the Shirtcliffe campaign account." Since the *Listener's* editorial stance openly advocated the adoption of MMP, the possibility that this claim is exaggerated cannot be discounted.

What is clear is that Shirtcliffe's commitment to promoting the case for the retention of FPP was sincere and genuine. He admits to having personally paid for the initial advertisements (estimated to have cost between $18,000 and $20,000) and to have established a bank account to get the campaign organisation under way. He made a family car available to Nicolle to enable him to carry out the campaign more effectively, he put "a few thousand dollars" into trailer hoardings, "put a bit of money into monitoring what people were thinking" after Janet Shirtcliffe had appeared on Television One's *Holmes* current affairs television programme, and devoted a good deal of his time to travelling around the country advocating the case for the retention of FPP (Shirtcliffe, 1996). While there can be no doubt that he did look to the business community to help the CBG maintain the momentum of his campaign (ibid.), he was adamant that neither the government nor the Labour Party was helping fund the CBG campaign, nor were funds coming from members of the Business Roundtable (*Ind.*, 9 July 1993). The ERC's claims that the CBG was "sitting on some huge war chest of corporate gold", was rejected as "a ridiculous fairytale concocted by the pro-MMP lobby", and the implication that all of the CBG's supporters were "right-wing and rich" was dismissed as "nonsense" (*Dom.*, 20 August 1993; *NZH*, 3 November 1993; CBG, 1993b:18 August 1993). Nevertheless, it is evident that the CBG's financial resources were much greater than those of the ERC; although it found it necessary to halt its newspaper advertising campaign for a period and dispense with the professional services of the advertising agency, Saatchi and Saatchi, because it did not have enough money to pay the costs involved, it was much more strongly placed, financially, than the ERC to mount a public advertising campaign promoting its views.

CBG and the politicians

When Shirtcliffe launched his campaign, the Prime Minister, Jim Bolger, congratulated him on his initiative but denied that the government was in any way involved. It was, he said, important for people other than politicians to "pick up the cudgels" and engage the debate on the issues surrounding MMP (*EP*, 26 April 1993). The next day and in another newspaper, however, his commendation was couched in more cautious terms, saying merely that Shirtcliffe was expressing a viewpoint that he held very strongly (*NZH*, 27 April 1993). Other MPs were not so kind: Winston Peters, for example, saw him as a creature of the "new right" business elite who wished to preserve the existing electoral system because it was advantageous to their interests (*Listener*, 11 September 1993).

The core problem confronting MPs, particularly those who were opposed to the adoption of MMP, arose from the abysmal failure of the MP-inspired Campaign for First-past-the-post the previous year. Most felt that they could not lend their overt support to the CBG in 1993 because the public would conclude that they were acting out of self-interest and not with the good of the country in mind. This presented the leaders of the CBG with a significant handicap: pro-MMP Members of Parliament could quite happily promote their preferred choice alongside the ERC lobby, but the majority of MPs who favoured the retention of FPP were unable to do likewise for fear that the slim chance of FPP winning majority support in the referendum would be irrevocably damaged.

For and Against — An Assessment of Two Campaigns

Undoubtedly the CBG campaign initiated by Shirtcliffe had a significant impact on the electorate's perception of the issues involved in the debate. Prior to the formation of the CBG, the Electoral Reform Coalition's advocacy of electoral change had gone largely unchallenged but, as the debate intensified and became more evenly balanced, public opinion favouring MMP noticeably declined (Figure 7.1).

Built as it was on the fears and uncertainties of people who were not quite sure of the desirability of change, the CBG's campaign was remarkably effective. It brought together people who were concerned about the impact of MMP on the

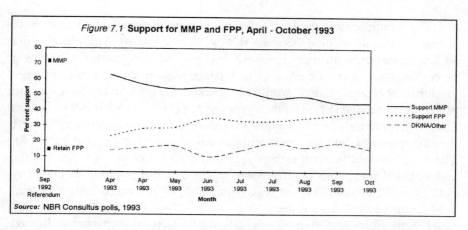

Figure 7.1 **Support for MMP and FPP, April - October 1993**

Source: NBR Consultus polls, 1993

future political and economic fabric but who were also concerned about improving the quality of the government. The evidence for this is in the shift from a largely negative, anti-MMP, stance in the early stages of its campaign to its more positive advocacy of parliamentary reform with its emphasis on 'better government', although, as Shirtcliffe admits, this change of emphasis "never really gained traction". The CBG's greatest handicap lay in its failure to convince the electorate that — despite Shirtcliffe's repeated protestations to the contrary — it was not simply a front for the Business Roundtable. Given the relatively short time it had to make its case to a suspicious and cynical public, Nicolle rated the CBG campaign as "reasonably successful" in terms of organisation but an "utter failure" in terms of its result. Tate rated it as unsuccessful because, at the end of the day, it failed to achieve its primary objective of thwarting the adoption of MMP (Nicolle, 1996; Tate, 1996; Shirtcliffe, 1996).

The ERC is a very good example of a highly successful lobby. A largely organic, grass-roots, almost anarchic organisational structure, it was a pressure group characterised by a single-mindedness of purpose that can only be admired. Although it did not have the resources to engage in market research or to engage focus groups, its spokespeople were articulate and believable. Highly populist in its approach, its campaign struck at a key moment in time when confidence in politicians and the political system was at an all-time low. Major reasons for its ultimate success were the depth and commitment of its active supporters and the fact that, with one notable exception, it picked up the Royal Commission's key recommendations and promoted them assiduously. It was successful in persuading the government to use these recommendations rather than those of the 1988 Electoral Law Select Committee as the basis for the 1993 *Electoral Act*. It could thus claim that its arguments were backed by the unanimous conclusions of the Royal Commission.

The months before the 1993 referendum were dominated by intense and, at times, vitriolic sniping between the two lobby groups. Shirtcliffe's first advertisement drew an angry response from pro-MMP supporters who saw it as confirmation that "a campaign of misinformation about mixed member proportional representation" would be mounted "by some in big business and politics who wanted to protect their privileges" (*Press*, 26 April 1993). But, as Donald observed, although the claim was not correct and was difficult to refute, the advertisement did help elevate public interest in the debate (Donald, 1996). The feud between the two groups persisted throughout the next six months and included allegations of infiltration, spying and disruptions of meetings by both sides.[50] The overall effect was, regrettably, to shed much more heat than light on the debate's core issues.

Despite Shirtcliffe's repeated denials that the CBG's campaign was funded by big business, and his several statements that the CBG had received a large number of unsolicited donations and offers of support, the organisation found the allegations very difficult to refute because it steadfastly refused to submit any financial records to public scrutiny. This conscious decision played into the ERC's hands, allowing it to establish an image in the electorate's mind of a David and Goliath struggle between its own slenderly resourced campaign and that of its opponent whose financial coffers were overflowing. Clark repeatedly reminded the public that the ERC did not have the corporate wealth of the CBG:

> We believe the bulk of this [advertising] money for the campaign they are waging must be coming from the corporate sector. All the indications are that big business and the businessmen who made a fortune out of the sale of public assets over the past ten years are backing the campaign to preserve the system and the politicians who made them so wealthy. (*NZH*, 28 September 1993.)

Clark believed that a spending cap, similar to the one included in the recently enacted *Citizens Initiated Referenda Act*,[51] should have been placed on each side of the electoral reform debate to guarantee that the debate was held on a level playing field. Most politicians were unmoved by this plea.

Because the CBG has declined to release its financial accounts it is difficult to determine the validity of the ERC's claims. What is clear, however, is that in the six months prior to the November 1993 referendum, the CBG outspent the ERC by nearly 8.5:1 on television, radio and print advertising. Based on advertising rate-card costs, the CBG spent just over $1.5 million, half of it on television advertising, compared to the ERC's figure of just under $181,000.[52] A large portion of these amounts appear to have been spent in the final week of the campaign — the CBG was reported as having "bought more than $500,000 worth of television advertising in the final week", compared with the ERC's expenditure of $85,000 in the same period (*SST,* 21 November 1993). The ERC sought to counter this expenditure disparity in the only way it knew — by creating an image that the debate was one of little people versus big money. One of its final print advertisements listed the names of its supporters (each of whom had contributed to the cost of the advertisement) to show that there were people behind the Electoral Reform Coalition, not 'bags on heads' (Donald, 1996).[53]

In the final few days neither side was confident that its view would prevail. The day before the referendum the *New Zealand Herald* (5 November 1993) reported that the ERC would continue the struggle for electoral reform and demand a citizens initiated referendum if it failed to secure majority support for electoral change, while the CBG repeated its promise that it would push for parliamentary reform if it was successful. Nicolle claims that on the Monday morning before the referendum, polls commissioned by the CBG had the supporters of FPP ahead; the next day, its tracking polls showed the CBG to be behind. At that point, Nicolle said, he knew that the CBG had lost "and there was nothing he could do to rescue it" (Nicolle, 1996). In retrospect, the final week's 'wall-to-wall' television advertisements were a mistake which, in effect, killed the CBG campaign. Donald substantially concurs with Nicolle's assessment; he believes that had the referendum been held a week earlier, the status quo may have prevailed (Donald, 1996).

Until the emergence of the CBG, the Electoral Reform Coalition had no serious opposition to contend with, but by mid-1993 it felt under pressure. In retrospect, according to Shirtcliffe, the CBG's main achievement was that it focused the community's mind on the judgment that had to be made. He believes that the ERC was 'shell-shocked' because the CBG emerged without warning to oppose it (Shirtcliffe, 1996).[54] The CBG sought to portray the ERC, and the Alliance which supported it, as "small factional interests ... (which) ... clearly do not make for effective government" (CBG, 1993b:13 July 1993). Although he concedes that the ERC's network strategy was 'brilliant,' Shirtcliffe was highly critical of its tactics. From day one, he said, the ERC "played the man, not the ball". The overriding characteristic of the campaign, from his viewpoint, was that it was very dirty and very personal from the outset: "We spent our time focusing on the issues and they spent their time attacking us. The whole thing reeked of highly organised pressure group tactics" (Shirtcliffe, 1996).

Perhaps predictably, ERC leaders have a different perspective. In a speech to the Democratic Party's annual conference in September 1993, Clark (1993) said that,

Up till now the ERC has always adopted a restrained and reasoned approach to the public debate on electoral reform, in stark contrast to the deliberate fearmongering and falsehood tactics of Shirtcliffe and the many anti-MMP politicians. ... The significant shift in the polls in recent months was forcing a review of ERC policy. It is time to take the gloves off about everything that is wrong with FPP.

Without doubt, the emergence of the CBG forced the ERC to rethink its strategy. No longer could it afford to sit back in the expectation that the support for electoral reform recorded in the 1992 indicative referendum would carry through unchallenged to the binding referendum. Its leaders knew that they had to further develop their organisation's strengths rather than try to compete in areas where they knew that they were weak. In this regard, the ERC's grass-roots network proved to be its greatest strength, and was almost certainly a decisive factor in the final outcome. Its biggest advantage was its strong group of people committed to MMP, a group that had been built up over a period of seven years through the networking process. Even with the best will in the world, the CBG had little chance of overcoming this in the short time available to it.

In each case the lobby groups' campaigns centred around strong-willed individuals, albeit with contrasting personalities and roles. Despite many assertions to the contrary, Peter Shirtcliffe was deeply and genuinely committed to the campaign he began and for which he was the principal spokesperson. Despite his claim that he was 'not a political animal' there can be no doubt that he strongly believed in the importance of localism in politics, and that MMP would destroy the link between constituent and MP that was a central element of FPP. His personal contribution, both financial and in personal time devoted to the CBG campaign, stamps him as a man of integrity.

Undoubtedly, however, Phil Saxby was *the* key figure. He was deeply involved in the campaign for electoral reform well before the Royal Commission presented its report, and he played a key role both in the formation of the Electoral Reform Coalition and throughout its long public campaign for electoral reform.[55] His commitment to the cause of electoral reform, which dates from the 1970s, appears to have stemmed from his belief that electoral reform provided the opportunity and the means of creating a better and more focused Labour Party (Saxby, 1996). Brian Nicolle, later to become a linchpin of the Campaign for Better Government organisation, and who was acquainted with Saxby through their Labour Party memberships, substantially confirms Saxby's own perception of his motives. Nicolle asserts that Saxby was a supporter of Rogernomics but that he did not believe that the Labour Party could be reformed from within because its membership was far too broad and the 'card vote' was a severe impediment to change. His solution was, therefore, to promote the adoption of a new electoral system that would encourage *all* political parties to change the way they operated. Saxby was, he said, "a very tenacious fellow" (Nicolle, 1996), a view supported by Donald (1996). John Terris, MP for Western Hutt at the time, described Saxby as "a wonderful electorate worker who did not let his commitment to proportional representation interfere with his work for the Labour Party". Saxby, he said, virtually ran the Electoral Reform Coalition: he "was the ERC; he guided the organisation from conception to final execution" (Terris, 1996). His single-mindedness of purpose, however, caused some embarrassment at times; David Lange was openly critical of him and this led Terris to distance himself from the ERC to some degree (ibid.).[56] According to Richard Northey (1996), the strength and effectiveness of the ERC lay in Saxby's persistence, but this handicapped its relationship with the Labour Party caucus: Saxby's personal style — repeatedly bombarding caucus members with fairly technical papers — frequently turned people away from him and his cause.[57] When coupled with his open identification with the Labour right (most of whom tended to support FPP) this made him an isolated figure within Labour Party politics. Even his colleagues within the ERC, although admiring his sheer tenacity and terrier-like qualities, acknowledged that he accentuated divisions within the Labour Party (Donald, 1996). Nevertheless, as Manning commented, "Saxby was always the driver; he was the one who picked up the [Royal Commission's] report and ran with it" (Manning, 1996). The advocates of electoral reform owe him a tremendous debt.

Both the Royal Commission's report and the Electoral Reform Coalition's dogged campaign were essential to the ultimate adoption of the MMP electoral system by the New Zealand electorate. Without the ERC's tenacious advocacy of the case for electoral reform in general and the MMP electoral system proposed by the Royal Commission in particular, the report might well have been left to gather dust on the shelves of academic libraries or have, at best, led to the reluctant adoption of a Supplementary Member electoral system. Without the Royal Commission's report, however, the activities of the ERC would have lacked both focus and authority. The Royal Commission provided the framework on which a campaign for electoral reform could be built; the Electoral Reform Coalition kept the issue before the public at a time when politicians were intent on defusing the report's recommendations. And, when the major parties both conceded the ultimate decision to the electorate, the Electoral Reform Coalition was crucially placed to spearhead the public debate for reform.

Notes

1   According to Antony Jay (ed.), in *The Oxford Dictionary of Political Quotations*, Oxford, OUP, 1996, what Lowe actually said was much less memorable. Speaking in the House of Commons on the passing of the *Reform Act 1867* he said: "I believe it will be absolutely necessary that you should prevail upon our future masters to learn their letters." Jay notes that this has been popularised in the form quoted here.

2   It should be noted, however, that in the broader constitutional arena, New Zealand assumed ownership of its constitution in 1947 (the *New Zealand Constitution Amendment [Request and Consent] Act 1947*, and the *New Zealand Constitution [Amendment] Act 1947*, passed by the United Kingdom parliament), and the Legislative Council was abolished with effect from the beginning of 1951.

3   Of the 22 seats won by candidates other than Labour and National, 12 were won in the three elections between 1935 and 1943.

4   Social Credit also promised to give electors the right to recall their MP if they were dissatisfied with his or her performance.

5   Social Credit changed its name to the Democratic Party in 1985.

6   In 1983 Social Credit MP, Garry Knapp, unsuccessfully sought leave to introduce a Popular Initiatives Bill into parliament. This bill provided for a referendum to be held within 100 days (or 150 days if a general election was to be held within this period) where a petition signed by more than 100,000 electors was presented to parliament and met the requirements of the bill (*NZPD*, 455: 4746–57).

7   It should be noted that NewLabour's founder, Jim Anderton, was a strong supporter of First-past-the-post while a member of the Labour Party.

8   Personal comment to one of the authors at the National Party's annual conference, Wellington, September 1987.

9   Wall's bill was closely modelled on the *Second Ballot Act 1908*.

10   Labour Electoral Reform Network, affiliated to the Wellington Labour Regional Council.

11   McGrath of the Nelson Electoral Reform Association had already tried, without success, to start a nationwide electoral reform organisation.

12   In addition to the coalition's 26 branches, there were contacts in Kaitaia, Orewa, Katikati, Dannevirke, Taihape, Parnassus, Rangiora, Geraldine, Queenstown, Blackball, and, though not listed, Foxton and Fox Glacier (ERC, 1993f).

13   Interestingly, the objective of advocating the use of the single transferable vote for elections to professional organisations, trade unions, school boards and local government was deleted because it was seen as likely to confuse.

14   According to Saxby, Democratic Party leader, Garry Knapp, played an important role in convincing some Democratic members present to support the decisions reached.

15   The letter was signed by senior representatives of ERC, WEL, CTU, NZ Democratic Party, The Greens (Green Party of Aotearoa), NewLabour, Social Credit NZ, Christian Heritage Party, Socialist Unity Party, Mana Motuhake Party, and Steve Maharey (MP for Palmerston North).

16   The Alliance, formed in 1991, was a grouping of five smaller parties — NewLabour, Greens, Democrats, Mana Motuhake and Liberal — all of whom supported the adoption of MMP.

17   Manning claimed that ERC had tried to stop the formation of the CPR because it did not like the idea of him "... operating on a semi-independent basis". When he ended his term as chairperson of ERC in late 1991, he set out to build the CPR organisation. A meeting he arranged at parliament for this purpose was attended by MPs Michael Laws,

Steve Maharey and Winston Peters, and a travelling roadshow was planned for 1992 but not held. He also stated that there were people who acknowledged the existence of CPR, linked up with it, and got on with the job of publicising the case for electoral reform outside of the ERC. This may well have been the case but there is no doubt that its role was very much subsidiary to that played by the ERC in 1992. Donald disputes Manning's interpretation of this last point. According to him, activists came primarily from the ERC, Alliance, and a small number of Labour Party stalwarts.

18 This submission relates to the Electoral Poll Bill then before the Electoral Law Select Committee.

19 Leading activists cited by Donald included Lowell Manning (Democratic Party), Marilyn Tucker (General Secretary, Socialist Unity Party), Louise Ryan (Federation of University Women and WEL), David Munro (secretary of the Northern Distribution Workers' Union), Helena Catt (University of Auckland politics lecturer), and Kevin Hackwell and Nicky Hager (Just Defence). According to Donald, the link to the Northern Drivers Union and the Socialist Unity Party connection to Ken Douglas helped pull the union movement back on board and put additional internal pressure on the Labour Party.

20 The report noted that Grey Power "has retreated from its previous support".

21 Throughout 1993, the *Listener* consistently supported the adoption of MMP. The factual basis of at least one of its articles was questioned when it claimed (9 October 1993) that "[v]oters have nothing to lose by having a fling with MMP this year. If MMP wins the referendum, voters can sample it in the 1996 and 1999 elections, then in 2002 they will get the chance to return to FPP if they wish". The 1993 *Electoral Act*, however, makes no mandatory provision for a referendum in the year 2002, or any other year for that matter.

22 This report was authored by Jonathan Boston, public policy lecturer at Victoria University, and Richard Randerson, Anglican Church Social Responsibility Commissioner.

23 With revisions, this leaflet lasted throughout the seven-year campaign (see ERC, 1993a).

24 Slogans included: 'Make your Vote Count' and 'MMP: a Fair Voting System'.

25 Saxby claims that the only setback ERC experienced at Labour Party conferences was when Jim Anderton attacked the concept of electoral reform.

26 The committee had recommended that the FPP system should be retained and that an indicative referendum be held to determine whether any increase in the number of MPs should be achieved through an extension of simple plurality or by a Supplementary Member system (AJHR, 1988:21).

27 Temple also wrote two booklets — *Making Your Vote Count* (Dunedin, John McIndoe, 1992) and *Making Your Vote Count Twice* (Dunedin, John McIndoe, 1993) — setting out the case for electoral reform in general and MMP in particular.

28 Organised by the Auckland branch of the ERC, this survey asked three questions: (1) Do you know that the Royal Commission unanimously recommended MMP as the best electoral system for New Zealand? (2) Do you think we could achieve better government through the present system? and (3) Do you have any concerns about MMP?

29 Saxby had proposed that ERC endeavour to develop lists of supporters under various sub-banners — business, teachers, farmers, students, lawyers, Christians, nurses, sportspeople, doctors, artists, retailers, and even National and Labour for MMP — but this met with only limited success.

30 ERC also benefited from help from what Saxby described as "friendly MPs" who made phone calls and assisted with mailouts. In 1992 the Public Service Association provided ERC with rent-free accommodation.

31 Both Saxby and Donald indicated that the largest donation was $5,000 but most were

	less than $100. Most donations came from targeted mailouts.
32	The television advertisements were put together hurriedly and fronted by two New Zealand television personalities, Annie Whittle and Ginette McDonald. Production was undertaken on a largely voluntary basis.
33	Government MPs branded this allegation "an outrageous lie" (see *NZH*, 26 July 1993).
34	This date (Anzac Day) is the day that New Zealand remembers those who served in past wars. Nationalism and patriotism are very much to the fore on this day each year.
35	Clark was correct. The newly adopted Italian electoral system was more akin to a Supplementary Member system (see *Press*, 27 April 1993 and *Dom.*, 27 April 1993).
36	Shirtcliffe's initial interest in different forms of electoral systems appears to have been aroused through his daughter's involvement in an inter-school debate some years previously. While he claimed to be not opposed to proportional representation *per se*, this early experience convinced him that New Zealand should avoid adopting the MMP electoral system because it was the wrong form of PR (see *Dom.*, 22 May 1993).
37	Both Nicolle and Tate had been members of the Labour Backbone Club (a right-wing group dedicated to supporting and promoting the reforms instituted by Roger Douglas between 1984 and 1988), but the club was dissolved before the CBG was founded. After the 1993 election and referendum, they became paid officials with the Act Party.
38	Jennings and Shirtcliffe had worked closely together on the Trade Development Board some years previously. According to Jennings (1996), during this period Shirtcliffe had prepared a plan that was subsequently ignored by the government, and he was left without any government and business community support. Jennings believes that Shirtcliffe carried some scars from this 'failure', but the more he reflected on the incident, the more he realised just how isolated Shirtcliffe had been and that this, in turn, had made it difficult for him to solicit support from the business community for the CBG campaign. Only when the business community itself realised that this was a campaign that they should be involved in, did support eventuate — but this was only three to four weeks before the referendum.
39	David Schnauer had been a National Party candidate in 1984 and 1987, and Dunleavy had been a National Party candidate in 1969. In 1996 Jennings and Patricia Schnauer entered parliament as Act Party list MPs.
40	According to Tate, Lange was not prepared to be associated with the CBG campaign because of his personal antipathy towards Nicolle.
41	In his advertisement, Shirtcliffe had claimed that Italy had recently overwhelmingly rejected MMP in favour of FPP.
42	When asked whether he thought his advertisement had contributed to the decline in support for MMP, Shirtcliffe responded: "People are starting to think about it more carefully."
43	The *New Zealand Herald*, 14 September 1993, reported that the CBG had paid for an hour of radio talkback on Radio Pacific — at a rate-card cost of $6,000 — to promote its opposition to MMP.
44	The group's membership was finally announced on 26 August. Along with Jennings, it included George Balani (a radio talkback host), Judith Bassett (historian), Pat Lynch (chair of the Independent Schools principals' group), Eru Pomare (Dean of the Wellington Medical School), former MPs Richard Harrison and Brian Talboys, Hilary Bennett, and Associate Professor G.A. Wood of the University of Otago.
45	The CBG welcomed the select committee's report on the Citizens' Initiated Referenda Bill as "a clear sign that Parliament can reform itself without having to throw out the current system of voting" (CBG, 1993l).
46	*The Dominion* (Wellington), 1 September 1993 reported Jennings as saying that the CBG vowed to make Jim Bolger change his mind on the need to reform parliament,

and that it was determined to get politicians to agree to improve the workings of the existing system. Bolger responded by saying that there would be no big changes if FPP was retained; the Leader of the Opposition, Mike Moore, said that Labour would introduce some changes.

47   Not everyone agreed with the CBG's proposals. David McGee (Clerk of the House of Representatives) indicated that, in his view, significant change was mostly a question of political will rather than the technical adjustments proposed (*Dom.*, 3 August 1993). Senior Labour MP, David Caygill, was even more caustic: reform was not an alternative to electoral reform; the proposed reforms to parliament's operating procedures amounted "almost to a diversion"; some suggestions "look distinctly recycled" while others were "charming on the face of it" but at the end of the day the government would retain its majority in the House (*Press*, 24 August 1993).

48   Towards the end of June Shirtcliffe announced that he proposed direct mailing an appeal for financial support "to businesses, organisations and individuals". The campaign's goal aimed at achieving a financial return of "well into six figures"(*Dom.*, 21 June 1993).

49   Myles had been elected as a National MP in the 1990 election but left to help form the Liberal Party in August 1991. Subsequently the Liberal Party became part of the Alliance.

50   For example, in September the CBG alleged that a member of ERC tried to infiltrate a private CBG function. In turn the ERC alleged that its offices had been broken into and computers removed (*Dom.*, 13 September 1993; *Listener*, 11 December 1993).

51   This Act set the maximum amount that could be spent on promoting a CIR issue at $50,000 for each individual or group promoting a point of view. This is in addition to the initiators of the referendum issue who could spend up to $50,000 in gathering support for the petition seeking the referendum.

52   These amounts are based on the standard rate-card for advertising and do not take account of possible deals and special discounts that may have been allowed. Figures calculated for the author by Philip O'Neill of Ogilvy & Mather Ltd. A similar expenditure ratio was arrived at by the *New Zealand Listener* for the September to November period (*Listener*, 11 December 1993). According to the advertising industry large advertisers could expect to receive discounts of between 25 and 30 per cent although the rate struck was likely to be closer to the standard rate where time was purchased at short notice.

53   The 'bags on heads' comment refers to a CBG television and print media advertisement depicting 21 faceless MPs — a reference to the proposed increased number of MPs under MMP and the fact that a large portion of MPs would be selected from lists prepared by parties, not the voters.

54   Donald (1996) agrees with this. He said that ERC believed that it had seen off the opposition forces after the 1992 referendum. Palmer, he said, kept telling ERC that a new organisation supporting the status quo would emerge but ERC leaders did not believe him.

55   Apart from a short period in 1991–92, Saxby was the ERC secretary from 1987 until 1996.

56   During the interview Terris said that he had always had strong sympathy with supporters of proportional representation and that these were strengthened when Saxby joined his Western Hutt electorate organisation.

57   Palmer wrote that "... Saxby tended to have turned a number of caucus members off by over-zealous lobbying" (Palmer, 1997). Saxby, himself, concedes that, to some extent, his persistence may have been counter-productive (Saxby, 1997).

8   The Maori Dimension

> [P]eople who are consistently under-represented may feel alienated and thus reject
> institutions that do not allow for the accommodation of their identity.
> — Canadian Royal Commission on Electoral Reform and Party Financing,
> *Reforming Electoral Democracy*, Final Report 1991, vol. 1, p. 93.

Because single-member, First-past-the-post, electoral systems award seats to
the candidates winning more votes than any other candidate (regardless of
their share of the total votes cast) they usually fail to provide legislative
representation for minority groups unless their numbers are sufficiently
concentrated geographically as, for example, in the French Canadian province
of Quebec. Where a country is overwhelmingly mono-cultural in its outlook
and perspective, this normally does not present any problem, but where a
significant minority exists, regardless of whether that minority is based on
race, ethnicity, religion, language, culture, or other criterion, the possibilities
of alienation from the society in which it is found, are greatly increased.

Some states include special provisions in their electoral rules to ensure
guaranteed representation for ethnic minorities; Lijphart points to Belgium,
Cyprus, Lebanon, Zimbabwe, and New Zealand as examples of states which
provide guaranteed representation for significant minorities living within their
borders (Grofman & Lijphart, 1986:113; see also, IDEA, 1997:98–100). Such
arrangements can also be applied at a sub-national level: the Danish-speaking
minority in the German *Land* of Schleswig-Holstein (ibid.) and, in the United
States, the provision made by the state of Maine which has guaranteed
representation to each of its two main Indian communities in the state legislature
since 1820 (CRC, 1991, 1:173), are two such examples.

Where a minority is a significant element of the population in one part of
a country, territorial representation may be adjusted to ensure that it receives a
share of seats in the legislature. The United States, where territorial and
geographic integrity has been largely abandoned in favour of numerical
considerations, is a good example. Where, however, this is not the case, the
quest for fairness suggests that other measures may need to be taken to ensure
that numerically important ethnic, racial, or other similarly identified groups
are not excluded from the political process. Grofman and Lijphart (1986:7)
have labelled the process of allocating seats to groups who would otherwise
tend to be severely under-represented or excluded from legislatures as
'enhanced representation'. The core problem, of course, centres around the

reconciliation of communal sentiment with majority rule (Mackenzie, 1958:35).

Today, the ideal of fair representation is one where significant political parties win a share of the seats in the legislature close to their overall share of votes won in the election. This goal does not, however, fit well with electoral systems based on single-member geographic districts. A system of representation which encompasses special criteria guaranteeing a voice for significant minority groups has, therefore, to be generally based on non-territorial considerations, that is, grouping populations on the basis of characteristics other than geographic territory. According to Derfner,

> [T]he crucial issue (of ethnic minority representation) is not simply that race is an important factor but that it is deemed more important than some other factors such as geography, test scores or seniority. (Grofman *et.al.*, 1982:67.)

If this is accepted, the underlying problem becomes one of identifying the community to be targeted — not always an easy task — and of designing an electoral system that is fair to electors belonging to the group which shares the distinguishing characteristics that have been identified and agreed upon.

The easiest and most direct way of achieving assured representation for ethnic minorities is to establish separate electorates for such groups. If such a course is followed there are two problems that need to be resolved: which ethnic group or groups should be recognised for separate representation, and on what basis should individuals be assigned to the electoral districts created for this purpose? (Grofman & Lijphart, 1986:117.)

History of Maori Parliamentary Representation

For nearly 130 years a distinctive characteristic of New Zealand's electoral system has been the provision of special electoral districts based on ethnic criteria and with separate electoral rolls. Described by Lijphart as "a simple and straightforward device"(ibid.), it has provided the country's indigenous Maori people with guaranteed representation in New Zealand's legislature. Nevertheless, separate Maori representation was not introduced as a consequence of any lofty or carefully considered principle: as one historian has noted, it "stumbled into being" (Ward, 1973:209) as a temporary measure pending the individualisation of native land titles which, when completed, would enable Maori to register as electors under the provisions of the then existing property qualification that all other electors were required to meet.[1]

The four Maori electorates were first established in 1867 and their number remained unchanged until the first MMP election in 1996. When the seats were first introduced, Maori were greatly under-represented on a population basis: in 1874, for example, they comprised approximately 13 per cent of the country's total population but elected only 4.5 per cent of Members of the House of Representatives. But with the steady decline in Maori population numbers during the remainder of the nineteenth century, coupled with a sharp reduction (from 91 to 70) in the number of European[2] seats in 1890, the four Maori seats gradually came to provide Maori with representation in reasonable proportion to their population numbers.[3] This remained the case until the early 1950s when the Maori population began increasing at a significantly faster rate than the non-Maori population.

From time to time Maori MPs argued that the number of Maori seats should be increased to a level that they believed was more closely proportionate to their peoples' share of the total population. In 1876, for example, H.K. Taiaroa, the Member for Southern Maori, introduced a bill in which he proposed that the number of Maori seats be increased to seven. In the same year, a petition containing nearly 400 signatures, and asking that the Maori parliamentary representation should be proportionate to its share of the total population, was presented to parliament. Six decades later Ratana MPs were advocating increasing the number of Maori seats to six to compensate for the growth in Maori population, and since the 1950s increasingly strident demands that Maori parliamentary representation be retained and expanded to reflect the increase in Maori population have been heard from Maori MPs and others (RCES, 1986a:B43–57). The response of successive governments was one of benign neglect.

In 1893 the separation of Maori and non-Maori parliamentary representation was reinforced by a provision requiring persons who were of more than one-half Maori descent to register in one of the four Maori electorates, while persons of less than one-half Maori descent were required to register and vote only in a European electorate. The separation of the two electoral systems was completed three years later when residence was made the sole determinant for registration as an elector. Henceforth all persons with more than one-half Maori ancestry could register and vote only in one of the four Maori electorates and all Maori with less than one-half Maori ancestry could register and vote only in a European electorate. Only those who were exactly one-half Maori and one-half non-Maori were eligible to choose on which of the two rolls — Maori or European — they would register.

In 1957 E.H. Corbett, then Minister of Maori Affairs, advised the First National Government's Minister of Justice (J.R. Marshall) that he believed that consideration should be given to allowing those Maori currently required to register on the Maori roll to register on the European roll if they so wished (quoted ibid., 1986a:B:47). National Party policy, reinforced by the recommendations of the 1960 Hunn Report (*AJHR*, 1961), was to adopt strategies designed to assimilate the two races. In 1965, during the debate on the *Electoral Amendment Act*, the Prime Minister, K.J. Holyoake, responded to E.T. Tirikatene's plea to increase the number of Maori seats by indicating "that the next step in Maori representation should be complete integration ..." (*NZPD*, 344:2708). Two years later the government amended the 1956 *Electoral Act* to permit Maori (that is, those of more than one-half Maori descent) to stand for election in European electorates, and in 1975 two National Party candidates of Maori descent were elected to represent General electorates.

Meanwhile, increasingly sensitive to its Maori constituency, the Labour Party had adopted Corbett's position (NZLP, 1966), and following its accession to the treasury benches in 1972, it instituted a comprehensive review of the *Electoral Act 1956*. During an intensive study by parliament's Electoral Act Select Committee the provisions for Maori representation came in for special attention and were the subject of much partisan debate. Although a number of public submissions advocated the immediate abolition of separate representation, none of those received from individual Maori or Maori organisations supported this position; on the contrary, the committee concluded that the number of Maori seats should be determined on the basis of total population in the same way as non-Maori seats. On the committee's recommendation the definition of 'Maori' included in the 1956 *Electoral Act*[4] was widened to include any descendent of the Maori race "who elects to be considered as a Maori for the purposes of this Act". Thus, for the first time Maori were able to choose on which electoral roll, Maori or General, they wished to register (*AJHR*, 1975:12–14). The committee (or, at least, its Labour majority) further recommended that future electoral redistributions should include the revision of the boundaries of Maori electoral districts and that these should be established using the same formula applying to the non-Maori seats. If implemented, the number of Maori seats would rise, fall, or remain static according to the number or Maori choosing the Maori roll. The committee's recommendations were adopted by parliament in 1975 and intended to apply to the redistribution following the 1976 quinquennial census.

Although heavily outvoted in the House of Representatives, the National Party continued to oppose most of these changes despite clear evidence that Maori society — whose numbers were increasing rapidly and many of whose members were exhibiting a renewed pride in *tikanga Maori* (Maori custom) — was becoming much more assertive and demanding in its determination to be acknowledged as a central player in all aspects of New Zealand society.

Following its victory in the 1975 general election, National repealed the provision which provided for the number of Maori parliamentary seats to be determined by the number of Maori (including a proportion of their children) opting to be included on the Maori roll. National's position, as expressed by its Minister of Maori Affairs, Duncan MacIntyre, was the traditional view that " ... the four Maori seats ... provide an essential Maori presence in Parliament. ...when the Maori people signify they no longer desire separate representation there should be a single electoral roll" (*NZPD*, 406:2852).

Nevertheless, the National government did not repeal the Maori electoral option provision, the first of which was held in conjunction with the 1976 census just three months after the 1975 election. Since then the Maori option has been conducted shortly after each five-yearly population census.

Between the mid-1970s and the mid-1980s both National and Labour held to their respective positions. The Maori option, a largely meaningless exercise since it served no other purpose than determining the size of the non-Maori general electoral population (and, as a consequence, the number of General electorates allocated to the North Island), continued to be held. Thus, although the number of General electorates rose from 83 in 1975 to 93 in 1987, the number of Maori electorates remained static.

The Royal Commission's Perspective

Among the Royal Commission's many terms of reference was a specific requirement for it to investigate "the nature and basis of Maori representation in Parliament" (RCES, 1986a:xiii[5]). This armed it with authority to undertake a wide-ranging examination of the separate Maori electoral system that had provided Maori with guaranteed representation in the New Zealand parliament for nearly 120 years.

The commissioners clearly recognised that this was an extremely sensitive matter, one that needed to be worked through very thoroughly if they hoped to reach conclusions and make recommendations that would achieve broad acceptability. As the Commission noted in its report, it made "a particular effort" to obtain the views of Maori, and those who made submissions were encouraged to do so in a way that reflected Maori custom. At a very preliminary stage in its work — even before the Commission's support staff had been appointed — it decided that all members who were able to do so should attend a hui at Ngaruawahia (headquarters of the Maori King Movement), "with a view to familiarising themselves with electoral issues currently being discussed by Maori people" (RCES 1986b:23 April 1985). Some months later, when public submissions were being heard, five hui were organised with the support and assistance of the New Zealand Maori Council, to allow Maori to present their views in a familiar and non-threatening atmosphere. In all, more than forty Maori individuals and groups responded to the invitation to make submissions, and all but six, who presented their submissions in person, did so in a *marae* (place of assembly) setting. In addition, the Commission noted that a number of Maori groups and individuals attended some of the Commission's ordinary hearings (RCES, 1986a:84–85). Maori who had long been agitating for significantly greater Maori parliamentary representation were given adequate opportunity to be heard.

At 12.5 per cent of the total population (Statistics, 1990:182), Maori were a highly visible minority. As tangata whenua whose forebears had entered into a treaty relationship with the British Crown, they occupied a special constitutional position. Since 1867 Maori had been guaranteed four seats in the legislature. A developing Maori renaissance had resulted in increasing demands that they be recognised as having a separate identity, and a unique cultural heritage which should be more fully acknowledged within the country's political and social framework. Yet, with only four out of parliament's 95 seats guaranteed to them, and with little evidence that either major party was prepared to select candidates of Maori descent for safe General seats, it was clear that Maori were substantially under-represented in the political arena. As the Commission noted in its report, its examination of the issues surrounding Maori representation required it "to confront some of the most complex and difficult issues of democratic politics" (RCES, 1986a:81).

After examining New Zealand's First-past-the-post electoral system against ten selected criteria (ibid., 11–12), the Commission concluded that the system of separate seats was "seriously deficient in providing for the effective representation of the Maori people" (ibid., 19). While it acknowledged that the separate seats provided guaranteed representation for Maori and helped ensure that their political interests were heard, they also created electoral and political separation which could not be satisfactorily overcome by addressing the difficulties arising from the fixed number, and unwieldy size, of Maori electorates (ibid., 89–97). In its view, the disadvantages of separate, though guaranteed, representation far outweighed their perceived benefits: "Maori seats under plurality have not given the Maori people a fair share of effective political power and influence. They have become a political backwater" (ibid., 98).

The Royal Commission identified five principles which, it believed, were:

... the conditions under which an important minority might reasonably expect to enjoy a just and equitable share of political power and influence in a decision-making system which is subject to the majority principle and over which the political parties hold sway: ...

(a) Maori interests should be represented in Parliament by Maori MPs;

(b) Maori electors ought to have an effective vote competed for by all political parties;

(b) All MPs should be accountable in some degree to Maori electors;

(c) Maori MPs ought to be democratically accountable to Maori electors; and

(d) Candidate selection procedures ... should be organised in such a way as to permit the Maori people a voice in the decision of who the candidates are to be. (ibid., 87–88.)

Application of these principles led it to conclude that a major test of any electoral system "... must be its capacity to provide for the effective representation of Maori interests on the basis of (these) principles" (ibid., 97). As a result, it recommended that "(t)he Mixed Member Proportional system should be adopted as the best means of providing effective Maori representation" (ibid., 106). While acknowledging that its proposed MMP electoral system could not provide guaranteed Maori representation, the Commission was satisfied that the number of MPs of Maori descent would rise substantially from existing levels, and that they would represent several political parties (ibid., 102). The key to this conclusion lies in the Commission's decision to recommend the establishment of a common electoral roll. Clearly, it believed that the existing electoral system with its separate rolls seriously inhibited the effective representation of Maori interests and concerns.

In proposing the adoption of an electoral system which had "no separate Maori seats, no Maori roll and no periodic Maori option" (ibid., 43–44,101), the Royal Commission was very well aware that its main recommendation flew in the face of the overwhelming weight of Maori opinion. It was convinced, however, that MMP would provide more effective representation for Maori than simple plurality. Members were unanimous in their view that Maori candidates would have a better chance of being elected through the national party lists — an integral part of their MMP proposal — if there were a single roll. Significant parties, they contended, would soon realise the advantages of including candidates of Maori descent high on their lists (ibid., 51), while the proposed common roll would increase the effectiveness of votes cast by Maori because all MPs would be in some way accountable to Maori electors (ibid., 98).

Another recommendation intended to enhance the prospect of Maori parliamentary representation was the Commission's proposal to waive its recommended threshold for parties representing primarily Maori interests. Here, its objective was two-fold: it wanted to encourage all parties to take Maori concerns seriously, and to increase the chances of electoral success for any Maori groups dissatisfied with the performance of existing parties and who wished to form their own party (ibid., 101). Although the Commission made no attempt to define the term 'Maori party', its members believed that it would be possible to establish criteria that would enable a Maori party to be identified. There is no evidence to indicate that it gave any serious consideration to the possibility of retaining separate Maori representation within its proposed MMP electoral system.

Nevertheless, the Commission was conscious that its MMP proposal might not find sufficient support among politicians and the electorate at large for it to be adopted. It therefore also addressed the question of what should happen to the provisions for Maori representation if FPP were retained. It concluded that if this eventuated, and no agreement could be reached with Maori on an alternative representational structure, the number of Maori electorates should be calculated using the same formula that determined the number of General electorates. Maori should continue to be given the choice of which electoral roll — Maori or General — they wished to be registered on, and the Maori electoral population, thus determined, should provide the basis for calculating the number of electorates to which Maori would be entitled. The adoption of this position would, of itself, go some way towards addressing the issue of the rapidly growing Maori-descent population being increasingly under-represented in parliament on a population basis. But, despite including this alternative in its report, the Commission emphasised that, in its view,

> ...this is a poor solution in that, notwithstanding the move from a fixed number of Maori seats, it perpetuates the electoral system which we regard as a particularly unsatisfactory form of Maori representation. (ibid., 107.)

The Royal Commission had proposed a radical solution to what was undoubtedly a highly complex and sensitive issue. In this regard the influence of the Commission's Maori member, Whetumarama Wereta, cannot be underestimated: in its report the Commission noted that her views "carried particular weight" (ibid., 81). While, personally, she believed that proportional representation would significantly increase Maori participation in politics, until the Commission accepted the concept of PR she was opposed to the abolition of separate Maori representation, although she admits that she did not hear any compelling arguments in favour of its retention. Her primary objective was to establish an electoral system that would encourage all political parties to accept that they had a responsibility for and commitment to issues that were of concern to Maori. Initially attracted to STV, she accepted MMP only after lengthy study and debate because she concluded that it would provide Maori with enhanced opportunities for participation and influence in politics through their greater involvement with a range of political parties. Although Wereta realised that many Maori were likely to be highly critical of her decision to agree to the abolition of the separate Maori seats, she believed that "if Maori wanted to retain separate seats they would have to argue for them" (Wereta, 1997).

The Royal Commission's study of the future shape of Maori parliamentary representation was the first comprehensive review of this aspect of New Zealand's electoral system in 120 years. By wrestling with an issue that had hitherto largely been avoided, it provided an essential baseline for the debate which followed. The big question still to be resolved, though, was how the politicians and the electorate would respond to its recommendations.

The Politicians' Response

Although neither the Labour Government nor the National Opposition welcomed the recommendations contained in the Royal Commission's report, it was inevitable that the question of Maori representation would again loom large when the report was referred to the Electoral Law Select Committee after the 1987 election. From the outset both parties maintained their long-standing and, as it transpired, inflexible positions. Labour remained committed to the retention of separate Maori representation with the number of Maori electorates determined periodically by the numbers of Maori (along with a proportion of Maori under the age of 18) who chose to be registered on the Maori roll. For its part, National remained equally committed to its policy, first expressly enunciated in 1975, that the number of Maori electorates should remain at four until Maori themselves signified that they no longer wanted separate representation, at which time the seats would be abolished.

Soon after it was appointed, the select committee met with members of the Royal Commission. Wallace reiterated the Commission's view that MMP would provide more effective representation for Maori because it "would give Maori a vote that counts". Separate representation, he believed, would be "ultimately divisive", and although he acknowledged that strong opposition to the abolition of the Maori seats existed — even if some form of proportional representation were adopted — he argued that the MMP electoral system proposed by the Commission would protect minority rights in a way that was not possible under New Zealand's existing electoral system.

In response to a question Wereta told the committee that proportional representation would result in a greater number of Maori being elected to parliament because "(t)he need to compete for the Maori vote will lead to a change in the parties", When Northey asked her what guarantee there was that MMP would result in more Maori MPs, she replied:

> Integrating Maori MPs into the system is very difficult. ... Effective political representation of minorities [and] indigenous groups is an outstanding matter, and in Europe proportional representation has been used as the means of dealing with communal differences. (ELSC, 1988d.)

In an interesting, if curious development, Wallace publicly indicated for the first time, that he was not totally wedded to the Commission's recommendation that separate Maori representation should be abolished. Although, in his view, MMP "would be highly likely" to give Maori more effective representation, he told the committee that "(i)f it is considered desirable, it is possible to maintain Maori seats in addition to the MMP system without upsetting the one-person, one-vote principle" (ibid.). Clearly, he had reached the conclusion that separate Maori constituency representation could be retained without detrimentally affecting the broad principle underpinning MMP, so long as a common roll existed and the overall composition of MMP parliaments was determined by the party vote.

As we have already seen the select committee was totally opposed to the MMP electoral system as proposed by the Royal Commission and, predictably, it unanimously recommended that the current FPP electoral system should be retained. When it came to consider the future of separate Maori representation, however, a deep gulf emerged between the committee's Labour and National members. In a background paper prepared by officials, the committee was told that while MMP could provide both the opportunity and incentive for increased Maori participation in the political system, as proposed by the Royal Commission it could not guarantee that MPs "with a special mandate to represent Maori interests" would be elected. The paper also noted that Maori opinion remained strongly in favour of retaining separate Maori seats, that if a new electoral system incorporated more constituency seats and fewer list seats it would be possible to retain separate Maori electorates — "either permanently or for an interim period until the Maori people could judge whether retention of separate Maori seats was desirable" — and suggested that if some form of list PR was decided upon, it could include a requirement that each party's nationwide list "give certain priority places to Maori candidates possibly selected by Maori members of those political parties" (ibid., 1988f).

Labour's Electoral Law caucus committee debated the matter at some length before recommending that separate Maori seats should be retained, that there should always be at least four seats guaranteed by law, and that the actual number should be determined by the number of Maori opting to be registered on the Maori roll, a position reached only after discussions had been held with the party's four Maori MPs (Palmer, H.100:17 July 1988 & 6 September 1988). Although this was largely a reiteration of the position adopted by the party since the early 1970s, there was one important difference. When Labour instituted the Maori electoral option in 1975, it accepted that the number of separate Maori seats could rise, fall, or remain static depending on the number of Maori opting to be included on the Maori roll; 13 years on, it proposed modifying this principle to prevent the number of Maori electorates falling below four.

For its part, National confirmed its previous position that the number of Maori seats should remain fixed at four until such time as Maori themselves decided, through their exercise of the Maori option, that they were no longer necessary. Doug Graham, the leading National member of the select committee, stated that he did not believe that separate Maori representation had served Maori well (ELSC, 1988c), and that prolonging the system of separate representation was not good for Maori (ibid., 1988b).

It was already clear that MMP, as proposed by the Royal Commission, did not have sufficient support among Labour MPs for it to be accepted as government policy. For his part, Northey was concerned to find an acceptable alternative that could win caucus support. Because he believed that the abolition of separate Maori representation could be seen as an attack on Maoridom, he proposed that the status quo remain until discussions could be held with Maori on the future of separate representation. Northey, who favoured limited reform, pushed for the adoption of a recommendation to introduce a Supplementary Member system (SM) because he believed that it would both assuage the growing demand for reform and permit the continuation of separate and guaranteed Maori representation.

Even before the select committee had reported back, Palmer sought cabinet's endorsement of a proposal to introduce either a modified form of MMP or, alternatively, an SM electoral system, both of which could be structured to incorporate separate Maori representation. He also sought Cabinet's endorsement of Labour's Justice and Electoral Law caucus committee's position that the Maori seats should be retained and their number determined by the proportion of Maori opting to be included on the Maori roll.

Both parties' overt opposition to any form of proportional representation system made it inevitable that the Royal Commission's central recommendation, the adoption of MMP, would be rejected unanimously. But, while members were agreed that MMP would not necessarily enhance Maori representation because it could not guarantee that MPs committed to representing Maori interests would be elected, the committee was sharply divided on the future of separate Maori representation. As a result, five of the report's six recommendations relating to Maori representation were endorsed only by the committee's Labour majority.

Taking on board the virtually unanimous view, expressed in submissions by Maori, that the separate Maori seats were spiritually and historically significant — even though it was arguable that they did not provide Maori with effective representation — the select committee concluded that the time had not yet arrived when separate Maori representation could be abolished. Labour members also concurred with the Commission's view that the constitutional position of Maori under the Treaty of Waitangi should be examined in consultation with Maori before any changes to existing arrangements were made. It recommended that a special select committee "whose composition reflects the partnership of the Treaty of Waitangi" should be established to undertake this task (*AJHR*, 1988:28).

The recommendations proposed by the Labour majority included support for a continuation of separate Maori representation with a statutory minimum of four seats, that the number of Maori electorates should be based on the number of Maori who chose to be included on the Maori electoral roll (plus their children and a proportion of Maori not included on any roll), and that the next electoral roll revision (scheduled for 1990) should ask all applicants to indicate if they were of Maori descent. This Maori descent data would then be able to be used in conjunction with future census data to estimate the Maori electoral population as well as, periodically, to invite registered Maori to confirm or change their choice of roll. The National minority opposed these recommendations, preferring to stick by their party's existing policy position (ibid., 24–29).[6]

Labour, which had dominated the four Maori electorates for more than four decades, was clearly seeking to use the select committee process to rectify what it regarded as an inequitable situation. Although, since 1976, Maori had been able to choose on which of the two electoral rolls they wished to be included, because the number of Maori electorates remained fixed at four the choice had no practical impact on Maori parliamentary representation. The party, or at least those few members who took a continuing interest in matters electoral, saw this review of the Royal Commission's report as providing a vehicle for instituting the change that had been denied when the Third National Government repealed the Third Labour Government's 1975 amendment which would have allowed the number of Maori seats to be calculated on a population basis, thus ensuring that Maori were represented in parliament in proportion to their number opting for the Maori electoral roll.

The government agreed with all recommendations pertaining to Maori representation apart from the proposal to establish a special select committee to inquire into the definition and protection of Maori political and electoral rights. It also foreshadowed the introduction of amending legislation to fix the minimum number of Maori seats at four, provide a new basis for calculating the Maori electoral population, and collect data on Maori descent when the next general electoral registration was held (ibid., 1990a:33–35). In the event, however, no amending legislation to establish four seats as the minimum entitlement for Maori parliamentary representation was ever introduced. This apparent lessening of commitment may be attributed both to the fact that the Labour caucus was deeply divided on the form any electoral reform should take, and that the party's chief constitutional reformer, Geoffrey Palmer, became Prime Minister in August 1989 and, in the cabinet reshuffle that followed, passed the Justice portfolio to Bill Jefferies. A government which was under considerable and increasing pressure from a variety of sources simply did not have the time or energy to devote to an issue, the benefits from which were likely to be small and not take effect, at the earliest, until the 1993 election.

With the defeat of the Labour government at the end of 1990, the future of Maori parliamentary representation returned to the back-burner. The National Party's 1990 election manifesto policy on Maori representation was no more than a reiteration of those put forward in the previous five elections: "...retain the four Maori seats in parliament, abolishing them only on the wishes of the Maori people" (NZNP, 1990). The question of Maori parliamentary representation did not arise again in any significant way until shortly before the September 1992 indicative referendum.

The Maori Perspective

More than once in its report the Royal Commission acknowledged the symbolic significance to Maori of separate representation as providing recognition and acknowledgment of the special status of Maori as indigenous New Zealanders (RCES, 1986a:18), and as "an important concession to, and the principal expression of, their constitutional position under the Treaty of Waitangi" (ibid., 85–86). Shortly after the Commission's terms of reference were announced, and before public submissions were invited, the New Zealand Maori Council convened a hui at Turangawaewae Marae to discuss the future of Maori parliamentary representation.[7]

The resolutions agreed to by those attending the hui, and which formed the basis of the Maori Council's submission to the Royal Commission, made clear the desire of Maori to retain and strengthen the separate representation that had been guaranteed to them since 1867. Outright opposition was voiced to any suggestion that separate Maori representation should be abolished; instead, those present agreed that it must be retained and the number of seats increased pro-rata to match the proportion of Maori in the total population. The hui recommended that all Maori should be registered on the Maori roll and insisted that the right to register should be available at all times, not just during the period set down for the Maori option.[8] The conference expressed its belief that all Maori representation must eventually be based on *iwi-runanga* (tribal council) and called for the establishment of a body comprising equal representation of Maori and non-Maori to examine all legislation passed by parliament prior to royal assent to certify that it was consistent with the Treaty of Waitangi. Finally, those present declared that "Maori representation shall not be reduced without the express approval of the majority of Maori electors" (RCES, 1986c). This letter, and the formal submission presented some months later, makes it very clear that in mid-1985, influential Maori leaders were not prepared to countenance the abolition of guaranteed Maori parliamentary representation: they believed that to surrender what Maori already had would be tantamount to surrendering their inalienable rights granted to them by the Treaty of Waitangi.

Of the 804 public submissions, only about 40 came from Maori, either as individuals or reflecting the collective views of groups. Because of the importance of the issue the Commission made strenuous efforts to ensure that Maori viewpoints were presented. In association with the New Zealand Maori Council, five regional hui were arranged to allow Maori to make their submissions — oral or written — in a non-threatening situation. Attendances were not large but the Commission was satisfied that it had listened to, and taken on board, a wide range of Maori opinion.

Even though the Commission freely acknowledged that the abolition of the Maori seats "could arouse strong feeling in the Maori community" (RCES, 1986a:108), it nevertheless proposed an electoral system which, if adopted, would result in their abolition. Why?

First, it is abundantly clear that the Commission was satisfied that MMP, even with the abolition of separate Maori seats, was the most appropriate electoral system for New Zealand.

> ...[W]e are all convinced [the commissioners wrote] that representation in the way we suggest through MMP is clearly the best solution. We believe MMP will produce real gains for Maori people in terms of effective representation. (ibid., 81.)

It believed, also, that under MMP, Maori would be represented in the main through the party lists, and that this would provide a positive inducement to all parties to take account of Maori concerns and to appeal for Maori electoral support across the entire country (ibid.). Second, the Commission appears to have concluded that, at the time Maori prepared their submissions, they had not considered, let alone examined, any alternative system. They were still wedded to the concept of guaranteed and separate representation because it provided Maori with a secure political anchor-point that they were not willing to surrender, and that this had restricted their perception of the broader issues involved. The commissioners appear to have expected that its MMP proposal would widen the debate among Maori, and provide an acceptable alternative solution which would satisfy demands for enhanced political representation.

Throughout its lengthy deliberations the Royal Commission was acutely conscious of the importance of the Treaty of Waitangi, and that its proposal to abolish separate Maori representation was likely to arouse significant controversy. In this context, Wereta's views assume major importance. She came to the Commission convinced that while, at first, separate representation had benefited Maori, "... of late it has not served our people very well". She believed strongly that *all* MPs must accept ownership of Maori issues; Maori MPs, she believed, had struggled for many years, with only limited success, over issues that were central to Maori well-being. The changes that they had been able to achieve

> were concessions made, not on their terms but by the non-Maori majority ... The Maori Affairs committee was dominated by non-Maori MPs who felt little sense of responsibility and commitment to Maori issues. ... The only way to go if you wanted to enhance Maori representation was to go for PR. (Wereta, 1997.)

The corollary to her conclusion that separate representation was disadvantageous to Maori, was that separate representation should not be included in the MMP model proposed by the Commission.

Why, then, did Maori take so long to react and voice their opposition to the MMP model proposed by the Royal Commission? The reasons appear to turn on Maori understandings of the partnership concept enshrined in the Treaty of Waitangi.

When, somewhat belatedly, Maori held a number of hui in the early months of 1993, it quickly became clear that they wanted their separate constituency representation retained even if MMP was endorsed by the electorate in the binding referendum later that year. Despite the Commission's arguments, they remained unconvinced that they would be better represented through the party lists. Since only a few Maori had ever been elected to parliament to represent

General seats, and those who were, were not generally regarded by Maori as the strongest advocates of the Maori perspective, the retention of the separate Maori seats was seen as much more than symbolic (Love, 1996).

In keeping with the electorate at large, few Maori had taken any real interest in the Royal Commission's recommendations when they were first published in December 1986. Lower levels of literacy, particularly where the written word was involved,[9] coupled with a paucity of financial resources and research skills, severely limited Maori society's ability to respond in depth. Further, this was only one of many reports affecting Maori lives, few of which had ever had any impact. By ignoring its mass of detail — a typical Maori response to government reports according to one prominent Maori leader — Maori were, in effect, saying that there were more important things demanding their attention. Largely for these reasons, Maori responses tend to be reactive rather than pro-active. For those who had read and understood the import of the Royal Commission's proposals for changing the nature of Maori representation, recommendation 7, which urged that:

> Parliament and Government should enter into consultation and discussion with a wide range of representatives of the Maori people about the definition and protection of the rights of the Maori people and the recognition of their constitutional position under the Treaty of **Waitangi**, (RCES, 1986a:112.)

seemed to provide an adequate bulwark against precipitate change. To many Maori leaders, this was a clear and unequivocal statement that the government and parliament had to consult fully with Maori and secure their agreement *before* any changes were made to the provisions for Maori parliamentary representation. Thus Maori appear to have been lulled into a sense of false security and inactivity until 1993.[10] Only when it became abundantly clear that the government's draft MMP legislation included the abolition of the separate Maori seats did Maori begin to organise themselves to fight for their retention (Love, 1996).

It is arguable, however, that Maori interpreted the Royal Commission's intentions correctly. The Commission's key recommendation was that its proposed MMP electoral system should be adopted only after extensive public discussion and public approval through a referendum (RCES, 1986a, 64). Since MMP was seen as "the best means of providing effective Maori representation" it can be argued that the Commission regarded its radical proposal for providing fair and equitable representation for New Zealand's indigenous people as an integral part of a total package. By this interpretation, recommendation 4 is in the nature of a caveat designed to prevent any changes to the form of Maori representation prior to a decision being taken on the introduction of MMP. Recommendation 6, which proposed that if MMP were rejected and no agreement was reached with Maori about the future of separate representation, the separate seats should remain and their number determined on the basis of population numbers, adds credence to this interpretation. In reality, recommendation 7, which appears to be regarded by Maori as the key one relating to Maori representation, suggests a mechanism whereby wider Maori constitutional and political interests might be addressed (RCES, 1986a:106–08). It does not appear intended to give Maori a veto over electoral change until these discussions had occurred, although given the climate of opinion in the late 1980s and early 1990s, any government that ignored Maori interests did so at its peril.

Maori Response to the 1993 Electoral Reform Bill

Both Labour and National entered the 1990s with their long-standing policies on Maori parliamentary representation unchanged but, as we saw earlier, National's determination to leave no stone unturned in its quest to win the 1990 election led to it promising a binding referendum on the electoral system (NZNP, 1990). Thus, reforming the electoral system, and with it the future of separate Maori representation, once again became a significant item on the political agenda. Once in office, however, and with the benefit of advice from Department of Justice officials, this policy was modified; instead of moving directly to a binding referendum held sufficiently early in the parliamentary cycle to enable it to implement any necessary changes to the electoral system before the 1993 general election, the government adopted a two-stage process — an indicative referendum towards the end of 1992 and, if a majority of those voting in that referendum supported change, a binding referendum in 1993.

The government refrained from adopting a position on either of the issues put to electors in the 1992 indicative referendum. Although it established an independent panel to oversee a state-funded public education and information programme, the panel was given no guidance as to the possible shape of the four alternative electoral systems included on Part B of the voting paper. Thus, with the government effectively sitting on the sideline, the panel was obliged to develop its own detailed descriptions of each reform option. Its decision that the Royal Commission's report should be regarded as background material only (McRobie, 1993:44) left it free to state that "[t]he Maori seats do not have to be abolished. All four reform options could still include separate Maori seats" (ERP, 1992a,b).

The panel's position did not, however, allay Maori uncertainty surrounding the future of the Maori seats. In mid-August the chair of the New Zealand Maori Council, Graham Latimer, advised voters to support the 'no change' option in Part A unless the government guaranteed the continuation of separate Maori seats (*Press*, 19 August 1992), and two weeks later the Council called on Maori to boycott the referendum because it failed to implement "the Treaty of Waitangi principle of equality between Maori and Pakeha" (*NZH*, 3 September 1992).[11] The same day the New Zealand Maori Congress announced that it had decided that the referendum was "irrelevant to Maori people", and that it would seek the establishment of a Maori House of parliament either as part of the New Zealand parliament or as an independent institution (ibid.).

Graham responded to the boycott clamour, calling it 'misguided' because the electoral system and Maori representation were, in his view, different issues which needed to be dealt with separately (*Press*, 4 September 1992). Nevertheless, he defended the government's decision not to guarantee the future of the four Maori seats under any of the reform options (*Dom.*, 4 September 1992). The Chief Ombudsman, who chaired the referendum panel, also stepped into the argument, reiterating the panel's earlier publicity which noted that Maori seats could exist under any of the four options included on the voting paper and, therefore, the adoption of a new electoral system did not necessarily mean the abolition of separate Maori seats.[12]

Opinion among Maori also appeared divided. Despite condemning any move towards abolishing the Maori seats as 'a betrayal' (*Press*, 16 September 1992), Eastern Maori MP, Peter Tapsell, publicly rejected the boycott call; his colleague, Bruce Gregory (Northern Maori), however, openly supported it because he believed that the referendum failed to guarantee the continuation of the four Maori seats (ibid., 4 September 1992). Dover Samuels, a senior member of the Labour Party's administrative wing, said that his party guaranteed that the four Maori seats would remain (ibid., 7 September 1992).

A few days later, Prime Minister Bolger contradicted both the official public education campaign and his Minister of Justice when he said that separate Maori representation would be abolished if voters favoured proportional representation in the referendum (*NZH*, 8 September 1992). Although, shortly afterwards, he sought to soften his stance with a press release which emphasised that any reform to the electoral system would be based on the recommendations of the 1986 Royal Commission (ibid., 9 September 1992), the government's credibility came under renewed scrutiny when John Armstrong, political editor of the *New Zealand Herald*, reported that the National Party's caucus had already resolved that any electoral reform legislation should be based on the Royal Commission's recommendations.

Armstrong concluded that this decision — which conflicted with National's 1990 manifesto pledge — meant that the caucus had "effectively agreed ... to abolish the four Maori seats if voters favoured proportional representation" (ibid.). The waters were muddied even further a few days later when Graham "hinted strongly" that he did not favour an MMP system which incorporated a weighting for Maori parties when he said:

> I am not sure you can just happily reduce the threshold that applies to everybody else... I find that the idea that political parties would find it necessary to put Maori on their lists to attract wide support was a convincing argument to the commission. I am not so sure I'm so sanguine about it. (*Press,* 12 September 1992.)

In parliament, four days before the referendum, senior Labour MP, David Caygill, moved to adjourn the House to debate what he described as a "significant confusion between the statements of the Prime Minister and Minister of Justice, and the contents of the material delivered to all households in July relating to the continuance of the Maori seats". Bolger responded to Caygill's call for clarification of the status of the National Party's 1990 promise that the Maori seats would be retained until Maori decided that they were no longer needed, by confirming that the bill, to be introduced if a majority voted in favour of change, would reflect the Royal Commission's recommendations, and that the Maori seats would remain only if the FPP electoral system were retained. This was reinforced by Graham who confirmed the government's intention to introduce a bill "along the lines of the Royal Commission's recommendations" if the electorate supported the 'change' option in the indicative referendum (*NZPD*, 529:10847–53).

Shortly after voters had overwhelmingly supported in principle a shift to a more proportional electoral system, the government introduced its bill setting out the structure of the new MMP electoral system and referred it to the Electoral Law Select Committee for study. When public submissions closed at the end of February 1993 only one of the 624 submissions received was positively identified as having come from a Maori source. In a memorandum to the Minister of Maori Affairs (Doug Kidd) the Chief Executive of *Te Puni Kokiri* (Ministry of Maori Development) suggested that his Ministry should notify Maori when the select committee would be visiting local areas so that oral submissions could be made (TPK, 1993:8 March 1993).[13] This concern was reinforced two days later when Professor Ngatata Love wrote to Kidd proposing a programme of "consultation and involvement of Maori on an issue [ie. the proposed abolition of separate Maori representation] that has major implications for constitutional and treaty rights" which, he indicated, had the backing of the National Maori Congress, the New Zealand Maori Council, and the Maori Women's Welfare League (ibid., 10 March 1993.)[14]

Government concern at the potential lack of participation by Maori was reinforced in an undated background paper prepared by Te Puni Kokiri. This set out a number of concerns surrounding the proposed abolition of separate Maori representation that it believed needed to be addressed: would the abolition of the four Maori seats be in breach of the Treaty of Waitangi; had adequate consultation taken place; had Maori been given adequate information about the implications of the proposed change (and, if additional information were needed, how should it be delivered); and whether an effective means of developing national Maori political parties could be achieved. Consistent with its belief that Maori should engage in "full and informed participation" in the electoral reform process, the Ministry proposed a nationwide consultation programme reflecting a partnership between the Crown, Te Puni Kokiri, and a steering committee representing the three pan-tribal Maori organisations (ibid.). In mid-April the government announced that it would fund a series of regional hui, culminating in a national hui, at a cost of more than $300,000 to the Crown, to enable Maori to determine their stance on the proposed abolition of the four Maori seats. Representatives of church, *kingitanga* (kingship), politicians, academics and other key Maori were also to be consulted (*NZH*, 15 April 1993). Overall responsibility for the programme was vested in a steering committee comprising representatives of the Maori Council, Maori Congress, and Maori Women's Welfare League, whose task was ensure that Maori were "fully and independently informed" on the implications of the Electoral Reform Bill — including the proposed abolition of the Maori seats — to gather Maori views, and to prepare a submission to the parliamentary select committee incorporating the views of Maori people on the future of Maori representation (Steering Committee, 1993a:1–2). The joint convenors, Love and William Katene, defined the steering committee's objective as developing "a strong and clear submission which reflects the views of how Maori people ... wish to be represented in Parliament" (*NZH*, 23 April 1993).

In the space of three weeks during the second half of April and early May, 21 regional hui were held. The consultation process culminated with a national hui, held at Turangawaewae Marae on 4–5 May, attended by some 250 *iwi* (tribal) representatives, the Minister of Justice, members of the Electoral Law Select Committee, and the chairman of the 1985–86 Royal Commission, Justice John Wallace. There, Maori speaker after Maori speaker identified what they believed to be the key issues relating to Maori representation:

   (1) that the Crown should recognise that the Treaty of Waitangi guarantees Maori the right to fair representation in parliament;

(2) that the four Maori seats should be retained "regardless of which electoral system is adopted";

(3) that the number of guaranteed Maori seats must be increased regardless of the electoral system finally adopted, that their number must be proportionate to the total Maori population and determined in the same way that the number of General electorates is determined;

(4) a new Maori option should be held before the 1993 election so that Maori had the opportunity of returning to the Maori roll; and

(5) the establishment of an electoral system which encouraged Maori to participate in the political process in a way that was consistent with the Treaty of Waitangi "and ... which acknowledges a unique constitutional status". (ibid., 22–25.)

Collectively, these views represented a resounding rejection of the government's draft bill — and, by implication, the Royal Commission's recommendation which proposed the abolition of guaranteed separate Maori representation. In his response, Graham indicated that it would be possible to retain the separate Maori seats but that Maori needed to be aware that their number might be reduced. He also pointed out that claims for separate representation that reflected the proportion of Maori to total population ignored "the fact that large chunks of the Maori people are on the General roll", and that it might be difficult to sustain an argument favouring the waiving of the threshold for Maori parties when Maori enjoyed separate guaranteed representation (*NZH*, 11 May 93). Justice Wallace also addressed the gathering, restating the Royal Commission's unanimous view that MMP, without separate seats, would provide Maori with much more effective parliamentary representation (Steering Committee, 1993a:22–35, 39). He was later also reported as saying that if Maori decided that separate Maori seats should be retained even if MMP were to be adopted,

> then that could quite readily be done. There could be separate seats under MMP based on the numbers of Maori and their children on the roll. ... But the Bill doesn't say that and if you wish that, you will need to say it. (*Press,* 4 May 1993.)

A constant Maori criticism was that the government had failed to consult adequately with them before preparing the Electoral Reform Bill. Resting their case on Article 3 of the Treaty of Waitangi, Maori argued that if the present form of representation is to be altered,

> ... it must be with the consent of Maori. If [this] is not obtained, then the legitimacy is not based on the consent of the people. Consent in this instance is not only

from the majority of the people, but specifically it must be obtained from Maori because of the obligations under the Treaty. (Steering Committee, 1993a:4.)

Some Maori believed that the government's belated move to fund a series of hui and allow Maori to make a late submission was little more than a token gesture because the timetable imposed on the steering committee did not allow for adequate publicity and information to be disseminated. According to one of the steering committee's convenors, the government had run ahead of itself by not previously consulting Maori: "It's put Maori at a great disadvantage", Katene was reported as saying. "I'm sure we are going to give them a lot to think about; it's not going to be as simple as they think. It can't go through in its present form" (*Press*, 4 May 1993).

When the steering committee finally presented its submission it drew the select committee's attention to the Royal Commission's view of the unique legal and constitutional status of Maori:

Members should be aware that there is an extraordinary measure of disquiet amongst Maori communities at a proposal which could eliminate Maori representation. ... hui throughout New Zealand have expressed concern over the process. ... it would be wrong as part of overall electoral reform to bring about a major constitutional change without clear evidence that the matter has been fully considered and canvassed by the indigenous peoples themselves... (ELSC, 1993d.)

The government, it argued, had to recognise not only the unique constitutional status of Maori, but also that the Treaty of Waitangi requires fair and effective representation for Maori within the parliamentary system. It recommended:

(1) that separate Maori seats should be retained regardless of which electoral system was confirmed in the forthcoming electoral referendum;

(2) that the number of constituency seats should reflect the proportion of Maori to the total population;

(3) that a separate Maori electoral Commission, which would express "a Maori cultural approach to (political) representation", be established to administer those provisions of the electoral system — such as the Maori electoral rolls, community of interest among Maori tribes, and any Maori political parties that might emerge — affecting Maori representation; and

(4) that an opportunity be given to Maori to exercise a choice of rolls before the 1993 election. (Steering Committee, 1993a:1.)

The whole tenor of the steering committee's submission makes it clear that Maori sought the fullest possible control over Maori parliamentary representation: they believed that this was the only way that Maori could ensure that their voice would continue to be heard in parliament. The educational role of the proposed Maori Electoral Commission, for example, was regarded as "fundamental and critical; to ensuring that Maori people are able to participate in the parliamentary system effectively" — that is through presenting the message *kanohi-ki-te-kanohi,* face to face (ibid., 5). What is equally clear is that the politicians were not prepared to countenance this degree of autonomy.

Nor did Maori share the Royal Commission's optimism that MMP, with its integrated electorates and common roll, would deliver significantly better representation for their people. Their clear preference was for the retention of the Maori electorates in addition to the opportunity for Maori to be elected to parliament through the party lists because, the steering committee argued, this would ensure "the just and proportional representation of Maori interests in parliament". In response to a question from a member of the select committee, the steering committee noted that many at the hui had felt "that if you identified yourself as a Maori then you should go on the Maori roll. ... A person cannot expect the benefits of education scholarships, or economic gains from Treaty of Waitangi settlements if one does not identify oneself as Maori politically" (ibid., 6–10).

While the steering committee's submission indicates that there was considerable orchestration of the resolutions agreed to by those attending both the regional hui and the national hui at Turangawaewae, few apart from the Royal Commissioners argued for abolition in 1993.[15] The virtual unanimity of agreement on the need to retain separate Maori representation, and for the number of seats to reflect the proportion of Maori in the total population, could not be denied. It cannot be doubted that these hui, and the submission which followed, were extremely influential in finally persuading the Electoral Law Select Committee to reincorporate separate Maori representation into the Electoral Reform Bill.

Agreement Reached

The Electoral Law Select Committee actually commenced its study of the Electoral Reform Bill early in March 1993, some two months before the pan-Maori organisations presented the results of the hui deliberations. Nevertheless, from the outset, its members were all acutely aware that the way in which they addressed the question of Maori representation would have an important bearing on the final structure of the proposed MMP electoral system. Thus, although the 1993 bill, as originally drafted, provided for the abolition of separate Maori parliamentary representation, the future of the Maori seats loomed large throughout much of the committee's deliberations.

Labour remained firmly committed to its long-standing policy on Maori seats, and once it was clear that there was overwhelming support for their retention it began to look for a mechanism whereby their number could be based on the Maori electoral population. If successful, it would mean that the number of Maori electorates would vary, up or down, depending on the number of Maori registering on the Maori roll. Nevertheless, Whetu Tirikatene-Sullivan (MP for Southern Maori) continued to press for the Electoral Act to incorporate a provision that would ensure that their number would never fall below four. Initially, National also maintained its established position although, as we noted above, its caucus — in direct contradiction of its 1990 manifesto commitment — had effectively agreed in July 1992 to the abolition of separate Maori representation if MMP were ultimately endorsed by the electorate (*NZH*, 9 September 1992; *Dom.*, 9 September 1992). Its ambivalence was obvious: despite the fact that the Royal Commission had argued cogently for the abolition of separate Maori representation National did not want to stand accused of breaking another election promise (*NZH*, 11 May 1993).[16] It would also be embarrassing if separate Maori representation were retained under an MMP system but the number of seats guaranteed to the Maori people was reduced as a result. Since no MP relished the prospect of being accused of using MMP as a lever to abolish the Maori seats, committee members ultimately strove to ensure that separate Maori seats were retained and their number did not immediately drop.

Even before final approval had been given to the proposed Maori hui consultation programme, the Department of Statistics prepared a background paper for the select committee setting out electoral population counts which could be used to prepare different sets of indicative electoral boundaries. This document is of considerable interest because it sets out a number of possible alternative scenarios for MMP:

(1) no separate Maori seats;

(2) a fixed number of four Maori electorates, separate from and in addition to the number of constituencies proposed by the Royal Commission;

(3) a fixed number of four separate seats included within the total number of constituency seats proposed by the Royal Commission; and

(4) a variable number of separate Maori seats over and above the number of constituency seats proposed by the Royal Commission, with their number determined by applying the prescribed New Zealand electorate quota to the Maori electoral population.

The data used to demonstrate the impact of each option had been used for the 1992 electoral redistribution and showed that if the fourth option were applied, only three Maori seats would result. Alternatively, if separate Maori seats were to be retained and their number fixed at four — as assumed in the second and third scenarios — the Maori electoral quota would, of necessity, differ significantly from that used to determine the size of the General electorates (ELSC, 1993f).

By mid-May, even though the Maori Steering Committee had still to present its submission, the select committee had progressed its deliberations to the point where it was examining possible formulae that could be used to calculate the Maori electoral population — an unmistakable indication that the weight of opinion within the select committee was moving in the direction of retention. A simplified formula, which would almost certainly increase the total number of people included in the Maori electoral population, was proposed by the Department of Statistics and, ultimately, adopted by the committee (ELSC, 1993g).[17]

A further paper prepared for the select committee by the Department of Statistics in mid-July showed that the application of this simplified formula to a range of population projections and Maori registration scenarios — and incorporating a fixed number of either 15 or 16 General electorates for the South Island — was likely to ensure that the number of guaranteed Maori seats would not fall below four in the immediate future (ELSC, 1993i).

In the wake of the Maori steering committee's strong recommendation that separate Maori representation should be retained, and evidence within the select committee that there was considerable and growing sympathy with the Maori viewpoint within the National Party caucus, Labour decided to press for the number of guaranteed Maori electorates to be calculated on the same basis as the General seats. It should be noted, however, that Labour also had a vested interest in ensuring that the party vote threshold was not waived for Maori parties because, as the party with the greatest number of Maori MPs at the time, it felt more threatened than any other party by this possibility. This opened the way for a trade-off: if the Maori seats were to be retained, there would be no need to legislate a threshold waiver (Caygill, 1996b). Labour strategists were well aware that they would need the National Party's support if the number of Maori constituency seats were to be determined on a population basis in the future. Although Tirikatene-Sullivan remained adamant that the number of Maori electorates should remain at a minimum of four (*NZPD*, 537:17224–25),[18] Labour's caucus was persuaded by the argument that if separate Maori representation were retained, with the number of seats being determined pro rata to Maori and non-Maori population ratios, there could be no fixed minimum. Not only was it convinced that such an arrangement would provide the best opportunity for securing an increase in the number of Maori seats, pressing Tirikatene-Sullivan's demand to the limit might also make it more difficult to persuade National to accept the proposed formula (Caygill, 1996a,b).

Not all submissions received by the select committee supported the retention of the separate Maori seats. Wallace and Darwin, members of the Royal Commission, reiterated that the Royal Commission's view was that MMP would result in better Maori representation and that the greatest benefits would come if the separate Maori seats were abolished (*NZH*, 18 March 1993).[19] Former Prime Minister Geoffrey Palmer also argued against the retention of the Maori seats: he believed that the arguments in favour of retention were "fundamentally misguided" because MMP "provides superior representation to minority groups than First-past-the-post" (ELSC, 1993c; *Press*, 10 April 1993), and that the Maori seats "have done almost nothing to help Maori people make progress" (*NZH*, 17 May 1993). In the final analysis, however, these views were overwhelmed by the strength and unanimity of Maori opinion.

The select committee's decision to recommend the retention of the separate Maori seats represented a significant change of direction from that proposed by the Royal Commission and included in the original draft of the Electoral Reform Bill. When Maori were confronted with the reality of the threat to abolish the seats that guaranteed them representation in the country's legislature, politically active Maori successfully mobilised the weight of Maori opinion to argue successfully for their continuance. That achieved, they could refocus their efforts on persuading Maori that support for the MMP electoral system, as finally passed by parliament, would prove advantageous for their people. This victory also brought another potential benefit: during the 1993 election campaign both Labour and National promised that if FPP won majority support in the binding referendum the 1956 *Electoral Act* would be amended to require the number of Maori electorates to be calculated using the same formula used to determine the number of General seats. Thus major party agreement had finally been reached on an issue that had divided them and had been a matter for periodic debate for nearly one-quarter of a century.

Conclusion

From the time of the Turangawaewae hui convened to discuss Maori parliamentary representation in mid-1985, until parliament passed the *Electoral Act 1993*, the one thing that stands out above all else is the constancy of the

Maori position. Although it can be argued that, as a group, Maori were slow to respond to the Royal Commission's recommendation that separate Maori representation be abolished, when the prospect of abolition became imminent, Maori elites demonstrated their ability to organise themselves, to network, and to develop a response that was overwhelmingly in favour of retaining the Maori seats. Taking their lead from the Royal Commission's report, they developed their own collective view of how best to maintain fair and effective political representation for their people. To them, the retention of guaranteed Maori representation was of paramount importance; if the separate Maori seats were preserved, they believed that the proposal to waive the threshold for parties that were primarily Maori would not be necessary (Steering Committee, 1993b:4). Nor were they as optimistic as the Royal Commission that the perceived advantages of a common roll and integrated electorates would outweigh the disadvantages they believed would result from the abolition of the separate Maori seats. In the final analysis, parliament's decision to retain separate Maori representation recognised that the Maori people have a unique constitutional position in New Zealand society. And while Whetu Tirikatene-Sullivan failed in her eleventh-hour attempt to have reference to the Treaty of Waitangi formally included in the *Electoral Act 1993* (*NZPD,* 537:17235), the Treaty did provide the constitutional and historical basis for the decision that was finally reached.

Although the commissioners were very well aware of the depth of feeling among Maori at their proposal to abolish the Maori constituency seats, they continued to advocate its adoption because they were convinced that MMP would provide Maori with fairer and more effective representation than they had ever achieved under First-past-the-post. We have already noted that the commissioners gave considerable weight to Whetumarama Wereta's views, perhaps to the extent that she effectively held a de facto veto over the argument and recommendations contained in the chapter on Maori representation. And, having reached its conclusions, the Commission appears to have been very reluctant indeed to concede that some modification might be desirable, or even necessary, if its central recommendation was to find general public acceptance. Although as early as 1987 Wallace accepted that it was feasible to retain separate Maori seats within an MMP electoral system without destroying its essence (ELSC, 1988d) — a point he reiterated to both the 1993 select committee and to Maori attending the hui at Turangawaewae in May 1993 — he remained adamant that the key to improving Maori parliamentary representation lay in the establishment of a common roll which, along with the party vote that would encourage all parties to select Maori candidates in high positions on their party list and compete for votes from all sections of the community, would determine the overall party composition of the House of Representatives.

Although the Royal Commission recommended against separate representation for Maori under MMP, the ultimate structure of the new electoral system is not inconsistent with the underlying principles of MMP as proposed in its report. The integrative political effects of the common roll through the party vote are still present and, if the results of the first MMP election in 1996 can be taken as a portent for the future, the new electoral system will deliver both an increased Maori presence in parliament, and greater representativeness across parties than was the case during the era of two-party politics. If this continues, Maori may become more confident that the parliamentary system is an appropriate and effective vehicle allowing them to participate fully in the political process. It seems highly unlikely, though, that even if a significantly increased number of Maori MPs are elected in future, Maori will countenance the eventual abolition of the separate Maori constituency seats because this may result in them facing the prospect of reduced parliamentary representation unless they can be assured of gaining at least as many MPs overall through extra list places.

The 1993 *Electoral Act* established a process in law that gave Maori choice as to the form of representation they preferred. It provided, for the first time, guaranteed representation on a proportionate basis for as long as Maori wished it to continue, but it no longer provided them with a fixed number of seats, or any guarantee that the separate Maori seats would remain a permanent feature of the electoral system. The future of separate Maori parliamentary representation now lies fairly and squarely in Maori hands.[20] As such, the provisions for Maori representation contained in the Act are likely to be viewed as integrative. They have provided a platform through which Maori and non-Maori can work together for the advancement of the whole New Zealand society.

Notes

1   Registration as an elector was made compulsory for non-Maori in 1924 but not till 1956 for Maori. Legislation authorising the preparation of Maori electoral rolls was first passed in 1914 but the first rolls were not completed and used until the 1949 general election.

2   The term 'European' was used to describe the seats not reserved for Maori electors. It remained in force until 1975 when it was replaced by the term 'General'.

3   In 1948, for example, Leslie Lipson was able to state that Maori were "equitably represented on a numerical basis" (1948:193).

4   Prior to 1974 a Maori was defined as "... a person belonging to the aboriginal race of New Zealand; and includes a half-caste and a person intermediate in blood between half-castes and persons of pure descent from that race".

5   Interestingly, this was one term of reference not included in the Labour Party's 1981 election manifesto policy, 'Open Government', although its Maori policy promised that the number of Maori seats would be determined by applying a formula that was "as close as possible" to the way that the number of General seats was calculated.

6   The select committee's Labour majority recommended that census data should be used to estimate the number of Maori who had failed to register so that a proportion could be included in the Maori electoral population.

7   The hui was attended by members of the Royal Commission. There appears to be some confusion as to when this hui took place. In a letter to Wallace dated 18 June 1985 Maori Council secretary, T.W. Parata, reported on the outcome of the conference held on 8 June. In its formal submission to the commission (presented on 28 November 1985) the dates of the conference are given as 26–27 April 1985.

8   When first registering as electors, persons of Maori descent choose which roll — Maori or General — they wish to enrol on. Once this choice is made, Maori can only change rolls during designated Maori option periods which occur shortly after each five-yearly census. (In 1993 the Electoral Act prescribed that the Maori option be held over a period of two months; in 1996, the Act was amended to allow four months.)

9   Many Maori contend that the most appropriate way to encourage Maori to consider and respond to issues of public importance is through the adoption of a kanohi-ki-te-kanohi strategy.

10   The Electoral Law Select Committee which studied the Royal Commission's Report in 1987–88 received a small number of submissions from Maori, all of which reiterated the main thrust of the New Zealand Maori Council's submission to the Royal Commission.

11   The boycott call was withdrawn after a few days.

12   In 1993 the New Zealand Maori Council noted that while the abolition of the Maori seats was implicit in the Electoral Reform Bill, the "publicity surrounding the system during the first (1992) referendum stipulated that the abolition of the four Maori seats was not a condition precedent to the implementation of a(n) MMP system" (ELSC, 1993c).

13   The number of submissions identified as coming from Maori sources was later raised to eight.

14   The New Zealand Maori Council is a statutory body, established in 1962, whose membership is based on a national, regional and local committee system, not iwi groupings. The New Zealand Maori Congress, formed in 1990, is iwi based. Its membership is tribal in nature, and it is independent of government. The Maori Women's Welfare League was founded in 1951 and seeks to promote the economic, social, cultural, physical and spiritual development of Maori. The League became involved in the issue of Maori representation because it believed that an important Treaty issue was under threat, and that if one right could be taken away then others could be removed just as easily. (The Maori Congress also warned MPs that since 1993 was the United Nations Year of Indigenous Peoples, the abolition of the four Maori seats carried with it the risk of international censure unless the matter was fully canvassed within Maoridom before any decisions were taken. See *NZH*,18 March 1993.)

15   Geoffrey Palmer was one who did, but his primary goal was to have MMP adopted.

16   It should be noted, however, that the Minister of Justice, Doug Graham, counselled Maori that they could not expect to retain the separate Maori seats *and* expect to have the proposed threshold waived for Maori parties.

17   In 1992, an opinion given by the Solicitor General (at the request of the Representation Commission) on the legality of the Department of Statistics' interpretation of the then existing formula for determining the Maori electoral population resulted in Parliament having to amend the Electoral Act before the 1992 redistribution could proceed. This

amended formula was always regarded as no more than a temporary expedient which would have to be dealt with more permanently before the next scheduled redistribution. (See also, ELSC, 1993f.)

18   During the committee stages of the Bill's passage through the House of Representatives, Mrs Tirikatene-Sullivan moved an amendment to set the minimum number of Maori electoral districts at four. Her amendment was defeated by 49 **votes to 21.**

19   It is important to note that their submission concerned itself solely with the need to ensure that democratic methods were used to select candidates. Their observation about Maori representation was made in response to a question from the committee.

20   It should be noted, however, that Maori representation has been designated as a specific topic for examination by a parliamentary select committee which is required to review aspects of the *Electoral Act 1993* between April 2000 and June 2002. See *Electoral Act 1993*, s.264.

9 The People Decide:
The 1992 and 1993
Electoral Referendums

> At the bottom of all the tributes paid to democracy is the little man, walking into
> the little booth, with a little pencil, making a little cross on a little bit of paper —
> no amount of rhetoric or voluminous discussion can possibly diminish the
> overwhelming importance of the point.
> — Winston Churchill, British Prime Minister, 1944.

Referendums, where a mass electorate expresses its collective view on a
particular public issue, are perhaps the ultimate expressions of participatory
democracy in a modern state for they are seen by their advocates as embodying
the principles of popular sovereignty, political equality, popular consent, and
majority rule (Butler & Ranney, 1994:11–12). In an earlier study, Butler and
Ranney identified three basic types of referendum:

(1) those controlled by the government which decides if a referendum
should be held, what the subject and precise wording of the
referendum should be, and whether its result should be binding or
merely advisory;

(2) those required by a country's constitution: here again, the government
holds the upper hand, the only difference being that the referendum's
result is binding if the proposal is endorsed by a majority of those
who vote; and

(3) popular initiatives (CIR), where citizens can propose a new law, or
changes to, or repeal of an existing law. In this case a referendum
may be binding or indicative depending on the provisions of the
statute under whose authority such a referendum is held. (Butler &
Ranney, 1978:23–33.)

Those who oppose the use of referendums as a means of determining
policy argue that governments are elected to govern and, by deferring to public
opinion, they abrogate that responsibility. Most decisions confronting
governments are complex and require a considerable input of knowledge,
expertise and time before the appropriate decision is reached. Ordinary citizens,
they contend, do not have the requisite level of expertise or understanding
which allows them to cast an informed vote. As a consequence, the referendum

Table 9.1   New Zealand National Referendums, 1908–90

Year	Issue	Outcome	% Support	% Turnout
1908–87[a]	Liquor Licensing (26 polls — at three-yearly intervals)	Status quo retained	—	—
1949[b]	Establishment of off-course betting on horse races	Endorsed	68.0	56.3
1949[b]	Allow licensed hotels to open beyond 6pm	Rejected	24.5	56.5
1949	Introduce compulsory military training in peace time	Endorsed	77.8	61.5
1967[b]	Allow licensed hotels to open beyond 6pm	Endorsed	64.5	71.2
1967[b]	Extend parliamentary term from 3 to 4 years	Rejected	31.9	71.2
1990[a]	Extend parliamentary term from 3 to 4 years	Rejected	30.7	82.4

[a.] Held in conjunction with general election.
[b.] Held on same day but not an election day.

Note: The 3-year parliamentary term could not, under the provisions of the *Electoral Act 1956*, be altered unless either 75 per cent of all MPs supported an amendment to change the law, or it was approved by a majority of those voting in a referendum on the issue.

(*Source:* Butler & Ranney, 1994:282–83; *AJHR*, 1991. For the 1949 and 1967 referendums, see Jackson, 1973:61–64.)

process is likely to be captured by special interest groups (RCES, 1986a:173–75; Butler & Ranney, 1978:34–37).

One scholar has described New Zealand as "an inveterate user of referendums" (Jackson, 1992). Triennial liquor licensing polls, a referendum device allowing voters to decide whether alcoholic liquor should continue to be sold in their home locality, were first instituted in 1881. Twenty-seven years on, in 1908, the first national triennial licensing poll was held in conjunction with the national election, a practice which continued without interruption until 1987. In addition, between 1949 and 1990, six other government-sponsored issues were referred to the electorate for decision (see Table 9.1). In both 1967 and 1990 the government published a neutrally-worded pamphlet, delivered to each household, outlining the benefits and drawbacks of each proposal (Cleveland & Robinson, 1972:134–35).[1] Throughout, successive governments controlled the referendum process at every point.

Despite the long history of government-controlled referendums in New Zealand, by committing themselves to a referendum on MMP in their 1990 manifestos, both Labour and National effectively let control of the future shape of the New Zealand's electoral system pass irrevocably to the electorate at large. As we saw earlier, Labour had reneged on the commitment made by David Lange late in the 1987 election campaign. But the avenues by which politicians could maintain control of the agenda had been effectively closed off once Labour had rejected the Electoral Law Select Committee's recommendation (pushed through by the committee's Labour majority) that an indicative referendum should be held to decide whether the number of MPs should be increased and, if so, whether the additional members should be elected from single-member electorates or through a Supplementary Member (SM) electoral system (*AJHR*, 1988:21). Undoubtedly, the new National Government would have preferred to return the question of electoral reform to the back burner, but this, too, was no longer possible. Other than wilfully breaking its promise to the electorate, the new government had no choice but to set wheels in motion that would lead, ultimately, to electors choosing to reject the First-past-the-post electoral system in favour of the Mixed Member Proportional electoral system, the principal features of which had been set out in the Royal Commission's report.

Informing the Public

It is axiomatic that whenever decisions involving choices between different options have to be made, they should be based on knowledge and understanding of the issues involved. Thus, when citizens are invited to choose between different electoral systems, it follows that some attempt should be made to ensure that they understand the options offered and their implications before they vote. Providing citizens with information in a readily digestible form is difficult enough, but developing even a basic understanding of a range of different options, is an extremely complex and difficult task. Inevitably, educational attainment levels vary widely amongst the voting public, as does their interest in politics generally. Putting information into the public domain is one thing; persuading the target audience to study the information provided and to work at it until it is clearly understood — in short, encouraging them to 'internalise' the message — is a vastly different proposition.

The independent panel and its responsibilities

When the Minister of Justice, Doug Graham, confirmed that an indicative referendum would be held in 1992, he said that the government would not adopt a position on the issue. At the same time, he announced that an independent, government-funded, publicity campaign would be conducted to provide electors with information about each option. The government, Graham emphasised, was determined that the various issues would be presented without bias. The panel, he said, would

> ... spend about $3 million to try to inform the public on the alternatives and what they mean. The government will go to extraordinary lengths to have independent unbiased reports and consideration of the programmes to be broadcast, so that at the end of the day people can say that they understand the single transferable vote system and the mixed member proportional system — or at least I hope the majority will be able to. (*NZPD*, 521:6006.)[2]

This decision, which represented a unique departure from earlier practice, was almost certainly prompted by earlier public criticisms of taxpayer-funded advertising campaigns by both National and Labour governments to publicise matters in a way that could be construed as promoting government policies. It is yet another indication that politicians had irrevocably lost control of the electoral reform process. Coincidentally, it freed Ministers to join other MPs in promoting their personal views without compromising the principle of collective ministerial responsibility. As far as we are aware, no other government has ever provided funding for a mass public information and education campaign while, at the same time, surrendering total responsibility for its content and presentation to an independent, non-partisan body.

The Electoral Referendum Panel was appointed in November 1991. Chaired by the Chief Ombudsman, John Robertson, whose appointment was designed to reinforce the panel's independence from political interference, it included David McGee, Clerk of the House of Representatives, Peter Blanchard, a member of the New Zealand Law Commission, Judith Aitken, a political scientist who was chief executive of the Ministry of Women's Affairs, and Hugh Kawharau, a prominent Maori leader and academic. Appointed to oversee the 1992 publicity campaign, and formally disbanded following its conclusion, the panel's perceived success in maintaining its independence from the government, resulted in the same strategy being adopted for the public information campaign which preceded the 1993 binding referendum.[3]

Even before the government had confirmed its intention to proceed with the promised, albeit indicative, referendum, the Department of Justice was well advanced with its preparations in the expectation that, as in past referendums, it would be the sole provider of official information to electors on the issues involved. The government's decision to appoint an independent panel, therefore, came as something of a surprise and effectively restricted the department's role to providing the panel with administrative support. It surrendered its involvement only reluctantly. Several times during the early months of 1992, the department endeavoured to recapture the initiative, actions which caused Robertson considerable concern to the point where he found it necessary to make clear that his panel had sole responsibility for the development and implementation of the public education campaign. As part of the executive arm of government, the Department of Justice could not be seen to be an active participant if the panel's independence from the government was to be established. Nevertheless, it seems certain that the decision to establish an independent panel, coming as it did after the department had already substantially developed its own programme, delayed the commencement of the public education campaign by a number of months (Justice, 1992a).[4]

The panel, which was not a statutory body, was responsible for supervising the preparation and dissemination of information about the referendum and the choices facing electors. In 1992 its terms of reference required it to familiarise the public with the concept of the indicative referendum and the different options included in it, to generate informed discussion and debate on those options and the issues surrounding them, and ensuring, as best it could, that the electorate was well-informed by the time votes were cast (*AJHR*, 1992a:5). At an early stage in this campaign, however, the panel appears to have adopted the additional objective: that of ensuring that electors knew that they had two votes, and that they should exercise their right to cast both votes regardless of whether they supported the status quo or the change option offered in Part A of the voting paper.[5]

The objectives of the 1993 campaign were broadly similar. Once again, the panel was required to familiarise electors with the choices facing them in the referendum, to generate informed discussion and debate throughout the community, and ensure that the electorate was well informed about the choices to be made (ERP, 1993a:13 July 1993). In addition,

> There was a caveat that was not part of the terms of reference for the 1992 referendum; the Panel was not to develop and present arguments in favour or against any one or both options. The task was to inform the public of the facts of the referendum options authorised in the statute, in an objective, impartial and

informative manner without entering the debate on the pros and cons of either option. (*AJHR*, 1993:5; CAB, 1993.)

When commenting on this directive (which effectively prevented the panel from becoming involved in the debate on the relative merits of FPP and MMP) Robertson confirmed that the panel would not take sides:

> There will be public expectation that the campaign should explain the advantages and disadvantages of either system. That expectation will not be met. People would have to look to the advocates of each option for advice. (*NZH*, 15 July 1993.)

Despite several attempts by the two competing lobby groups, the panel resolutely maintained this position throughout the course of the referendum campaign.

The 1992 campaign — a smorgasbord of options

As we have already noted, the referendum process ultimately decided upon by the government was a complex two-stage one, although its logic — majority support for the status quo ending the debate forthwith; majority support for 'change' resulting in a second, binding referendum — was undeniable.

The 1992 indicative referendum posed two distinct questions, the first involving a relatively simple choice between support for the status quo and change, and the second inviting a choice between four options — Preferential Voting (PV), a Supplementary Member system (SM), MMP, and the Single Transferable Vote (STV) — none of which were familiar to more than a minute handful of New Zealanders. To complicate matters even further, the government declined to legally define any of the alternative electoral systems or provide detailed descriptions of how they might operate within the New Zealand context. In justifying the government's position, Graham, said:

> There's no point in the Government spending a great deal of taxpayers' money developing up in detail all the options when three of them at least aren't going to be ever introduced, and possibly the whole lot. (*Dom.*, 4 September 1992; cf. *NZPD*, 1993, 529:10851–52.)

The panel, which considered that it was not its function to decide such matters, was thus constrained to providing only very generalised information about each of the alternatives to First-past-the-post based on knowledge of similar systems used in other countries, and to give some indication of how each might work if it were adopted by New Zealand.

Initially, according to one panel member, it was expected that the panel's role would be confined to approving tender documents, awarding the campaign contract, and approving campaign publicity material prepared by the successful tenderer before it was published. Notwithstanding, the panel, led by its chairperson, became actively involved in the control and co-ordination of the campaign from the outset because it recognised only too well the challenges that would confront it. Following its first meeting, towards the end of January 1992, Robertson frankly acknowledged the potential difficulties his panel faced in presenting a taxpayer-funded programme involving four reform options "in a fair and unbiased way". At the same time, however, he noted that "the creativity of the country's advertising agencies knew no bounds" (*Dom.,* 30 January 1992). According to Robertson, the panel knew that public relations and advertising agencies had little or no experience of public information campaigns, and were not fully familiar with the machinery of government and politics; it had, therefore, to manage the campaign within these constraints (Robertson, 1997).

Early in its work, the panel took a number of decisions which played an important part in the way the campaign was developed. In addition to selecting the advertising and public relations strategy to be used in promoting awareness and explaining the options facing voters, it determined that each option must be presented impartially and neutrally. As it later noted in its report to parliament, it resolved not to become actively involved in any public debate or "act to correct or dispute any irresponsible or errant information put forward by proponents of any particular system". It viewed its task as one of informing electors about the options, not persuading them if, or how, they should cast their votes (*AJHR,* 1992a:5). One particularly significant decision was that the Royal Commission's report would be treated as background material only: the panel agreed not to promote its recommendations because it believed that to do so would effectively promote support for MMP (Robertson, 1997). Thus, although the Commission's report discussed each option included in the referendum at some length, the two agencies involved in preparing material for public release were constrained in their ability to use its descriptions of how each option might work in the New Zealand context. In keeping with its strictly neutral stance, the panel also decided that the descriptions and explanations of each option (including the description of FPP) should stand alone and not be compared with any of the other options, nor would it comment on the way that the different voting systems were presented to the public by others. The priority given to achieving balance in its presentation of the different options reinforced the panel's determination to preserve its political independence and impartiality (Justice, 1992b; ERP,1992c: 11 May 92; Robertson, 1997).[6]

Another important early decision related to the question of separate Maori representation. Although, as an integral part of its MMP proposal, the Royal Commission had recommended that the separate Maori electorate seats should be abolished (RCES, 1986a:43–44), the panel resolved:

> ... that in the absence of any indication from Parliament to the contrary, since all reform options could be implemented with separate Maori seats and could be implemented with a Parliament of the same size as the present one, it would state this in its publicity. (*AJHR*,1992a:6.)[7]

Clearly, while it could not pre-empt decisions that were properly the responsibility of politicians, the panel's decision to work on the basis of the status quo, itself a direct consequence of the government's determination to not spell out any of the four reform options in detail, muddied already murky waters still further. By suggesting that there was no need to abolish separate Maori representation, Maori were lulled into a sense of false security and, as a group, took very little active part in the 1992 referendum debate. Second, by inferring that the number of MPs could remain at approximately 100, the panel raised, but did not answer, questions about the structure of MMP as proposed by the Royal Commission. Effectively, the panel was in a 'no win' situation — damned if it did and damned if it didn't!

These issues came to a head four days before the referendum when Labour MP, David Caygill, sought clarification of recent public statements made by Ministers, including the Prime Minister. Prefacing his remarks by saying that the government had a duty to ensure that all electors were "fully and fairly informed about ... the consequences of the vote they are being invited to exercise", Caygill asked what guarantee there was that a second referendum would be held in 1993 if a majority of voters supported the change option, but that that support was not overwhelming. He also asked whether the indicative referendum related solely to the structure of the House of Representatives or also envisaged the possibility of establishing a second chamber; whether the legislation introduced would provide for 120 seats as proposed by the Commission or differ from this recommendation if MMP were the most favoured option; and whether the status of the government's 1990 manifesto commitment to retain the separate Maori seats had changed in the light of the Prime Minister's statement that majority support for MMP in the indicative referendum would mean that the electoral reform bill would reflect the Royal Commission's recommendation and would, therefore, "not contain any specific proposed mechanism to retain the Maori seats". He widened the debate still further by asking how far the government was committed to the Royal Commission's recommendations, particularly with respect to the registration of political parties and disclosure of donations (*NZPD*, 529:10849–51).

Graham's response was that the government's commitment to hold the second referendum was a moral, not a legal one, that the Royal Commission's recommendations would be followed because it was "[t]he obvious starting point", and that the possibility of a second chamber should, perhaps, be considered only after the future structure of the House of Representatives had been decided. This meant, he said, that any draft bill would follow the Royal Commission's recommendations:

> We will not drift away from the Royal Commission on the Electoral System after it has spent years looking at the matter and, in turn, the select committee has spent years looking at the commission's report. (**ibid.**, 10851–53.)

It is doubtful, however, whether this debate contributed at all to clarifying the issues exercising the mind of the electorate.

The panel commenced its campaign three months before the referendum. A pamphlet, aptly titled *We're Taking it to the People* and delivered to nearly every household at the beginning of July, summarised the five options facing voters, including First-past-the-post. Also included was a simple list of ten criteria intended to help electors assess the different electoral systems, although nowhere did it acknowledge that these were the same criteria used by the Royal Commission to test the efficacy of different voting systems (RCES, 1986a: 11–12; ERP 1992a). Another more detailed publication, *The Guide to the Referendum*, was distributed to libraries, information centres, and electorate secretaries, and made available to the public on request. Special interest groups were also catered for: Maori and Samoan language versions of the householder pamphlet were printed; a special brochure outlining the implications of the different reform options for the Maori electorates was prepared; audio tapes and braille translations were prepared for people with impaired vision; and key parts of the householder pamphlet and sub-titles to referendum programmes shown on television were made available through teletext to assist people with impaired hearing.

Television, radio, the daily press, and selected periodicals were all used extensively, both to alert electors to the referendum and to describe the key elements of each option. At first the campaign concentrated on raising public awareness about the referendum, and this was followed during late August and early September by a second wave of advertising designed to encourage electors to study the householder pamphlet. Television was also used to disseminate more detailed information: during the first half of September three informational programmes were broadcast — a specially-commissioned documentary, *A Voter's Guide*, set out to explain the different voting options in a light-hearted manner; *Counterpoint*, a television current affairs programme, linked New Zealand journalists and politicians, and an Australian journalist, with overseas commentators in West Germany and Ireland and, on the Sunday prior to the referendum, a special *Marae* programme designed to explore the reform options and their implications for Maori electorates was broadcast (Tully, 1993:52–56). When the panel found that it was unable to meet an unanticipated public demand for speakers, it prepared a videotape, keyed closely to the detailed *Guide,* and distributed it on request to community and other interested groups.

From the outset, the panel was concerned to ensure that special efforts were made to reach Maori voters, particularly in the preparation and presentation of material. After consultation with Maori, the Department of Justice proposed a four-pronged approach involving local and regional hui, radio programmes specifically targeted at Maori through iwi radio stations, in-depth discussions, and the provision of specific information on voting. For the campaign to make a significant impact among Maori, it was accepted that "good and credible spokespeople for radio, TV, and hui — preferably Maori ... [and] ... [e]ffective and creative use should also be made of the blossoming Maori radio network," were necessary (Justice, 1992b:27 February 1992). Because the panel believed that Maori electors warranted special attention, it invited representatives from the New Zealand Maori Council, the Maori Congress, and Maori Women's Welfare League to meet with it "to discuss strategies for providing information to Maori voters". The Congress refused to become involved because it concluded that "the referendum did not address Maori concerns", and after discussions between the panel and the New Zealand Maori Council, the latter also declined to participate, its chairman, Graham Latimer, subsequently calling on Maori to boycott the referendum. In the end the only Maori input, other than from Te Puni Kokiri, came from members of the Maori Women's Welfare League (though not its executive) who assisted the panel by reviewing prepared material and helping with its distribution. In its report to parliament the panel noted: "[t]he loss of the iwi network otherwise available through the Congress and the Council was a setback for the panel in its proposed work" (*AJHR,* 1992a:13).

Despite these efforts to meet Maori needs, a number of Maori leaders were not impressed. At least one even went so far as to suggest that the referendum issues, as presented by the panel, were not sufficiently interesting to attract and hold the attention of Maori. Other, more particular, criticisms were also voiced and responded to: for example, the panel's concern at the standard of the translation of the Maori language version of the householder pamphlet resulted in it delaying publication to allow a new translation to be prepared. Nevertheless, Maori dissatisfaction with the quality of information prepared for them remained, and shortly before the referendum was due to be held, Te Puni Kokiri, supported by its Minister, Doug Kidd, approached the panel with a request for $69,000 to help fund the preparation and publication of its own newsletter detailing FPP and the reform options. Robertson bluntly declined the request because he believed that if the panel provided funds to a government agency responsible to a Minister of the Crown it would compromise its political independence (TPK, 1992). Despite this sharp rebuke, the Ministry proceded with the publication of its planned newsletter. When it appeared, the panel simply noted it as another contribution to the public debate (Justice, 1992b; ERP, 1992c:14 September 1992).

New Zealand's third largest ethnic group, people of Pacific Island descent, were also specially targeted. The Ministry of Pacific Island Affairs had recommended that a Samoan language version of the householder pamphlet was all that was necessary, but the panel felt that this might cause offence so it produced an English language version incorporating front page greetings in six Pacific Island languages. Subsequent consultations, and a plea by a prominent member of the New Zealand Samoan community, resulted in the panel authorising a Samoan language translation. In addition, three meetings were held to inform Pacific Islanders about the different voting options.

1993 — a clear choice between two alternative electoral systems

Unlike 1992, the Electoral Referendum Panel had two well-defined, though contrasting, electoral systems to describe and explain to the electorate. To this extent its terms of reference were much more straightforward because both systems were detailed in legislation — First-past-the-post in the *Electoral Act 1956* and its many subsequent amendments, and MMP in the *Electoral Act 1993*.[8] This is not to infer that the panel's task was a simple one; as the panel and its advisers discovered during the development and implementation of the programme, the goal of achieving balanced, neutral, and informative statements of fact about both electoral systems presented a number of diverse challenges which, at times, severely tested their abilities.

Although, after the 1992 campaign, Robertson was adamant that he would not be involved in any future panel, in May 1993, after the government confirmed that it would fund another public education campaign in the lead-up to the binding referendum, he was again approached to accept the position of chairperson. Initially reluctant to commit himself — he did not finally accept the appointment until 23 June (*AJHR,* 1993:4)[9] — he drew attention to the limited time-frame within which the campaign would run, and disputed the government's view that the panel's work would be simpler than in 1992 because there were only two options to publicise (*NZH,* 18 May 93; *Press,* 18 May 93). At its first meeting on 13 July, the panel noted with concern that delays in passing the electoral reform legislation could restrict the public education programme, and that there was "little the panel can do with confidence", by way of detailed planning until the final shape of the new Electoral Act was known (*NZH,* 15 July 1993; ERP 1993a:14 July 1993).

When the panel held its first meeting the Electoral Law Select Committee was still deliberating on the legislation authorising the referendum and detailing the structure of MMP. It invited the panel to meet with it " ... to discuss the proposed publicity campaign ... prior to the arrangements for the campaign progressing to an advanced stage" (ERP, 1993a:13 July 1993).[10] Following this meeting, which took place on 14 July, Robertson publicly reiterated his concern that the panel's preparations would be constrained until the legislation was finally passed. He argued, with some justification, that until the bill had passed through all its stages (which was not expected until early August) the panel would not know for certain what parliament's decisions were on key issues (*Dom.,* 15 July 1993). This drew a terse response from Murray McCully, the committee's chairperson, who complained that the short time-frame available for the proposed public education programme had never been raised with his committee, and said that he would be very concerned if the panel was delaying the development of its advertising campaign (ibid., 16 July 1993). Robertson was far from impressed with McCully's comments and wrote to him to express his disappointment at the "adversarial mode" implicit in his public statement. He reminded McCully that the panel had a responsibility to avoid "half-baked ideas", and that since a major difficulty confronting the panel in 1992 had been parliament's failure to define the options adequately, he thought it was reasonable to expect that the select committee would support the panel in its work "rather than publicly question it" (ERP, 1993a:16 July 1993).[11]

The format of the 1993 programme was similar to 1992, and built on that experience. A pamphlet (ERP, 1993b) setting out the basic facts of both FPP and MMP was distributed, mainly through community newspaper networks, at the beginning of September. The information contained in this pamphlet was expanded in a 16-page publication, *The Referendum: The Guide* (ibid., 1993c), which was widely distributed through public libraries, local authority information offices, citizens' advice bureaux, MPs' electorate secretaries, and made available to individuals on request. Towards the end of the campaign a further pamphlet (ibid., 1993d), which addressed the main issues that had arisen during the public debate in the form of questions and answers, was sent, personally addressed, to all 2.34 million registered electors. A comprehensive handbook designed for use by media was also produced (ibid., 1993e).

Television, radio and print media was again used extensively. At an early stage the panel identified six central themes — the number of votes, number of seats, issues of proportionality, Maori seats, the place of minor parties, and the formation of governments — which formed the basis for a structured advertising campaign comparing FPP with MMP. All were presented using a 'mirror-form' strategy: the key features of each theme were introduced and developed for both electoral systems by a single character. A measure of the perceived effectiveness of this comparative advertising strategy was its utilisation by others towards the end of the campaign. Paralleling the advertising programme, research was commissioned to monitor the development of electors' understanding of the two systems. These findings were used to fine-tune the programme where necessary. For example, the weekly research barometers identified proportionality as the concept electors found by far the most difficult to understand, and this enabled the panel to adjust its original programme by increasing public exposure to the proportionality concept, and to present it in different ways (ibid., 1993a:15 October 1993).

For those who sought more detailed information and explanation a video expanded on the six key concepts at the heart of the public education campaign (ibid., 1993f).[12] A Chinese language translation of the video commentary was prepared and distributed to Chinese communities throughout the country by the New Zealand Chinese Association. A 24-hour free-of-charge telephone inquiry service which operated during the eight weeks leading up to the referendum responded to over 16,000 calls. Special interest groups were again accommodated: sight-impaired persons were able to access audio tapes describing the two options and study it by means of a braille translation, a summary of the basic pamphlet was published as a teletext page, and information kits were sent to all secondary schools.

As we have already seen, in 1992 the panel had endeavoured, with little success, to develop a working relationship with three disparate Maori groups. In 1993 it sought to involve representatives of the three pan-Maori organisations[13] from the outset. The steering committee's co-convenors, Ngatata Love and Wiremu Katene, met with the panel at its first meeting where they presented an initial proposal involving extensive use of existing institutional and customary Maori networks such as Maori Trust Boards, iwi-runanga, *Whare Wananga* (houses of instruction), and *Kohanga Reo* (language nests), to disseminate information, principally using time-consuming but arguably more effective kanohi-ki-te-kanohi strategies (ibid., 1993a: 8 October 1993; 29 October 1993; 1 November 1993). Robertson was concerned to ensure that the activities at the core of this proposal were consistent with the broader campaign and that the panel's impartiality would be maintained, and he sought assurances that this would be so (ibid., 23 July 1993). He also sought written confirmation that all three pan-Maori groups were committed to the proposed programme. On the same day, Robertson wrote to Wira Gardiner, Chief Executive of Te Puni Kokiri to stress the need for close co-operation between the panel and the Ministry (ibid., 30 July 1993). Gardiner's reply, which implied that Love and Katene had gone their own way the previous year, offered assistance in calling hui through his Ministry's regional offices. Two months later, however, Te Puni Kokiri withdrew its resources at the direction of its Minister, who did not want an organisation representing executive government involved in any way (ibid., 24 September 1993).

The Maori sub-programme eventually delivered 137 local and regional presentations to an estimated 6500 people — principally in the North Island where most Maori live — two networked Aotearoa Radio talkback programmes (the second on the night before the referendum) involving 25 iwi radio stations, a television programme using the Maori version of the panel's video, and information stalls staffed by Maori which were set up in 46 major shopping centres in Auckland, Wellington, and Hamilton where urban Maori were concentrated. When measured solely in monetary terms on a 'cost-per-person-present' basis, the kanohi-ki-te-kanohi strategy (which averaged out at $46 per head) appeared very expensive, and Robertson believes that "it is not cost effective, and may not be technically efficient unless it is associated with a strong multi-media campaign" (Robertson, 1997). This, however, fails to take into account flow-on benefits arising from any subsequent discussions between those who had attended sub-programme presentations and had later discussed what they had learned with others. Nor does it allow for the impact of the programme's less formal promotion through the medium of information stalls. Neither of these aspects is capable of being measured in monetary terms.

Pacific Islanders also received special attention. The panel again sought guidance and assistance from the Ministry of Pacific Island Affairs (ERP, 1993a:30 July 1993), the basic pamphlet was translated into six Pacific Island languages,[14] and 31 single-language ethnic meetings were held. The average attendance at these meetings was a lowly 23, with Samoan numbers in particular, proportionately much lower than other Pacific Island ethnic groups. Ethnic radio, however, had a large following and appears to have been an effective means of communicating with these groups.

Although both electoral systems were clearly defined in law by the time the 1993 public education campaign commenced, the panel still encountered significant difficulties in preparing for and promoting the public debate (*AJHR*, 1993:6).[15] Although it was able to commence work on its programme after the bill had been reported back to parliament by the select committee, the panel still had to be mindful that further amendments were possible (and did occur) as it continued its progress through the House of Representatives. A further complicating factor was that the date of the general election (and, therefore, the referendum) was still not known. This announcement finally came on 14 September, the day that the panel commenced its advertising programme. The effect was to make the referendum secondary to the election campaign in the minds of many electors.

The government muddied the waters even further with its eleventh-hour announcement — coming as it did after the panel's publicity material had been finalised and, for the most part, printed — that if FPP won majority support over MMP, it would amend the 1956 *Electoral Act* to provide for the number of separate Maori electorates to be determined on the same basis as General electorates. Since it would have been wrong for the panel to have anticipated a promised future change to the 1956 *Electoral Act*, all of its information included reference to a fixed number of Maori electorates under FPP but a variable number under MMP.

The future form of Maori representation was one of several issues that surfaced frequently during the panel's campaign. Arguably, it was the most important one. As we have seen, the Electoral Law Select Committee recommended (and parliament subsequently adopted) that, under MMP, the number of Maori constituency seats should be calculated by applying the same formula used to determine the number of North Island General constituency seats. In providing its example of how the number of Maori electorate seats might be calculated in an MMP environment, the panel elected to base its statements on the Maori Electoral population used by the 1992 Representation Commission (*AJHR*, 1992b:14)[16] because this was the only official data readily available in the public domain. When its first pamphlet, which included the words "[o]n the basis of the 1992 Maori electoral option, there would be only three Maori electorates" (ERP, 1993b) appeared, the panel's statement was challenged both by Labour Party politicians and Department of Justice officials because the select committee had been assured that "if there was no change in the ratio of Maori enrolled on the Maori [and] General rolls after the 1994 Maori roll option there would be four Maori seats, not three as mentioned in the panel's publicity material" (ibid., 1993a:14 September 1993). This was not the end of the matter. Near the conclusion of the campaign one of the panel's statements relating to the future number of Maori electorate seats was again challenged, this time by the Department of Statistics. The department alleged that the panel was remiss in not using the information presented to the select committee on 16 July 1993 which subsequently provided the basis for the calculation of electoral populations and the new definition of Maori electoral population (ibid., 15 October 1993).[17] In reply Robertson restated the panel had "stuck to known facts" (ibid., 22 October 1993). What followed was a series of increasingly terse communications between the Government Statistician, Len Cook, and the panel, which ended only after Robertson forcefully asserted the panel's independence. Replying to a letter from Cook (ibid., 27 October 1993) containing — according to Robertson — the "clear implication... that if the panel did not accept your views and calculations and do something about it, you would ...", Robertson responded:

> No panel specifically set up to act independently in the conduct of this campaign could possibly accept such an approach. This is especially so when its terms of reference made it clear that it did not accept directions from the instrumentalities of Executive Government in carrying out its operations. (ibid., 29 October 1993.)

Not for the first time, Robertson had strongly asserted the panel's independence from government influence. In fairness to Cook, however, it must be noted that the Government Statistician is, by statute, responsible for all of New Zealand's official statistics and is totally independent of government direction, and his objection to the panel's published material was made on that basis. Interestingly, a major spin-off effect of the panel's handling of this question, and the public debate it generated, may have been to direct more attention to the new method of determining guaranteed separate Maori representation than might otherwise have been the case.

At the outset the panel resolved, as it had in 1992, that it would monitor the public debate by correcting errors of fact but would not get involved in the debate itself because it would thereby run the risk of promoting one electoral system against the other (ibid., 13–16 August 1993). Several times during the course of the campaign, issues were raised by members of the public to which the panel found it necessary to respond. Early in its work the panel had realised, that under certain circumstances, an MMP parliament could have more than 120 MPs although its first publication did not make this clear (ibid., 1993b).[18] A number of electors challenged this, pointing out that since the *Electoral Act 1993* provided for a party or parties which won more constituency seats than the number of seats their party vote entitled them to (referred to as the 'overhang'), there could be occasions when the number of MPs exceeded 120. One even suggested that future MMP parliaments could have as many as 185 MPs, thus destroying the proportionality concept on which MMP was based.[19] Another MP went even further by suggesting that parties could engage in deliberate manipulation in order to subvert the MMP electoral system. The panel's response was to note that this could only happen if an individual party or parties set out to make it happen (ibid., 1993a:15 September 1993).[20] It also found it necessary to issue a press release warning the media not to misinterpret the provision in the *Electoral Act 1993* that required a select committee to be set up after 1 April 2000 to review the operation of MMP should it be endorsed by electors in the referendum, to remind electors that the proposed Electoral Commission was not empowered to "oversee the process of democratic candidate selection", and to point out that the 60:60 split of constituency and list seats proposed by the Royal Commission had not been incorporated in the 1993 *Electoral Act* (ibid., 14 October 1993).[21]

One quite unanticipated development occurred shortly before the public education campaign was launched when the Governor-General, Dame Cath Tizard, touched on the Governor-General's possible role in an MMP electoral system. During a speech to the Friends of the Alexander Turnbull Library, she was variously reported as saying:

> The frequent exercise of the Governor-General's reserve powers would not only damage the office but also, I suspect, seriously undermine the democratic basis of our system. (*NZH*, 7 July 1993) ...What the situation might be if New Zealand votes for some system of proportional representation, I don't know. I do know though, that I'm just as happy not to have to find out. Should the vote this year be for MMP, by the time of the first election under the new system I will no longer be the Governor-General. (*Dom.*, 7 July 1993.)

This seeming intervention into the debate drew critical responses from several advocates of MMP and at least one academic. Electoral Reform Coalition chair, Colin Clark, described her comments as "very disappointing", and said that it was unfortunate that they had gone so far (*NZH*, 6 July 1993), while Alliance leader Jim Anderton criticised her comments, claiming that she had undermined her political neutrality (ibid., 7 July 1993). University of Auckland constitutional law expert, Bill Hodge, noted that Tizard's expression of an opinion on a political issue was without precedent, certainly within the previous 20 years. She had, Hodge said, "defied the convention that the Governor-General does not comment on political issues" (ibid.). In the face of such criticism, damage control became the order of the day: a spokesperson for the Governor-General said that Tizard had not intended to speak out on the merits of either First-past-the-post or MMP (ibid.), while the Governor-General herself observed: "I support neither side in this debate and it would be improper for me to do so" (*Dom.*, 8 July 1993). There the matter rested, but it did little to assuage the fears of MMP supporters that last-ditch attempts would be made to torpedo the drive for electoral reform.

The 1993 publicity campaign was dominated by the two diametrically opposed lobby groups, the Electoral Reform Coalition (ERC) and the Campaign for Better Government (CBG). Because it was clear that these two groups would drive much of the public debate, the panel consciously sought to work with them and persuade them to use the panel's material as the factual basis for the debate (*AJHR*, 1993:6; *NZH*, 2 September 1993). If this could be achieved, a common starting point would, at least, have been established. This was consistent with the panel's view that if "a valid, informed and effective decision" was to be achieved, it must be grounded on an "unbiased, factual information campaign" (*AJHR*, 1993:18–19). With this in mind, and conscious of the fact that "a strong public debate is essential to develop the public's understanding of the two options" (*NZH*, 2 September 1993), Robertson invited the leaders of both lobby groups to meet with the panel at an early stage to discuss the broad structure of the public education programme (ERP, 1993a:23 July 1993).

At the meeting, on 3 September, 10 days before the panel's campaign launch, Robertson emphasised that the referendum was about electoral reform, not parliamentary reform. Despite this, the CBG representatives, Owen Jennings and Brian Nicolle, pleaded with the panel to promote the wider issues of political accountability. Robertson reiterated that responsibility for this lay with the parliament and the government, and, as such, did not fall within the panel's terms of reference. The ERC representatives, Colin Clark and Phil Saxby, sought to persuade the panel to include the Royal Commission's recommendations and argument in its campaign. Robertson rejected this outright, stating that much of its content had been superseded by later developments. Nor would he countenance offers from both groups to assist the panel by vetting its draft material before final approval; the panel, Robertson reminded them, was independent and it, alone, would be accountable for its campaign material (ibid., 3 September 1993).[22]

Although the meeting with the lobby groups was amicable, it did little to prevent the two groups from repeatedly criticising each other's attempts to persuade the electorate to support its point of view. Many were of a tit-for-tat nature. When, for example, the CBG broadcast a television advertisement depicting 21 hooded MPs (designed to draw attention to the cost to the taxpayer of an enlarged parliament), the ERC complained to the Advertising Standards Complaints Board. The CBG responded swiftly by lodging a complaint with the same board over an ERC advertisement that erroneously claimed, the CBG alleged, that Italy had recently adopted an MMP electoral system (*NZH*, 30 September 1993). The Complaints Board responded by upholding the CBG's complaint because it "agreed that the Italian system was a type of proportional representation but it was not MMP as proposed for New Zealand", and rejecting the complaint by the ERC because the CBG's advertisement was "factually correct" (ibid., 5 October 1993). This sniping between the two groups continued unabated throughout the seven weeks of the public debate, keeping the Complaints Board busy throughout. While, for the most part, the ERC's and CBG's complaints were pursued through the Advertising Standards Complaints Board, some were also referred directly to the Electoral Referendum Panel which took the view that the issues raised fell "within the parameters of robust debate" (ibid., 21 October 1993).[23]

In large measure these spats occurred because the CBG was assumed to have an inexhaustible 'war chest' while the ERC's financial support base was strictly limited. When the first CBG television advertisement was screened, the ERC — which accused the CBG of using "subliminal messages to turn people away from MMP" (*Press*, 6 October 1993)[24] — wrote to the Minister of Justice alleging that big business was being permitted to buy television advertising time to manipulate the referendum when political parties were barred from buying election advertising. As a means of levelling the playing field, the coalition suggested that each side of the referendum debate should "be given equal time on television and radio to promote their case and that neither party be allowed to buy additional time". Graham's response was short and to the point: there was nothing he could do, he said, to prevent one or other side from buying broadcasting time. The CBG's reaction was equally predictable: the ERC's attacks were well rehearsed and failed to recognise or acknowledge the big response to the CBG's appeal for donations (*NZH*, 27 September 1993).

All the major metropolitan daily newspapers devoted space to supporters of both camps to promote their case. Notable contributors on the MMP side were two members of the Royal Commission, John Wallace and Ken Keith (*Dom.*, 14 October & 4 November 1993; *NZH*, 26 October 1993; *Press* 3 November 1993). Among those ranged against MMP were Australian academic, Malcolm Mackerras, Canberra journalist, Crispin Hull, and politicians David Lange and Simon Upton (*Dom.*, 13 August, 19 October & 4 November 1993; *Press,* 7 September & 4 November 1993). The same papers also devoted many column inches of editorial comment and advice to electors — Auckland's *New Zealand Herald* supported MMP, Wellington's *Dominion* and Dunedin's *Otago Daily Times* both advised their readers to vote for the retention of the existing electoral system, while Christchurch's *Press* left its readers to decide for themselves.

In marked contrast to 1992, politicians as a group were strangely quiet as the binding referendum approached. Very few members of either major party were prepared publicly to take a firm position because most believed that the active intervention by MPs in support of First-past-the-post the previous year had been counterproductive. Perhaps in a forlorn, last-ditch attempt to swing public opinion back towards FPP, the Prime Minister, Jim Bolger, broke his silence when he predicted that New Zealand would experience a "very unstable three years of politics if MMP was adopted" as MPs jostled for a reduced number of constituency seats (*Press,* 28 October 1993). Like so many other statements from MPs on the subject of electoral reform, this one was almost certainly regarded as self-serving by a sceptical electorate.

Voters Speak Out Twice — The Results

1992 — an overwhelming rejection of the status quo[25]

Some months after the 1992 referendum British psephologist, David Butler, observed that the result was an extraordinary example of electors "cocking a snook at authority ... the biggest slap in the face of the establishment that you can think of in any referendum. ... It is a surprise that it should come in New Zealand which one thinks of as a very stable, orderly society" (*NZH*, 24 March 1993).

True to all predictions, the 1992 referendum, a stand-alone poll in which just over one-half of all registered electors voted, produced a not unexpected show of support, both for changing from the existing First-past-the-post electoral system and for MMP as the most preferred alternative. What was surprising was the overwhelming nature of that support for both options — 84.7 per cent supported the 'change' option in Part A of the voting paper, and 70.5 per cent endorsed MMP as the preferred reform option despite the fact that, in part B, electors were presented with a choice of four diverse options. Detailed results are set out in Table 9.2.

Although this was a national referendum, the results are amenable to aggregate analysis because they are collated on an electorate-by-electorate basis. What stands out is a remarkable geographic and political consensus for both 'change' and MMP. In every electorate, at least 70 per cent of those who went to the poll supported the 'change' option,[26] although differences emerge when electorates are considered on the basis of their geographic characteristics and incumbent party.[27] Overall, electorates held by opposition parties voted more decisively for 'change' than did electorates whose incumbent MP

Table 9.2 Results of the Indicative Referendum, September 1992

	Votes	%
Part A – Status Quo or Change:		
Retain First-Past-the-Post:	186,027	15.3
Vote for Change to the Electoral System:	1,031,257	84.7
	1,217,284	
Part B – Preferred Alternative:		
Supplementary Member (SM):	62,278	5.5
Single Transferable Vote (STV):	194,796	17.4
Mixed Member Proportional (MMP):	790,648	70.5
Preferential Voting (PV):	73,539	6.6
	1,121,261	
Valid vote as a percentage of registered electors		
Part A	53.4	
Part B	49.2	
Number of registered electors and percentage turnout:	2,279,396	53.5
Informal Votes:		
Informal Votes – Part A:	2,606	0.1
Informal Votes – Part B:	97,708	4.3
Disallowed Special Votes:	37,840	

Source: AJHR, 1993a

represented the governing National Party even though these electorates still recorded decisive support for 'change' (Table 9.3). In 23 of the 29 Labour-held electorates, support for 'change' was greater than the mean of 84.7 per cent, while 35 of the 41 electorates where support for 'change' was below the mean had elected National Party MPs in 1990. When ranked according to the level of their support for 'change', all but one of the 24 lowest-ranked electorates were won by National in 1990, 16 (66.7 per cent) were rural, three (12.5 per cent) were centred on a single rural service centre, while only four (16.7 per cent) were wholly urban. Conversely, the 14 electorates that supported the 'change' option most strongly were located in one or other of the country's three largest cities, ten of them in Auckland. It is clear from these data that dissatisfaction with FPP was greatest amongst urban dwellers, and in electorates that had returned opposition MPs in 1990.

Table 9.3   1992 Indicative Referendum: Voter Support for the 'Change' Option and for MMP as the Preferred Option by Party (%)

	Alliance	Labour	National	Mean
Support for 'change' (%)	87.6	86.8	83.7	84.5
Support for MMP (%)	75.0	71.9	69.7	70.5

Source: AJHR, 1993a

A similar pattern is evident when voter support for the MMP option is analysed. Levine and Roberts (1993a:162) explain the overwhelming support for the MMP reform option in these terms:

> New Zealand's voters, accustomed to an uncluttered ballot paper, coped with the unfamiliar two-part menu by displaying an unmistakable preference for the option generally regarded as most damaging to the interests of the country's two dominant parties. Despite some pre-referendum speculation about a possibly divided pro-change vote, with perhaps only a plurality being secured by one of the four alternatives, the part B result was a stunning 70.5 per cent in favour of the mixed member proportional option (MMP) recommended by the Royal Commission.

As with the support for 'change', while voters in all electorates opted decisively for MMP as the most preferred reform option there were, inevitably, variations in that support between electorates with different characteristics. Of the 14 electorates which endorsed MMP most strongly, seven were represented by MPs who openly favoured that reform option. In rural electorates, most of which were won by National in 1990, support for MMP lagged behind urban electorates by between 5 and 7 percentage points. As Levine and Roberts concluded, "[t]he electorate's unprecedented near-unanimity of outlook meant that it was perceived as speaking with almost a single voice ..." (ibid., 163). Given the comparatively low voter turnout (53.5 per cent) compared with previous referendums held outside the normal general election cycle, the level of support for MMP ensured that the result could not be dismissed as irrelevant.

Of the other reform options, the Single Transferable Vote (STV) was clear second choice among those who voted. At 17.4 per cent, its support was greater (and higher in absolute terms) than that recorded for the 'no change' option in Part A. This was little short of remarkable in view of the fact that it was a late addition to Part B of the voting paper, and suggests that, in 1992, voters favoured what they believed to be electoral systems that were fairer to political parties, particularly those smaller and newer parties who were consistently disadvantaged by FPP. In comprehensively rejecting both other options, voters clearly recognised that neither the Supplementary Member system nor Preferential Voting would go anywhere near to achieving this objective.

At 32.7 per cent, electoral turnout by those on the Maori roll was extremely low. Of those who did vote, 82.6 per cent supported the 'change' option (slightly lower than the overall mean) but a significantly higher 75.6 per cent supported MMP as the most preferred reform option. The low level of turnout supports the view that the 1992 referendum offered nothing to Maori by way of substantial electoral reform despite the best efforts of the Referendum Panel to keep the door to reform at least slightly ajar. The general perception appeared to be that a continuation of FPP would mean that the number of dedicated Maori seats would stay fixed at four while the adoption of MMP — assuming that the Royal Commission's model was adhered to closely — would result in the abolition of separate representation. Either way, any potential benefits to Maori appeared minimal, despite the firmly held and assiduously promoted views expressed in the Royal Commission's report and subsequently promoted actively by some of its members.

Although Levine and Roberts' explanation for the overwhelming support for MMP is convincing, it overlooks one important point. MMP was the reform option unanimously recommended by the Royal Commission and, for nearly six years, its adoption had been promoted assiduously by the Electoral Reform Coalition. No other reform option — or, for that matter, FPP — had any comparable organisation advancing its cause by consistently keeping it in the public eye. This, coupled with the fact that electors had almost totally lost faith in politicians and the political parties they represented, created a climate of opinion that persuaded voters to send MPs a strong and unequivocal message demanding change. Thus although the 1992 referendum was non-binding, the comprehensive nature of its message forced politicians to take the prospect of change to the electoral system seriously and to design an MMP electoral system that would be broadly acceptable to the electorate.

1993 — a narrow but conclusive vote for change[28]

As expected, the 1993 referendum, held in conjunction with the general election, resulted in a much higher voter turnout than 1992. This guaranteed that the final outcome would much more accurately reflect the real strength of public opinion than had the indicative referendum.

Nevertheless, while MMP was supported by a clear majority of those who voted, its margin over the existing electoral system was not nearly as decisive as it had been the previous year. In fact, when the number of electors who voted for the 'change' option in 1992 is set against the number who supported the adoption of MMP in 1993, the difference between the two is a minuscule 1,662 votes or 0.16 per cent. At the same time support for the status quo (retention of FPP) rose by 30.8 per cent. The result of the 1993 binding referendum is set out in Table 9.4.

Analysis of these aggregate results highlights the presence of considerable regional differences. Support for MMP was much stronger among North Island and Maori electorates than South Island electorates. All four Maori electorates, and 82.9 per cent of the 70 North Island's General electorates, voted in favour of MMP compared with only 48.0 per cent of South Island General electorates.[29] An even more detailed analysis (by region and type of electorate) reveals a general decline in support for MMP from north to south, and a sharp cleavage between urban and rural voters.

Table 9.4   Results of the Binding Referendum, November 1993

	Votes	%
Valid Votes:		
For First-Past-the-Post (FPP):	884,964	46.1
For Mixed Member Proportional (MMP):	1,032,919	53.9
	1,917,883	
Number of registered electors and percentage turnout:	2,321,664	82.6
General Election —		
Total valid votes and percentage turnout:	1,934,160	83.3
Informal votes cast:	11,364	0.6
Disallowed votes:	43,932	2.3

Source: AJHR, 1994

Although it is tempting to conclude that virtually all who supported the 'change' option in 1992 voted for MMP in 1993, and that the upsurge in support from the status quo option in the binding referendum came almost totally from those who had abstained in 1992 because they knew that they would have a second opportunity to voice their opinion should the second, binding, referendum be held, it would, nevertheless, be quite wrong to do so. While aggregate data can throw some light on the collective behaviour of the electorate at a given point in time, they do not allow such inferences to be drawn. For insights into reasons underpinning the decisions reached by electors we must turn to the findings of survey research.

Survey data gathered immediately after the 1993 election (Vowles, *et al.,* 1995:175–80) tends to confirm the stability of support for MMP across both referendums: 71 per cent of those who voted for MMP in 1993 indicated that they had voted for the 'change' option in the 1992 referendum, compared with a mere 4 per cent who had supported the 'status quo' option and 26 per cent who had not voted. Conversely, of those who voted for FPP in 1993, 94 per cent had supported the 'no change' option the previous year, while 41 per cent of those who did not vote in 1992, opted for FPP in the binding referendum. Thus, overall there appears to have been only a moderate shift of opinion among those who voted in both the 1992 and 1993 referendums. A pre-election survey by Levine and Roberts (1994:245–49) showed that 92.8 per cent of those who voted in favour of retaining the status quo in 1992 intended to vote for FPP in the 1993 referendum while 75.6 per cent of electors who supported the 'change' option in 1992 intended voting for MMP.[30] Support for the two options was, however, much closer amongst respondents who had abstained in 1992: 57.6 per cent said that they would vote for FPP compared with only 42.4 per cent for MMP. This, combined with the nearly seven voters who shifted back to FPP after having supported the 'change' option in 1992 for every two voters who switched from supporting the status quo in 1992 to MMP in 1993, resulted in a substantial closing of the gap between the existing and proposed new electoral system. The final margin of 7.8 percentage points was, however, sufficiently large to dissuade the proponents of FPP from challenging the result through recourse to legal action.

How might these differences be explained? Levine and Roberts (1994) note that a number of trends apparent in the results of the 1992 referendum were again present in 1993: the strongest support for MMP was recorded in electorates which returned Labour, Alliance or New Zealand First MPs in the 1993 general election;[31] that 19 of the 25 electorates recording majorities in favour of FPP were won by the governing National Party; and that, as in the indicative referendum, voter perceptions of the quality of the government's performance had a significant bearing on the way that electors cast their votes.[32] It is also clear that support for a continuance of FPP among South Island voters, particularly those living in rural areas, reflected concerns that MMP would mean geographically much larger electorates (and, therefore, less effective representation of their interests), a fear that was cultivated by the Campaign for Better Government in its advertising blitz.[33] The strong Maori endorsement of MMP on the other hand, may be attributed, at least in part, to the fact that although the government had belatedly — albeit reluctantly — promised that it would amend the 1956 *Electoral Act* to provide for the number of Maori electorates to be calculated on the basis of population numbers, a vote for MMP would guarantee that this would happen, at least as far as it was possible to do so. It was a case of one *kereru* (native wood pigeon, a protected species) in the pot being worth two or more kereru in the bush!

Why Did Voters Rebel?

After the Royal Commission's report was published most commentators held out little hope that its main recommendation, the introduction of a new, proportional representation, electoral system, would be embraced. What, then, led voters to rebel against their political masters? What were the factors that led electors to reject the electoral system New Zealand had used for close to 140 years? And, finally, to what extent did the National government's decision to pass control of the public information and education programmes across to an independent panel contribute to what Lijphart suggested was the 'demise of the last Westminster system'?

In their more recent study of referendums Butler and Ranney (1994:259) point out that although politicians usually dislike referendums, there are occasions when they resort to them "as last-ditch devices for resolving issues" that have become so contentious that they cannot be solved by ordinary political mechanisms. They note that when this occurs, decisions are effectively taken "out of established hands, and elected leaders can never control — or be responsible for — their outcomes". New Zealand's experience strongly supports their view: by 1992 politicians had effectively surrendered, to voters, responsibility for determining whether a major electoral reform should take place and, if so, which one of a smorgasbord of alternative electoral systems should be adopted.

But, as we have already seen, the origins of the 'voter revolt' lay in the collective and individual experiences of the late 1970s. National's success in winning parliamentary majorities in both the 1978 and 1981 general elections, even though it did not win a plurality of the popular vote, prompted growing unease about the ability of FPP to fairly reflect the public will, an unease that was compounded by the failure of a third significant party to win more than minimal parliamentary representation, despite capturing at least one in six of all valid votes cast in each of these two elections.[34] Nor was that all, for during the years of the Muldoon administrations (1975–84) the quality of government decision-making came increasingly into question. This centralised democracy model, dubbed the 'elective dictatorship' by Lord Hailsham (1978:9–11), led directly to Labour's 'Open Government' commitment, first set out in its 1981 election manifesto. The establishment of the Royal Commission, its intensive study of New Zealand's electoral system and those of a number of other countries, and its recommendation that New Zealand adopt MMP, flowed inexorably from this pre-1984 commitment.

When faced with the reality of the report and its implications for electorally dominant parties, the Labour Government drew back, only to have the issue of electoral reform return to haunt it after Lange's gaffe during the 1987 election campaign. The Fourth Labour Government's virtual meltdown during its second term in office (1987–90), and growing public cynicism about its ability to govern effectively in the interests of all citizens, helped undermine electors' confidence in the ability of the electoral and political systems to deliver. And although the levers of power were entrusted to National in 1990, its economic and welfare prescriptions reinforced the electorate's view that the First-past-the-post electoral system offered them little genuine choice. Increasingly, electors came to distrust their governments. Add to this, the developing tendency of both major parties to splinter in the face of growing internal tensions and the emergence of several new parties, and the public mood of cynicism with politics and politicians was ripe for exploitation. The new parties, in particular, had nothing to lose by promoting an electoral system that had been recommended because it was likely to provide them with fairer representation.

Just how effective were the two taxpayer-funded public education campaigns? Inevitably, such programmes are notoriously difficult to plan and present, especially where the issues involved are technically complex and lie largely outside the mainstream of most recipients' experience. In this context, the government's decision to establish a panel was a significant departure from previous practice. What made it even more unusual was that, although the panel's programme would be funded by the government, the panel was totally independent of government direction.

Both the 1992 and 1993 panels were charged with responsibility for overseeing the development and presentation of a mass public education programme for some 2.3 million potential voters with widely varying levels of literacy,[35] within an extremely short period of time — less than eight months in 1992 and half this time in 1993. Although people are generally most attentive when they recognise that they have a need for information and knowledge — interest generally increases as the time for making decisions draws close — the complexity of the issues encapsulated in the two referendums pointed to the desirability of a significantly longer public phase in both years. Without precedents to guide it, the 1992 panel was faced with a very steep learning curve. The 1993 panel, with its substantial continuity of membership and significantly fewer options to explain, was able to build on the experience gained the previous year to develop strategies that targeted the key issues much more closely.

In order to reach some assessment of the impact of the two campaigns we must turn to survey research commissioned by the Independent Referendum Panel in both years, a survey commissioned by the Department of Justice in the wake of the 1992 referendum, and published public opinion polls commissioned by newspapers. Since the issues explored and the questions asked differed between surveys their results cannot be readily compared. At best, we are left with a rather hazy overall picture of the impact of the two campaigns and differing impressions of their effectiveness.

In both years the panel commissioned Phoenix Research of Auckland to monitor electors' awareness of the referendums and knowledge of the reform options to be included on each voting paper. In 1992 three surveys were conducted: a 'benchmark' survey in May 1992 (well before the panel commenced its advertising campaign) and two 'monitor' surveys, one shortly after the householder pamphlet had been delivered in early July and the second at the end of August, some three weeks before the referendum. The 'benchmark' survey revealed that only 22.2 per cent of respondents were aware of the referendum but awareness had risen steeply (to 87.8 per cent) by the first monitor survey, after which it plateaued. A similar, though not so marked, pattern was evident when respondents' knowledge of the four reform options was tapped: MMP was by far and away the best known option (27 per cent in the 'benchmark' survey, rising to 47 per cent by the time of the second 'monitor' survey), well ahead of preferential voting (4.3 per cent rising to 6 per cent), SM (0.6 per cent; 6 per cent), and STV (0.4 per cent; 7 per cent) (Justice, 1992b).

The panel's 1993 'benchmark' survey, conducted in September, revealed a 69 per cent awareness of the forthcoming binding referendum, much higher than in 1992. By the final 'barometer' survey this had increased to 90 per cent. Knowledge of the options was also much greater than in the previous year, rising from 40 per cent in the 'benchmark' survey to over 80 per cent in the last survey when 96 per cent of respondents were able to identify First-past-the-post as one of the options, and 90 per cent identified 'Mixed Member Proportional' as the other. Interestingly, most respondents referred to the Mixed Member Proportional electoral system by its initials, MMP. This was cause for some concern among the panel and its advisers because the voting paper included only the full names of each electoral system, but their fears were allayed when research showed that nearly all respondents were able to associate the two when prompted (*AJHR,* 1993:12–15).

In 1992, public opinion polls conducted on behalf of newspapers focused on whether electors had sufficient information to be able to make an informed choice. Responses indicated that even though they had received the panel's householder pamphlet, electors still did not feel as though they had sufficient information to make an informed choice,[36] although one survey noted that many claimed to have put the pamphlet to one side for later reference. These same surveys also recorded mixed responses to the householder pamphlet: in July, 26 per cent of respondents to a *National Business Review* Insight survey indicated that the brochure had left them more confused (*NBR,* 24 July 1992), and the paper's August survey reported that 61 per cent of respondents thought that the panel's publicity campaign 'had not helped' (ibid., 14 August 1992).

Following the 1992 referendum the Department of Justice commissioned a survey of voter registration and turnout. In a briefing paper to the Electoral Law Select Committee in March 1993, the department noted that there was evidence of a lack of understanding of the options involved, which may have influenced non-voters — three-quarters of non-voters said that on the day before the referendum they felt that they did not know enough to decide how to vote. The most common reasons for not voting were given as apathy, disillusionment and a lack of knowledge about the different options (ELSC, 1993a).

What are we to make of these conflicting signals? The adage, 'you can lead a horse to water ...' readily comes to mind. Although the 1992 Phoenix Research surveys recorded a rising level of public awareness, this was a superficial measure because it did not tell how many electors really understood the different reform options and the issues surrounding them. Increased public awareness was not sufficient, in itself, to guarantee an informed electorate. In 1992 the panel's campaign was seriously handicapped by the fact that the legislation authorising the referendums did not detail any of the reform options to be placed before the electorate. This was compounded by the panel's decision to publicise each option in the order that they were balloted to appear on the voting paper: FPP, SM, STV, MMP and PV.[37] Although Robertson (1997) argues that any departure from the order established by the process set out in the *Electoral Referendum Act 1991* would have increased public confusion, and would have been a decision that the panel was not authorised to make, the result was that there was no logical progression across the reform options — from simplest to the most complex — to help voters to understand their intricacies. The lack of detail, and the fact that the referendum was non-binding, undoubtedly contributed to the comparatively high level of disinterest evident.

The 1993 campaign, on the other hand, was simpler and more focused even though its time-frame was probably still too brief, particularly given the distractions of the concurrent general election campaign. Disseminating information is essentially a one-way process; education, on the other hand, usually involves some degree of interaction between teachers and learners and, wherever possible, should be largely free from distractions. To be successful, community education programmes should also be sufficiently stimulating to encourage the target audience to study the material provided and discuss the issues involved with others. For many, the most appropriate environment is in small, non-threatening gatherings where questions can be asked, and ideas exchanged and debated. All of this, of course, takes time, and the government's failure to allow sufficient time for the public to absorb abstruse concepts means that it must accept primary responsibility for any shortcomings arising from what were extremely brief programmes. Community-based facilitators, trained under the auspices of the panel and encouraged to work alongside community networks and informal local groups to stimulate interest and encourage debate among equals, would undoubtedly have required significantly greater financial resources than the government allocated, but it may have led to greater community understanding than subsequent research, undertaken on behalf of the Electoral Commission, reported (*AJHR*, 1997:9).[38]

The fact that support for the 'change' option in 1992 was substantially replicated in the vote for MMP in 1993 seems to indicate that many electors decided on their referendum voting intentions well before the panel's campaign. This observation is supported by anecdotal evidence from a number of those involved in explaining the options at the public meetings held in both 1992 and 1993; they reported that attendances in 1993 were well below those of 1992, perhaps as low as 50 per cent. For this reason, if for no other, the publicly-funded education and information campaign probably made little or no difference to the final result, most elector's minds had been made up, based on a variety of factors, well before the 1993 campaign was launched.

In its 1993 report to parliament the Independent Referendum Panel argued that an unbiased and factual information campaign was essential if

[A] valid, informed and effective decision is to be realised. ... [The panel believed] that it was able to exert an impartial constraining influence on the national debate by ensuring that the facts of both referendum options were aired and were available to the individual voter. (*AJHR*, 1993:18.)

This approach inevitably prompted criticism from a number of quarters: the *New Zealand Herald* (28 October 1993), for example, commented that the panel was "so neutral as to be unhelpful to the public", while, at different times, members of the Electoral Reform Coalition castigated the panel for not mentioning the Royal Commission's recommendations in its material ("this may have unwittingly biased the polls towards FPP" [*Press*, 23 October 1993]), and "for not doing enough to explain MMP" (*NZH*, 3 November 1993).

The bottom line, however, is whether the government — and society in general — is prepared to provide the resources necessary to allow programmes of public education to be conducted on a scale that allows the development of comprehensive programmes designed to encourage positive participation and interaction by electors. While there will always be those whose interest in politics is minimal or even non-existent, if future governments are serious about wanting to encourage electors to participate actively in programmes intended to help them understand the issues before they cast their vote, much greater resources than those made available to the 1992 and 1993 electoral referendum panels will need to be allocated.

In the wake of the referendum Mackerras, a persistent and trenchant critic of MMP (which he had earlier described as 'a ratbag scheme') asked: "How did over a million ordinary New Zealanders vote for such an awful system?" He concluded that those who voted for MMP probably thought that it was fairer than FPP, and their suspicions of the motives of the people openly opposed to MMP persuaded them to vote for change (Mackerras, 1994:36–40). This is a highly simplistic view. Another explanation has been proposed by political geographer, Ron Johnston, who suggests that people voted for MMP in the hope that the country would return to the cultural norms of the welfare state era. Citing Nagel (1994:525–29), he wrote that it was not:

> simply a response from those disadvantaged by the reforms [of 1984–93], with those who had benefited most arguing for the status quo. ... The vote was a call for an end to the dismantling of the state apparatus and social structure erected over a century or more; New Zealanders wanted to return to the (perhaps rather staid) stability and security of their recent past. (Johnston, 1994:64.)

There can be little doubt that support for the change option in 1992, and a vote for MMP in 1993, was a reaction to the policies of recent Labour and National governments. The study by Vowles, *et al.* (1995:180–92), shows that a vote for MMP correlated closely with electors' "views on democracy as well as a range of policy stances usually associated with left-wing parties", and they conclude that, "[c]ontrary ... to allegations about voter ignorance and confusion made during and after the referendum, the vast majority of voters made choices that can be rationally and logically explained".

The twin referendum process which resulted in New Zealand adopting a new electoral system by public endorsement was "an exercise in popular sovereignty" (Brookfield, 1992:20[39]). Having surrendered the decision for change to the electorate on this occasion, it will be exceedingly difficult for a future government or parliament to ever again change the country's electoral system without first securing the electorate's approval through another referendum.

Former British Prime Minister, James Callaghan, once described the referendum mechanism as "a rubber life raft into which we all may have to climb" (quoted, Butler & Ranney, 1994:260). Callaghan was, of course, referring to politicians but, in New Zealand's case, in 1992 and again in 1993, it was the voters who abandoned First-past-the-post for the life raft of electoral reform because a majority believed that the MMP electoral system might just give them the means of persuading inherently untrustworthy governments to be more directly accountable to those who put them in a position of power in the first place.

Notes

1   See Cleveland & Robinson (1972) for the text of the ministerial statement on the 1967 electoral referendum. In 1990, the pamphlet authorised by the government and distributed to all households prior to the referendum was headed 'Important Information. Referendum on Term of Parliament: This leaflet summarises the arguments for both sides'.

2   Cabinet allocated a total of $3 million to the panel for its 1992 campaign and $5.085 million for its 1993 campaign (*AJHR*, 1992a:16 and 1993:15).

3   Membership of the two panels differed only slightly. Blanchard was appointed to the High Court bench in July 1992 and was not replaced. Aitken was appointed Chief Executive of the Education Review Office towards the end of 1992, and Margaret Clark, Professor of Political Science at the Victoria University of Wellington, was appointed to the 1993 panel.

4   The Department of Justice had envisaged a **six-month campaign,** divided into two distinct phases — a three-month campaign to increase public awareness followed by a second three-month campaign explaining the different options.

5   The Bill, as introduced, provided that both parts of the voting paper be completed in order for it to be treated as formal, but this requirement was dropped on the recommendation of the Electoral Law Select Committee (*AJHR*, 1992a:6–7).

6   Throughout, the panel was very conscious that its credibility could have been undermined had its neutrality and independence been brought into question. For example, before it let a contract to the Gibson Group (a television programme maker bidding for a contract to make a special television documentary programme, *A Voter's Guide*) it inquired whether the company or its principals had had any previous political involvements that could prove embarrassing.

7   The householder pamphlet (ERP, 1992b), included the sentences: "None of the options

necessarily involves enlarging parliament", and "The Maori seats do not have to be abolished. All four reform options could still include separate Maori seats."

8   Although enacted in August 1993, this Act would not become operative unless a majority of those voting in the referendum supported the adoption of MMP.

9   One factor in his eventual acceptance was that parliament recommended the appointment of a temporary Ombudsman to cover the referendum period. This allowed Robertson to relinquish some of his casework while, at the same time, not impeding the work of the Ombudsman's office.

10   The Bill was finally reported back to parliament on 22 July.

11   In his letter Robertson also said: "I have never at any time since the panel met (on 13 July) said I was concerned about the short amount of time available."

12   Nearly 2,000 copies of the video, including 500 copies of a Maori version, were circulated on request. The Maori version was identical to the standard version apart from being prefaced by an introduction in the Maori language.

13   The New Zealand Maori Council, Maori Women's Welfare League, and Maori Congress. A steering committee representing these organisations had been instrumental in persuading the government to allow more time and provide financial resources to enable Maori to consult with their people before making a submission on the 1993 Electoral Reform Bill.

14   Cook Island Maori, Tongan, Samoan, Nuiean, Tokelauan, and Fijian.

15   In 1993 the panel's over-riding objective was "to communicate to every registered voter sufficient factual information on the two referendum options to enable an informed choice to be made on Referendum day".

16   The Maori Electoral Population was set by statute for the 1992 redistribution after the Representation Commission had questioned the basis and, therefore, the validity of the Government Statistician's original declaration.

17   The statement challenged was: "Based on the 1991 census there would be 64 electorate MPs (16 South Island General electorates, 45 North Island General electorates and 3 Maori electorates) if MMP was used in this [1993] election. However, if MMP is used in future elections new electoral boundaries would be needed. Before these are set, Maori will be given a chance to say if they wish to be on a General or Maori electoral roll. This could change the electorate balance." (See *The Referendum: The Guide*, Wellington, 1993, p 6.) By shifting from the de facto (census night) population count to the de jure population count and redefining the definition of Maori Electoral Population, the Maori population was significantly increased.

18   The brochure stated that there would "immediately be 120 MPs in parliament under MMP".

19   While this was theoretically possible, it could only eventuate in the extremely unlikely event that one party won all the constituency seats but only a minuscule (approximately 0.4 per cent or less) share of the party vote. Furthermore, that party would also have to be registered otherwise its constituency MPs would be treated as independent candidates and deducted from 120 before list seats were allocated.

20   National Party MP, Bruce Cliffe, argued that this could be achieved by a party dividing into 'town' and 'country' parties for the purposes of an election, and that the Electoral Referendum Panel should draw this to public attention. A 1995 amendment to the Electoral Act which requires 'component parties' to be identified has gone some way towards reducing the potential for this kind of manipulation.

21   A number of pro-MMP media had indicated that this review would provide electors with an opportunity to change back to the First-past-the-post electoral system if they did not like the way MMP worked in practice. The 1993 *Electoral Act* provided only that the select committee had to 'consider' the provisions in the act relating to the

procedure for defining the General electoral districts (including the 5 per cent tolerance allowed) and the provisions made for Maori representation. A further 'catch-all' provision empowers the select committee to decide whether to recommend whether any further changes to the electoral system should be decided by referendum.

22   Notwithstanding Robertson's rejection, the ERC again pursued the question of including the content of the Royal Commission's report in the panel's advertisements (ERP, 1993a:11 October 1993). The CBG also offered its help by reviewing drafts of the panel's material after it had "noticed a couple of factual errors in the panel's advertisements" (ibid., 5 October 1993). And, even before the panel had met with the protagonists, ERC vice-chair, Rod Donald, telephoned the panel's executive secretary, David Flux, to tell him that he had a copy of the draft television advertisement scripts and that he "wished to influence the final version to ensure that there was no perceived bias" (ibid., 27 August 1993).

23   In response to earlier complaints from the CBG, the panel concluded that they "lacked substance", were "time wasting", and "did not warrant a detailed response". (ERP, 1993a:8 October 1993.)

24   The ERC described its own pamphlets as "factual and unemotive", a view not shared by the CBG which accused radio broadcaster and MMP advocate, Pam Corkery, of disseminating misleading information (CBG, 1993q).

25   For a more detailed analysis of the result of the 1992 referendum see Levine & Roberts (1993a,b); Harris (1992).

26   The greatest support (90.5 per cent) in favour of change was recorded in Avon, while the Wallace electorate (71.1 per cent) recorded the lowest level of support for change.

27   In 1992 there were three parties represented in the New Zealand parliament: National, 65; Labour, 29; and the Alliance, 3, 2 of whom had left the party they had been elected to represent in 1990.

28   For a more detailed analysis of the result of the 1993 referendum see Levine & Roberts (1994); Harris (1993); McRobie (1994); Vowles, *et al.* (1995).

29   Overall, 55.2 per cent of voters in North Island General electorates supported MMP compared with 50.1 per cent of voters in South Island General electorates. Support for MMP among voters in Maori electorates was 65.8 per cent.

30   Pearson's (r) correlation coefficient between the support for MMP in both 1992 and 1993 for the 36 electorates which were unchanged or only minimally changed as a result of the 1992 electoral redistribution is 0.708, indicating a high level of consistency across both votes. For the classification of the 1993 electorates see James & McRobie (1993).

31   In a survey of 998 electors conducted in the six days immediately prior to the referendum, 79.6 per cent of National Party voters indicated support for FPP, but 89.1 per cent of Alliance voters, 79.0 per cent of New Zealand First voters, 62.7 per cent of Labour voters, and 51.6 per cent of other party voters indicated support for MMP.

32   80.8 per cent of electors who rated the government's performance as 'very good' voted for the retention of FPP compared with only 21.9 per cent of those who rated its performance as 'very poor' (Levine & Roberts, 1994:249).

33   In the face of declining parliamentary representation, the number of South Island electorates was fixed by law at 25 in 1967 (effective from the 1969 election). This change, however, did little more than temporarily arrest the continued expansion of the South Island's already large rural electorates.

34   In 1978 Social Credit won 16.1 per cent of the vote and one seat. Three years later it won 20.7 per cent of the vote and two seats. In 1984 its support fell to 7.6 per cent of the valid vote but it retained two seats. Also, in 1984, the New Zealand party won 12.3 per cent of the vote but no parliamentary seats.

35   According to the report of the International Adult Literacy Survey (Education, 1997), conducted in March 1996, literacy is defined as the ability to use "printed and written information to function in society, to achieve one's goals, and to develop one's knowledge and potential". This report noted that "[l]iteracy forms a continuum from those people in society who have only minimal or basic reading skills to those who possess highly developed skills to allow them to comprehend complex information". According to the report, "20 per cent of New Zealand's adult population was found to have very poor literacy skills. ... [and] ... could be expected to experience considerable difficulties in using many of the printed materials that may be encountered in daily life".

36   The *New Zealand Herald*, 13 August 1992, recorded that 64 per cent of respondents felt that they did not know enough. A comparable question in the *National Business Review*, 18 September, indicated that 66 per cent felt that they still did not have sufficient knowledge to make an informed choice.

37   As required by the *Electoral Referendum Act*, the order was determined by lot.

38   It should be noted, however, that there was considerable evidence in the Commission's 1994 survey to indicate that a considerable residual of latent knowledge about MMP was still present in many electors.

39   Brookfield's comment relates to the 1992 referendum but is equally apposite here.

10 The Transition to MMP

> The interval between the decay of the old and the formation and the establishment of the new, constitutes a period of transition, which must always necessarily be one of uncertainty, confusion, error and wild and fierce fanaticism.
> — John C. Calhoun, *A Disquisition on Government*, 1850.

The electorate's decision in favour of MMP, coupled with the narrowest possible victory for the incumbent National Government in the 1993 general election, put pressure on the government to commence the process of transition to the new electoral system as soon as it was administratively possible to do so. Several matters had to be addressed before the first MMP election could be held, some of which were constrained by statutory time-lines that could not be avoided. It was abundantly clear that the absolute minimum time required to carry out the statutory and administrative requirements dictated by the adoption of MMP was at least 12 months. Taking the summer holiday period for both 1993/94 and 1994/95 into account, this meant that earliest the first MMP election could be held was May 1995. Had the National Government lost the support of the House of Representatives before the statutory requirements or administrative arrangements had been met, another election would have had to have been held under the provisions of the *Electoral Act 1956* — an event that no one wanted. This chapter examines the statutory and other changes that took place before the first MMP election, the process of coalition building, and formation of the first MMP government.

The Maori Electoral Option

The first step in the transition to MMP was the determination of the Maori electoral population through the Maori option. Until this figure was known, work could not start on defining the new, larger MMP electoral districts. The Maori option was held between 15 February and 15 April 1994, at the conclusion of which the number of Maori registered on the Maori roll had increased by a net 32,294 persons. As a result of the application of the new formula for calculating the Maori electoral population,[1] five Maori constituency seats would need to be established for the first MMP parliament.

The Maori option provides Maori with a mechanism to allow them to decide the future of separate Maori representation. Although the option had first been held in 1976, until the *Electoral Act 1993* came into force it had had no practical significance other than helping determine the number of General electorates to which the North Island was entitled. The way that these data had been gathered had also changed several times during this period: in 1976, it had been gathered along with the five-yearly census; in 1982, a special declaration card was sent to all registered electors (although recipients who were not of Maori descent were instructed to "do nothing with this card"); in 1986, the option was combined with the regular roll revision; in 1990, ethnicity (self-ascribed) was sought at the same time as the roll revision; while in 1992, Maori option cards were sent only to those registered electors who had declared Maori descent.

The Royal Commission had been highly critical of the manner in which the 1982 option had been carried out. Describing the practice of sending option cards to all registered electors as expensive and potentially confusing, it suggested that cards should be sent only to electors who were entitled to exercise an option (RCES, 1986a:96 & 150). Subsequently, the Electoral Law Select Committee — after seeking advice from the Electoral Enrolment Centre — recommended that a Maori descent question should be included in the next roll revision to enable future Maori option exercises to be targeted at electors who had declared Maori descent (*AJHR*, 1988:29). This recommendation was inserted into the *Electoral Act 1956* in 1990 in the expectation that all qualified Maori would be captured on the database. Thus, in 1992, Maori option cards were sent only to electors registered on the Maori roll, and those on the General roll who had acknowledged Maori descent. Although the referendum on the future shape of the electoral system was still a long way off, this essentially administrative decision was to have far-reaching implications for the special Maori option held in 1994 because persons of Maori descent who had not declared their Maoriness were unwittingly excluded from the option unless they took the initiative to obtain and complete an option card.

In 1994, for the first time, Maori were given a genuine opportunity to determine the immediate future and shape of their parliamentary representation. Maori leaders, especially those who had been actively involved in the special Maori voter information campaign prior to the 1993 election, were well aware of the importance of the legislative change, and shortly after the election, the joint convenors of the 1993 Steering Committee (Katene and Love) approached officials of the Department of Justice to press for a comprehensive, government funded, awareness and information campaign to be conducted by Maori prior to the Maori option period. A minimum of three months was suggested for this campaign. The two men met with the Minister of Justice late in November, and again on 7 December 1993, when they presented a proposal to develop Maori awareness of and knowledge about the Maori option through a kanohi-ki-te-kanohi strategy (HC, 1994a:17–20).

A significant difference of opinion soon emerged: whereas the Minister and his officials regarded the Maori option as no more than providing an opportunity for Maori who were already registered as electors on either roll to restate their choice, Steering Committee members believed that the 1994 Maori option had to be promoted in a way that would encourage all qualified Maori to exercise their right of choice, regardless of whether or not they were currently registered as electors and regardless of whether they had previously acknowledged Maori descent. The official view prevailed and the government declined to find additional financial resources for a Maori option education campaign, although it did — rather reluctantly — agree to transfer $150,000 from the Electoral Enrolment Centre's Maori option budget to the Steering Committee to assist it with its campaign to inform Maori of the importance of the Maori option (ibid.). The dates for the option were gazetted on 22 December 1993.

Dissatisfied with the government's stance, Maori convened a national hui at Turangawaewae on 14 January 1994. There, it was decided to seek an urgent hearing before the Waitangi Tribunal to test the claim that the Crown had

> an obligation under the Treaty of Waitangi to protect the right of Maori to be represented in Parliament and that there are special needs in promoting Maori enrolment and education on the option. (WT, 1994:1.)

Taking its lead from a recent Privy Council decision (ibid., 13–14),[2] the Tribunal held that the Crown had a Treaty obligation to "actively protect" Maori citizenship rights, including the right to political representation conferred by the *Electoral Act 1993*, and that the relationship between the two should be based "on reasonableness, mutual co-operation and trust" (ibid., 15). To the question of whether the Crown had allocated sufficient resources to meet its Treaty obligations, the Tribunal held that the amount of funding allocated was "substantially less than is required..." (ibid., 35). After considering the report, the government declined to provide a further $250,000 to the programme on the grounds that it had already made approximately $1.6 million available during the previous 12 months (including nearly $600,000 for the Maori option) to promote electoral issues among Maori (HC, 1994b). By the time this decision was announced the Maori option period had already commenced.

Despite what it regarded as a lack of government commitment, the Steering Committee (by now renamed Inco — Information Co-ordination — Services) pressed ahead with its programme of regional hui designed to elicit local volunteer help in disseminating information about the Maori electoral option. As with the referendum education campaign the previous year, the principal strategy adopted was that of face-to-face discussion and explanation.[3] Although, as a result of the Maori option, the Maori roll increased by over 32,000 electors, including an estimated 10,000 new enrolments, the task Inco Services tackled was altogether too large for the resources it had at its disposal and the results were, at best, patchy. Initially, Te Puni Kokiri saw its role as no more than providing support for Inco Services, but it soon became apparent to it that a coherent strategy was lacking. Put simply, Inco Services did not have the resources or the local networks to mount the kind of effective immersion campaign that was essential for it to succeed.[4] As the campaign unfolded, the uneven and inconsistent participation levels by the three pan-Maori organisations persuaded the Ministry that it had to become more actively involved. For example, it organised training and strategy sessions which, it believed, "resulted in a more focused and disciplined information dissemination process than would have been the case without (the Ministry's) involvement". Even so, its participation appears to have been largely reactive, and targeted to plugging gaps wherever they appeared. "In some regions", the Chief Executive wrote, "it was clear that were it not for the involvement of TPK there would not have been an information campaign at the local level" (HC, 1994c).

Predictably, Maori were disappointed at the outcome of the option for the campaigners had confidently expected that they would achieve their objective of a significant increase in the number of Maori seats (Steering Committee, 1993). The three pan-Maori organisations therefore challenged the outcome in the High Court where it sought a declaration that the Maori option notice, promulgated on 17 December 1993, was invalid and should be quashed. The High Court found for the Crown (HC, 1994d) whereupon the plaintiffs appealed to the Court of Appeal. In its judgment (CA, 1995:411–18) the Court of Appeal upheld the decision of the High Court, ruling that the notices sent to registered electors of Maori descent were "sufficient to comply with the statutory requirement ..."; publicity about the Maori option was adequate (the fact that some Maori — those not registered and those who qualified to register during the option period — had not received a personally addressed, written notice did not make the conduct of the option unreasonable); and that the government's decision to reject the Waitangi Tribunal's recommendation (that additional funds should be allocated to publicising the option) was "not unreasonable [since] reasonable steps to publicise and explain the option were taken...". It also concurred with the High Court's view that the Minister of Justice had not breached his statutory duties in any material way (ibid., 412). The essential test, according the President of the Court of Appeal who delivered the judgment, was reasonableness, not perfection. No more can be legally required than what was reasonable at the time. What was done was far from perfect but it passes the test of reasonableness. (ibid., 418.)

The Court also upheld Justice McGechan's concern that "... the Crown was and is under a Treaty obligation to protect and facilitate Maori representation" (HC, 1994d). In its view, the lessons learned from the conduct of the 1994 Maori option would need to be taken into account when programmes for promoting Maori awareness of future options were being planned (CA, 1995:418).

The eleventh hour inclusion of separate Maori seats in the *Electoral Act 1993* assured Maori that, henceforth, separate and guaranteed representation would remain an integral part of New Zealand's electoral system for as long as they wished. This was a significant development: not only did it provide Maori with a secure parliamentary platform through constituency representation, but they could also enter parliament through party lists.[5] The prospect of a significantly increased Maori parliamentary presence was, therefore, very real. Why, then, were Maori so obviously disappointed with the outcome of the 1994 Maori option?

Undoubtedly, a major reason lay in the unrealistically high expectations of many Maori that a substantial increase in the number of Maori electorates would eventuate because, they believed, most Maori would want to transfer to the Maori roll. Claims made at various hui held during 1993 suggested that as many as 20 Maori seats might be possible if all Maori opted to be registered on the Maori roll.[6] These outrageously high estimates appear to have been based on the proportion that those who acknowledged Maori ancestry in the 1991 census bore to the total population (Statistics 1991)[7], and by calculating the Maori seat entitlement as a proportion of all 120 seats in an MMP parliament. What does not appear to have been taken into account is the fact that 116,907 of those acknowledging Maori ancestry at the time of the 1991 census had not identified themselves as belonging to the New Zealand Maori ethnic group.[8] Because this latter group had chosen not to identify themselves as such, it seems likely that few would have chosen to transfer their electoral registration to the Maori roll if they were not already on it. Realistically, therefore, the size of the available pool was more likely to have been around 400,000 of whom approximately two-thirds would have been aged 18 years or over.

But even if, at the time of the 1994 option, all eligible Maori had chosen to register on the Maori roll, the maximum number of Maori electorates could have been no more than ten. This is because the *Electoral Act 1993* stipulates that the South Island's electorate quota is the critical determinant of both the number of

North Island General electorates and the number of Maori electorates. Even if all persons who had declared Maori ancestry in 1991 had chosen to be included in the Maori electoral population, the electoral quota for South Island electorates would have been sufficient to restrict the number of Maori electorates to no more than ten. It must also be remembered that the Maori option allows Maori to transfer both to and from the Maori roll during each Maori option period. Any overall gain or loss in Maori enrolments that does occur is, therefore, a net figure which incorporates movements in both directions.

Could the government have done more to ensure that Maori leaders had a greater opportunity to promote the case for a shift to the Maori roll? Although the government and the Electoral Enrolment Centre were careful not to take sides on which roll Maori should register, the answer is almost certainly 'yes'. What the government failed to recognise was that the 1994 Maori option was a unique occasion in that, for the first time, Maori had a genuine opportunity to influence the number of Maori constituency seats in the New Zealand parliament. It also failed to comprehend fully the significance of the procedural change to the Maori option requirements incorporated into the *Electoral Act* in 1990. Thus, at the time of the 1992 Maori option the number of Maori seats was still fixed at four and any decision made by Maori would have no effect on the number of Maori seats. But by the time the special Maori option was held between February and April 1994, the rules had changed; the choice facing Maori was a very real one, one that was regarded as being of fundamental importance to Maori political participation by many Maori. While the government was technically correct in arguing that the Maori option was solely concerned with providing Maori who were registered as electors, it erred in not fully recognising that, because the outcome would determine the number of Maori seats in the next parliament, there was an additional incentive for Maori to encourage electorally qualified but unregistered Maori to enrol as electors and to choose on which of the two electoral rolls they wished to be included. The importance of the 1994 option warranted this additional attention.

What could the government have done to alleviate this basic problem? First, while it was important that the transition to the MMP environment commenced as soon as practicable, parliament could have passed amending legislation to extend the Maori option period.[9] It is most unlikely that such a move would have encountered any opposition. And even if the commencement of the option period could not be delayed, an additional month would have given Maori more time to mobilise, train volunteers, and promote the option among those directly affected by the new provisions. Second, given the fundamental change to Maori representation incorporated in the *Electoral Act 1993*, the government should have given more serious consideration to providing increased financial resources to allow a more extensive promotional campaign to be undertaken. Had the cabinet approved the recommendation of the Minister of Maori Affairs that an additional $250,000 — which, according to the Minister, could have been found from within existing financial approvals (HC, 1994b:App.J) — be allocated to promoting the Maori option at least some of the pressures faced by both Inco Services and Te Puni Kokiri would have been eased. Cabinet, however, believed that the 1993 Electoral Referendum Panel's campaign, which incorporated a special sub-programme targeted specifically at Maori, should have made Maori sufficiently well aware of the changes that would result from the adoption of MMP to enable them to make an informed decision as to which electoral roll they should choose. Once again, the government had underestimated the intensity of Maori feeling surrounding the issues of parliamentary representation.

And what of Maori: could they have done more to ensure that the significance of the Maori option was disseminated as widely as possible amongst those most directly affected? Here, the answer must be a qualified 'yes'. Had the three pan-Maori organisations been prepared to invest even a portion of the money they spent subsequently in pursuing the issue through the courts, and had they been prepared to seek the assistance of expertise that was available within the wider community, it may have been possible to establish a much larger pool of Maori volunteers who understood the importance of the option and of the choices facing their people. Maori, quite appropriately, wanted the programme to be conducted in a way that was consistent with tikanga Maori, but while the kanohi-ki-te-kanohi strategy of communicating information had been effective during the 1993 electoral referendum and electoral enrolment sub-campaigns, it is an extremely expensive strategy in terms of finance and personnel required. The basic problem facing Maori in the weeks immediately prior to the option period was establishing a sufficiently large group of trained and enthusiastic volunteers to ensure that Maori communities, particularly those in the more remote rural areas, were covered. As it turned out, there were insufficient Maori volunteers with the necessary expertise to meet the programme's demands in the time available, and those that did contribute were often literally run off their feet.

The 1994 Maori option did, however, mark the beginning of a new era in Maori politics for, despite disappointment at its outcome, for the first time Maori were able to influence directly the number of parliamentary seats guaranteed to them. No longer could Maori argue that they were under-represented in the nation's parliament. The *Electoral Act 1993* and the option which followed is, therefore, likely to be seen by future generations as a watershed in Maori-pakeha political relations, where a fixed number of seats regardless of population numbers gave way to a process which gave Maori people the power to determine the nature of their political representation.

Defining the MMP Electoral Districts

For more than a century New Zealand's electoral districts have been redrawn shortly after each five-yearly census of population to maintain the approximate equality of each electorate's total population. Since the adoption of MMP meant that the number of electorates would need to be reduced from 99 to 65 before the first MMP election could be held, the Representation Commission (the statutory body responsible for the regular reviews) which had last redrawn the electoral map in 1992, was required to reconvene. For only the second time since 1887[10] the Representation Commission was required to define a second set of electorates using the same census data.

With fewer but geographically larger electorates, it was inevitable that the country's electoral map would differ significantly from the previous one. The average population for each new electorate rose to c.51,800, 57.3 per cent larger than for the last First-past-the-post electorates. Nevertheless, the rules governing the redistribution were essentially the same as previously; provided each electorate's total population was within ±5 per cent of the prescribed electorate quota,[11] the Commission is able to take four other discretionary factors into account when making its decisions — community of interest, communications links, topography, and "[a]ny projected variation in the ... electoral population of those districts during their life". There was also a prohibition on any General electorate including territory in both the North and South Islands.[12] As a result of the reduction in the number of electorates, rural constituencies in particular became considerably larger geographically, but in practice New Zealand's insular character and mountainous topography left the Commission with little room for manoeuvre. External constraints such as the country's lengthy coastline, the South Island's mountain backbone and the North Island's main mountain range, and the fact that the last electorate in each island, and the last Maori electorate to be drawn, must all conform to the electorate quota, all served to restrict the Commission's flexibility. It was therefore inevitable that following the first MMP redistribution the country's electoral geography would broadly reflect past patterns.

The Commission's procedures also closely followed those of previous redistributions although, because it was obvious that the electoral map would experience far greater change than in any previous redistribution in living memory, it was given eight months rather than the normal six months to complete its task. Once the Government Statistician had determined the North Island, South Island and Maori electoral populations and calculated the number of seats to which each was entitled, the Surveyor-General's office aggregated mesh block[13] data into a series of options based purely on numbers. Provisional boundaries were then drawn by applying the discretions included in the *Electoral Act* to resolve the constraints of population numbers (RC, 1995b). The maps thus produced (there were several alternative scenarios) provided the starting point for the Commission's deliberations. The end result was the publication of proposed boundaries open for public scrutiny and comment.[14] Once the period for objections and counter-objections closed, the Commission reviewed its earlier proposals, and made changes where necessary or appropriate in the light of public input. Publication of its final report in April 1995 gave the Commission's decisions the force of law. The impartiality of a majority of its members, and the finality of its decisions are major contributors to public acceptance of the integrity of New Zealand's redistribution process (*AJHR,* 1995a; McRobie, 1989:10–19).

Inevitably, politicians are always keenly interested in the outcome of the Representation Commission's deliberations. Their interest was particularly acute as the first MMP redistribution approached because one-third of incumbent MPs would be without constituency seats when the current parliament was dissolved. The political context of the redistribution process had long been recognised: in 1956 the composition of the Representation Commission had been amended to include two political representatives — one to represent the government of the day and the other, the opposition — and, in 1981, provision was made for political parties and independent MPs to make submissions to the Commission before it commenced its work. Before the Surveyor-General unveiled his provisional boundaries to the Commission in 1994, National, Labour and the Alliance each presented submissions, and they made a further oral submission after they had been shown the provisional boundaries in confidence (*AJHR,* 1995a:10). New Zealand First, which also had MPs, chose not to make a submission because "it was not prepared to be represented by the opposition representative" (RC, 1995a:8 August 1994). New Zealand First's decision highlighted a problem that had been evident for some years: minor parties' lack of confidence in the ability of political appointees to represent the interests of several, often competing, political parties (McRobie, 1990:23–46). The Representation Commission was sufficiently concerned to suggest to parliament that it might consider how parties should "be represented on the commission in the MMP environment" (*AJHR,* 1995a:18).

The presence of commissioners representing political interests makes it very difficult to keep the Surveyor-General's initial suggestions out of the public gaze. Following its previous practice, the Commission, at its initial meeting in March 1994, confirmed its long-standing position on confidentiality:

> It was agreed that the work of the commission will and must remain completely confidential, subject only to the right of members appointed to represent the government or opposition consulting as to statutory criteria with a small limited number of persons (no more than 3–5 in each case) provided the persons consulted with are prepared to give undertakings of complete confidentiality. Such consultations will cease prior to the commencement of the objection process so that no member of the commission can be alleged to have had any part in formulating any objection to the proposals of the commission.
>
> Such confidentiality is essential to ensure the independence of the commission from political or public pressure.
>
> In relation to Commission members who are employees of a government department, it was agreed that it would be quite inappropriate for any Minister to seek information from any such employee (whether a chief executive or otherwise), and if any such approach was made it should be resisted and brought to the notice of the Chairman of the Commission immediately. (RC, 1995a:2 March 1994.)

Despite this, the appointed members subsequently advised the full commission that before they could consult on the statutory criteria with the parties they represented, those with whom they were consulting would need to be given an opportunity to view the provisional boundaries. The commission resolved that affected parties could be shown the provisional boundaries but that maps would not be supplied.

The Surveyor-General tabled his initial proposals on 15 August 1994. They were shown to the nominees of parties a week later, and the next day parliament was "awash with rumours" allegedly detailing the provisional boundaries (*Press*, 23 August 1994). The next day the *New Zealand Herald* published what purported to be a map showing the provisional boundaries (*NZH*, 23 August 1994; *Dom.*, 25 August 1994), and this was followed by detailed descriptions of provisional boundaries in different parts of the country (*Press*, 24 August 1994). The Prime Minister, Jim Bolger, accused the opposition parties of leaking the information to the media, an action which, he claimed, had made the situation intolerable (ibid.). Bolger called on the Commission to release the provisional maps to the public, but the Commission rejected this demand following a lengthy meeting (held by telephone conference call) at which it discussed the "extreme leakage" that had occurred (RC, 1995a:23 August 1994).[15] Although it acknowledged

> the high level of public interest in the new MMP boundaries ... speculation was not a reason to release the provisional boundaries. ... The Commission remains

committed to the goal of promoting electoral justice — fair electoral boundaries, produced according to law, and by fair process. (RC, 1995c:24 August 1994.)

As further details emerged, another attempt was made, this time in parliament, to force the publication of the provisional boundaries, but this was fended off by the Minister of Justice, who told parliament that

> [t]he Representation Commission is a statutory body with statutory duties, and is not subject constitutionally to a direction from Parliament. To allow Parliament to intimidate the Representation Commission would be quite wrong and cannot be tolerated ... .

Graham's stance was supported by David Caygill, deputy leader of the Labour Opposition and its spokesperson on electoral matters (*NZPD*, 542:3100–02).

Although publicity surrounding the leaks soon died down, undercurrents remained. At the beginning of October a special telephone conference call meeting of the Commission was convened in response to complaints of continuing leaks made by John Slater, chair of the National Party's Auckland Division; the Party's Canterbury-Westland Division; and information provided by two National Party MPs, Jim Gerard and Brian Neeson. At this meeting Lloyd Falck, the commissioner appointed by the opposition parties, reported that he had been approached by Labour MP, Mike Moore, who described in general terms the provisional electoral boundaries in his local area. When Falck refused to confirm their accuracy, he received a lecture from the MP! (RC, 1995a:4 October 1994.) The Commission believed that a prima facie case warranting investigation had been established, and appointed Dr Mervyn Probine, retired Chief Executive of the States Services Commission, to investigate further, although Falck questioned whether the Representation Commission had the power to conduct such an inquiry (ibid., 14 October 1994). After an investigation extending over five months Probine reported that he had been unable to identify the source of the alleged leaks (RC, 1995a:13 March 1995).[16] The Commission therefore resolved that a paragraph should be included in its final report recommending that the *Electoral Act* be amended "to impose an obligation of confidentiality on all members of the Commission and other persons entrusted with the work of the Commission" (RC, 1995a:13 March 1995; *AJHR*, 1995a:20).[17]

This stance reflected the long-held view of previous Representation Commissions that if it were to achieve the objective of impartiality and political neutrality in reaching its decisions, total confidentiality must be preserved. This had already proved increasingly difficult to maintain as the redistribution process became increasingly politicised; the increasing volatility of the political arena since the early 1970s had resulted in both the Labour and National parties consciously seeking to gain an electoral advantage through the redistribution process (McRobie, 1978:255–69; 1990:23–46). While the distribution of constituency seats among competing parties assumed a lesser importance in an MMP environment, incumbent MPs were, nevertheless, vitally interested in the fate of 'their patch' in the period before the first MMP election.

Two other matters caused the Representation Commission concern. When the Surveyor-General first presented his provisional boundaries to the full Commission they were questioned on the ground that he may not have applied the requirements of the *Electoral Act 1993* correctly, in that he appeared to have taken existing electoral boundaries into account when preparing his provisional maps, whereas the transition provisions included in s.269 of the Act expressly excluded such consideration. The Commission referred the matter to the Solicitor-General who accepted the Surveyor-General's explanation that "where there is a coincidence between a provisional boundary and the corresponding existing boundary, factors other than the mere existence of the boundary may be relevant", and concluded that because the transitional provisions recognised the problem arising from one-third fewer electorates, as well recognising that, in practice, many boundaries are dictated by topographical features, there was "no legal basis for questioning the validity of the provisional maps on the ground that the Surveyor General took into account or was influenced by the existing boundaries" (RC, 1995b).

Hanging over the Commission like the sword of Damocles was the Maori Option case, the hearing of which commenced at the end of August 1994. As we have already seen, the plaintiffs' arguments were rejected at all levels but the Commission could not know when it commenced its work what the outcome would be. Nor could it justifiably delay its deliberations until the outcome was known because the next election had, by law, to be held no later than the second half of November 1996, and commissioners, Ministry of Justice officials, and political parties were all acutely aware of the need for the new MMP electoral districts to be defined at the earliest possible date. Had the court found in favour of the plaintiffs, a new Maori option would have had to have been conducted and, depending on its outcome, the Representation Commission would almost certainly have had to return to square one. As it transpired, the plaintiffs failed in their attempt to have the 1994 Maori Option overturned and the Commission was able to complete its work without further interruption.

When the final boundaries of the new electoral districts were made public at the end of April 1995, politicians and political analysts generally agreed that the new electoral map marginally favoured Labour (*Press*, 28 April 1995; *SST*, 30 April 1995; McRobie, 1995). Although, as noted above, the shape of electoral districts under MMP was not as critical as they had been in the FPP era, two factors which had important implications for both Labour and National stood out. For incumbent Labour MPs the pressure to find a winnable constituency seat was reduced while the pressure on incumbent National MPs was correspondingly increased. There were also other implications for both major parties: the more constituency seats they won the fewer list seats they would gain, and the expected flexibility in constructing their lists would be constrained as a consequence. The two smaller parties, the Alliance and New Zealand First, were also affected but in a different way; although the redistribution appeared to have cost the Alliance one constituency seat, both it and New Zealand First each seemed likely to go into the following election with at least one seat where they could claim incumbency. This was important because, under MMP, victory in one constituency seat would guarantee them a parliamentary presence even if they did not reach the 5 per cent threshold.

The formal announcement of the 65 MMP electoral districts marked the final administrative step in the transition to MMP. The Representation Commission's decisions are final, and once they are released they become effective from the dissolution of the current parliament. Before the new boundaries were released nearly all sitting MPs had indicated a preference for representing a constituency. It was thus inevitable that competition would occur between MPs from the same party during candidate selections, and also between incumbent MPs from different parties at the next election. The effects of the redistribution were soon apparent as MPs from both Labour and National began jockeying for position, and the administrative wings of both parties moved quickly to reassure those who were likely to miss out on being selected for a winnable constituency seats that a high ranking on the party's list could be expected (*NZH*, 29 April 1995 [NZLP President]; *Dom.*, 29 April 1995 [NZNP President]).

Candidate Selection

Before 1993 political parties had been regarded as private organisations and the processes for selecting parliamentary candidates had been left entirely in their own hands. Reviewing this situation, the Royal Commission on the Electoral System had pointed out that as most voters express a preference for a party rather than an individual candidate, " ... it is the parties' prior selection of candidates which, especially in safe seats, effectively determines who is to become the electorates representative" (RCES, 1986a:239).

The Royal Commission made no complaint about the manner in which the system had worked before 1986 other than the under-representation of women and ethnic minorities. The Commission believed, however, that the adoption of the MMP electoral system with its requirement for placing candidates in order of priority on a nationwide party list would require safeguards to ensure that democratic procedures for the selection of candidates was maintained (ibid., 240).

Under the list system parties become responsible for determining, in effect, nearly half the membership of the House of Representatives. As a result, the Royal Commission advocated certain controls over selection procedures recommending that:

> ...the law should specifically require that anyone who stands as a candidate for a particular political party should be selected according to procedures which allow any member of the party, either directly or through representatives themselves elected by members of the party, to participate in the selection of candidates for whom they are eligible to vote, such procedures to be adopted by an Annual General Meeting of the party. (ibid., 240.)

These rules were to be subject to challenge by a member of the party and, ultimately, appeal to the High Court. Predictably, the 1988 Electoral Law Select Committee (*AJHR*, 1988) rejected the recommendation, both on principle, and because it also rejected the Commission's recommendation in favour of MMP.

Despite the recommendations of the 1988 Select Committee, MMP was chosen by a majority of the public at a referendum in 1993. Similarly, the recommendations of the Royal Commission regarding candidate selection, cavalierly dismissed by the 1988 Electoral Law Select Committee, were supported by its 1993 counterpart and incorporated in the *Electoral Act 1993* (section 71). This Act included a provision requiring every registered political party to ensure participation in the selection of candidates by those current financial members entitled to vote and/or by delegates elected or otherwise selected by current financial members. These candidate selection requirements in the new *Electoral Act* were hardly onerous, the chairman of committee pointing out that, " ... those rules are sufficient to enable the three current major political parties to select their candidates the way they do at present" (*NZPD*, 537:17123).

Despite these loose requirements, no doubt prompted by the need to devise candidate selection methods for the party list, and to ensure that their rules were not open to challenge, most parties undertook a thorough review of their candidate selection processes. In the case of the Labour Party, in particular, there had been a number of criticisms and difficulties ranging over several years despite the opinion of the Royal Commission that candidate selection practices under FPP were generally satisfactory. Hence, before the end of 1993 the Labour Party established a joint party organisation-parliamentary party working party on MMP which elicited some 200 responses from constituent organisations and some individuals, about their wishes in regard to the candidate selection process.

A report based on these responses, together with some key options, was then circulated to members before further discussion at the six regional conferences in 1994. Following that, a final report, with new rules framed as constitutional amendments, was circulated to constituent groups six months prior to the 1994 annual conference and passed at that conference. Apart from providing for the selection of list candidates, these new rules also altered the balance on constituency selection panels in favour of the local delegates while maintaining central representation on the panels (Street, 1995).

The National Party, no doubt more satisfied with its existing candidate selection arrangements, was less ambitious in the changes undertaken. It, too, established a working party in 1993 to look at the organisational changes likely to be required by the introduction of MMP but decided against any major structural changes, preferring to concentrate instead on the new rules required for the selection of list candidates (Thompson, 1995).

The problem lay not so much in the formal requirements, or the longer term constitutional arrangements of the parties, as in the transition process from one electoral system to another and the consequent need to ensure a minimum of internecine conflict. Candidate selection is a sensitive process fraught with the possibility of conflict at the best of times, but in conditions of electoral system transition it has the potential to cause serious division unless handled with the greatest possible care. It is partly because of the threat of such problems that so many MPs are reluctant to embrace electoral reform.

Considering the possibility of electoral reform in Britain, the *Economist* pointed out that "there is no point in advocating a system MPs will never accept" (*Economist*, 28 October 1995:72). The journal suggested that attempted adoption of the German system or Single Transferable Vote (STV) would involve:

> ...many fewer Tory and Labour MPs. Moreover, no one of them can know whether they will be among the reduced ranks. Perhaps as few as half the MPs who now have constituency seats would then have them. ... If they failed to get one, they would have to hope the party machine placed them high on its list for a seat, making them beholden to national party headquarters. ... [T]he conclusion is stark. Most Members of the House of Commons have a powerful self-interest in preserving the existing system.

That situation certainly applied in New Zealand and, as we have seen, the fact that this form of obstruction was overcome was due to the mixture of accident and design which led to the holding of two public referendums both of which the two major parties, in effect, lost.

In practical terms, the transition process was eased somewhat by the simultaneous increase in the size of the House of Representatives from 99 to 120 MPs. Even so, the number of single member constituencies was reduced from 99 to 65. The need to redraw electoral boundaries into larger electorates inevitably resulted in a number of potential conflicts between MPs in the same political parties. Various strategies were used to reduce the incidence of these conflicts:

(i)   *Volunteering for the party list*: Some MPs voluntarily gave up their constituency seats, mainly in cases where there were too many established MPs in the party competing for too few seats. Such actions were mainly confined to a limited number of senior MPs who would thus be assured of a high placing on the list. In the case of the Labour Party this contributed to the fact that, according to then party president, Maryan Street, "In the end, the Labour Party had no difficult choices to make over constituency selections between sitting MPs" (Street:1995). The Deputy-Leader and Senior Whip both relieved pressure in this way, giving up safe seats and agreeing to stand in National-held seats. A third senior MP in a safe-seat opted for the list anyway. In the National Party, the Deputy-Leader also moved to the list to relieve electoral congestion. It is noteworthy that in both major parties the leaders remained firmly anchored in their electorates despite being assured of the top list placing, and despite the fact that, in both cases, their opting for the list would have helped to relieve electoral congestion.

(ii) *Retirements*: These accounted for a larger group although it is not always easy to attribute causes in this category with any precision. Some, prompted by the need for electoral rationalisation may simply have decided that this was a good time to end their parliamentary career, or, it may have been suggested to them that it was an appropriate time to leave the political scene gracefully. The retirement of senior National Party MP Warren Cooper, for example, was expected to relieve electoral pressures and leave the way open for sitting MP Alec Neill to take the new Otago seat. Contrary to expectations, however, Neill failed to win selection and was forced to rely upon any subsequent list selection. Other retirements openly conceded a lack of enthusiasm for working under the new system.

These included Burdon for National and Lange for Labour (both of whom were 'early' retirements in terms of age). Others may have been more directly influenced by a lack of optimism both about their chances for re-selection for the new constituencies and their chances of a high list placing. Of the National MPs retiring, five were sitting ministers — Philip Burdon, Warren Cooper, John Falloon, Robin Gray, and Roger McClay while a sixth, Rob Storey, was an ex-minister. In the case of the Labour Party, one of the four, Koru Wetere, who had reached 60 years of age and suffered ill-health, can be considered a normal retirement.

(iii) *Transference to local government*: Three MPs sought to further their careers in local rather than national government. This was a relatively new development although Labour MP Fran Wilde had resigned in 1992 to take-up the high profile Wellington mayoralty. In 1995 no fewer than three sitting MPs stood for mayoralties, two National — Warren Cooper and Katherine O'Regan — and one Labour — Elizabeth Tennet. The assumption may well have been that with the introduction of MMP, there was likely to be a steady devolution of powers to local authorities. In practice, only one of the three, Cooper, aged 62 and ranked sixteenth in cabinet, was successful in the mayoral elections. It might be thought that Cooper was a likely candidate for retirement anyway. Unlike O'Regan, Tennet's retirement was not dependent upon the result of the mayoral election.

(iv) *Defection*: In Dunedin where three Labour MPs were competing for two seats, a frontbencher and former cabinet minister, Clive Mathewson, obligingly cleared the way by leaving Labour to help form the United New Zealand Party. In Christchurch, former cabinet minister Margaret Austin also defected from Labour to United, while in Wellington earlier defector and former cabinet minister, Peter Dunne (who had left Labour to form the Future New Zealand Party) joined United along with four National MPs, one from Wellington (Pauline Gardiner) and three from Auckland (Bruce Cliffe, Peter Hilt and John Robertson). At the time of his defection Cliffe was a sitting cabinet minister who became Deputy-Leader of the new party. Subsequently, he retired from parliament in 1996, aged 50. Ross Meurant, Under-Secretary in the Bolger Government, left the National Party to form his Right of Centre (ROC, later Conservative) Party but retained his Under-Secretaryship for some time, causing the government to claim that it was now a coalition. Subsequently, Meurant left the Conservative Party and became an independent.

Another National MP, Trevor Rogers, also left National to join ROC. A former National minister outside cabinet, Graeme Lee, left to form the Christian Democrat (CD) Party while Peter McCardle and long-time disaffected MP, Michael Laws, both left National to join New Zealand First. Thus, the National Party lost nine MPs by defection alone.

Partly as a result of these activities, serious conflict within the major parties was reduced to a minimal level. In the case of the Labour Party the most serious remaining constituency conflict was passed over to the list selections when sitting MP Jack Elder, out of favour with the central party organisation, decided not to stand for either of two new electorates, Titirangi or Waipareira. This meant that the avoidance of immediate conflict was at the cost of longer-term recriminations over the list. Elder eventually transferred his allegiance to New Zealand First. In the National Party, a head-on collision between fourth ranked cabinet minister, Paul East, and leading backbencher Max Bradford was resolved when Bradford, who had declined to be considered for the list, was selected as the constituency candidate. East was then selected as number 5 on the National Party's list. One useful by-product of the conflict was that the National Party's membership in the new constituency was boosted quite dramatically! Given the scale of the reduction in the number of parliamentary constituencies and the consequent radical changes to boundaries, the change of electoral system passed off with remarkably few serious problems at the constituency level for either of the two major political parties.

Ironically, one of the more serious problems with constituency selections took place with the Alliance which had only two sitting MPs and was not expected to win many constituency seats but to be mainly a list party. Because it consisted of five distinct political parties — the Democrats, Greens, Liberals, NewLabour and Mana Motuhake — candidate selection, whether at the con-stituency or list level, presented it with particularly difficult problems. These problems were enhanced when the party's National Director, Matt McCarten, made it clear that rankings on the Alliance's list would be heavily influenced by candidates' ability to win selection for a constituency seat (*Press*, 11 October 1995). In one particular case, the favoured Christchurch Central electorate candidate, Alliance education spokesperson and NewLabour member Elizabeth Gordon, was unexpectedly beaten by Manu Motuhake candidate Joanna Waiwai Ryan at a meeting with a Democratic Party chairman. Under Alliance rules, membership of at least a month was required before qualifying to vote at a selection meeting. It was claimed on this basis that some who voted at the meeting were not eligible to do so. The Alliance national executive reviewed the case along with two others and decided that in the Christchurch case the selection would have to be rerun. Gordon won and Ryan left the party.

The party list system posed a different order of problems. The concept itself was new in New Zealand and the provisions in the *Electoral Act 1993* were very broad, making no distinction between the selection of candidates for electorates or for the list. All that was required was that registered parties should "follow democratic procedures in candidate selection" with participation by:

(a) Current financial members of the party who are ... entitled to vote for those candidates at any election; or

(b) Delegates who have (whether directly or indirectly) in turn have been elected or otherwise selected by current financial members of the party; or

(c) A combination of the persons or classes of persons referred to in paragraphs (a) and (b) of this section. (*Electoral Act, 1993*, s.71.)

Accordingly, the political parties were left largely free to devise both the criteria upon which list candidates were to be selected and the methods by which this would be best achieved.

All parties were broadly agreed upon the general criteria involved. In the case of Labour, for example:

We charged ourselves with the task of compiling a list which reflected our support base, that is, balanced gender, ethnicity, geography, age and skill. In addition to that, we needed to balance familiar, recognisable faces with new, up and coming faces... (Street, 1995.)

Ms Street admitted that this process "had the advantage of patent transparency and the disadvantage of being quite brutal" (ibid.).

After early differences between the parliamentarians and the party organisation National adopted a different strategy with its decision to produce an 'integrated list' (Thompson, 1995). This involved the possibility of having over 80 per cent of the constituency candidates also standing on the list — a process known as 'doubling,' the idea being that the party fights one integrated campaign, thus avoiding the danger of two different sets of candidates giving different signals about a party's intentions. At the same time, party president, Geoff Thompson, claimed that the party also intended to use the party list to boost the number of women MPs. Despite the quest for gender and racial balance, however, the party rejected the idea of quotas with Thompson emphasising that "Our list is going to be built on the basis of talent" (*Press*, 10 October 1995).

The third and minor parties with far fewer constituency problems to deal with, were less inhibited in their range of list choice than the major parties.

The Association of Consumers and Taxpayers (Act), for example, devised a list in two sections. The first consisted of persons who wished to register as Act candidates, while the rather improbable and impracticable second section consisted of outstanding New Zealanders, whom they would like to see as part of Act's team in parliament, nominated by other New Zealanders from all walks of life (*NZH,* 19 August 1995).

For the major parties, the list provided the site for battle between various groups and factions within a party. The main distinction was that between the parliamentary party and the party organisation. Clearly, the parliamentary parties had a vested interest in defending their own. Initially, until a change of party president and consequent adoption of the 'integrated list' approach, this attitude was at its strongest in the National Party where the careers of a greater number of MPs were at risk. Despite the fact that the number of sitting National MPs was reduced by over 25 per cent through the processes of retirement and defection, a further 18 per cent had either failed to win nomination for a constituency, or were required to contest marginal seats and were thus potential candidates for the list. At least four National MPs declined to be considered for the list, but as two of these (Banks and Ryall) were likely to win their seats this did not materially affect the issue. From the point of view of a parliamentary party in New Zealand, it is important to look after your own in order to maintain morale and the strong team ethos which characterises the cohesive nature of New Zealand political parties.

In both major parties provision had to be made for party leaders and for a number of MPs left without seats in the boundary changes. A party like the Alliance with only two MPs, or New Zealand First with only four, were untroubled by such concerns. On the other hand, the party organisations, no doubt influenced by the animus against politicians which had contributed so powerfully to the introduction of MMP, were more conscious of the need to introduce new talent.

In the case of the Labour Party, in particular, this also had an ideological aspect. During the 1980s the 'Rogernomics' market-led policies espoused by the parliamentary Labour Party had largely alienated the party organisation, which had been waging a campaign to regain control largely through the candidate selection process. The introduction of the party list system gave that process a powerful boost.

It may have been no accident that the Labour Party was the first to produce its candidate list; its president, Maryan Street, was anxious to have the process completed before she stepped down from the position in November 1995 (*SST,* 5 November 1995). Although Ms Street herself has suggested that this was to ensure that the party was ready to contest an election whenever it might be called, there was an inevitable suspicion that she wished to be assured of the outcome. In September-October 1995 the party's regional committees picked and ranked their own regional preferences when voting delegates met to hear speeches from each candidate and rank their lists.

These lists were then submitted to a national moderating committee of 32 which had the task of whittling down 92 nominations for 60 list positions. The order of the first 30 was decided by exhaustive ballot, an order which largely reflected the preferences submitted by Labour's regional committees. Fifteen of the top twenty positions were filled by sitting MPs. These included the leader, Helen Clark; her deputy, David Caygill; Labour's finance spokesperson, Michael Cullen; two other front bench MPs, Lianne Dalziel and Annette King. Three of these were in safe seats, the exceptions being Caygill who, as we have seen, had volunteered for the party list to avoid congestion, and Dalziel who had chosen the list on principle. The Chief Whip, Jonathan Hunt, had also sacrificed his seat, while the three remaining MPs represented a mixture of insurance policies, where their seats were marginal, or cosmetic purposes, e.g. representing trade unions and agriculture, where their seats were safe. Six backbenchers first elected in 1993 were also included; all of them were MPs with seats at risk, thereby helping to safeguard the future of the party.

Interspersed among these were five new faces including the Maori Vice-President of the party; a prominent, outspoken, trade unionist; and a female Maori archivist and researcher; a school principal who had earlier been a high profile by-election candidate; and a prominent Maori former protester. The list represented an interesting blend of talent but was, inevitably controversial. The problem with any such list is not so much who is included as who is left out. No fewer than 13 MPs decided not to stand for the list for a variety of reasons. One, Chris Carter, dissatisfied with his 25th ranking, pulled out immediately. MP Jack Elder, who had chosen not to stand for one of the two new constituencies when his old seat disappeared, was incensed at being ranked at number 40, declaring that the list looked like a dream ticket for the politically correct (*Press*, 30 October 1995).

The party list appears to have been designed to achieve two objectives. Given that most senior Labour MPs were standing in safe seats, their presence near the top of the list was symbolic, emphasising the known Labour Party 'branding'. Their ranking would not adversely affect those lower on the list. At the same time there was a concern to cope with popular alienation from the party by distancing itself from its record in the 1980s, introducing new talent and boosting the chances of the 1993 intake.

Labour's difficulties exemplified the problems of producing an ideal list although, once again, the examples cited are accentuated by the process of transition. All the parties were, in effect, feeling their way. Once the smaller number of constituencies becomes the established pattern, and the principle of the party list becomes more familiar with broadly expected patterns, it might be expected that future difficulties will be of a lesser order.

Legislative Changes

Although the electorate had endorsed the *Electoral Act 1993* which set out the detailed structure of the MMP electoral system, further legislative changes were made before the first MMP election was held. Two existing acts were involved — the *Electoral Act* itself, and those sections of the *Broadcasting Act 1989*, which established the regime allowing state funding of political parties' television and radio advertising during election campaigns. Apart from a small number of clauses, both pieces of amending legislation were generally supported across party lines. The issues that were contested in the select committees and on the floor of the House of Representatives, however, were disputed vigorously; in most instances, National and Labour supported the proposed changes while, for the most part, the smaller parties — including Act New Zealand and the Progressive Green Party, neither of whom were represented in parliament — strenuously opposing them. In the end, however, weight of numbers prevailed.

Many of the amendments were largely technical and administrative in nature, and arose from — ironically — the Electoral Law Select Committee's review of the last FPP election. These were readily approved. Yet others were designed to address anticipated problems arising from the wording of the, as yet untested, MMP provisions. Most of these were also passed without rancour: there was, for example, no opposition to an amendment requiring parties forming part of a larger grouping to declare this when they nominated their own separate lists of candidates,[18] or to an amendment requiring parties to have at least 500 financial members who were *eligible electors* before they could be registered. Another amendment approved gave electors, once again, until the afternoon before the election to register, instead of writ day (20 to 27 days before election day) as previously provided. More important were the agreements reached in the Electoral Law Select Committee to require parties to disclose donations received at both electorate and national level where these exceeded $1,000 (in the case of a donation, or multiple donations from the same source, to a particular electorate) and $10,000 (in the case of one or multiple donations to a party's national campaign), and to establish a ceiling on parties' campaign expenditure (cf. RCES, 1986a:185–202).[19]

The issue which resulted in the deepest divisions arose from the select committee's recommendation to alter the structure of the ballot paper. The second schedule to the *Electoral Act 1993* had provided for two separate ballot papers — one for each of the electorate vote and the party vote.[20] The select committee recommended that it be redesigned as a single ballot paper with both votes side by side, and with the party vote to the left of the electorate vote. This, a majority of the committee believed, would emphasise the importance of the party vote in determining the overall composition of the House of Representatives following the election (*NZPD*, 551:9942). Other changes were also proposed: each party's name and logo would be placed alongside the name of its constituency candidate with the party vote being randomised in each electorate by the alphabetical order of constituency candidates,[21] and the voting boxes for each vote would be set out side by side down the centre of the paper.

Supporters of the proposed change — National and, with one exception, Labour MPs — argued that that the basis of the committee's recommendation was to be found in the Royal Commission's report (RCES, 1986a:76),[22] and that it followed the German model. David Caygill, who did not regard the proposed change as "a matter of enduring significance", told the House that:

> [n]o less than three members of that delegation ... from three different parties, came back from Europe with a copy of the German ballot paper they had been shown and remarked to colleagues on various sides of the House how sensible they thought it was to look at that particular proposal. (*NZPD*, 551:9942.)

Both he and McCully believe that the crucial change occurred when three MPs (Wyatt Creech, Michael Cullen, and Winston Peters) from different parties, independently of one another, each returned with a copy of the German-style ballot paper (Caygill, 1996; McCully, 1996). Although Peters subsequently denied that he had ever supported amending the ballot paper format (*NZPD*, 551:9952 & 10067), Caygill is adamant that Peters was initially a strong supporter of change. In response to accusations that changing the ballot paper was the real reason for the sub-committee's visit to Europe, Cullen retorted that the German ballot paper "... turned up by chance. It was a mere by-product of a visit to look at the Standing Orders of other parliaments. The notion that about 12 people went overseas to discover one ballot paper is slightly ludicrous." And, in justifying the change, he pointed to support from the Electoral Reform Coalition and Professor Richard Mulgan, a member of the Royal Commission, who, he claimed, was "concerned that a two-paper system would confuse people and mistakenly give them the impression that the constituency vote was as important or more important than the party vote" (ibid., 10108). Other

MPs supported the change because it physically represented the way that the electorate voted and how the "party vote will actually work under the MMP system ..." (ibid., 10119).

For the members of the smaller parties opposed to the change, the arguments were quite different. Describing the proposed new ballot paper as "an outrageous case of gerrymandering" (*NZH*, 9 September 1995), and "unfair, unethical, unconstitutional and unprecedented ... it is blatantly and unarguably about vested interests" (*NZPD*, 551:10114), Christian Democrat leader (and former National MP), Graeme Lee, accused National and Labour of collusion, a view echoed by New Zealand First leader, Winston Peters, while the Progressive Green Party claimed that the new form of the paper was designed to prejudice list parties by encouraging voters to 'tick' the same party twice — a clear reference to National's pre-election 'two-tick' campaign to encourage its supporters to vote both for National Party in the party vote and for the National Party's candidate in the electorate vote (*NZH*, 9 September 1995).

Although the opposition's objections focused primarily on the second schedule of the *Electoral Act 1993* the crucial problem for the government was that section 168, which described the method of voting, required amendment to delete all references to 'Part A' and 'Part B' of the ballot paper. Since section 168 is one of the six reserved provisions it could be amended only with the support of at least 75 per cent of all MPs or by a majority of those voting on the question in a referendum. United (and former National) MP, John Robertson, for example, described the proposed change as "an outrage" and "an abuse of the privilege of power" because the 1993 legislation had entrenched the simple form of ballot paper which National and Labour now proposed to change "out of political expediency" (*NZPD*, 551:10106–07). Further, opponents argued, somewhat unconvincingly, that since the 1993 *Electoral Act* had been approved by voters in a referendum, the same mechanism should be used to amend it. Several members, among them, Matthewson, Lee, Jim Anderton and Sandra Lee, cited the Independent Referendum Panel's public education programme which, they claimed, quite clearly showed two ballot papers (ibid., 10111) — an argument that conveniently ignored the panel's responsibility to present the MMP electoral system as it was defined in law at the time of the 1993 referendum.

In a last-ditch attempt to forestall change, the Christian Democrat and Act parties mounted a legal challenge in the High Court where they sought an interim injunction to prevent parliament from voting on the issue. Declining to rule on the question (the challenge was struck out in Chambers), the High Court noted that "because the courts and Parliament do not interfere with each other's processes, any challenge should await the completion of the parliamentary process, so that any court action could not inhibit that process" (*NZH*, 24, 28 & 29 November 1995).

Although this legal challenge failed, it forced the government to amend the definition of "Members of Parliament" contained in section 27 of the *Electoral Act 1993*. Here, MPs were defined as "persons who are elected from time to time in accordance with the provisions of *this* Act..." (emphasis added), but since all but one incumbent MP had been elected under the authority of the *Electoral Act 1956* (which had been repealed with effect from 1 July 1994) some doubt existed as to whether the House was competent to amend the reserved provisions of the 1993 *Electoral Act*. Acting on the advice of the Solicitor-General, the government introduced an amendment to section 27 to make it clear that members of the 1993–96 parliament had undisputed authority to change the form of the ballot paper. Although the opponents of the change to the ballot paper staged a fillibuster in an attempt to embarrass the government further, the amendment to section 27 was divided out as a separate bill and passed. United (and former National MP), Peter Hilt, then sought to have the proposed change to the ballot paper voted on during the Committee stage before the amendment to section 27 was signed into law. This strategy failed because Hilt had already spoken in the debate, and the Minister of Transport, Maurice Williamson, then occupied the House until the tea adjournment with a Ministerial Statement. The Electoral Amendment Bill was signed into law during the evening meal break and the Electoral Reform Bill, now renamed the Electoral Amendment Bill (No. 2) was passed later that same evening.

Caygill believes that the sub-committee which went to Europe during the first part of 1995 was "enormously significant" in changing the thinking of the Labour and National caucuses on a number of aspects of the ballot paper, especially once it was realised that party discipline would become even more strict than hitherto (Caygill, 1996). Both caucuses, then, saw advantages for their party in the proposed new ballot paper layout with its randomised party vote. At first, Ministry of Justice officials opposed any change, arguing "... that such a layout could tend to invite voters to cast both their votes for the same party on both parts of the paper rather than encouraging separate consideration of each vote" (*NZPD*, 551:9947), but "once officials grasped that a deal had been struck, nearly everything else was done on the basis of official recommendations" including the addition of coloured party logos (Caygill, 1996). What is clear is that the smaller parties' complaints— that the change was dictated by National and Labour self-interest — have some validity. This was the first occasion that an entrenched provision had been amended by parliament without the support of all MPs; in every previous instance since 1956, unanimity had been reached or the proposed amendment had been dropped. It appeared as though, having lost control of the process of electoral change between 1990 and 1993, parliamentarians — or at least those who were members of the numerically largest caucuses — were endeavouring to, once again, reassert control.

One other piece of legislation which also shows evidence of parliamentarians attempting to regain the initiative in electoral matters — and which also divided the House along major party-minor party lines — was the Broadcasting Amendment Bill, introduced by the Minister of Broadcasting, Maurice Williamson, in October 1995. Some months earlier, Williamson had tested the waters by announcing that the government proposed removing existing restrictions which prevented parties from using their own funds to purchase radio and television time during election campaigns. If enacted, parties would be permitted to spend up to 25 per cent more than the largest allocation made to a party under the state funding formula currently administered by the Broadcasting Standards Authority. According to the Minister, the intention was to allow small or emerging parties, which were either ineligible for state funding and broadcasting time, or whose entitlement was minimal, to advertise their policies. It would also, he said, create a more level playing field for political advertising between broadcasting and the print media which was totally unrestricted (*Press*, 6 June 1995).[23]

Labour's response was fully predictable with Helen Clark promising that her party would move amendments designed to force parties to disclose the source of party donations because it wanted to prevent the secret funding of parties by wealthy interests (ibid.). Caygill condemned the proposal as "a complete perversion of MMP", one which would allow small parties with a minimal entitlement to state funding to "spend $500,000 or more, perhaps, if the money was made available to it by another party" (*NZPD*, 556:13377). Public criticism, and strong opposition during the Finance and Expenditure Select Committee's deliberations, forced the committee to recommend deleting the provision from the bill, and Williamson subsequently announced that the government would drop the clause, a decision Caygill described as a "significant back-down on the government's part" (ibid.). Faced with the very real possibility of a Labour filibuster, the government conceded defeat on this issue although the Minister of Justice indicated his displeasure with the tactic when he said "[b]ecause we have to pass the legislation (expeditiously) we have little choice but to go along with it" (ibid., 13379).

An important factor in the government's change of heart was the decision to transfer responsibility for allocating state funding to parties for election broadcasting purposes from the Broadcasting Standards Authority (which had carried out this function since 1989) to the Electoral Commission. Central to this change was a move to increase the Commission's membership by two persons, one to represent the government and the other the opposition, when it carried out this task. While the proposal was supported by Labour and National, it was opposed by most of the smaller parties. When the Bill was introduced, it had not included any provision for an augmented Electoral Commission (Harris, 1997a; *NZPD*, 556:13484), and while Labour supported transferring responsibility for allocating state funding to the Commission, it did not support it "...as it (the Electoral Commission) is currently constituted, having the sole discharge of that jurisdiction. ... [I]t is not right that this function should be discharged without any representation from political parties", because decisions as to how much money each political party is entitled to at election time is "a highly political judgment" (*NZPD*, 551:9976).

In its report the Finance and Expenditure Select Committee[24] unanimously recommended that the Electoral Commission should be augmented when the allocation of state funding for election broadcasts were determined. Caygill found it hard to understand why this should be controversial since the Broadcasting Standards Authority had always been expanded when it allocated state funding to parties at election time. Both he and the chairman of the Electoral Law Select Committee (Tony Ryall) also pointed out that that committee had always intended that when the Electoral Commission assumed responsibility for the funding allocations the two political representatives who joined the Broadcasting Standards Authority for this purpose would simply be transferred to the Electoral Commission (*AJHR*, 1993:9). The committee's decision, Caygill claimed, "would make the system more open, more accountable, and more democratic". He also drew a comparison with the composition of the Representation Commission "which clearly exercises a very important political function" (*NZPD*, 556:13377–78, 13385 & 13522).

MPs from the smaller parties were strongly opposed. At one point United's John Robertson alleged that a 'deal' had been struck between National and Labour outside the committee, and at another he accused them of "a huge abuse of power" which reflected the former environment where there were effectively only two parties in the House. "The future", he argued, "involves a system of many parties in this House" (ibid., 13478 & 13520). Alliance MPs expressed opposition to political appointees, with Anderton accusing Labour of having 'vested interests' in supporting the augmentation of the Electoral Commission "because it will have a representative on the Electoral Commission directly influencing the amount of money given to political parties" (ibid., 13383). The overall mood of those opposed to the inclusion of two political appointees was perhaps best expressed by the United Party leader, Clive Matthewson, when he said:

United New Zealand does not trust either of the old parties on electoral matters. We distrust both of the old parties equally on matters of electoral law. The evidence we have for that distrust is the changes they made to the ballot papers. What that change told us, and the process of that change — where those parties ganged up to pass something that was an entrenched provision in our electoral law, against the opposition of every other party, not only in this Parliament but outside this Parliament — was that both National and Labour rather liked the cosy old arrangement where they had turns at being the Government, and they want to continue it and they will try to put down newer parties. That is the context in which we have to consider this Bill. (ibid., 556:13381.)

The Electoral Commission was also highly critical of the move with its President, John Wallace expressing reservations to the select committee. In the first place, he believed that the proposed political appointments "could be seen to compromise the principles of independence and impartiality on which the Commission was established". Second, Wallace questioned whether two political representatives "could satisfactorily represent a number of parliamentary parties which might have opposing interests concerning the allocation of broadcasting time and funds". While he acknowledged that political parties "have a vital interest in the allocation of election broadcasting time and funds, and have relevant expertise to contribute to those matters", he did not consider that political representatives were necessary to provide that expertise or to satisfy themselves, and the parties involved, "that the allocations are the result of a fair and impartial application of the criteria specified in the law" (EC, 1996). In defending the select committee's decision Caygill emphasised that Wallace's views had not been ignored; "they were not accepted" (Caygill, 1996a). The augmented body, he added, had been modelled on the independent and impartial Representation Commission whose composition made any distortion of outcome impossible. The appointees, he said in conclusion, would be representing the government and the opposition, "not the political parties from which they may have come" (*NZPD*, 556:13522–23). After a lengthy debate, the House passed the bill by weight of numbers, 74–14, with Labour, National and the lone Christian Democrat MP supporting the measure and United, New Zealand First, Alliance, and Conservative MPs voting against it.

While in no way critical of the way in which the two additional members contributed to the task of allocating the state funding pool the Electoral Commission, in its post-election report to the Electoral Law Select Committee (EC, 1997), reminded it that when the legislation was being considered, it had objected to the principle of including two political appointees because "it was important that the Commission maintained the appearance and reality of independence", and reiterated its view that it was inappropriate (ibid., 31). It also noted that several parties had objected to the presence of the two additional members, and one even went so far as to invite them "to disqualify themselves" (ibid., 5). The two 1996 appointees, the report noted, had questioned whether such appointments could be sustained in future, especially given "the difficulty of finding a representative of a coalition government and a representative acceptable to all opposition parties" (ibid., 32).[25]

For the past forty years, at least, political input to the machinery issues of, first, redistribution and, more recently, the state funding of election campaigns, has been an accepted part of the process. It is understandable, therefore, that politicians, particularly those whose attitudes have been moulded during the era of two-party dominance characteristic of New Zealand's First-past-the-post electoral system, would want to maintain a position of perceived influence. To argue, as some MPs have, that without political input the Representation and Electoral Commissions would not have the knowledge or experience to carry out the functions required of them, simply begs the question. Without doubt, their functions would still be concluded within the framework of the law; their absence would, however, leave them open to uninformed criticism that they had not acted fairly. The presence of political appointees — in a minority on both Commissions — acts to protect their members from such criticism. But while the appointment of two persons to represent government and opposition worked reasonably satisfactorily in the era of two-party dominance, it is questionable whether it can be made to work satisfactorily in an MMP environment. With a multiplicity of parties now represented in parliament, it is likely to be difficult to reach substantial agreement on who is to represent government and opposition parties on the two Commissions. The first test of parliament's willingness to resolve this matter in a way that is acceptable to all parties is likely to come when the political appointees to the next Representation Commission are due to be nominated.

The Registration of Political Parties

One of the great ironies of the adoption of proportional representation in New Zealand is the extent to which voters who had become, for the time being at least, deeply alienated from the two major political parties, proceeded to vote for an essentially party-based electoral system. One explanation might be that it was the *parliamentary* parties, and parties as *governments*, that had lost public confidence and there was, therefore, no objection to greater powers being vested in the extra-parliamentary organisations which were seen as a limiting influence upon the parliamentary parties. It is questionable, however, how many voters draw such fine distinctions. For most voters, the concept of party is all-inclusive. That political parties would have greater control over the selection of parliamentary candidates under the party list system was overshadowed by the fact that third and minor parties were likely to be more adequately represented in the House of Representatives and this was seen as likely to curb the power of single party majority governments.

Whatever the reason for the decision, a change of electoral system to MMP clearly involved the political parties themselves making adjustments in order to adapt to the new electoral environment created by MMP. Although under FPP political parties came to dominate the political process, this had been an essentially evolutionary process, and electoral legislation largely ignored the existence of political parties in any formal sense. Political parties were free to register under the *Incorporated Societies Act 1908*, which provided that voluntary bodies such as sporting bodies, charitable organisations and others not existing for pecuniary gain could become incorporated. The Act provided for their management, control and dissolution in a regulated manner while avoiding the more complex provisions of the *Companies Act*. There was, however, no requirement to be registered and little control of any sort over their activities.

The assumption upon which FPP was based, and continued to function, was that candidates would be nominated and elected as individuals; make their electoral deposits as individuals; have their electioneering spending in the electorate limited as individuals; name scrutineers as individuals and apply for recounts or lodge electoral petitions as individuals rather than as representatives of parties. Under the *Electoral Act 1956* even the constitution of the Representation Commission responsible for the highly sensitive process of drawing the electoral boundaries referred merely to representatives of the Government and Opposition.

Nevertheless, although legally the electoral process dealt almost exclusively with individuals, over the years it had proved impossible to wholly exclude the all-pervasive influence of parties. A 1981 amendment (section 15C) to the Act goes on to state that "Any political party to which a member of the House of Representatives belongs ... may make submissions to the [Representation] Commission" provided they have obtained 5 per cent or more of the valid votes at the preceding general election. For a short time, too, between 1975 and 1980, provision existed under the Act for the party name to appear on the ballot paper. The *Broadcasting Act 1989*, Part VI, dealing with parliamentary election programmes also dealt with the role of political parties at a general election providing, *inter alia*, for the allocation of time to parties and the amount of money to be allocated to them.

Under MMP any remaining vestiges of dissemblance cease entirely for with a party list system of representation it is necessary to vote *directly* for political parties. As a result, the Royal Commission in its report on the electoral system considered whether or not the registration of political parties was desirable. Numerous arguments were advanced in favour. The Commission pointed out, for example, that apart from the role of political parties in an MMP system, registration would clearly be needed if state funding of political parties (also favoured by the Commission) were to be adopted, or if limits were to be introduced on party, as distinct from candidate, spending. The Commission believed that the introduction of party registration would be advantageous whether or not MMP was introduced, suggesting that difficulties could arise under the existing system in respect of party designations at polling booths or appearances before the Representation Commission (RCES, 1986a:266-8). Last, but not least, two fellow Commonwealth countries, Australia and Canada both registered their political parties without any important difficulties arising.

Against registration, was the argument much favoured by the two major parties when matters such as the size of their memberships, or their financial affairs is raised, that they are voluntary, private organisations. As the Royal Commission commented:

> ...such a view of their character is very difficult to square with their actual position in our constitutional and political system, and their vital role in presenting to voters the choices which they make at the election. They have a critical public function. (ibid., 267.)

The 1988 Electoral Law Select Committee further considered the matter of registration although, as with its consideration of the type of electoral system to be adopted, this too became entangled with other issues. In this case it was the question of state funding, for it was clear that registration of political parties would virtually be a requirement if state funding were to be introduced. For those National Party MPs opposed to state funding, registration appeared as the thin end of the wedge. Registration, however, was seen as an advantage in helping to clarify who, or what organisations, might make submissions to the Representation Commission where more than two parties existed in parliament.

The committee endorsed the findings of the Royal Commission that political parties should be free to register themselves; that the minimum number of members required to qualify for registration should be 200 (eventually enacted as 500 *financial* members and, in 1995 amended to 500 financial members *who qualified as electors*); and that registration should be cancelled if membership fell below that figure. A second ground for cancellation recommended by the Royal Commission — "if the party has not endorsed at least 3 candidates at the most recent general election" — was modified by the provision, "except where it has had a candidate successfully elected at the most recent election" (*AJHR*, 1988:64). The committee went beyond the recommendations of the Royal Commission in recommending, by majority, not only the registration of political parties but also independent candidates, although this recommendation was not included in the subsequent 1993 Act.

The Electoral Law Select Committee further proposed some restrictions upon the names of political parties which might be registered. These included limitations on:

(a) the length of name;

(b) whether it is offensive;

(c) whether it is identical with, or very similar to, the name, or abbreviation, or acronym of an existing registered political party;

(d) whether it contains or comprises the word 'independent' in addition to the name, abbreviation or acronym of a registered political party;

(e) whether it contains words such as royal that are protected under other Acts, unless they are already the name of a political party, such as New Zealand, National (*AJHR*, 1988: 63-4).

The substance of these recommendations was eventually incorporated into the 1993 Act, although in much broader, simpler terms.

With the passing of the *Electoral Act 1993* formal registration became a fact, with the newly established Electoral Commission responsible for the registration of parties. The increase in the number of members required to register a party, from 200 to 500, and the refinement of the term 'members' proved to be an effective hurdle. When, for example, MP Peter Dunne left the Labour Party in 1994 to form his Future New Zealand Party, he clearly failed to achieve the 500 financial members necessary for registration as a party despite the fact that his pending defection from Labour had been signalled well in advance. Subsequently, Dunne became a founder member of the United Party when it was formed in July 1995. This party, made up of seven sitting MPs, had little difficulty in overcoming the hurdle, passing the 500 member threshold within its first week of existence (*NBR*, 14 July 1995).

Similarly, the introduction of the registration of political parties took place with few problems. The most controversial decision was that permitting the registration of the component group, the Alliance, *as well as* the individual parties which made it up. That precedent was subsequently followed by the Christian Democrat and Christian Heritage parties, which formed a relatively short-lived electoral umbrella group — the Christian Coalition. In all, 21 registered parties appeared on the ballot paper in 1996, with another 11 unregistered parties contesting some electorate seats.

Coalition Building

New Zealand attitudes toward coalitions are largely inherited. The British tradition, which provided the model, was summed up by Disraeli in the mid-nineteenth century when he declared that "England does not love coalitions". If England does not love them then the record shows that New Zealand loves them even less. New Zealand has, in effect, inherited an *anti-coalition* culture. In the popular mind coalitions have been associated with governmental instability. Italy has been a favourite example. Very occasionally a preference may be expressed for a grand coalition of the two major parties but this usually amounts to an impracticable plea for a return to a pre-party situation. To move, therefore, from the relative certitude of the FPP system to one in which coalition and minority governments were likely to be the norm is a remarkable leap involving what amounted to a revolution in popular attitudes. But the problem is wider than that, for the personnel required to work the system, the politicians, lacked any real insights into coalition behaviour, even how or why coalitions operate overseas. Pre-MMP, New Zealand's political culture was antipathetic to the whole concept of coalition.

One might well question why, in these circumstances, was such an electoral system adopted? Clearly, it was not a system favoured by a majority of politicians but it may well have been a response to deeper changes taking place within New Zealand society. It has to be remembered that PR systems do not *cause* the formation of political parties, they merely *facilitate* it.

Successful political parties in the past have tended to be related to underlying societal cleavages. In New Zealand the predominant major cleavages tended to be socio-economic. Labour had its urban-city strongholds in the poorer areas of cities, National in the more well-off. The rural-urban cleavage was also important, with National predominating in the mainly rural electorates, Labour more in the urban, with a struggle between both for the more evenly balanced provincial centres.

Those cleavages still exist but there has been a shift in emphasis. Race has moved more to the fore; religious issues have surfaced; post-modernist issues such as gender, moral, and environmental issues, have cut across traditional party loyalties with the result that the two major parties have found it more and more difficult to provide adequately for the representative needs of a modern society. The change of electoral system can, therefore, be seen not only as an implied criticism of the adequacy of the two major parties but also a device for facilitating a wider range of views in parliament. New Zealand is no longer a simple type of society where views can be adequately covered by two highly cohesive political parties, however diluted their policies and philosophies have become.

The problem is that the broader range of views represented in legislatures using PR systems tends to be associated by many with inherent political instability. Yet political stability is not dependent upon the electoral system alone. Apart from other considerations, deeply divided societies are more prone to choose PR systems and countries such as Switzerland demonstrate that even deeply divided societies can maintain a high level of political stability using PR.

What *is* one key factor in political stability is the type of party system which develops and the resulting type of coalitions. Instability tends to be a characteristic of extreme polarised pluralism. This the type of system where large, extreme, non-coalitionable parties are found, such as post-1945 Italy; the Fourth French Republic, or Chile between 1961 and 1973. Yet these are the exceptions rather than the rule. New Zealand is an unlikely candidate for such a system. Another possibility was, and still is, Moderate Unpolarised Pluralism with four to eight parties in which no party is big enough to form a government alone but most are willing to form a coalition with others. This type of system, which used to be regarded as the European standard type, usually proves moderately stable to stable (Kolinsky, 1987:16–22).

Increasingly, however, the tendency seems to be towards Moderate Polarised Pluralism systems in which parties coagulate into groups of potential coalitions and elections become a plebiscite, a choice between Government and Opposition parties, not unlike the traditional two-party system. So, where polarisation is low, as it tends to be in New Zealand, there is the possibility of greater co-operation and compromise between parliamentary parties, resulting in a greater likelihood of majority coalitions, and thus a greater likelihood of stability. This is the form that characterised the first coalition formed under MMP in 1996.

Ironically, the old FPP system made an invaluable contribution to the learning curve associated with the new MMP system. At the 1993 general election, after some uncertainty on election night, the National Government was returned to power with a majority of only one seat. This seemed likely to produce a 'hung' parliament as, if according to the usual practice the government provided the Speaker of the House, it would be left without a clear majority. In a statesmanlike address on election night the Prime Minister met what was, in FPP terms, a 'crisis' by reflecting on the greater need for co-operation and looked forward to the new MMP era. The situation was saved when, most unusually in New Zealand where the speakership is viewed as a winning party 'perk', an opposition member agreed to accept the position.

This government by a 'hair's breadth' single party majority was then transformed by a series of defections which plagued National between 1993 and 1996. This was all part of the party realignment process as MMP approached. For practical purposes, this process had started in 1989 when Jim Anderton broke away from the Labour Party to establish NewLabour, and ultimately the Alliance. The process had continued in 1993 when Winston Peters, his candidacy for Tauranga vetoed by the National Party, left National and formed the New Zealand First Party.

Unlike most previous break-away parties in New Zealand, both the Alliance and New Zealand First established themselves as viable, if very small, parties under FPP. The approaching advent of MMP with its promise of a fairer deal for smaller parties clearly was a temptation to others to follow the same course.

As a result, in less than three years even under the old FPP system and without any further election, New Zealand successively had a single party majority government, a majority coalition government, a minority government, another majority coalition, a minority coalition and a further majority coalition. Only a grand coalition was missing. All of this with virtually the same government!

In this swiftly moving situation, together with doubts about how the electorate would be likely to exercise the novelty of having two votes, constituency and party, under the MMP system, speculation about possible coalition outcomes tended to revolve largely about opinion poll surveys. These started to follow the two vote format well before either the constituency candidates or party lists were named and the results were highly speculative. Nevertheless, what did become clear was that, apart from the Alliance and New Zealand First which had established themselves earlier, the newer small parties, whether with MPs or not, had largely failed to capture public support.

National always appeared likely to emerge as the largest single party but lacking the coalition partner necessary to produce a majority. Labour and the Alliance on the other hand, appeared complementary on a raft of issues and seemed to offer the possibility of a minority, or majority, coalition. For its part, the Alliance stipulated early on that if there was to be a coalition between them following the first MMP election, the broad policies involved would have to be agreed *before* the election or there would be no coalition. The rationale offered was that of transparency: that the electorate needed to know before the election what sort of government it would be voting for. The Alliance also enunciated 12 principles which it stated were fundamental to its purposes and which were declared non-negotiable. In the circumstances of the time, with Labour the second largest political party in the House of Representatives and the Alliance with only two seats, this had all the appearance of the tail attempting to wag the dog.[26]

Before the 1996 general election however this strategy had much to do with building-up the status the Alliance. With only two sitting MPs in the House but with a high poll rating, it succeeded for a time in presenting itself as one of the 'big three' parties, instead of accepting the dominance of Labour and National. Labour was hardly likely to enter into any pre-election coalition deals on terms set by a junior partner when it was far from clear just how well that party was likely to fare at the election. Moreover, Labour, with a poorly polling leader, was wary of any entanglement with the then high-polling Alliance leader. Discussion of any such 'pre-nuptial' agreement therefore, although of obvious advantage to the Alliance, hardly amounted to a serious attempt at coalition-building.

Obviously aware of this, the Alliance defined its non-negotiable principles more in terms of its internal needs for cohesion than as a serious negotiating position. Firm adherence to publicly stated and reiterated principles was designed to ensure a clear-cut image of a party which stood by its word, in contra-distinction to Labour portrayed as a pragmatic party which had departed from its principles when in government in the 1980s. Such stances, together with the conflicting positions of the two parties — the Alliance only prepared to negotiate prior to the election and Labour only afterwards — not only amounted to deadlock but to a fundamental unwillingness to accept the nuances of coalition-building.

Instead, Labour sought to cultivate New Zealand First which, ideologically, might have been thought nearer to National. This involved no deals but a growing habit of consultation and co-operation, the best basis for any possible coalition deals. While it might have been thought that a more logical linkage was New Zealand First and National, this was complicated by personality clashes between the two leaders (a factor, too, in Alliance-Labour relationships).

The National Party as government expressed a general readiness for co-operation with others but was slow to take third and minor parties into consideration. There were exceptions, such as a multi-party accord on superannuation, which had the effect of partly depoliticising the issue, but that was very much to the government's advantage. Apart from that, while it held a narrow majority the Bolger Government continued to behave much like any other majority government under an FPP system.

It was only as a minority government that National was forced to consider more carefully the views of the other parties in the legislature. This led to temporary, one-off coalitions for particular pieces of legislation such as the Sale of Radio New Zealand Bill which the government was only able to pass after the United Party came into being and agreed to support it, or co-operation with the Labour Party over the form of the electoral ballot paper, a common interest which the two major parties shared but which was opposed by all the third and minor parties. More common were the temporary coalitions of non-government parties either to defeat unacceptable clauses in legislation, such as the secrecy provisions of the Overseas Investment Bill, or to send Private Members' Bills, such as the Registration of Teachers Bill, to a parliamentary select committee against the wishes of the government. Simple as these arrangements may seem, they represented an unusual innovation for MPs in the New Zealand parliament and, in terms of inter-party co-operation, provided some valuable preliminary experience of the type of activity which might be required as a result of the introduction of the MMP system.

Once again, however, an important caveat is the transitional period between the two systems where the informal rules and practices of coalition techniques are being acquired and there has not been time for conventions to become established. In such circumstances, and particularly in a small legislature, such as that in New Zealand, personalities play a disproportionate role — for good or bad. With the 5 per cent electoral threshold proving to be such a significant hurdle, the 1996 general election resulted in the representation of six parties in parliament (one less than in the last parliament under FPP). The MMP system is the closest any form of PR can come to the original FPP system. That, combined with a tradition of strong party cohesion and prevailing two party culture, suggests that in future New Zealand will continue to have two major parties with strictly limited third parties — both in number and size — with the continued likelihood of two party majority coalitions made up of a major-minor party combinations, an outcome not dissimilar to that in Germany.

Forming the First MMP Government

The 1996 general election marked the end of the first stage in the transition to the MMP environment. Since, as expected, no party won a clear majority of parliamentary seats[27] a coalition government, or perhaps a single party minority government needed to be negotiated. The formation of the government took nine weeks and was not completed until just before the House of Representatives was scheduled to reconvene. This delay caused some frustration for voters who, in the past, had been accustomed to knowing which party would govern New Zealand for the next three years late on the night of the election.[28]

Throughout the 1993–96 parliamentary term the leaders of New Zealand First, Winston Peters, and Northern Maori MP, Tau Henare, repeatedly criticised the National Party's philosophy and leadership. Henare had even said that he was not prepared to work with the National Party in a coalition government that included key National figures — a statement he later drew back from (*Press*, 15 October 1996) — and Peters had been reported as saying that the price of New Zealand First coalescing with National would be the 'dumping' of three of its very senior members — Prime Minister, Jim Bolger, the Minister of Finance, Bill Birch, and Health Minister, Jenny Shipley — a statement he later denied making (*EP*, 25 June 1996; *Listener*, 12 October 1996). Peters' continuing criticism of National, in particular, during the election campaign led commentators to conclude that New Zealand First supporters were making it clear that they did not want their party to enter into a coalition with National although, three days before the poll, *The Press* (9 October 1996) reported that the party was split over whether it should seek a coalition with National or Labour.

Unlike the Alliance leader, Jim Anderton, Peters resolutely refused to give any indication of whether New Zealand First would be interested in entering into a coalition with either of the largest parties (*Dom.*, 27 July 1996).[29] Although Peters acknowledged that this stance would probably cost New Zealand First votes, it did guarantee the party flexibility in the negotiations that would follow the election. This was especially important since electoral support for the Labour Party increased noticeably as the campaign developed. Ten days before the election, however, Peters claimed that New Zealand First "would be part of the next government" (*Press*, 2 October 1996), thus clearly indicating his primary objective.

Since this was the first experience New Zealand politicians had had of coalition formation across parties, the nine weeks taken to complete coalition negotiations cannot be considered to be unreasonable. What made the process quite unusual, however, was that New Zealand First, the third largest party, conducted coalition negotiations separately but simultaneously with both the incumbent National Government[30] and Labour, the major opposition party in the previous parliament. Never before in the democratic world have separate coalition negotiations taken place simultaneously with two different parties.

On the night of the election Peters told New Zealanders that they "would have to be patient" while coalition negotiations took place. With this statement he effectively seized the initiative, and he maintained it through the entire negotiating period. It was he who set the agenda for the negotiations and, despite his insistence that all negotiations take place in secret, it was he who made virtually all public statements detailing progress. There were also a number of bizarre incidents — for example, a room in which negotiations were taking place was swept for listening devices, and demands were made to remove a television camera from the roof of an adjacent building which (it was alleged) was directed at the room where New Zealand First was meeting to make its final decision — underscoring the atmosphere of paranoia surrounding New Zealand First's determination to become a key part of the first MMP government. Even the party's decision to enter into a coalition with National was expressed in terms of New Zealand First as the dominant partner (*EP*, 11 December 1996).

Shortly after the election each of the parties established a small negotiating team which was augmented by specialist spokespeople when specific policy details were worked through. Initially, discussions focused on establishing agreed procedures, including the maintenance of confidentiality and, once these were agreed to, the broad principles governing the operation of the proposed coalition were worked through. According to a member of National's negotiating team, the party, however, spent little time discussing broad principles because it had already gone through New Zealand First's manifesto policies in considerable detail and had matched them with its own policies to identify where modifications might be made and concessions granted (Bradford, 1997). Detailed policy discussions took place in small sub-committees of portfolio specialists (*Press*, 22 November 1996) which were interspersed with formal meetings. Only when issues were well advanced did the respective parties' caucuses become involved, and it was not until the two draft agreements — between New Zealand First and National and New Zealand First and Labour — had been finalised were they referred to the separate party caucuses for examination and ratification. Throughout this process Peters and the New Zealand First negotiating team were working towards securing a detailed coalition agreement which set out exactly the coalition government's programme for the next three years (ibid., 15 October 1996).

As the fourth-largest parliamentary party, the Alliance was not part of the negotiating process but its presence could not be totally ignored. Since a Labour-New Zealand First coalition government would be a minority one, the post-election position adopted by the Alliance towards such an arrangement was crucial. Three days after the election Anderton provided Labour with a 20-page issues paper which, while not setting out demands, made it clear that a Labour-New Zealand First coalition would not have total freedom of action. It was obvious, however, that at least some New Zealand First MPs regarded the Alliance as a potential barrier to such a coalition. Peters said that he saw no reason to talk with the Alliance although he conceded that Labour would have to do so before any coalition proposal involving Labour was put to his caucus for approval (ibid., 21 November 1996). For its part, Labour indicated that it did not trust the Alliance to maintain confidentiality (ibid., 23 November 1996), and it was not until the end of November before representatives of the two parties met to discuss the terms under which the Alliance might offer support to a Labour-New Zealand First coalition. At this meeting Anderton advised that Alliance support would be forthcoming so long as the coalition's policies moved in the general direction favoured by his party (ibid., 28 November 1996). Subsequently, Labour was reported to have agreed to show him details of any coalition agreement in confidence because, as Anderton pointed out, the Alliance could not be expected to sign up to any deal without knowing its contents (ibid., 29 November 1996). Nevertheless, Anderton made it crystal-clear that the Alliance was not prepared to support any aspect of a Labour-New Zealand First coalition agreement it found unacceptable (ibid., 2 December 1996) — an unmistakable signal that, where necessary, any agreement would need to be amended to meet Alliance concerns or its support would not be forthcoming. For his part, Peters had already indicated that he would not tolerate any Alliance input into a coalition deal (ibid., 29 November 1996). Finally, on the morning that the New Zealand First caucus met to make its decision, the Alliance delivered signed copies of a two-page agreement with Labour, which guaranteed that a Labour-New Zealand First coalition would have the support on confidence and supply issues that it needed to form a government, but that the Alliance retained the right to promote its own policies "vigorously" and to oppose legislation it disagreed with. In releasing this agreement, Anderton said that the Alliance was "offering constructive support ... (and) ...absolute authority to form a government without having a blank cheque to do anything they like" (ibid., 11 December 1996).

While the negotiations were being undertaken, New Zealand was governed by a caretaker administration. Ministers from the 1993–96 National Government remained in office but, by convention, refrained from taking any new policy initiatives or making significant policy decisions (CAB, 1996:20–23). Even so, it was not long before decisions on major state sector projects began piling up, and the Chairman of the State Services Commission (Don Hunn) instructed departmental chief executives to discuss with their Ministers how they might deal with the growing backlog of items requiring decision because "the normalities of government must proceed" (*SST*, 10 November 1996). One example of the caretaker government delaying a decision occurred when the Minister of Health, Jenny Shipley, directed the Southern Regional Health Authority not to release its decision on the southern cardio-thoracic unit planned for Christchurch while the coalition talks continued (*Press*, 28 November 1996).[31] The cabinet also agreed that Ministers would clear requests for negotiators to talk with officials, but that they were not to be apprised of the details of what those talks were about (Dunne, 1997).

The day that the New Zealand First caucus met to debate the details of the two agreements brokered by their negotiators was marked by high tension and drama. Wellington's *Evening Post* reported a continuing flow of phone calls, sorties and haggling between the New Zealand First caucus room and the leaders of the Labour and National parties which continued until late in the afternoon. The New Zealand First's caucus was clearly divided — understandably, because many of its members had earlier belonged to one or other of the two major parties. Around 5pm Henare, who had earlier favoured entering into a coalition with Labour (*Dom.*, 27 July 1996), telephoned Helen Clark and asked her to reconsider the cabinet position she was prepared to offer Peters. "Peters wanted finance. She (Clark) declined," the *Evening Post* reported the next day (12 December 1996).

The agreement signed by the leaders of National and New Zealand First on 10 December 1996 resulted in the formation of a majority coalition government which aimed "to provide sound and stable Government for New Zealand for a three year term concluding with the 1999 General Election" (Coalition Agreement, 1996:5). Nevertheless, the agreement recognised the right of each party to its own identity and organisation (ibid., 4), and prohibited either coalition partner from supporting

> ... any policy advanced by any other non-Coalition party or private member and, if a bill is introduced to the House, shall not vote in favour of such bill or abstain upon the vote unless and until the consent in writing has been obtained by both Parties to the Coalition. (ibid., 7.)

New Zealand's equivalent of the 'three-line whip', a dominant feature of New Zealand's parliamentary process during the FPP two-party era, was clearly still alive and well despite the expectations of many electors that MMP would result in a more consensual type of government.

A number of other aspects of the coalition agreement are also noteworthy. Despite New Zealand First's pre-election stance that the number of cabinet's members should not exceed 15 (NZF, 1996, Democracy Policy:9), the coalition agreement provided for a total Ministry of 26, twenty inside cabinet and another six outside. In this way the problem facing Bolger in reducing the size of his existing Ministry was lessened.[32] Initially, National's allocation comprised 15 cabinet Ministers and two Ministers outside cabinet, compared with New Zealand First's five cabinet posts and four Ministers outside cabinet. It was agreed, however, that this ratio would change no later than 1 October 1998, when National's cabinet representation would be reduced to

12, with the three vacancies thus created being reallocated to New Zealand First MPs (Coalition Agreement, 1996:8). Provision for the resolution of disputes between the coalition partners was also made: the agreement defines a "fundamental dispute" as one "... which could lead to substantial injury to the Coalition and which appear on reasonable grounds to be incapable of satisfactory long term resolution by negotiation" (ibid., 10). If this occurs, a disputes committee, consisting of the leaders, deputy leaders and presidents of the coalition partners is required to seek a resolution through negotiation. If agreement cannot be reached, either party may give written notice to the other "... that unless the matter is resolved within ... seven days the Coalition will be terminated" (ibid., 11).

A 50 page schedule attached to the agreement spelt out 36 policies that the coalition government proposed implementing during its three-year term of office.[33] Policy statements varied widely in the amount of detail included — health, for example occupied five pages,[34] while 25 other policies each occupied less than one page — and, in many instances, commitments were qualified by words and phrases such as "to consider...", "consult with...", "accept in principle..." and "strengthen commitment to...". In encapsulating the compromises each party had made to reach agreement, this document effectively superseded the election manifestos they had presented to the electorate during the election campaign. Superficially, it appeared that New Zealand First had achieved most: Winston Peters became Deputy Prime Minister and took up the newly created position of Treasurer,[35] and a number of its key policy planks — superannuation (including the deferral of tax cuts scheduled for July 1997 and a referendum on a compulsory retirement savings scheme), a widening of the Reserve bank's inflation target, a ban on the sale of a number of key strategic assets,[36] increased expenditure on health and education and, perhaps most significant of all, the removal of the $NZ1 billion cap on Maori grievance settlement claims imposed by the previous government — were included. Crucially, however, National was able to preserve, largely unaltered, the key elements of the *Reserve Bank Act*, *Fiscal Responsibility Act* and *Employment Contracts Act* which collectively lay at the heart of the economic reforms of the previous 12 years.

Several undercurrents were apparent throughout the period of negotiations. Some National Party MPs privately aired concerns that their party might concede too much in the talks, and indicated that they wanted an opportunity to debate the agreement before it was signed (*Press*, 3 December 1996). Backbench MP Christine Fletcher opined that National "should have ruled out any negotiation on the *Employment Contracts Act* and other fundamental economic policies before entering coalition talks", and that National's negotiating team would need to satisfy its backbench MPs that it had not traded away too many policies (TV1, 1996), while Agriculture Minister, Lockwood Smith, signalled that some members of National's caucus would rather sit in opposition than compromise on what they regarded as National's fundamental principles (*Press*, 6 November 1996). There were also reports that some senior National Party politicians were concerned that a smaller cabinet which included New Zealand First MPs would block their own advancement (*SST*, 20 October 1996). Similar pressures were evident within the Labour caucus where senior MPs were reported to have begun lobbying for a dwindling number of cabinet posts (ibid., 10 November 1996).

To most observers, New Zealand First's decision to join National as a coalition partner was something of a surprise. For years, personality clashes between Peters and the National Party's parliamentary leadership suggested that Labour was his logical ally. In an interview, John Henderson, a former head of the Prime Minister's Department when David Lange was Prime Minister, stated that he believed that New Zealand First's policies had more in common with Labour's than with National's policies but, with considerable prescience, he added: "Never underestimate what could happen when you take an ambitious politician and put him together with a pragmatic party" (*ST*, 18 October 1996). Why, then, did New Zealand First — and Peters in particular — bury the hatchet and decide to enter into coalition with National?

With the benefit of hindsight it seems clear that, psychologically, Winston Peters was always likely to be more comfortable with National, the party he left in 1993 after representing it in parliament for more than a decade. There is some, admittedly tenuous, evidence to suggest that he may have decided to go with National about two weeks before the final decision was made, and that he may have made it subconsciously even before the election (Kirton, 1997). If this is correct, it is a case of Peters returning home to his political roots. Why, then, did the negotiations take so long? Without doubt, Peters was the dominant figure in the New Zealand First caucus for, without him, few if any other New Zealand First MPs would have made it to parliament. The explanation lies in Peters' recognition of the fact that New Zealand First held the whiphand while the negotiations were in progress, although Bradford (1997) has stated that the New Zealand First negotiators did not seem to have much idea about how to go about negotiating; once they were concluded New Zealand First's position would become less powerful. Prolonging the coalition process enabled Peters to keep New Zealand First in the public spotlight for as long as possible.[37]

Before talks between the parties began, Peters had announced that New Zealand First hoped to hold a "dual negotiating process, not a competitive bidding war" (*Press*, 16 October 1996). It is clear, however, that New Zealand

First used its pivotal position to play National and Labour off against one another. Nowhere is this more clear than in the events surrounding National's concession of the new position of Treasurer to Peters. Clark had confirmed Labour's Finance spokesperson, Michael Cullen, as her choice as Minister of Finance in mid-November (ibid., 20 November 1996), and refused to alter her position when the issue was put to her for the last time in the late afternoon of 10 December. Some months later, one of the New Zealand First negotiators, Tuariki John Delamere, confirmed that the last-minute offer by the National Party negotiators to appoint Peters as Treasurer resulted in the New Zealand First caucus agreeing to enter into a coalition with National. Delamere said that as late as 5.30pm "New Zealand First MPs were 'very much' leaning towards Labour". Two issues — the position of Treasurer and the stance of the Alliance — were, he said, the decisive ones (*Press*, 30 April 1997). What New Zealand First's decision would have been had National also refused to offer Peters the position of Treasurer must remain an open question.

In an interview published in the *New Zealand Listener* (12 October 1996) National Party president, Geoff Thompson, had said "... what you could say is that we are very conscious of the broad interests of the party in any (coalition) discussions that are held". In this instance, the "broad interests" of the party clearly included retaining the levers of power; National's caucus members did not learn of its negotiators' concession until Peters announced it on television a few hours later. One consequence which flowed from the strategy adopted by New Zealand First's negotiators was that it left a substantial residue of bitterness with the rejected party.

There is some evidence, too, that the prospect of the perquisites of office played a significant part in New Zealand First's ultimate decision. As we noted earlier, the coalition agreement gave New Zealand First a disproportionate number of Ministerial positions — eight out of 26, or 30.8 per cent — and that this number was scheduled to rise to 11 (42.3 per cent) by 1 October 1998. According to Kirton, a report that appeared in *The Press* on 11 October 1997, and which claimed that "[t]he number of ministerial posts secured by New Zealand First in the coalition agreement was one of the main factors that persuaded the party to seal its deal with National instead of Labour", is accurate. Peters' strategy, he said, was to obtain "the trinkets of office" for his caucus and, as a result, a large amount of negotiating took place on the number of cabinet and other ministerial positions to be allocated to New Zealand First (Kirton, 1997; Bradford 1997). This must be seen as an attempt to bind New Zealand First caucus members, particularly those who were rewarded with appointment to ministerial positions, even more closely to Peters because he was, effectively, their patron.

Although the first MMP election has been safely negotiated and a majority coalition government emerged as a result of protracted negotiations, the transition to MMP is far from complete. Effective working relations between coalition partners are still being developed, all members of parliament, both returnees and the newly elected, have had to adapt to the new political environment where several divergent points of view are likely to be expressed in public, and coalition partners have to accept that not all of the policy positions they put to electors in the election campaign are likely to be implemented. The first MMP parliament threw up evidence of some discomfort among members, particularly those belonging to the newer parliamentary parties, so some realignment of individuals' allegiances is still a real possibility. The many registered parties that did not win parliamentary representation because they failed to surmount the stipulated threshold or win a constituency seat also still need to consider their political future. Some will fold their tents and steal quietly off into the night never to be seen again, while others may seek to regroup through amalgamations in preparation for another attempt to storm the barriers to a parliamentary presence. One thing, however, is certain: the MMP environment, and the style of politics that results from it, will be the subject of continuing study and discussion during the next few years as politicians, political activists and the electorate at large assess the benefits and costs of the MMP electoral system in preparation for the parliamentary review scheduled for the first years of the new millennium. What can be safely said is that the jury is still out on whether New Zealand's change to MMP has delivered the benefits the public expected of it.

Notes

1   The algebraic representation of the formula is:
$$MEP = [MR / (MR+MGR)] * MCP$$
where MR is the number of electors registered on the Maori roll,
     MGR is the number of Maori on the General roll, and
     MCP is the census Maori population (declared ancestry basis).
The number of Maori electorates is determined by dividing the Maori electoral population by the General electoral quota for the South Island (which is, itself, determined by dividing the South Island's General electoral population — the 'Usually Resident' population less the South Island's Maori electoral population — by 16, the number of General electorates allocated to the South Island by the *Electoral Act 1993*).

2   Broadcasting Assets case.

3   The programme also included 17 regional and one national hui, an advertising campaign on Aotearoa National radio, and a presence at the Aotea Cultural Festival held at Hawera.

4   Many Maori networks have little or no formal structure and, overwhelmingly, they are

	very decentralised and largely autonomous. The most effective grassroots networks are those of the Maori Women's Welfare League.
5	It should be noted, though, that at the time the results of the Maori option were announced, Maori did not know the number or distribution of Maori list candidates, or how many of them were likely to be elected. All they knew was that their guaranteed representation had increased by one seat.
6	Most estimates by Maori ranged from 14 to 17 seats.
7	The 1991 Personal Questionnaire (Question 8) asked: "Have you any New Zealand Maori ancestry?" (Responses totalled 511,278 or 14.9 per cent of the total population.)
8	Question 7 asked: "Which ethnic group do you belong to?" The figure of 116,907 was provided by the Department of Statistics in 1994.
9	Parliament met for the first time after the 1993 general election on 21 December 1993.
10	The previous one was in 1890 after Parliament had decided to reduce the number of 'European' MPs (and, therefore, the number of electorates) from 91 to 70.
11	The key determinant of the three electoral quotas (North Island, South Island, and Maori) is the South Island's General (ie. non-Maori) electoral population.
12	One other criterion normally included in the Representation Commission's terms of reference, the boundaries of existing General electoral districts (though not the existing Maori electoral districts), was specifically excluded from the first delineation of MMP electorates.
13	A mesh block is the smallest statistical unit of population. Each usually contains up to c.200 people.
14	Of the 1,331 objections and counter-objections received, 60.3 per cent related to proposed boundaries and nearly all of the rest to the proposed electorate names. According to the Representation Commission's own analysis, 28.4 per cent of objections and 57.0 per cent of counter-objections were allowed wholly or in part. (It should be noted, however, that counter-objections often supported the commission's original proposals.)
15	The commission voted by 7 votes to 3 against releasing the provisional maps, with two appointed members, Ian McLean (representing the government), and Lloyd Falck (representing the opposition parties), and one other member voting against the resolution.
16	Probine's investigation focused on the Labour Party. Although the commission was satisfied that leaks had occurred (because of "a close correlation between the apparently leaked information ... and the actual boundary changes"), when Probine interviewed David Caygill (who was overseeing the Labour Party's input), Caygill, somewhat disingenuously it appears, "suggested that what appeared to be leaks might be nothing more than informed guesses".
17	On the day that Probine's interim report was received the commission's chairman reaffirmed the need for confidentiality and "suggested that any member who was unable to resist even the temptation or outside pressure to breach that confidence should resign from the Commission. There was no disagreement with that proposition" (see RC, 1994a:14 October 1994). Some indication of the seriousness with which the commission demanded total confidentiality can be gauged from instructions issued to the small group of public servants responsible for preparing the commission's final decisions for publication: their attention was drawn to section 39(2) of the *Electoral Act 1993*, which placed a heavy restriction on any information conveyed to them in the course of their duties, and was accompanied by a warning that "... persons infringing this provision are likely to be charged under s.244 of the Act with committing a corrupt or illegal practice" (RC, 1994a:2 March 1995).
18	The aim was to prevent the formation of 'umbrella' parties designed to manipulate the

provisions of the new electoral system by, for example, one party contesting only constituency seats while an associated party contested only the party vote, in which case both parties would receive separate seat entitlements that, together, might exceed their combined entitlement if they were a single party.

19   The Royal Commission's proposals for controlling parties' campaign expenditure differed from that finally agreed to by Parliament. The commission had recommended that campaign expenditure by parties should be related to the number of constituencies contested but the select committee adopted a formula which allowed each registered party contesting the party vote to spend a maximum of $1 million (including GST) plus $20,000 for each electorate contested. Registered parties which chose to contest only constituency seats would be permitted to spend the equivalent of a maximum of $20,000 (including GST) multiplied by the number of electorates it contested in addition to each of its candidates' electorate expenses. The select committee concluded that this arrangement would be fairer to parties which chose to contest only list seats than the one proposed by the Royal Commission. (See *NZPD*, 551:10061 and 10077.)

20   As prescribed, the electorate vote was to be printed above the party vote and the two parts were to be separated by poll clerks before being handed to voters. This format had been adopted in 1990 (for the general election and referendum on the term of Parliament), in 1992 (for the indicative referendum on the electoral system), and in 1993 (for the general election and the binding referendum on the electoral system). According to Moore (1996), then Senior Legal Adviser with the Department of Justice, it was included in the *Electoral Act 1993* "because it had been found to work in 1990".

21   Registered parties choosing not to contest a constituency seat would appear in alphabetical order below those parties which did, and a blank space would be included in the party vote side where an independent candidate contested the constituency seat.

22   However, although a sample MMP ballot paper was included in its report, the Royal Commission made no explicit recommendation as to what form it should take.

23   There can be little doubt that this proposal was closely related to Williamson's suggestion that the full impact of MMP's proportionality might be minimised if an 'umbrella party' contested the party vote and used associated parties to stand in electorates.

24   The committee comprised three National MPs, two Labour MPs and two United Party MPs.

25   The Electoral Commission proposed that if Parliament decided that they should be retained, the appointments should be the nominees of the Prime Minister and Leader of the Opposition, as prescribed in the *Broadcasting Act 1989*.

26   By 1997 the Alliance was appearing more open to negotiation in preparation for the next election.

27   National won 33.8 per cent of the party vote and 44 of the 120 parliamentary seats; Labour, 28.2 per cent and 37 seats; New Zealand First, 13.4 per cent and 17 seats; the Alliance, 10.1 per cent and 13 seats; Act, 6.1 per cent and 8 seats; and United, 0.9 per cent and 1 seat. Fifteen other parties won 7.5 per cent of the party vote but no seats.

28   In only two of the twenty elections between 1935 and 1993 was there any doubt the day after the election about which party would form the next government.

29   During the second, nationally televised, leaders' debate on 8 October he once again appeared to distance himself from the prospect of entering into coalition with National despite Bolger stating — no fewer than three times — that he agreed with Peters on policy matters and that the two parties had much in common.

30   Strictly speaking, a coalition government — formalised through a written agreement — comprising National and United, governed in the months prior to the election. (See Boston, *et al.*, 1996:201–02.)

31   Shipley's directive was based on the caretaker convention that she no longer had a mandate to make the decision. The next day, New Zealand First's health spokesperson, Neil Kirton, announced that the preferred proposal was a joint public-private one that included an element of profit-making to which New Zealand First was strongly opposed.

32   Although four Ministers had retired from politics at the election, 18 Cabinet Ministers and two Ministers outside Cabinet remained. With a total of only 17 ministerial positions available, and a number of able backbenchers in the wings, some adjustments needed to be made. One Minister (John Banks) resigned from the caretaker Ministry before the coalition agreement was finalised and another, United Party's Peter Dunne, was seen as expendable (despite his publicly stated desire to be part of the new ministry). This effectively reduced the number of current Cabinet Ministers to 16, still more than the number of places available even without allowing for the introduction of new talent. Bolger dealt with this problem in two ways: he nominated Kaikoura electorate MP, Doug Kidd (Minister of Labour in the previous government), as Speaker — pushing aside the current Deputy Speaker, Jim Gerard, in the process — and dropped two Cabinet Ministers and both remaining Ministers outside Cabinet to allow him to promote a small number of National backbench members. In this way, Bolger was able to meet the terms of the coalition agreement and promote four of his party's MPs to Ministerial positions.

33   A supplementary agreement identified a further seven issues for consideration.

34   New Zealand First's spokesperson on health, Neil Kirton, fought to include both the principles underpinning his party's health policy (public health and non-profit) and detailed policies "because he did not trust National to stick with the broad principles enunciated" (Kirton, 1997).

35   The Coalition Agreement designated the newly-created position of Treasurer as the 'senior' position in the finance portfolio, the other position being that of Minister of Finance. Speaking to a meeting of Wall Street bankers in April 1997, the Minister of Finance differentiated their roles by describing the Treasurer as having 'major responsibilities on the economic and macro side, while ownership and financial accounting matters rested with the Finance Minister'. (See *Press*, 5 April 1997.)

36   These included electricity generation, and distribution, public television and New Zealand Post, all of which were State-owned Enterprises.

37   Theoretically, the coalition talks could have continued for some months. By law, however, Parliament was required to meet no later than six weeks after the date set for the return of the writs. Undoubtedly, all parties involved in the negotiations preferred that they be completed and decisions made before Parliament met. This was achieved with two days to spare.

11 Consequences and Causes

It is an error to imagine that evolution signifies a constant tendency to increased perfection. That process undoubtedly involves a constant remodelling of the organism in adaptation to new conditions; but it depends on the nature of those conditions whether the direction of the modification effected shall be upward or downward.
— Thomas Henry Huxley, *The Struggle for Existence in Human Society*, 1888.

It is perhaps hardly surprising that in 1993 the New Zealand voting public found itself more opposed to what had gone before than alert to the consequences of change. Voters knew that the existing system was both unfair and backed by many, apparently self-interested, politicians. In short, they knew what they did *not* want. New Zealand voters had been reacting in this way for generations. That, however, does not imply that this form of reaction is unqualified. Governments in New Zealand have rarely been defeated unless the electorate has believed that there was a credible opposition ready to replace them. The same applied to FPP. It is interesting to speculate whether it would have been defeated but for the role of the Royal Commission and the continuing campaign of the Electoral Reform Coalition. The Royal Commission succeeded in putting a 'face' on the otherwise vague and intimidating concept of proportional representation. The public generally might not know much about it but name recognition for MMP was high. At least voters knew *of* it and having been carefully assessed by experts in the Royal Commission, it had been invested with a degree of credibility. That proved sufficient — just.

Vowles (1993:23) may be correct when he argues that "a desire for more responsive government and democratic representation was the major impulse behind New Zealanders' support for a proportional electoral system", but this was largely an inchoate desire, a reaction less to specific government policies than to apparent inflexibilities, attitudes and processes. New Zealand, in effect, was passing through an economic and social revolution at this time. It is hardly surprising that the ordinary citizen who was being dragged through massive changes at breakneck speed, felt disoriented and deprived of democratic anchors which it was believed, rightly or wrongly, had provided protection in the past.

What the politicians, in particular, may have underestimated was a sense, not exactly of alienation, but of profound public mistrust of recent governments, both Labour and National. While declining, turn-outs at general elections remained high — 85.2 per cent of registered electors in 1990 and 85.2 per cent in 1993 (*AJHR*, 1991a:167;1994:163) — but a 1993 *Time* 'Morgan' poll reported that politicians ranked with car sales people as the least-respected occupations in New Zealand (*Press*, 2 June 1993).

In this sense, then, the result of the 1990 general election may have served to produce a misleading impression. The landslide National Party victory, when it won 70 per cent of the seats, appeared to be an overwhelming endorsement of both National and the electoral system. Yet National's victory, in an election in which 85.2 per cent of electors voted, was based on only 47.8 per cent of the vote while Labour's electoral support dropped to a critically low 35.1 per cent. The 'softness' of this support was to be revealed clearly in 1993 when both major parties sank to unprecedented lows of 35.0 percent and 34.7 per cent respectively.

The public mood was one of betrayal. By 1993 two successive governments had broken electoral promises. Both had been responsible for major economic and social changes during a painful period of reconstruction. Both had followed broadly similar economic policies despite the fact that the dramatic fall in support for Labour in the 1990 general election could be construed as a sharp public rebuke for that government and its policies. That rebuke was a lesson the successor National government chose to ignore. Thus, in 1993, National, too, suffered a similar fate with an almost identical decline in voter support (–12.8 per cent), while Labour's support dropped a further 0.5 per cent. For a disillusioned public, changing governments had had little effect. In a two-party system, when a government displeased its constituents the normal reaction was to punish it at the next general election, but with both major parties out of favour in quick succession, that remedy alone no longer appeared adequate. Hence blame fell on the electoral system.

In a poll conducted shortly before the 1992 indicative referendum, two out of three New Zealanders who were eligible to vote claimed that they did not know enough to make an informed decision while 51 per cent of those supporting electoral change claimed that they were motivated by the poor performance of politicians rather than conviction of the merits of another voting system (NBR, 18 September 1992). Thus, despite the best efforts of the Electoral Referendum Panels set up to provide impartial information for the referendums, few would argue that the public generally were well-informed beyond the basics about what the MMP system was likely to involve. While it is true that, before the second referendum was held 6 November 1993, an *NBR-Consultus* poll (22 October 1993) reported that 60 per cent claimed to know 'A Lot' or 'A Fair Amount' about MMP, misunderstandings about the significance of the role of the party vote were to persist through to the first MMP election in 1996 (*NBR*, 27 September 1996).

By 1993, therefore, whether the public believed that the electoral system was the *cause* of its distrust in the two major parties no longer mattered. Both major parties had forfeited public confidence and, if they were to be punished and shown the error of their ways, the only decisive means of achieving this appeared to be through changing the electoral system. A poll taken shortly after the 6 November 1993 referendum showed that "…more than four out of 10 of those who voted MMP did so because they were fed up with MPs' **performance"**. Just 32 per cent said they were "positively convinced" another voting system would lead to better government. (*NBR*, 19 November 1993.)

Expectations

The problem with reactive politics of this nature is that when change does occur it is often associated with a tendency to raise exaggerated expectations which are incapable of achievement. Some indication of New Zealanders' expectations of a change of electoral system may be gained from a survey of the expected benefits from MMP conducted by UMR-Insight Research shortly after the 1993 referendum. Table 11.1 sets out the reported results of this poll.

Grouping the 'very likely' and 'somewhat likely' categories shows a logical sequence of expectations. A total of 85 per cent of respondents believed that it would be "easier for minor parties to get representation". This ties in with the 80 per cent who believed that there would be "more consensus in government decision-making". That, in turn, leads to the third most important category in which 73 per cent expressed a belief that "governments [would] not [be] able to introduce unpopular policies". On the other hand, expectation that "MPs' behaviour will improve" was never high.

The expectation that it would be "easier for minor parties to get representation" was realistic but that of 'consensus' much less so. A greater degree of co-operation than hitherto, possibly, but not consensus. The 1993 referendum, which resulted in the adoption of MMP, thus involved two diametrically opposed sets of expectations. Those who supported the introduction of MMP tended to pitch their expectations too high with a tendency to identify MMP with consensus. Such beliefs ignored the type of coalition arrangements likely to ensue, and hence the extent to which governments were likely to be constrained in introducing unpopular policies. The mere existence of a greater number of minor parties — in any case limited by a high electoral threshold — does not in itself produce consensus. MMP is merely an electoral system which may form *part* of a consensual system. Certainly, MMP may *facilitate* development towards consensus, but it cannot, of itself, produce or guarantee a consensual system.

On the other hand, opponents of MMP tended to predict disaster, particularly for the economy, which, it was believed, the new electoral system would undermine. That exaggerated expectations were widespread is not surprising for, remote from other countries and with a strictly limited knowledge of PR systems or coalitions and how they work, New Zealanders were embarking upon a quite extraordinary 'leap into the dark'.

Table 11.1   The Benefits of MMP

There have been a number of arguments made by supporters of MMP about the benefits it will bring to New Zealand. How likely do you think these benefits will be under MMP? (Responses recorded as percentages.)

	Very likely	Somewhat likely	Not that likely	Not likely at all	Don't know
Easier for parties to get representation	50	35	8	3	4
There will be more women MPs	24	37	21	7	11
Minorities better represented	22	46	21	4	7
MPs' behaviour will improve	19	33	20	23	5
Governments not able to introduce unpopular policies	34	39	14	6	7
Party lists will mean higher-quality MPs	14	29	24	22	12
Will adopt sound, stable, centrist economic policies	14	44	18	13	11
More consensus in government decision-making	40	40	9	5	5

Source: NBR-Consultus poll, 19 November 1993

Here, however, it is salutary to bear in mind what can be achieved through electoral systems and what their limitations are, for it is all too easy to attribute undue influence to the system itself. A good example of this is the majoritarian system which, in New Zealand, worked in an entirely different fashion in the second half of the nineteenth century, before the advent of cohesive political parties, than in the second half of the twentieth century.

There is undoubtedly a widespread tendency to associate multi-party systems with proportional representation, and two-party systems with simple plurality electoral systems. While there is plenty of empirical and anecdotal evidence to support such conclusions, it is now generally accepted that the relationship between electoral and party systems is that electoral systems facilitate rather than determine particular outcomes and that, in the words of Duverger over forty years ago: "...on the whole PR maintains almost intact the structure of parties existing at the time of its appearance" (Duverger, 1954:252). The adoption of a proportional representation system, therefore, does not automatically mean a multi-party outcome even though that is a likely result. Austria and Germany, for example, both with proportional systems, tend to have what are predominantly two and a half party-type outcomes.

But it is also true that there may be serious problems in making assumptions about the transferability of systems. Political parties, in particular, may be profoundly influenced by pre-existing social and political cleavages such as class, religion, urbanisation, language, religion, or ideology. Thus divided societies are more likely to choose PR systems because such systems facilitate the possibility of multi-party outcomes. The system adopted does not, in itself, *cause* a multi-party outcome. In this sense, the fact that New Zealand chose to adopt a PR system may well be seen in part as a reflection of the fact that no longer does it regard itself as such a homogeneous society as it once did.

Even so, the particular form of PR chosen to adopt is far removed from the type of 'pure' list PR systems found in Israel or the Netherlands. With its inclusion of a substantial number of single-member electorates, MMP represents a system which is as close as it is possible to remain to simple plurality while adopting a fully proportional system. Moreover, with the inhibiting effect of the 5 per cent threshold, what might be regarded as the excessive number of political parties associated with 'purer' forms of PR are severely curtailed from the outset.

One of the main fears expressed about PR was that it was likely to lead to undue fractionalisation of political parties. Already, while still using FPP but in the penumbra of change, the number of political parties represented in the House of Representatives increased to a total of seven, although it would be tempting to label at least some of these as independents rather than developed political parties. MMP ensures that third, or minor, parties receive seats in proportion to the votes that they win, assuming that they can qualify with 500 members and clear the 5 per cent threshold or win an electorate seat. At the 1993 general election the Alliance and New Zealand First parties instead of each holding 2 per cent of the seats, under MMP would have been entitled to approximately 18 per cent and 8 per cent of the seats, respectively, in a 120 seat parliament, with the result that no party would have held a majority in the

House. Before the 1996 general election, however, there was no certainty that voters, when faced with casting the two votes available in the new electoral system, would behave in the same way that they had in the past. Indeed, at the 1996 election a very high 37 per cent of voters decided to split their vote.

Some Consequences

In considering whether there is likely to be a permanent proliferation of third and minor parties represented in the House of Representatives, we need to distinguish the novel situation immediately following the 1996 general election, a transitional stage, from likely outcomes in future elections.

The manner in which the initial transition was handled by the main players is likely to have an important influence on the subsequent climate for negotiation. Parties insisting upon inflexible terms, or positioning themselves in virtually non-coalitionable situations before the election, not only affected short-term, but also longer term expectations and attitudes. A key factor in the transitional stage is the extent to which pre-existing attitudes seem destined to persist. Clearly, third and minor parties need to proceed cautiously, charting a course between domination by a major party partner or, if too intransigent, bringing the new system into public disrepute to their own subsequent detriment. Dodd claims that it is not the number of parties that matters so much as the degree of difference between them. The critical factor for cabinet durability, "is not the existence of majority party or multi-party parliaments; rather it is the existence of low to moderate fractionalisation rather than high fractionalisation" (Dodd, 1976:239).

Some PR systems with a very low, or no threshold, can result in as many as fourteen or fifteen political parties. Theoretically, it is possible for New Zealand to have as many as 20 political parties meeting the 5 per cent threshold represented in parliament (Nagel, 1994b:144).[1] In practice, any great multiplicity of parties was always unlikely in a nation with a limited number of significant social cleavages and with such a strongly established two party tradition.

Under FPP, the average vote won by a majority party over the last 10 general elections had been 41.7 per cent of the total valid votes cast, the highest proportion being 48.4 per cent for Labour in 1972. Comparing this with the first MMP general election in 1996, Labour's party vote reached a record major party low of 30.5 per cent. National, the largest single party, won 36.6 per cent. This compares with the all-German MMP-type elections for the Bundestag in 1994 where the key coalition partner, the Christian Democrat/Christian Social

Union had a combined vote of 41.5 per cent supplemented by its coalition partner, the Free Democrat Party, with 6.9 per cent and the main opposition party, the Social Democrats won 36.4 per cent.

If Germany is taken as a guide it is noteworthy that although government change is often a result of coalitional rather than electoral change, the overall political system has proved remarkably stable. As Norpoth (1981:31–32) has concluded:

> Both the exercise of power by the major party in office and occasionally the temptation to abuse that power have been curbed by the presence of the minor party in government. As a built-in opposition within the government, it was able to act more effectively than was true for the major party in opposition... On balance, the negative points of coalition performance, i.e. the constant jealousies among the coalition partners, the disproportional weight of the minor partner, and the corresponding frustrations endured by the major partner subtract little from the overall positive score... Thus coalition government in the Federal Republic is just one small step away from pure majority rule and hardly any less commendable than the latter.

The existence of six political parties in parliament opens the possibility of a choice between minority or coalition governments. (A minority coalition government is also possible but is treated here merely as a minority government). The possibility of a minority government which may be brought down at any time and is associated with less stable conditions traditionally raised fears among New Zealanders long accustomed to the certainty of outcome provided by the FPP system. In an ironic twist of fate, however, the last election held under the old FPP system turned out to be so close that, coupled with defections from the government party preceding the introduction of MMP, voters were treated to a remarkable range of types of government, all within a single parliamentary term. This provided a graphic illustration of how minority government could work. Although considerable uncertainty and suspicion remained about the stability and representative nature of coalitions under MMP, with particular concerns about the nature of deals likely to be cut in the now 'smoke-free' rooms, New Zealand was fortunate to approach MMP with a remarkable series of experiences provided by the last days of FPP. Even so, suspicion persisted. Minority government is not a popular form. As Butler has pointed out: "If the price is not too high, governing parties would always prefer to have the assurance of the sustained tenure of office that a solidly-based coalition will give them but the price may be too high" (Butler, 1983:96).

Another **feature of the 1993-96 period was a concern about whether or not,** a viable coalition partner would be available for a National government under MMP. Although National enjoyed a healthy, but not absolute lead in the opinion polls throughout the 1993-96 parliamentary term, there was no obvious future coalition partner. While aspirants such as the United Party appeared, new political parties formed during this 'phoney war' period experienced — as evidenced in the public opinion polls — considerable difficulty in obtaining political traction. The principle enunciated by political scientists, Hauss and Rayside (1978:54), that "institutional facilitators including the much ballyhooed electoral law have little effect on the development of new **parties", was endorsed**. This, however, was restricted to the *formation* of new parties, for the authors also note that "there is evidence that parties which did poorly under plurality systems would do better under proportional representation" (ibid., 43).

The problem, however, was not simply that coalition partners were unavailable, but a certain lack of 'fit'. As Dahl and Tufte (1974:93) hypothesise:

> In the smaller system, any conflict among organised groups is likely to entail personal conflicts among the individuals in the groups... Hence a group conflict, particularly if it endures for long, is likely to reinforce — and be reinforced by — personal antagonisms.

The two most important third parties whose existence preceded the decision to adopt MMP, the Alliance and New Zealand First, were both led by men who had broken away from the two major parties and strong *personal* antipathies developed. Moreover, any gains made by the Alliance were likely to be at Labour's expense, while New Zealand First also damaged National electorally. Thus, if there was a slowly emerging acceptance of the possibilities of government inherent in coalitions, there was little appreciation of the range of choices covered by that term or of the fact that some types were likely to be more stable than others. New Zealanders instinctively tended to look forward to a situation not too far removed from that to which they had been accustomed. They tended to assume a form of Moderate Polarised Pluralism and that electoral outcomes would result in some form of 'minimum-winning connected' coalitions (Axelrod, 1970) of closely aligned parties.

Theoretically, although Browne and Dreijmanis (1982:353) found insufficient evidence to discern any general correlation of coalition characteristics with cabinet durability, there is some evidence to suggest that minimum-winning connected coalitions do tend to be the most stable (Dodd, 1976:161; Browne & Dreijmanis, 1982:29). Dodd (ibid., 239), however, believes that:

(A)n important substantive change occurs when a nation moves from a parliament possessing a majority party to a parliament lacking one. In a highly polarised and/or unstable party system, this transition can virtually guarantee minority government... On the other hand, the minimum winning party coalitions of moderate multipartism may allow a more flexible response to short-term electoral fluctuation than majority partism.

Given the strength of New Zealand's two-party system in the past, together with the particular form of PR adopted, it could be presumed that while it was unlikely that any single party would win a clear majority, two major parties would win approximately two-thirds of the vote and seats. In practice, in 1996 they won 67 per cent of the party vote and 67.5 per cent of the seats.

The pre-election situation was complicated by the fact that, at this time, the Labour Party appeared to be a party in decline. MMP meant that it was vulnerable to a challenge for second party status, from either the Alliance or New Zealand First. That struggle for second party status divided the support of the centre left and opened the way for a centrist party, an opportunity which both United and New Zealand First sought to exploit. With New Zealand First also threatening the status of Labour as a possible second major party, the possibilities of instability appeared to increase. Despite winning only 28.2 per cent of the party vote Labour easily surmounted the third party challenge. At 25 per cent, the combined support for the two third parties only modestly exceeded what had been achieved on occasions under FPP despite the luxury of a second vote with MMP. Only one new party (Act, formerly the Association of Consumers and Taxpayers) qualified by crossing the 5 per cent threshold.

If, as seems likely, New Zealand continues to maintain a relatively low degree of party fractionalisation, and the party leaders acquire the art of successfully maintaining their separate party identities while collaborating as a coalition government, the outcome could well be semi-permanent coalitions of the type found in Germany. If this does occur the system could prove to be as stable as FPP. Even if that does not occur and minority governments prevail, that does not in itself lead to instability. As Butler (1983:69) has pointed out: "They have been tried in almost every country and have often lasted a considerable time. Sometimes (but by no means always) there is an explicit deal by which other parties agree not to bring them down."

There are a variety of techniques that could be introduced if necessary, such as the constructive vote of no-confidence, or fixed term parliaments, both of which are likely to enhance government stability. Minority governments have been common in Scandinavia and in a number of other countries. While they do lead to increased political uncertainty they are not necessarily unstable.

On the other hand, it must be considered doubtful whether a majority of New Zealanders would wish to pass from what has been undue certainty in the past, to the higher degree of uncertainty associated with minority regimes, at least for any protracted period of time. Hence, while minority government is always possible, for most New Zealanders concerned about governmental stability it is the least desirable option. Third and minor parties may believe that it maximises their influence but there are always constraints. In particular there is always the danger that the creation, or undue exploitation, of political uncertainty for partisan advantage may backfire on its proponents and prove to be a dangerous political tactic.

The difficulties implicit in a transitional situation are not limited to those directly resulting from the electoral system, particularly in the short-run in New Zealand where, with the combination in 1996 of a House enlarged from 99 to 120 members and a large increase in new members representing third and minor parties, many of the accepted conventional practices were readily called into question. This can be politically healthy as well as risky. There may well be advantages in questioning why various, albeit time-honoured, practices are followed, and whether they are still applicable in modern circumstances. In such circumstances, good, sound advice from parliamentary and public servants is at a premium. It is important that they should be knowledgeable, both about procedures associated with PR systems as well as the type of problems that may cause them to be called upon for advice. In this sense the period from 1993 to 1996 was put to good use with both politicians and public servants acquainting themselves with European practices and engaging in a continuous round of meetings and seminars which did much to help promote a smooth transition.

Change inevitably begets change. Change to the new PR electoral system inevitably involved some critical scrutiny of the adequacy of the existing role of the Governor-General and the nature of the conventions taken for granted in the past. In turn, these developments fed into a growing debate about the monarchy. Clearly, in a situation where minority or coalition governments are likely to become the normal political arrangements, it was necessary to decide whether or not, or to what extent, the Head of State would be required to participate in the selection of governments, or what alternative arrangements were desirable. Such questions have been left for the House of Representatives to resolve. If agreement cannot be reached there, the Governor-General is a backstop with largely unspecified powers — the so-called 'Reserve Powers'. Thus, although there has been some clarification of the Governor-General's role by the present incumbent, there has been virtually no change, with lack of specificity seen as an advantage, to be equated with flexibility.

The hitherto largely unquestioned ascendancy of the cabinet has also been largely maintained during the first year of MMP. Certainly, the increase in the size of the House of Representatives has made it more difficult to maintain the previous high levels of party cohesion but, once again, it is the type of coalition structure which is the ultimate determinant. If minimum-winning connected majorities can be maintained, as in Germany, or with the Liberal and National parties in Australia, any reduction in the ascendancy of the two parties constituting the coalition will be considerably less than that taking place in the case of a minority government. With minority governments the importance of the House of Representatives is likely to be substantially enhanced.

In either case, governments are more open to the defeat, or substantial amendment of particular bills introduced to the House. It is arguable that this is a long overdue improvement, for government legislation is not always well-considered. There has been a steadily developing tendency in recent years for select committees to exercise increased influence over legislation, but governments can all too easily consider that changes to their legislation involve loss of face, and they have succeeded in maintaining overall control. When judged in terms of certainty of policy outcomes there may be some advantages in government control, but this can prove to be counter-productive if it becomes entangled in the games of political one-upmanship which became such a feature of two-party politics in New Zealand under FPP. The persistence of these practices was seen from the outset of MMP, with the new coalition cabinet dominating the selection of chairpersons of select committees and generally maintaining government majorities on them.

Given advances such as the development of communications, greater education, and changes of life styles, political parties today tend to be 'sold' as 'products' by professional marketing organisations. As a result, during the latter part of this century, the major political parties have steadily moved away from the mass party democracy model and back toward a more cadre type organisation. Falls in the membership of political parties have been a world-wide phenomenon and hopes of any permanent reversal of this trend may well represent a triumph of hope over expectation.

The major New Zealand political parties, like their European counterparts, have also suffered important declines in membership spread over a considerable period. This means that they have become less and less representative as membership organisations and, at the same time, more and more professional as election-winning organisations. This raises important questions about their roles, particularly in relation to the candidate selection processes under the party list system. In Germany, we are assured, little distinction is drawn between local and list MPs but Germany is a federal system where 'local' MPs in the regional *Lander* (states, provinces) are much more the focus of popular attention than those in the federal parliament. In New Zealand, the likely future role of party list MPs is still far from clear.

It remains to be seen in practice just how well these broad rules succeed in ensuring that New Zealand political parties manage to avoid the oligarchic label. Even with democratic forms of candidate selection for party lists, there must be concern about the representative claims of New Zealand political parties when their memberships are less than that of some pressure groups. At the electorate level in particular, it is not easy to see how electorates, substantially increased in size, are likely to stimulate increased local participation. Whether the participatory possibilities inherent in this process are likely to lead to increased membership of political party organisations must, therefore, be a matter of some doubt.

On the other hand, as we have seen, proportional systems may eventually encourage a move away from the government/opposition mentality and help to facilitate more effective representation of third and minor parties than is usually found with FPP systems. With a consequential move away from 'catch-all' type parties (Kirchheimer, 1966:177–200) to what might be dubbed 'niche-market' types, it is often assumed that this will lead to more clearly defined parties of principle which, in turn, will help boost party membership figures. Once again, however, it is yet to be proven that a return to an emphasis upon principles by political parties (assuming that this is a practical electoral possibility) or, indeed, a greater role for memberships in such matters as candidate selection, will succeed in reversing the decline of mass membership type parties. Party membership decline is certainly not restricted to FPP systems alone. The long-term impact of MMP in this context is, therefore, difficult to anticipate.

But perhaps one of the most important consequential changes likely to result from MMP concerns race relations. Once again, the form of MMP adopted by New Zealand is a recognition, rather than a cause, of change. Clearly, a system of Maori representation which improves upon the inadequate representation which existed under the FPP electoral system has to be welcomed by both main races, but it was implicitly conceded, even by the Royal Commission, that MMP alone was not an adequate replacement for FPP and the four Maori seats. Although the Commission believed that MMP involving a party list would improve the political representation of Maori by establishing a common electoral roll, it also believed it necessary to have a special provision that the 5 per cent threshold required for list representation should be waived for "parties representing primarily Maori interests" (RCES, 1986a:44).

In its report the Royal Commission recommended that there be "no separate Maori constituency or list seats, no Maori roll, and no Maori option". Instead, it recommended that the Representation Commission be required to take "community of interest among the members of the Maori tribes" into account in determining constituency boundaries (RCES, 1986a:101). But, following strong Maori pressure to retain and allow for an increase in the number of separate Maori seats, the Royal Commission's recommendation that separate Maori representation be abolished was rejected. It seems unlikely that, given their previous experience from the Treaty of Waitangi onwards, Maori would ever have contemplated giving up their existing representation without much firmer guarantees of enhanced representation under the new system. The retention of separate constituency seats, together with the Maori Option and provision for the number of seats to increase as numbers on the Maori roll justify this, does raise important questions. The 1994 Maori Option campaign, particularly the attempts to persuade Maori, not only to enrol but also, reportedly, to leave the General in favour of the Maori Roll, might be seen as serving to heighten differences between the races. Yet, MMP, in the form proposed by the Royal Commission, was intended to lead to a more integrated society.

Despite the 1961 Hunn Report, important differences continue both between, and among, Pakeha and Maori, over whether the common object is integration, segregation, or symbiosis (*AJHR*, 1961:15). The shift of terminology to such terms as sovereignty, autonomy, self-government, *kawanatanga* (governance) and *te tino rangatiratanga* (unqualified exercise of leadership), resulting from a renewed emphasis on the Treaty of Waitangi, has served further to confuse the issue. Judged in terms of differences between the races, the 1993 referendum might be seen as representing a test of whether New Zealand was attempting to purchase biculturalism 'on the cheap' by attempting to maintain a fundamentally homogeneous society with more generous provision for minority concerns, or accepting the consequences of becoming a genuine bi- or multi-cultural society.

It is by no means clear that either race saw the choice in those terms or even that there is any certainty about the best answer. Without doubt, adequate provision has to be made for the representation of a permanent minority, such as the tangata whenua, whether formally or informally, at all levels. Certainly, in order to produce justice for Maori it is necessary to convince Pakeha that there is a problem, whether in matters of unemployment, cultural sensitivity, or political representation. Whether subsequent generations of both races will come to see persuading Maori to leave the General roll for the retained separatist Maori roll as a step towards promoting, or hindering, the future harmonious development of race relations in New Zealand is a matter for speculation. This, however, is a change not directly attributable to the introduction of MMP. It is a change which might have occurred whether or not there had been a change of electoral system. MMP with its party list system does at least ensure that both Maori and Pakeha will be on a common roll for the crucial party vote. Moreover, this will require political parties to pay greater attention to all parts of the country, whether Maori or Pakeha safe or marginal seats, if they are to maximise their chances of participating in government.

Although the change of electoral system is the focus of attention, and in many ways has provided the catalyst for change, other associated changes have also been of considerable importance. The impact of the increase in the size of the unicameral House of Representatives is one example. Although, logically, it can be associated with the introduction of MMP, it is likely to have important consequences in its own right, particularly upon party cohesion. The sudden increase in the size of the House of Representatives from 99 to 120 seats at one election would have had important repercussions regardless of the change of electoral system, but it is particularly significant when seen in relation to the introduction of MMP and the transition process. Not only did the introduction of MMP contribute to the retirement of no fewer than ten MPs (including six sitting ministers, one former Prime Minister and one former minister), but also brought about an increase in third party representation via the party list. The result is the most inexperienced House to be elected for decades. This, in turn, contributed to a strong public backlash, both to the increased number of seemingly well-paid MPs — many of whom were plainly lacking in experience — and the electoral system with which the increase was associated in the public mind.

Another product of the same sentiments that produced MMP rather than a direct consequence of its introduction, the *Citizens Initiated Referenda Act 1993*, is of considerable potential importance. New Zealand has been the third most frequent user of national referendums after Switzerland and Australia, although Switzerland's use of the system outnumbers virtually all other democracies combined (Lijphart, 1984:202). Since the failure of prohibition by referendum in 1919 the system has not been highly regarded as a means of governance. The majority of the New Zealand referendums have been liquor licensing polls, a system now abandoned. It has also been used mainly for 'conscience issues', that is matters upon which politicians themselves are reluctant to take decisions, such as state betting facilities for horse-racing, public house opening hours, or peace-time conscription. In addition, there have been occasional uses as a means of deciding whether there should be a three or four year term of parliament.

Although initially taken to by some groups with enthusiasm, it is not at all clear how the system of citizens' initiated referendums is likely to work out. The first referendum, posing the question, "Should the number of professional firefighters employed full-time in New Zealand in the New Zealand Fire Service be reduced below the number employed on 1 January 1995?" attracted an 87.8 per cent vote opposing the cuts in a turn-out of 26.9 per cent of voters (*AJHR*, 1997a:349). How useful such a $10 million exercise was in helping to resolve what was an essentially industrial relations problem is a moot point. However, despite petitions proposing such matters as full state-financing for health and education, halving the military budget by the following decade, or refusal of separate funding for Maoridom, few managed to negotiate the substantial hurdles. Moreover, governments are protected by the fact that such referendums are only indicative. If they were binding, as was proposed at the time, the role that governments have enjoyed in the past would have come under threat from a very blunt instrument indeed.

Reform by Misadventure?

The first hurdle for any would-be reformer is to manage to get the topic for reform onto the political agenda. This is a far from easy task and there is no certain way of achieving it. There are few really new ideas in politics, and frequently the reform in question will have been vaguely in the public consciousness for years, or sometimes decades, without being seriously considered. What then causes it to move, if not to the forefront, at least into the general currency of public debate?

The most likely causes are changed circumstances making reform more appropriate than previously. Such circumstances may include, for example, an economic or political crisis. Alternatively, reform may be driven by a leader or other highly placed influential political figure, or powerful group interests single-mindedly promoting the issue. Change may arise as a by-product of other changes, economic, social or political; or it may be a combination of two or more of these. As we saw in chapter 1, Longley (1989:3) identified six specific factors as important in examining the processes by which institutional or constitutional change come about. These factors were: events, individuals, organisations, the media, issues, and perceptions of self-interest.

Events

Events encompasses the question of how and why the issue of change surfaces onto the political agenda. As Longley points out, if ideas for change are seldom new, what gives them currency at any particular time? In particular, institutional and constitutional change of any magnitude is a relatively rare and frequently difficult occurrence, so agenda setting is particularly important. Possible causes advanced by Longley are electoral deadlocks, such as 'hung' parliaments; elections which highlight discriminatory effects on third parties; the emergence or disintegration of a new (or older) party; revolutionary situations; or influence by the example of other countries.

As we have seen the concept of PR was not new in New Zealand, dating back at least to the beginning of the twentieth century. It was not, however, taken seriously until near the end of the century. One reason for this is that it was originally espoused largely by third parties which felt disadvantaged in what emerged as a two party system. But few saw any good reason for change. In Europe at that time, some more conservatively inclined major parties had favoured PR as a means of moderating the potential threat of socialist governments. New Zealand, however, had been a British settler colony inheriting British institutions which were widely admired at that period of its history. Thus there was little reason to change a system that worked and was familiar.

Logically, it might be thought that PR could, and should, have been introduced when New Zealand departed from the British model and abolished its upper house of parliament in 1950. Such a move would have helped to maintain a wider spread of representation. But the Legislative Council had become such an inconsequential and powerless body that abolition could be presented as merely a recognition of what was virtually the status quo. New Zealand was strictly a practical democracy with little concern about what *should* or *might* be? PR, in particular, was viewed as an alien, continental form of representation which few bothered to understand and which had little application.

Even with the introduction of a new *Electoral Act* in 1956, the form of electoral system was hardly questioned. And although a third party, the Social Credit Political League, campaigned for PR in the 1970s, it was not until the two successive general elections in 1978 and 1981, in which a governing party won a majority of seats with fewer votes than its main opponent, that the system began to be seriously questioned. It was not, therefore, until the level of public satisfaction with FPP began to drop that attention began to turn to possible alternative methods of election. Thus *events* initially encompassed the general election results of 1978 and 1981 followed by growing disillusionment with the two major political parties, Labour and National. As governments, both parties had uncharacteristically pursued unpopular policies which they believed necessary for the economic health of the nation even at the cost of breaking electoral promises. Accordingly there was a decline in support for the two party system and the electoral system upon which it was based.

It was the Royal Commission which was instrumental in having proportional representation recognised as a viable alternative to the existing system. Such was the degree of disillusionment with government and politicians that the issue of reform was turned on its head. If public knowledge of MMP was limited, the fact that the Royal Commission had carefully considered the matter and come to a clear conclusion obviously carried considerable weight. And if doubts remained, the fact that politicians were fiercely opposed to the findings of the body that they had themselves created merely served to reinforce public scepticism. Thus, instead of having to justify an alien 'continental' type electoral system, the roles were reversed. It was essentially FPP that was evaluated by the public and found wanting, not PR.

Individuals

Longley argues that:

> A key governmental or political leader may ... through his power of personality and leadership prove to be a major catalyst for the proposal moving onto the political center stage ... the politics and processes of change initiation are deeply shaped by the actions and stands of key individuals. (Longley, 1989.)

He also stresses, however, that individuals may just as easily be responsible for thwarting reform proposals as for promoting them. In the case of MMP the role played by one man, Geoffrey Palmer, in establishing the issue on the political agenda, is pre-eminent. Using an amateur/professional typology, Gomibuchi has demonstrated that Palmer displayed "strong amateur dispositions", that he possessed a clearly identifiable set of principles in relation to the constitution and parliament which he retained throughout his eleven-year parliamentary career; and that his political involvement was motivated by a desire to see his ideals materialised (Gomibuchi, 1995:118).

These principles relate to Palmer's role as a Professor of Law, both prior to, and after, his parliamentary career. In this sense, he raised the issue of electoral reform in relation to his concerns about executive dominance even before the aberrant general elections of 1978 and 1981. From the point of view of the success of MMP, the right man was in the right place at the right time. A respect for his knowledge, status, and dedication rather than any enthusiasm amongst his colleagues helped to ensure success in surmounting the successive party hurdles required to place the issue in the party's election manifesto, thereby ensuring its place on the political agenda at the general election. Even so, this was not an advocacy of PR, merely a pledge to investigate this question, amongst others.

By the time that Labour became the government in 1984, Palmer had become Deputy-Leader of the party and was in a position, not only to expedite his reform proposals, but also to determine the all-important nature of the Royal Commission which was to consider it. As with other bodies, the process of appointment to Royal Commissions is as important for who is excluded, as for who is appointed. In particular, the fact that Palmer managed to resist attempts to include MPs or ex-MPs was crucial. Once the composition of the Royal Commission was settled, he does not appear to have made any attempt to influence it, confident in a carefully considered, rational outcome.

That Palmer was sufficiently confident to leave the Royal Commission to its own devices is due to the fact that it was largely hand-picked, and particularly to the choice of chairman, Justice Wallace. Without Wallace's careful, reasoned, open-minded approach it is doubtful whether the Commission would have had the courage to reach such a radical conclusion. This is not a case of a zealot dragging others in his wake, rather it is much more a matter of process, weighing and balancing without fear or favour, acutely cross-questioning those making submissions but, above all, following the logic of the evidence. If Wallace came to favour MMP strongly it was because his team did. Once convinced, he became a strong proponent of the system and had little hesitation in advocating the case for change long after his formal duties as chairman had ceased. The choice of chairman of this particular Commission was crucial. Wallace was essential to Palmer's design, not because he was going to produce 'the' answer that Palmer might want but because he could be relied upon to ask the right questions.

Despite what Palmer obviously regarded as a highly favourable outcome, given the adverse response of the cabinet to the Commission's key recommendation there appeared to be little chance that MMP would be implemented. In one of the great ironies of New Zealand's electoral history, the man who helped to save that situation, Prime Minister David Lange, was one of those most strenuously opposed to the recommendation. What caused Lange's mistaken statement of Labour Party policy in the 1987 general election television Leaders' Debate is less important than the fact that it occurred. Until then, politically, it seemed probable that the introduction of MMP was likely to be a long-term option at best. Lange's public promise of a binding referendum on the issue, however, placed it high on the political agenda — and this was reinforced by his deputy's prompt public confirmation of his leader's statement.

Lange's mistake was a high (or low!) point of individual influence in the policy process. But it also appears to have had another consequence. It was, after all, the National Party which eventually promised, and implemented, a binding referendum on the electoral system. In the same Leaders' Debate, opposition leader Jim Bolger was promising an indicative referendum, Lange had poured scorn on the proposal. No doubt stung by this, National upgraded its proposal to a binding referendum in 1990 while Labour became more cautious, advocating the indicative form.

At a lower level, MPs Richard Northey as chair of the Electoral Law Select Committee, and John Terris with his Private Member's Bill, also played important secondary roles. The extent to which the role of the individual was limited in seeing the issue through to a conclusion, however, is clearly shown when, following the rejection of a referendum on the issue by cabinet and caucus, Palmer declared the issue to be "effectively dead for the immediate future", adding that it might be revisited in another 20 years (*Press,* 17 April 1989).

Up to that point, the role of individuals in promoting MMP appears to exemplify the principle that "It is easier to get a constitutional [change]...on the political agenda than it is to win. The predominant pattern is of frustrated demands" (Banting & Simeon, 1985:5).

Organisations

Longley makes the point that organisations are inherently interwoven with individuals' actions. This is certainly the case with the two principal pressure groups involved with the adoption of MMP. Unusually, the process of reform preceded the formation of the groups. In both cases, the pro-MMP Electoral Reform Coalition, and the anti-MMP Campaign for Better Government, the groups formed around founder-leaders. Philip Saxby, founder of the Electoral Reform Coalition (ERC), made a submission to the Royal Commission favouring MMP before forming the ERC. Similarly, Peter Shirtcliffe, Chairman of Telecom, was the driving force in the Campaign for Better Government (CBG).

The ERC played a crucial role in rallying the various supporters of PR behind the banner of MMP. It played an important role in disseminating information through its newsletters, lobbying MPs, encouraging letters to newspapers, and holding meetings. The overall effect was to help ensure that the issue continued to be placed in front of the public and, equally, important, that the focus remained upon *proportional* representation. By contrast, the CBG developed at a very late stage when it appeared as if the issue was going to be lost by default. By then it looked, and was, an expensive, desperate, last-ditch attempt to turn public opinion around with the use of scare-tactics. Not only did these tactics in themselves create considerable scepticism, but the CBG was also associated in the public's mind with big business — those who had been the principal beneficiaries of the Rogernomics (economic) revolution of the 1980s.

Thus there were none of the umbrella-type organisations with the diverse and prestigious organisational membership of the type cited by Longley, although there is no question that the CBG was generously financed. Overall, however, the impetus for reform came, not from pressure groups, but from the report of the Royal Commission. The major contribution of the ERC was to keep the issue before the public as the politicians prevaricated and while the CBG provided a late spoiling campaign.

Media

Longley argues that the impact of the media occurs in two ways: by media attention to a political or constitutional problem or proposed change, and by media coverage of various key arguments and issues surrounding such proposals. He makes the point that advocates of change are often dependent upon the media as means of gaining credibility as well as the use of newspaper advertisements containing prominent names supporting the cause. In addition, there are always unforeseen circumstances: on the day after the Royal Commission's report was made public, it was overshadowed by dramatic political news of what was to become known as the Maori Loans Affair.

On the whole, the media played a low-key, responsible role. Of the major metropolitan newspaper editorials, Wellington's *Dominion* and Dunedin's *Otago Daily Times* supported the status quo. The *New Zealand Herald* (Auckland) eventually supported change, and the *Press* (Christchurch) proved to be even-handed. All the newspapers carried informative articles on the issues. The weekly *Listener* was the journal which campaigned most actively for change. One unusual feature, however, was to find the Royal Commission's chairman subsequently writing articles and playing an active role, both at a variety of meetings and in the media more generally, in support of his Commission's findings.

Radio and television devoted time to the issues, and were generally unbiased in their coverage. Overall, the media played an important role in informing, rather than promoting, or obstructing, change.

Issues

This is perhaps the least satisfactory of Longley's criteria. He admits that issues are shaped by events, articulated by individuals, pressed by organisations, and communicated by the media. Perhaps better described as *assumptions* or *beliefs* these may be expressed, for example, as the notion that FPP is a particularly *British* arrangement in striking contrast with various proportional electoral arrangements used in continental political systems. Longley believes that such arguments, even when unarticulated, can have a subtle conditioning impact on the interpretation placed on reports of the experiences of other political systems. Without doubt, this would have been an issue if the question of change had been discussed in 1950, but the second half of the century had seen important changes taking place. Britain's entry into the European Community and New Zealand's growing emphasis upon its status as a small nation in the South Pacific meant that the significance of the British example, although still important, had declined considerably.

This issue was loudly articulated by visiting Australian political scientist, Malcolm Mackerras, brought to New Zealand by the CBG to campaign against MMP. Perhaps not surprisingly, the argument appeared to carry little weight. Not only had the Royal Commission's recommendation served to give MMP authoritative backing, but the fact — where known — that the British had had a hand in the design of the original German system; that a not dissimilar system had been recommended in Britain in 1976; and, above all, that it appeared to be a stable system, reduced the impact of that form of argument. It is a measure of how far New Zealand had travelled from the "off-shore British farm" mentality of the 1950s to the multi-cultural world trader stance of the 1990s that 'British' *versus* 'continental' aspects of the issue failed to become a matter of serious debate.

Much more serious as a practical issue was the general public mind-set in relation to proportional representation. Few understood what it was or how it worked but it was widely perceived as complicated, convoluted and an unsatisfactory form of government. PR was 'what happened in Italy' — it was associated above all with government instability. That this deeply held prejudice was overthrown was due to the extent of the disillusionment with the existing form of party government in New Zealand under MMP plus the careful work carried out by the Royal Commission which seemed to recommend a credible alternative system.

Perceptions of Self-Interest

The argument here is that: "Unless major parties, factions or interests become convinced that a suggested change will be beneficial to them, such proposals are unlikely to start to move through the processes of change initiation..." (Longley, 1989).

According to Longley, perceptions of self-interest, may be explicitly articulated. A New Zealand example was that separate Maori seats should be retained because they enhance Maori influence. More frequently, however, self-interest is disguised by other issues. Hence, as New Zealand politicians lost control of the reform issue to the electorate, major political party leaders, convinced that electoral reform would harm their parties, preferred to stress instead the need for strong single party government rather than sounding as if they were motivated only by self-interest. Similarly, third parties backed electoral reform, not on the grounds that it would advance their own interests but on the principle of fairness in the electoral system.

The debate in New Zealand was certainly carried on in this way with a clear delimitation of interest between the third parties backing reform, and the major parties backing the status quo. What was truly exceptional about the situation, however, was that one of the major parties could have set up a commission which served to help undermine its own interests. This was not a case of a commission 'bolting'; rather, it was a government which allowed itself to endorse a commission which, from the first, was capable of producing a recommendation with which the government was to profoundly disagree.

It was not a government which found itself misled; there was no one to blame but itself. Yet, perhaps most surprising of all, it was *not* the Labour government which introduced the legislation providing for the binding referendums which led to the adoption of MMP, but the more conservatively inclined National Party government. In this sense, *both* major parties had become entangled in the net. As far as the major political parties were concerned, by 1991 the processes of change had acquired all the inevitability of a Greek tragedy.

Yet, politicians rarely yield totally. Although the leaders of the major New Zealand political parties failed to prevent the adoption of PR they have never ceased trying to claw back control. Thus, the form of ballot paper (with party and candidate votes adjacent, making it easy to tick across for the same party) was adopted by the two major parties despite the opposition of third parties. Despite the expressed wishes of the Electoral Commission, the two major parties also insisted upon political representation on that Commission when it dealt with the allocation of election broadcasting funding allocations. And, in 1997, capitalising upon widespread public dissatisfaction (Figure 11.1), there were increasing demands by politicians for further changes, both to the size of the House of Representatives and to the electoral system, although no one was publicly advocating a return to FPP.

Thus, for both major parties the introduction of MMP was reform by misadventure. This is no copy-book model of how reform can be achieved.

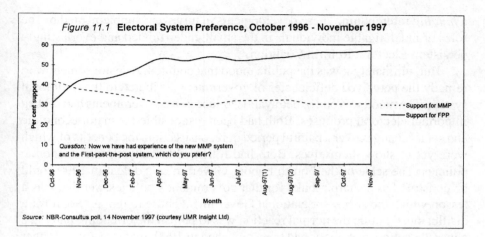

Figure 11.1 **Electoral System Preference, October 1996 - November 1997**

Question: Now we have had experience of the new MMP system and the First-past-the-post system, which do you prefer?

······ Support for MMP
—— Support for FPP

Source: NBR-Consultus poll, 14 November 1997 (courtesy UMR Insight Ltd)

Ultimately, even the voting population surprised itself. Nevertheless, there was always the feeling that, right or wrong, popular sovereignty had been re-asserted, not necessarily in the *form* of the new voting system (which suffered a rapid decline in popularity even before it had had a fair trial), but in the fact that a *majority* had demonstrated the ability to change the system *despite* the politicians.

So — Accident? Design? Or Evolution? The original outline for change was unquestionably the work of one innovating individual, Geoffrey Palmer. Viewed in the longer term development of New Zealand's constitutional system it is surprising that some such development did not occur earlier. If Palmer had not seized the initiative when he did, it is difficult to avoid the conclusion that almost certainly a 'Palmer clone' would have occurred at some point in the not too distant future. The stage was set for such a development.

It was Palmer who succeeded, virtually single-handedly, in placing the issue on the political agenda. It was to Palmer's choice of Justice Wallace as Chairman of the Royal Commission, and the membership of that team, that credit must go for converting vague preferences into a specific, radical alternative. Even so, matters of such weighty consequence can frequently take decades of discussion before they are implemented — if ever. It would have been surprising if the MPs of both major parties had *not* sought to strangle the proposal at birth. That they failed to do so must be attributed at least partly to accident. Lange's spectacular mistake at the 1987 general election served to keep the matter prominently before the public gaze. To that has to be added the extraordinary vicissitudes of competitive party politics which caused the opposition National Party to take up the issue and campaign on the promise of a *binding* referendum. These developments in turn were supplemented by the roles of indefatigable individuals in the small under-funded and everlastingly persistent Electoral Reform Coalition.

But, ultimately it was the public mood that counted. A desire somehow to remedy the perceived deficiencies of government attributed to the traditional system. The mood was one of betrayal. Two successive governments had broken important electoral promises. Both had been responsible for major economic and social changes over a painful period of reconstruction, the benefits of which were yet to show themselves. Both had followed broadly similar economic policies. The scale of the Fourth Labour Government's defeat in 1990 could be construed as a sharp rebuke for that government's policies, yet that was a lesson which the successor National Government chose to ignore. So, if for a disillusioned public the normal reaction was to punish the offending party at a general election, as Labour had been punished in 1990, that remedy no longer appeared adequate where both major parties were involved in quick succession. Some other solution seemed to be required.

That solution was at hand. It is one of the ironies of the situation that this public mood of betrayal had not existed when the Royal Commission originally produced its report, yet that report was available just when it was needed.[2] Moreover that report had contained an important 'sting in its tail' with its recommendation that the issue be resolved by a public referendum. As much as any other single factor, it was this report of the Royal Commission which helped to create the intellectual receptivity necessary for the adoption of a particular alternative electoral system and, by a trickle-down process, helped to *reassure* the public that proportional representation was indeed a viable alternative to a system from which so many had become disaffected. The report did not itself lead to change so much as serve to channel its direction when the time was ripe, and provide the all-important suggested mechanism — popular referendum — by which change might be achieved despite the politicians. Even so, the overall effect was *not* to convince the New Zealand public that MMP was necessarily the better system but rather that it was worth a try given the wholly unsatisfactory pass that FPP had reached some seven years after the report was written.

Notes

1   Indeed, Nagel argued that in abstract theoretical terms the figure could even be as high as 85 parties.
2   Albeit not always physically, for many copies had been dumped some years earlier when the Government Printing Office was privatised. As a result, the report had to be reprinted, and went out of print, all within the space of ten years. (On the initiative of the Electoral Commission, it was reprinted again in 1997.)

Appendix

The Development of the Electoral Act 1993

Appendix: The Development of the *Electoral Act 1993*

Item	Royal Commission (1986)	Electoral Bill (as introduced)	Bill (as reported back)	1993 Electoral Act	Amended Act (1995)
Voting paper	Single paper	Divided paper (above/below)	No change	No change	Single paper
	Party and Constituency sections side by side with party vote on left	Part A: Constituency vote Part B: Party vote			Party and Constituency parts side by side with party vote on left
	White circles (black background down centre of paper)	White circles (black background down right hand side of each paper)		No change	White circles (black background) down centre of paper
	Party logos included	No party logos		No change	Party logos included
	Party name and party constituency candidate side by side (random order?)	Candidate names and party names in alphabetical order on each part		No change	Candidate names in alphabetical order; Party names listed in same order as candidate names
	Top 5 party candidates listed in order	Top 3 party candidates listed in order	Party name only to be shown	No change	No change
Number of MPs *Constituency:*	120 60	No change No change	No change Fixed number for South Island; variable number for North Island and Maori	No change No change	No change No change
List:	60	No change	Variable number (depending on number of constituency seats)	No change	No change
Number of South Island Constituency seats	Minimum of 15 seats	No change	Fixed at 16	No change	No change
List MPs	Closed national lists No independents	No change	No change	No change	No change

Item	Royal Commission (1986)	Electoral Bill (as introduced)	Bill (as reported back)	1993 Electoral Act	Amended Act (1995)
	Constituency candidates can be included				
Number of Votes	2 — party and constituency	No change	No change	No change	No change
Threshold	4% of Party vote or 1 Constituency seat	No change	5% of Party vote or 1 Constituency seat	No change	No change
Maori Representation	No separate representation No Maori roll No periodic Maori option Maori parties exempt from threshold	No change	Separate representation for Maori Separate roll Maori option taken after each census Number of Maori constituencies based on proportion of Maori choosing Maori roll Threshold to **apply to** Maori parties	No change	No change
Method of seat allocation	Modified St Laguë formula — total party vote divided successively by 3, 4, 5, 7, 9, 11 ... etc	No change	Standard St Laguë formula — total party vote divided successively by 1, 3, 5, 7, 9, 11 ... etc	No change	No change
Registration of Parties	Parties should have opportunity to register Minimum of 200 financial members required for registration Cancellation **if number falls** below 200 or less than 3 candidates at last election	Chief Electoral Officer to register parties Cancellation if number falls below 200 or no MP	Electoral Commission to register parties Minimum of 500 current financial members Cancellation if number falls below 500 or no MP who is current financial member	No change	At least 500 current financial members who are eligible to register as electors

Item	Royal Commission (1986)	Electoral Bill (as introduced)	Bill (as reported back)	1993 Electoral Act	Amended Act (1995)
Voter Registration	Qualified electors should be able to register as electors until (and including) day before election	Rolls close day following issue of Writs: no registrations allowed between this date and day after date set for return of Writs	No change	No change	Registration permissible up until (and including) day before election
Electoral Commission	4 members — Secretary for Justice, Secretary for Maori Affairs, 2 persons appointed by Governor-General (1 to be a judge) Functions — administer electoral law (esp. enrolment and conduct of elections), review electoral system, educate public about electoral and parliamentary matters	Proposal omitted from Bill	4 members (Chief Judge of Maori Land Court instead of Secretary for Maori Affairs) Functions — registration of parties, public education, advise Minister of Justice and parliament, research electoral matters	No change	Functions extended to include allocation of party broadcasting money and time during election campaign (*Broadcasting Amendment Act, 1996*)
Representation Commission	Each parliamentary party should have representative (appointed by Governor-General on nomination of House of Representatives) but without vote National quota for electorates	Party membership restricted to representative of Government and Opposition only (to retain vote) No change	South Island quota the basis for calculating North Island General electorate and Maori quotas	No change	No change

Item	Royal Commission (1986)	Electoral Bill (as introduced)	Bill (as reported back)	1993 Electoral Act	Amended Act (1995)
	±10% tolerance	±10% tolerance but able to be widened where necessary to accommodate fixed number of South Island electorates	±5% tolerance		
Chatham Islands Representation	Not mentioned (1992 Electoral Commission questioned statutory restriction requiring Chatham Islands to be included in Lyttelton or Western Maori electorates)	Chatham Islands to remain included in Lyttelton or Western Maori electorates	Chatham Islands able be included in any appropriate General and Maori electorate at discretion of Commission	No change	No change
Citizens' Initiated Referenda	Opposed		Introduced and passed as separate law, 1993		

References

Alley, R.M. & Robinson, A.D.(1971), 'A Mechanism for Enlarging the House of Representatives', *Political Science*, 23:2, Wellington, School of Political Science and Public Administration, Victoria University of Wellington.

Andrew, P. (1996), Correspondence, 18 November 1996.

Appendices to the Journals of the House of Representatives [*AJHR*] (1858), F.1, 'Report of a Select Committee of the House of Representatives on the Amendment of the Electoral Law'.

— (1891), I.10, 'Report of the Constitutional Reform Committee'.

— (1961), G.10, 'Report on the Department of Maori Affairs'. (The Hunn Report.)

— (1975), I.15, 'Electoral Act Committee, 1975: Final Report'.

— (1977), I.1, 'Report of Petitions Committee'.

— (1980), I.17, 'Report of the Select Committee on Electoral Law'. First Report.

— (1981), I.17, 'Report of the Select Committee on Electoral Law'. Second Report.

— (1986a), H.3, 'Report of the Royal Commission on the Electoral System: Towards A Better Democracy'.

— (1988), I.17B, Electoral Law Committee, 'Inquiry into the Report of the Royal Commission on the Electoral System'.

— (1990a), I.17, Electoral Law Committee, 'Report on the activities of the Committee for the Forty-Second Parliament'.

— (1990b), I.20, 'Further Government Response to Report of Electoral Law Select Committee on Inquiry into the Report of the Royal Commission on the Electoral System'.

— (1991a), E.9, 'The General Election, 1990'.

— (1991b), I.17A, 'Report of the Electoral Law Committee on the Electoral Poll Bill'.

— (1992a), E.9A, 'Report of the Electoral Referendum Panel, 1992'.

— (1992b), H.1, 'Report of the Representation Commission, 1992'.

— (1993a), E.9, 'The Electoral Referendum, 1992'.

— (1993b), E.9A, 'Report of the Electoral Referendum Panel, 1993'.

— (1993c), I.17C, 'Report of the Electoral Law Committee on the Electoral Reform Bill'.

— (1994), E.9, 'The General Election and Electoral Referendum, 1993'.

— (1995a), H.1, 'The Report of the Representation Commission, 1995'.

— (1995b), I.21A, Electoral Law Committee, 'Inquiry into the 1993 General Election'.

— (1997a), E.9, 'The General Election, 1996'.

— (1997b), E.57, 'Report of the Electoral Commission for the Year ended, 30 June 1997'.

Axelrod, R. (1970), *Conflict of Interest: A Theory of Divergent Goals with Applications to Politics*, Chicago, Markham Publishing Co.

Banting, K.C. & Simeon, R. (1985), *The Politics of Constitutional Change in Industrial Nations*, London, Macmillan.

Bassett, M.E.R. (1996), Correspondence, 22 June 1996.

Beetham, B.C. (1993), Correspondence with P.R. Harris, 12 March 1993.

Bills Thrown Out (1858), Representation Apportionment Bill (National Archives, LC 1/1858/1).

— (1902), Elective Legislative Council Bill.

Bolger, J.B. (1987), 'Address to the Society of Accountants', Hamilton, 18 September 1987.

— (1988), 'An Upper House for New Zealand'. Text of a speech given to the Rotary Club of Auckland, 18 April 1988.

— (1992), 'Speech to National Party Wellington Division Conference', 7 June 1992.

Boston, J. (1987), 'Electoral Reform in New Zealand: The Report of the Royal Commission', *Electoral Studies*, 6:2.

Boston, J.& Holland, M., eds. (1987), *The Fourth Labour Government*, Auckland, Oxford University Press.

Boston, J., Levine, S., McLeay, E. & Roberts, N.S. (1996), *New Zealand Under MMP: A New Politics?*, Auckland, Auckland University Press/Bridget Williams Books.

—   (1997), *From Campaign to Coalition: New Zealand's First General Election Under Proportional Representation*, Palmerston North, Dunmore Press.

Bradford, M.R. (1997), Telephone interview, 19 November 1997.

Brook-Cowen, P., Cowen, T., & Tabarrok, A. (1992), *An Analysis of Proposals for Constitutional Change in New Zealand*, Wellington, Business Roundtable.

Brookfield, F.M. (1992), 'Referendums: Legal and Constitutional Aspects', in Simpson (1992).

Brown, B. (1962), *The Rise of New Zealand Labour*, Wellington, Price Milburn.

Browne, E.C. & Dreijmanis, J., eds. (1982), *Government Coalitions in Western Democracies*, New York, Longman.

Bryant, L. (1997), Correspondence, 25 September 1997.

Burdon, R.M. (1965), *The New Dominion*, Wellington, A.H. & A.W. Reed.

Butler, D.E. (1963), *The Electoral System in Britain Since 1918*, 2nd edition, Oxford, Clarendon Press.

—   (1983), *Governing Without a Majority*, London, Collins.

Butler, D.E. & Ranney, A., eds. (1978), *Referendums: A Comparative Study of Practice and Theory*, Washington, DC, American Enterprise Institute.

—   (1994), *Referendums around the World*, London, Macmillan.

Cabinet [CAB] (1990a), CAB(90)526, 'Proportional Representation — Indicative Referendum', 27 July 1990.

—   (1990b), CAB(90)M26/14, 'Proportional Representation — Indicative Referendum', 6 August 1990.

—   (1990c), CAB(90)M27/33, 'Proportional Representation — Indicative Referendum'.

—   (1992), Papers (CAB) (1992), CAB(92) 795.

—   (1993), CAB(93)M21/19, Annex I.

—   (1996), *Cabinet Office Manual*, August 1996.

Campaign for Better Government [CBG] (1993a), *Referendum Review* (4 issues).

—   (1993b), Press Releases.

Campaign for Proportional Representation [CPR] (1991), letter to Hon Douglas Graham, 12 July 1991.

Canadian Royal Commission [CRC] (1991), Canadian Royal Commission on Electoral Reform and Party Financing (1991), *Reforming Electoral Democracy*, Ottawa (4 volumes).

Canterbury Digest (1993), July 1993.

Catt, H. (1995) 'Representation and CIR'. Paper presented at New Zealand Political Science Association Conference, Wellington, 1995.

Caygill, D.F. (1996a), Interview, Christchurch, 22 July 1996.

—   (1996b), Correspondence, 29 November 1996.

—   (1997), Correspondence, 14 July 1997.

Chen, M. (1993), 'Remedying New Zealand's Constitution in Crisis: Is MMP part of the answer?', *New Zealand Law Journal*, January 1993.

Clark, C. (1993), Speech to the Democratic Party Annual Conference, 5 September 1993.

—   (1997), Correspondence, 30 September 1997.

Clark, H. (1996), Interview, Wellington, 17 June 1996.

Cleveland, L. & Robinson, A.D. (1972), *Readings in New Zealand Government*, Wellington, Reed Education.

Coalition Agreement (1996), Wellington.

Collinge, J. (1992), 'Keeping a Watch on Democracy by Use of Public Referendums', in Simpson, A., ed. (1992).

Court of Appeal [CA] (1995), *New Zealand Law Review*, 1 *NZLR* [1995], Taiaroa v Minister of Justice.

Cullen, M.J. (1996), Interview, Wellington, 19 June 1996.

Dahl, R.A. & Tufte, E.R. (1974), *Size and Democracy*, Stanford & Oxford, Stanford University Press/ Oxford University Press.

Dictionary of New Zealand Biography [*DNZB*] (1990–), ed., Claudia Orange, Wellington, Department of Internal Affairs (3 volumes to date).

Dodd, L.C. (1976), *Coalitions in Parliamentary Government*, Princeton, Princeton University Press.

The Dominion (Wellington).

Dominion Sunday Times (Wellington).

Donald, R. (1996), Interview, Christchurch, 12 July 1996.
— (1997), Correspondence, 21 October 1997.
Dunne, P.F. (1997), Interview, Wellington, 29 September 1997.
Duverger, M. (1954, 1964), *Political Parties: Their Organisation and Activity in the Modern State*, 1st and 3rd edns., London, Methuen.

Eagleson, W. (1997a), Correspondence, 3 April 1997.
— (1997b), Telephone interview, 7 April 1997.
Easton, B. (1994), 'Royal Commissions as Policy Creators: The New Zealand Experience', in Weller, ed. (1994).
Education, Ministry of (1997), *Adult Literacy in New Zealand: Results from the International Adult Literacy Survey*, Wellington.
Electoral Act, 1956.
Electoral Act, 1993.
Electoral Commission [EC] (1996), Media Release, 11 June 1996.
— (1997), 'Report to the Electoral Law Select Committee on the Electoral Commission's exercise of its statutory functions in relation to the 1996 general election'.
Electoral Law Select Committee [ELSC] (1988a), EL88/488, Submission to Electoral Law Select Committee by Electoral Reform Coalition.
— (1988b), EL88/628, Notes of Committee Consideration, 20 September 1988.
— (1988c), EL88/629, Notes of Committee Consideration, 13 September 1988.
— (1988d), EL88/630, 'Notes of the Meeting of the Electoral Law Committee with Members of the Royal Commission on the Electoral System', 24 November 1987.
— (1988e), EL88/668, Secretary of Justice to Electoral Law Committee, 'Maori Representation: Background Paper', 3 May 1988.
— (1993a), '1992 Referendum Review', 17 March 1993.
— (1993b) (Submissions EL/93/4, 35, 39, 57, 73, 73(a), 84, 97, 97(a), 99, 101, 109, 118, 125, 126, 166, 312w, 360w, 417w, 644, 655).
— (1993c), EL233C/32, Submission of Geoffrey Palmer.
— (1993d), EL232H/163 'Electoral Reform Bill — Maori participation'.
— (1993e), EL93/422, 'Submission of New Zealand Maori Council'.
— (1993f), R.F. Welply, Deputy Government Statistician, to L. Tukaki-Millanta, Clerk, ELSC, 12 March 1993.
— (1993g), SCADM/ERB593, F. Nolan, Department of Statistics, to W. Moore, Department of Justice, 13 May 1993.
— (1993h), EL233B, J/13, Department of Justice, 'Maori Representation', 18 May 1993 (background paper).
— (1993i), EL233D, Department of Statistics, 'Seat Distribution Calculations', 16 July 1993.
— (1993j), EL/93/644, Department of Justice Report J2, 'Electoral Reform Bill—Summary of Submissions', 8 March 1993.
— (1993k), EL/93/648, Department of Justice Report J6, 'Open Regional Party Lists: Preliminary Report', 29 March 1993.
— (1993l), EL/93/655, Department of Justice Report J11, 'Electoral Reform Bill Report of the Department of Justice', 3 May 1993.
— (1993m), EL 233B, Department of Justice Report J16, 'Addendum to Report— Open Regional Lists', 25 May 1993.
— (1993n), EL/93/651, Department of Justice Report J9, 'Establishment of an Electoral Commission', 26 April 1993.
Electoral Referendum Coalition Files [ERC] (1988a), Letter to ERC Convenors, 5 December 1988.
— (1988b), Press release, 9 December 1988.
— (1988c), Report to convenors, 13 December 1988.
— (1989a), Report to convenors, 2 February 1989.
— (1989b), Saxby to Sandra Ewan (Executive member, Democratic Party), 8 February 1989.
— (1989c), Saxby to Sandra Girvan, 8 February 1989 and Christopher Leitch (Democratic Party president), 23 March 1989.
— (1989d), Report to convenors, 12 March 1989.

— (1990a), Saxby to Matiu Rata, 7 March 1990.
— (1990b), Withers & Donald to Palmer, 20 June 1990.
— (1991a), Annual Report for 1990/91, 14 September 1991.
— (1991b), Draft of Constitution, 28 June 1991 (adopted 14 September 1991).
— (1991c), Saxby to Helena Catt (fax), 23 September 1991.
— (1991d), Saxby to Manning, 26 September 1991.
— (1991e), Notes of a meeting with incoming ERC chairperson, Colin Clark, 30 September 1991.
— (1992a), 1992 Broadsheet.
— (1992b), Minutes of Annual General Meeting, Wellington, 24–26 October 1992.
— (1992c), Management Committee Minutes, 27 October 1992.
— (1992d), Catt to Bush, 12 December 1992.
— (1993a), *What is MMP? A Guide to the Mixed Member Proportional (MMP) Voting System.*
— (1993b), 1993 Budget.
— (1993c), *Progress Report: Campaign 93!*, 5 September 1993.
— (1993d), Kevin Hackwell, 'Campaign Report to ERC Executive', nd (probably September 1993).
— (1993e), *Referendum Roundup*, 12 October 1993.
— (1993f), Circular Letter, 28 October 1993.
Electoral Referendum Panel [ERP] (1992a), *We're Taking it to the People: The Electoral Referendum, 19 September 1992*, Wellington.
— (1992b), *The Guide to the Electoral Referendum*, Wellington.
— (1992c), Panel Records, 1992.
— (1993a), Panel Records, 1993.
— (1993b), *The Referendum: The Facts*, Wellington.
— (1993c), *The Referendum: The Guide*, Wellington.
— (1993d), *The **Referendum**,* **Wellington.**
— (1993e), *Referendum'93: Media Handbook*, Wellington.
— (1993f), *The Referendum: Explaining the **Options**,* **Wellington.**
Evening Post (Wellington).

Flux, D. (1997), Correspondence, 26 September 1997.
Forster, J. (1969) 'A Note on the Background of **Parliamentarians'**, *Political Science* 21:1, **September 1969.**

Gobbi, M.W. (1992), 'We the Sovereign: Clarifying the Call for Direct Democracy in New Zealand', in Simpson (1992).
Gold, H. ed. (1992), *New Zealand Politics in **Perspective***, 3rd edn, Auckland, Longman.
Gomibuchi, S. (1995), 'An Amateur Labour? Geoffrey Palmer and his Contribution to the Electoral Reform Policy', unpublished MA thesis, University of Canterbury.
Graham, D.A.M. (1992a), Correspondence, 9 March 1992.
— (1992b), Interview, Wellington, 10 November 1992.
Grimshaw, P. (1972), *Women's Suffrage in New Zealand*, Auckland, Auckland and Oxford University Press.
Grofman, B., Lijphart, A., McKay, R.B. & **Scarrow, H.A.** (1982), *Representation and Redistricting **Issues***, Lexington, Massachusetts, Heath.
Grofman, B. & Lijphart, A. (1986), *Electoral Laws and their Political Consequences*, New York, Agathon Press.
Gustafson, B. (1980), *Labour's Path to Political Independence*, Auckland, Auckland/Oxford University Press.
— (1986), *The First 50 Years. A History of the New Zealand National Party*, Auckland, Reed Methuen.

Hailsham, Lord (Quintin Hogg) (1978), *The Dilemma of Democracy: Diagnosis and Prescription*, London, William Collins.
Hamer, D.A. (1988), *The New Zealand Liberals: The Years of Power, 1891–1912*, Auckland, Auckland University Press.

Hanham, H.J. (1968), *The Reformed Electoral System in Great Britain, 1832–1914*, London, The Historical Association.

Hansard Society (1976), *Report of the Hansard Society Commission on Electoral Reform*, London.

Harris, P.R. (1992), 'Changing New Zealand's Electoral System: The 1992 Referendum', *Representation*, 31:115.

— (1993), 'Electoral Reform in New Zealand: The 1993 Referendum, New Zealand Votes for Change', *Representation*, 32:117.

— (1996a), Correspondence, 20 February 1996.

— (1996b), Correspondence, 30 April 1996.

— (1997a), Interview, Wellington, 20 October 1997.

— (1997b), 'Changing New Zealand's Electoral System: Continuity or Crisis' in Boston, *et al.*, (1997).

Harris, P.R. & Levine, S.I., eds., with Clark, M., Martin, J., Mcleay, E. (1994), *The New Zealand Politics Source Book*, 2nd edition, Palmerston North, Dunmore Press.

Harrop, M. & Miller, W.L. (1987), *Elections and Voters*, Macmillan Education, Basingstoke.

Hauss, C. & Rayside, D. (1978), 'The development of new parties in western democracies since 1945', in Maisel, L. & Cooper, J., eds. (1978).

Hawke, G.R., ed. (1993), *Changing Politics? The Electoral Referendum 1993*, Institute of Policy Studies, Wellington.

Henderson, J.T. (1995), Interview, Christchurch, 25 September 1995.

Herron, D.G. (1960), 'The Franchise and New Zealand Politics, 1853–58' in *Political Science*, Wellington, Department of Political Science and Public Administration, Victoria University of Wellington, vol. 12, no. 1, March 1960.

Heylen Full Trust and Confidence Poll.

High Court of New Zealand, Wellington Registry (HC) (1994a), CP99/94, Affidavit of R.H.N. Love, 1 July 1994.

— (1994b), CP99/94, Affidavit of D.A.M. Graham, 1 August 1994.

— (1994c), Chief Executive, Te Puni Kokiri, to Minister of Maori Affairs, 13 May 1994 (Background paper for CP 99/94).

— (1994d), Reserved Judgement of McGechan J, 4 October 1994.

Holland, M. & Boston, J. (1990), *The Fourth Labour Government*, 2nd edn., Auckland, Oxford University Press.

Hughes, C.A. (1991), Report to Department of Justice, 10 December 1991.

— (1996), Interview, Brisbane, 12 April 1996.

Hunn, J.K. (1961), *Report On Department of Maori Affairs*, Wellington, Government Printer (*AJHR*, 1961, G.10).

Hunt, J.L. (1996a), Telephone interview, 26 February 1996.

— (1996b), Interview, Wellington, 17 June 1996.

Huntington, S.P. & Moore, C.H., eds. (1970), *Authoritarian Politics in Modern Society*, New York, Basic Books.

International Institute for Democracy and Electoral Assistance (IDEA) (1997), *The International IDEA Handbook of Electoral System Design*, 2nd edition, Stockholm.

Jackson, W.K. (1972), *The New Zealand Legislative Council: A Study of the Establishment, Failure and Abolition of an Upper House*, Dunedin, University of Otago Press.

— (1973), *New Zealand: Politics of Change*, Wellington, Reed Education.

— (1987), *The Dilemma of Parliament*, Wellington, Allen & Unwin/Port Nicholson Press.

— (1991), 'The Abolition of the New Zealand Upper House of Parliament', in Longley, L.D. & Olson, D.M., eds., *Two into One: The Politics and Processes of National Legislative Cameral Change*, Boulder, Westview.

— (1992), 'Commentary on "Referendums: Legal and Constitutional Aspects" ', in Simpson.

James, C. (1986), *The Quiet Revolution*, Wellington, Allen & Unwin/Port Nicholson Press.

James, C. & McRobie, A. (1993), *Turning Point: The 1993 Election and Beyond*, Wellington, Bridget Williams Books.

Jennings, O.R. (1996), Interview, Auckland, 13 March 1996.

Jesson, B., Ryan, A. & Spoonley, P. (1988), *Revival of the Right: New Zealand Politics in the 1980s*, Auckland, Heinemann Reid.
Johnson, N. (1975), 'Adversary Politics and Electoral Reform: Need We Be Afraid?', in S.E. Finer (ed.), *Adversary Politics and Electoral Reform*, London, Anthony Wigram.
Johnston, R. (1994), 'New Zealanders and Electoral Reform: An Alternative Perspective', *Representation*, 32:119.
Joseph, P.A.(1993), *Constitutional and Administrative Law in New Zealand*, Sydney, The Law Book Company.
Justice, Department of (1992a), File P&D 3-14-3-1.
— (1992b), File P&D 3-14-3-3.

Kaase, M. (1983), 'The West German General Election of 6 March 1983', *Electoral Studies*, 2:2.
Kirchheimer, O. (1966), 'The Transformation of the Western European Party **System'**, in LaPalombara, J. & Weiner, M., eds. (1966).
Kirton, N. (1997), Telephone interview, 30 October 1997.
Kolinksy, E., ed. (1987), *Opposition in Western Europe*, London, Croom Helm.

Lange, D.R. (1994), Transcript of interview with S. Gomibuchi, 17 August 1994.
LaPalombara, J. & Weiner, M. eds. (1966), *Political Parties in Western Development*, Princeton, Princeton University Press.
Levine, S.I., ed. (1978), *Politics in New Zealand: A Reader*, Sydney, Allen & Unwin.
Levine, S.I. & Roberts, N.S. (1993a), 'The New Zealand Electoral Referendum of 1992', *Electoral Studies*, 12:2.
— (1993b), 'The Referendum Results: "The People Screamed" ', in McRobie, ed. (1993).
— (1994), 'The New Zealand Electoral Referendum and General Election of 1993', *Electoral Studies*, 13:3.
Lijphart, A. (1984), *Democracies. Patterns of Majoritarian and Consensus Government in Twenty-One Countries*, New Haven, Yale University Press.
— (1987), 'The Demise of the Last Westminster System? Comments on the Report of New Zealand's Royal Commission on the Electoral System', *Electoral Studies*, 6:2.
Lijphart, A. & Grofman, B. (1984), *Choosing an Electoral System: Issues and Alternatives*, New York, Praeger.
Lipson, L. (1948), *The Politics of Equality*, Chicago, University of Chicago Press.
Longley, L.D. (1989), 'Changing the System: Anticipated Versus Actual Results In Electoral and Legislative Reform'. Paper presented at the Midwest Political Science Association Meeting, Chicago.
Longley, L.D. & Olson, D.M. (1991), *Two into One: The Politics and Processes of National Legislative Cameral Change*, Boulder, Praeger.
Love, N. (1996), Interview, Wellington, 18 June 1996.

Mackenzie, W.J.M. (1958), *Free Elections*, London, George Allen & Unwin.
Mackerras, M. (1994), 'Reform of New Zealand's Voting System, 1985–1996', *Representation*, 32:118.
— (1996), Interview, Canberra, 15 April 1996.
McCully, M.S. (1996), Interview, Wellington, 11 December 1996.
McGee, D.G. (1993), Draft Opinion, Draft./3 (nd).
— (1997), Correspondence, 19 June 1997.
McLay, J.K. (1993), Correspondence with P.R. Harris, 19 March 1993.
McLean, I., ed. (1996), *The Concise Oxford Dictionary of Politics*, Oxford, Oxford University Press.
McLintock, A.H. (1958), *Crown Colony Government in New Zealand*, Wellington Government Printer.
McRobie, A. (1978), 'The Politics of Electoral Redistribution', in Levine (1978).
— (1984), *Election '84*, Christchurch, MC Enterprises.
— (1989), *New Zealand Electoral Atlas*, Wellington, GP Books.
— (1990), *Defining Electoral Districts: Three Essays on Electoral Redistribution*, Christchurch, MC Enterprises.

— (1993), *Taking it to the People: The New Zealand Electoral Referendum Debate*, Christchurch, Hazard Press.

— (1994), 'Final and Binding: The 1993 Electoral Referendum', in Vowles & Aimer (1994).

— (1995), 'The 1995 Electoral Redistribution' (xerox).

— (1997), 'New Zealand's First MMP Election', *Agenda*, vol. 4, no. 3.

Maisel, L. & Cooper, J., eds.(1978), *Political Parties: Development and Decay*, Beverly Hills, Sage.

Manning, Lowell (1996a), Telephone interview, 22 July 1996.

— (1996b), Correspondence, 23 July 1996.

Marshall, J.R. (1948), 'The Faith of a Liberal', *Journal of Political Science*, 1:1.

— (1983), *Memoirs. Volume One: 1912 to 1960*, Auckland, Collins.

Moore, W. (1996), Interview, Wellington, 27 June 1996.

— (1997), Telephone interview, 9 July 1997.

Muldoon, R.D. (1974), *The Rise and Fall of a Young Turk*, Wellington, Reed.

Mulgan, R. (1980), 'Palmer, Parliament and the **Constitution'**, *Political Science*, **32:2.**

— (1984), *Democracy and Power in New Zealand: A Study of New Zealand Politics*, Auckland, Oxford.

— (1992), 'The Elective Dictatorship in New Zealand', in Gold, **H., ed. (1992).**

— (1995), 'The Democratic Failure of Single-Party Government: The New Zealand Experience', *Australian Journal of Political Science*, vol. 30 (Special Issue).

— (1996a), Correspondence, 27 February 1996.

— (1996b), Interview, Canberra, 16 April 1996.

— (1997), Correspondence, 11 April 1997.

Nagel, J.H. (1994a), 'What political scientists can learn from the 1993 electoral reform in New Zealand', *PS: Political Science & Politics*, 27.

— (1994b), 'How Many Parties will New Zealand have under MMP?', *Political Science*, 46:2.

National Business Review (Auckland).

New Zealand Constitution Act, 1852 **(UK), 15 and 16 Vict., Ch. 72.**

New Zealand First (NZF) (1981), Tauranga. (A publication of the New Zealand League of Rights.)

New Zealand First [NZF] (1996), Election Manifesto.

New Zealand Government Gazette (NZG), Auckland.

New Zealand Herald (Auckland).

New Zealand Insight, Wellington, UMR Insight Research (Monthly).

New Zealand Labour Party [NZLP] (1966), *1966 Election Manifesto*, Maori Affairs Policy.

— (1981), *Getting New Zealand Working Again* (1981 election manifesto).

— (1987a), *The Next Three Years: Labour's Plan for the Future* (1987 election manifesto).

— (1987b), *Official Policy Document.*

— (1990), *Labour: Our Policies for the 90s*, Wellington.

New Zealand Listener (Auckland).

New Zealand National Party [NZNP] (1990), *1990 Election Policy.*

New Zealand Parliamentary Debates [NZPD].

Nicolle, B. (1996), Interview, Auckland, 13 March 1996.

— (1997), Correspondence, 3 September 1997.

Nohlen, D. (1984), 'Changes and Choices in Electoral Systems', in Lijphart & Grofman (1984).

Norpoth, H. (1982), 'The German Federal Republic: Coalition Government at the Brink of Majority Rule', in Browne, E.C. & Dreijmanis, J., eds. (1982).

Norris, P. (1997), *Electoral Change Since 1945*, Oxford, Blackwell.

Northey, R.J. (1995), Correspondence to S. Gomibuchi, 21 June 1995.

— (1996), Interview, Wellington, 26 June 1996.

Palmer, G.W.R. (Palmer papers, deposited with the MacMillan Brown Library, University of Canterbury), H.39 (Royal Commission, 1984–85).

— H88 (General Files — Electoral Law Reform).

— H.100 (Electoral Law Reform).

— CH 93/3/12a (Electoral Law Caucus Committee).

— CH95/3/126a (Electoral Law).

—   CH95/3/372 (Proportional Representation).
—   CH95/3/546 (Cabinet papers, meeting 24).
—   CH95/3/547 (Cabinet papers, meetings 25 & 26).
—   (1979), *Unbridled Power? An Interpretation of New Zealand's Constitution and Government,* Auckland, Oxford.
—   (1992), *New Zealand's Constitution in Crisis: Reforming our Political System,* Dunedin, John McIndoe.
—   (1996), Telephone interview, 29 February 1996.
—   (1997), Correspondence, 4 August 1997.
Peaslee, A. (1985), *Constitutions of Nations,* Vol.II, Asia, Australia and Oceania, 4th edition (revised), The Hague, Dordrecht for Nijhoff.
The Press (Christchurch).

Representation Commission [RC] (1995a), Minutes, 1994–95.
—   (1995b), J.J. McGrath (Solicitor-General) to F.W.M. McElrea (Chairman), 18 August 1994.
—   (1995c), Press Releases.
Richardson, R.M. (1995), *Making a Difference,* Christchurch, Shoal Bay Press.
—   (1996), Interview, West Melton, 16 July 1996.
Riker, W.H. (1962), *The Theory of Political Coalitions,* New Haven, Yale University Press.
Robertson, J.F. (1997), Correspondence, 26 September and 15 October 1997.
Royal Commission on the Electoral System [RCES] (1986a), *Report of the Royal Commission on the Electoral System: Towards a Better Democracy,* Wellington *(AJHR,* 1986, H.3).
—   COM Series 70 (New Zealand National Archives).
—   (1986b), ACC W3042 (Box 2), Royal Commission on the Electoral System, Minutes.
—   (1986c), ACC W3047, General Correspondence 1–4.
—   (1986d), ACC W3047, Submissions 1–635.
—   (1986e), ACC W3047, Research Papers; Miscellaneous papers.

Saxby, P.J. (1996), Interview, Wellington, 18 June 1996.
—   (1997), Correspondence, 19 and 24 September 1997.
Shirtcliffe, G.P. (1996), Interview, Wellington, 17 June 1996.
—   (1997a), Telephone interview, 12 August 1997.
—   (1997b), Correspondence, 15 August 1997.
Simpson, A.C. (1978), 'Commissions of Inquiry and the Policy Process', in Levine, S.I. (1978).
—   ed. (1992), *Referendums: Constitutional and Political Perspectives,* Wellington, Department of Politics, Victoria University of Wellington, Occasional Publication No. 5.
Skene, G. (1987), 'Parliamentary Reform', in Boston & Holland (1987).
Smith, V. (1996), Interview, Wellington, 26 June 1996.
Social Credit/Democratic Party, Election Manifestos, 1954—1990.
Southland Times (Invercargill).
Spoonley, P. (1987), *The Politics of Nostalgia. Fascism and the Extreme Right in New Zealand,* Palmerston North, Dunmore Press.
Statistics, Department of (1990), *New Zealand Official 1990 Yearbook,* Wellington.
—   (1991), *New Zealand Census of Population and Dwellings, 1991,* Wellington.
Steering Committee (1993a), Report of Steering Committee to parliamentary select committee, 'Implications for Maori of the Electoral Reform Bill', May 1993.
—   (1993b), 'Implications for Maori of the Electoral Reform Bill: Addendum', May 1993.
Street, M. (1995), 'Implications of MMP — Labour Party Viewpoint', AIC Conference, Wellington, 9–10 November 1995.
Sunday Star (Auckland).
Sunday Star-Times (Auckland).

Taranaki Daily News (New Plymouth).
Tate, P. (1996), Interview, Auckland, 13 March 1996.
—   (1997), Correspondence, 3 September 1997.
Te Puni Kokiri [TPK] (1992), Robertson to Harrison, 27 August 1992.

— (1993), File 3300.
Television One [TV1] (1996), *Meet the Press*, 27 October 1996.
Temple, R.P. (1992), *Making Your Vote Count*, Dunedin, John McIndoe.
— (1993), *Making Your Vote Count Twice*, Dunedin, John McIndoe.
Templeton, H.C. (1995), *All Honourable Men: Inside the Muldoon Cabinet 1975-1984*, Auckland, Auckland University Press.
Terris, John (1996), Interview, Wellington, 19 June 1996.
Thompson, G.W.F. (1995), 'Implications of MMP. How National Is Adapting To This New Political Environment', AIC Conference, Wellington, 9-10 November 1995.
— (1996), Correspondence, 13 March 1996.
Thomson, A.S. (1859), *The Story of New Zealand*, 2 volumes, London.
Tully, Jim (1993), 'The Media and the Referendum', in McRobie (1993).
Turner, I. (1983), 'Electoral System Innovation: A Comparison of the Lower Saxony Electoral Laws of 1946 and 1977: their Origins and Effects', *Electoral Studies*, 2:2.

Upton, S.D. (1994), Telephone interview, 4 April 1994.
— (1996), Interview, Wellington, 12 December 1996.

Values Party, Election Manifestos, 1972–81.
Vowles, J. (1995), 'The Politics of Electoral Reform in New Zealand', *International Political Science Review*, 16:1.
Vowles, J. & Aimer, P. (1993), *Voters' Vengeance: The 1990 Election in New Zealand and the Fate of the Fourth Labour Government*, Auckland, Auckland University Press.
— eds. (1994), *Double Decision: The 1993 Election and Referendum in New Zealand*, Wellington, Department of Politics, Victoria University of Wellington.
Vowles, J., Aimer, P., Catt, H., Lamare, J. & Miller, R. (1995), *Towards Consensus? The 1993 Election in New Zealand and the Transition to Proportional Representation*, Auckland, Auckland University Press.

Waitangi Tribunal [WT] (1994), WAI 413, *Maori Electoral Option Report* (Report 7 **WTR**), **Brooker's**, Wellington.
Ward, A.(1973), *A Show of Justice: racial 'amalgamation' in nineteenth century New **Zealand**, Auckland, Auckland University Press and Oxford University Press.
Weller, P., ed. (1994), *Royal Commissions and the Making of Public Policy*, Brisbane, Macmillan for Centre for Australian Public Sector Management.
Wereta, W. (1997), Interview, Wellington, 30 April 1997.
Wilson, J.O. (1985), *New Zealand Parliamentary Record 1840-1984*, Wellington, Government Printer.
Wilson, M. (1989), *Labour in Government 1984-1987*, Wellington, Allen & Unwin/Port Nicholson Press.
Wood, G.A. (1969), 'The Electorate's Verdict' in Peter Munz, ed., *The Feel of Truth*, Wellington, A.H. & A.W. Reed.
Wright, W.E., ed. (1971), *A Comparative Study of Party Organisation*, Colombus, Charles E. Merrill.

Zwaga, W.E.R. (1992), 'Delivering Television Audiences to Advertisers? Impressions from the Living Room', *Marketing Bulletin*, 1992:3, 9–17, Palmerston North, Massey University.

Index

References from Notes indicated by 'n' after page reference